# Jakarta

# Jakarta
## The City of a Thousand Dimensions

*Abidin Kusno*

NUS PRESS
SINGAPORE

© 2023 Abidin Kusno

*Published by:*
NUS Press
National University of Singapore
AS3-01-02, 3 Arts Link
Singapore 117569

Fax: (65) 6774-0652
E-mail: nusbooks@nus.edu.sg
Website: http://nuspress.nus.edu.sg

ISBN 978-981-325-226-4 (paper)
ePDF ISBN 978-981-325-227-1
ePub ISBN 978-981-325-228-8

**National Library Board, Singapore Cataloguing in Publication Data**
Name(s): Kusno, Abidin, 1966- author.
Title: Jakarta : the city of a thousand dimensions / Abidin Kusno.
Description: Singapore : NUS Press, [2023] | Includes bibliography and index.
Identifier(s): ISBN 978-981-325-226-4 | 978-981-325-227-1 (ePDF) | 978-981-325-228-8 (ePub)
Subject(s): LCSH: Urbanization--Indonesia--Jakarta. | Construction industry--Indonesia--Jakarta. | City planning--Indonesia--Jakarta.
Classification: DDC 307.7609598--dc23

Cover image: Drawing courtesy of Suryono Herlambang.

Typeset by: Ogma Solutions Pvt Ltd
Printed by: Mainland Press Pte Ltd

*In memory of*
Anthony D. King
1931–2022

"How or what we write, for whom, and with what
political agenda, to bring about what political and policy
transformations, clearly depends on what we believe
to be important."*

* Anthony D. King, "Actually Existing Postcolonialisms: Colonial Urbanism and Architecture after the Postcolonial Turn", in *Postcolonial Urbanism: Southeast Asian Cities and Global Processes*, ed. R. Bishop, J. Phillips, and Wei Wei Yeo (London: Routledge, 2003).

# Contents

List of Figures ............................................................ ix

Preface .................................................................... xi

Introduction: The City of a Thousand Dimensions: Theory,
Practice, Subjectivity .................................................... 1

1.  Middling Urbanism ................................................... 23
2.  The Rule of Many Orders ............................................ 40
3.  Roads, Rhizomes and Regimes ........................................ 48
4.  Where Will the Water Go? ........................................... 71
5.  A New Assemblage City .............................................. 108
6.  Urban Politics ..................................................... 128
7.  Islamist Urbanism .................................................. 149
8.  Escape from Jakarta: The Future Redux .............................. 169
9.  Jakarta: A Conversation ............................................ 181
10. Our Streets: Reflections on a Pandemic City ....................... 206

Afterword: On "Multitude" and the Urban Question:
A Reading in a Time of Pandemics ........................................ 218

Bibliography ............................................................. 228

Index .................................................................... 246

# List of Figures

1.1     Street scene in *Kampung* Pulo                                      26

1.2a    A cut in the wall                                                   28

1.2b    Entrance from a *kampung* to condominiums and mega-commercial
        superblocks in Jakarta's CBD                                        28

1.3     An analytical map of *kampung* settlements                          30

1.4a, b The emergence of "middle-class" rental spaces in a *kampung*        38

3.1     *Bemo*: A traditional means of public transportation influenced
        by the *jitney* of Indian origin                                    49

3.2     *Mikrolet*                                                          53

3.3     Traffic congestion and billboards advertising cars and promoting
        the war on drugs and the MCU "Civil Wars" movie                     58

3.4     *Ojek* and their makeshift terminal                                 65

3.5     Motorcycles vs. cars: Motorbikes use forbidden busway lane
        to escape traffic                                                   67

3.6     "Ini Loh Jalanku!" [This is *my* road!]                             68

4.1     *Banjir* Jakarta                                                    72

4.2     The flood greets Jokowi                                             77

4.3     Community-funded extra pumps and pipes in North Jakarta            79

4.4     Van Breen's 1917 Map                                                85

4.5     Flood Alert: Disaster Response Post—*Siaga Banjir:
        Posko Tanggap Bencana*                                              86

4.6     Publicity campaign linking *banjir*, garbage and the river during
        the time of Governor Jokowi                                         94

4.7     River scene in *Kampung* Pulo                                       95

4.8     Raising the house entryway (*kaki lima*)                            99

4.9     "Pluit City: A World Class Waterfront City—The New City
        in North of Jakarta"                                                99

| 5.1 | Map of the location of Meikarta | 109 |
| 5.2 | Meikarta showroom in a shopping mall | 122 |
| 6.1 | A banner of Forum Betawi Rempug (FBR), Jakarta | 134 |
| 7.1 | Masjid Al Safar, Bandung | 153 |
| 7.2 | *Alun-alun* Bandung | 155 |
| 7.3 | Reunion of the anti-Ahok rally at the National Monument, Jakarta, 2 Dec. 2017 | 159 |
| 7.4 | 212 Mart | 160 |
| 7.5 | A *musholla* in the middle of a *kampung* near housing complexes in West Jakarta | 163 |
| 7.6 | Plan to build a *musholla* | 165 |
| 10.1 | Barricades in Bandung's major Asia-Africa Street | 208 |
| 10.2 | Mobile stall in Tangerang | 210 |
| 10.3 | Motorcycle courier riding through the streets in Tambora, West Jakarta | 211 |
| 10.4 | Scene on the street near a Police HQ in Bandung, 25 April 2020 | 215 |

# Preface

The essays in this book were written between 2012 and 2020, around the time that the Governors of Jakarta included Joko Widodo, Basuki "Ahok" Purnama and their eventual successor Anies Baswedan. The essays represent my view of a city that has become ever more multi-dimensional as the unifying nationalist discourses have given way to practices of informality, neoliberal capitalist development and identity politics. Jakarta has become a "city of a thousand dimensions", according to Indonesian writer, Seno Gumira Ajidarma. A thousand dimensions suggest not so much a picture of "messy urbanism", "emergent urbanism", "incremental urbanism", or a "megacity", concepts which have been used to depict a city like Jakarta. Instead, the term suggests a form of governmentality (a political rationality, for better or worse) about which we still know very little although it has been formed through sedimented layers of time and has shaped substantially the socio-cultural and political life of the city. This book is an attempt to tease out some dimensions that have given shape to this urban condition and the political culture that structures it. The city's expanded flexibility in accommodating capital and labour, the formal and the informal, and the consistent lack of planning can be understood, as this book argues, as an art of governing.

Since the last decade, contemporary Jakarta has become an important site for the exploration of a range of critical concepts and issues in urban studies.[1] Scholars from Anthropology, Sociology, Geography, Politics, Planning and Asian Studies continue to engage with and contribute to the study of contemporary Jakarta. They have advanced scholarship on comparative postcolonial urbanism in and through their studies of the city. I seek to complement this ongoing exploration of

---

[1] Monographs include Hellman, Thynell and van Voorst, eds., *Jakarta: Claiming Spaces and Rights in the City* (2018); Silver, *Planning the Megacity: Jakarta in the Twentieth Century* (2008); Simone, *Jakarta: Drawing the City Near* (2014); Van Voorst, *Natural Hazards, Risk and Vulnerability* (2016); Wilson, *The Politics of Protection Rackets in Post-New Order Indonesia* (2015) and Shatkin, *Cities for Profit* (2017). Recent articles on Jakarta include the works of Eric Sheppard and Helga Leitner in collaboration with members of their research team, such as Sheppard, "Globalizing Capitalism's Raggedly Fringes" (2019), Herlambang et al., "Jakarta's Great Land Transformation" (2018), Leitner and Sheppard, "From Kampungs to Condos?" (2018) and Liong et al., "Space Grabs" (2020).

the city, but instead of viewing the city through the lens of a specific community or a theoretical framework and focusing on a topic, I explore multiple sites and cover various issues that, when brought together, constitute a socio-political dimension that is neither formal nor disorderly. I interpret the contemporary passage and transformation from an earlier establishment to the mental revolution of Jokowi and Ahok, from a dissolution of a political cultural norm to counter-revolutionary responses to reconfiguring the city. Along the way, I pick up a historically determined dynamism of many orders or dimensions which continues to shape the way the city is understood, governed and left alone.

Building on insights from critical geography and anthropology of infrastructure among others, I seek to make sense of a city where gaps and discrepancy have led to both disasters and opportunities as well as a mode of governing society. I examine a number of social groups such as policy makers, business groups and commoners, and analyse their responses to the range of urban issues they are facing in and through the sites of their intervention and practices to show how they are implicated in the shaping of the built environment, in the development of statecraft and the formation of identity politics; how their disparate concerns discursively intersect, creating a complex convergence of a power relation that has brought about the way of a city of a thousand dimensions.

This is my fourth book about what people and their built environment have done to each other. My primary concern is still limited to a city, namely Jakarta, with some references to nearby Bandung and a region in West Java. The reason that I keep focusing on this city is both intellectual and personal. My extended family members live there and so every time I go to Jakarta, my visit encounters everyday materials that give rise to such concerns and reflections that it is difficult to focus on just one topic or stay consistent within a certain theoretical approach. The routine of everyday life is always subjected to flexibility, creativity and discursivity. But events that surface from the banality of everyday life are not to be neglected for they are often governed by a spatial configuration that is inescapably political. If we move between different urban configurations, we may be able to connect the everyday with the structure that gives it meaning. An interpretation can then be made, and a story can be told. Yet Jakarta can be approached in so many ways because its urban configuration has many dimensions, many formal and hidden rules and many historical layers. So, it can have many stories. This does not mean that Jakarta is a special case of urbanism. I am not sure how exceptional it is. The city can be compared with many cities in the Global South even though some parts of its urban form and life resemble cities in the Global North. I think however one could have more interesting conversations about the city if one approached Jakarta in terms of fragments (i.e. moving between different configurations) that when they are put together, as this book will show, give a feel of an architectonic form of a thousand dimensions. This form again is always in formation, always changing, but it is also always at once, social and political. It has power to govern and transform subjectivities.

How has my own thinking changed as Jakarta continues to change so much? I started, as in *Behind the Postcolonial* (2000), with moving architecture from its domain of self-expression to the realm of social and political commentaries. I saw Jakarta as a phantom *polis* of the colonial past and a product of both postcolonial state violence and capitalist modernisation which ended badly with the massive riots against ethnic Chinese and the urban poor. But was the fall of Suharto a result of awakening from a dream (or a nightmare)? Did the Suharto generation even dream the one to follow?

My subsequent works seek to respond to these questions by moving forwards and backwards in time, not in search of a lost time, but to see if Jakarta "after Suharto" is a residue of a dystopian dream world that continues to haunt the present. Alternatively, if we are entering a new era, to what extent have we moved on still accompanied by the earlier ones? *The Appearances of Memory* (2010) and *After the New Order* (2013) were written in this mood of wondering. They shared a similar concern over the meaning of "after Suharto" or "moving forward" or "movement" itself: Where to start, what remains, and how to tell a story, no matter how fragmentarily and, as much as possible, from perspectives other than those of the victors. Such questions required me to pace back and forth across time, retrieving forgotten history, discarded objects and utopian pasts to respond to questions concerning the future. The mood of these two books however cast doubts on the possibility of a new time. If there was a new time as suggested in the title *After the New Order*, the atmosphere was rather gloomy.

The present book, *Jakarta: The City of a Thousand Dimensions*, belongs to another epoch, I would like to assume, to the time of a new political regime led by Jokowi and Ahok. I am among those who want to see hope in their era. I want my narrative of the city to respond to Jokowi's call for "mental revolution", from which a different form of urbanism could hopefully emerge. This book therefore seeks to consider what is worth salvaging in the city they once governed, along with what they managed to do in recovering what they could from the mess they inherited from the previous regimes. To both appreciate and problematise their struggles, I track the urban configuration that informs the political culture of governance. It has become apparent to me that Jakarta in the time of Governors Jokowi and Ahok offered opportunities as much as challenges to political entrepreneurs. As much as they wanted to create a "new Jakarta", the past, alas, has survived as a tradition that is far from easy to uproot or transform. Before anything new was established, Jakarta fell back into the hands of political opportunists and supporters of an order that reminds me of the old, with a different configuration which still needs to be analysed. For sure, the fall of Ahok ended the dream of a possible new alliance between the city and the nation which for Jokowi was the road to revolution.

This book ends with dystopian Jakarta (once again) and the utopia of a new capital city; both of these dream places however soon got caught up in the storm of pandemic. I have not been able to visit Jakarta since early 2020. By 2021, at least half of the population in Jakarta had suffered from COVID-19. They included my extended family as well as relatives and friends. The COVID map of the city had moved from patches of different colours to a single colour consisting of a dark field. I have never seen such a monochromatic map of Jakarta. The city was unified by COVID-19 at least at the surface. It has become one dimensional if that means the opposite of a thousand dimensions. The one-colour map with no other details is a colour of death for some, but for many, it is also a color of solidarity.

As a coda, this book presents a short account that I collected from friends to express my shock and solidarity. We assembled experiences and observations in the form of a "pandemic notebook". It seems to me that the COVID-19 pandemic is already defining an era. It is still hard to imagine the one to follow, but whatever it is, it demands a historical awakening from what has gone wrong in the previous eras.

The pandemic notebook underscores how great a debt I owe to many generous friends who shared their insights or informed this book in many ways. The brief mention of names cannot begin to repay such a debt. Deep apologies to anyone I have forgotten. I will always be grateful to Suryono Herlambang for our ongoing conversation over many years. I can no longer distinguish his thinking and concerns from my own. Seno Gumira Ajidarma, Teti Argo, Wahyu Astuti, Melani Budianta, Manneke Budiman, Gunadi Darmono, Herlily, Dian Tri Irawati, Miya Irawati, Lilawati Kurnia, Rita Padawangi, Frans Prasetyo, Jo Santoso and Regina Suryadjaja generously shared ideas and notes, many of which I have tried to assimilate into the texts often without knowing how to acknowledge them. They have offered more good advice than I have accepted. They are in no way responsible for any erroneous claims, omissions, or shortcomings which I'm sure readers will find. Outside Indonesia, I have had the good fortune in the recent past to learn on various occasions from fellow scholars with similar interests: Joshua Barker, Bülent Batuman, Greig Crysler, Andy Fuller, Sheri Gibbings, Liette Gilbert, Jörgen Hellman, Roger Keil, Philip Kelly, Stefan Kipfer, Nancy Kwak, Michael Leaf, AbdouMaliq Simone, Luisa Sotomayor and Lauren Yapp. I am grateful to them all. I would also like for Terry McGee and Anthony D. King, my former mentor, to know my deep appreciation of their work and support. With compassion, Tony King taught me a great deal of what I know about knowledge, subjectivity and the built environment (Kusno 2022). Tony King passed away a few days before the manuscript went to the Press. I therefore dedicate this book in memory of him.

Thanks are due to the publishers of the following journals and books for allowing me to include in this monograph revised versions of previously published articles: "Middling Urbanism: The Megacity and the Kampung", *Urban Geography* 41, 7 (2020): 954–70; "Where will the Water Go?", *Indonesia* 105 (April 2018): 19–51; "Escape from Jakarta?", *Current History*, 118 (809), (September 2019): 235–40; "Tradition and Its Aftermath: Jakarta's Urban Politics", in *Whose Tradition? Discourses on the Built Environment*, ed. Nezar AlSayyad, Mark Gillem and David Moffat (New York: Routledge, 2017); "Jakarta: A Conversation", in *Jakarta: Claiming Spaces and Rights in the City*, ed. Jörgen Hellman, Marie Thynell and Roanne van Voorst (New York: Routledge, 2018); "Manhattan in Orange County: Lippo and the Shenzhen of Indonesia", in *After Suburbia: Urbanization in the Twenty-first Century*, ed. Roger Keil and Fulong Wu (Toronto: University of Toronto Press, 2022) and "Islamist Urbanism and Spatial Performances in Indonesia", in *Cities and Islamisms: On the Politics and Production of the Built Environment*, ed. Bülent Batuman (New York: Routledge, 2020). Acknowledgements are due to Frans Prasetyo and Yen Tzu-Chien for permission to reproduce photographs from their collection.

The Social Science and Humanities Research Council of Canada supported this work financially. I thank the council for its generosity. The York Centre for Asian Research, via Alicia Filipowich, dispensed all kinds of research support and administration. I am also thankful to Peter Schoppert and Qua Lena from NUS Press, and anonymous reviewers for their helpful comments, encouragement and support. Farhan Karim, Lee Kah Wee and Anoma Pieris generously supported the publication of this book by including it as a volume in their book series *Across the Global South: Built Environments in Critical Perspective*. Barnard Turner edited the manuscript with knowledge and enthusiasm. His comments have helped me clarify what this book is about. Yasir Hameed, Sabika Zaidi and participants of my graduate courses at York University keep me periodically on my intellectual toes, exercise for which I am grateful. Hong and Leia in Canada, Isabel and Christine in somewhere, have shared living through the period of writing of this book. They gave me more understanding and affection than I deserve.

Finally, without my extended family in Jakarta the essays collected in this book could not have been written. With such a view, I open this book with a reflection on an episode of my life in Jakarta before *merantau* (moving and thinking outside Indonesia), and when I was able to occasionally stay in the city as a "builder" of our family house.

# Introduction

## The City of a Thousand Dimensions:
## Theory, Practice, Subjectivity

In the last decade, there has been large-scale urban construction in the major cities of Southeast Asia. A UK architectural website, *Building.co.uk*, reported in 2014 that "the region boasts three of the world's top 10 most rapidly growing construction economies—Indonesia, Vietnam and the Philippines, each growing between 6–9% each year. Three other construction economies in the region—Singapore, Malaysia and Thailand—are also growing strongly, at 3–5% a year" (Withers 2014). The magazine recommended that the UK's construction industries should consider the region an attractive destination, perhaps more so than China and India even though "there's a shortage [there] of engineers and of contractors" (Withers 2014).

Yet, as is characteristic of professional magazines, *Building* said nothing about the building workers, as if they were just readily available, presumably coming from rural Southeast Asia. It said nothing about the variety of the undocumented "informal sector", including the small-scale auto-constructions of the urban majority. It also ignored an earlier pattern of city building established by post-independence Southeast Asian cities, especially in the 1980s which contributed to the Asian financial crisis. The current surge of construction economies, as scholars in the field have pointed out, is part of the longer "real estate turn" (Shatkin 2017), sustained by a set of ecologies of governance which has given rise to "neoliberal exceptions" in the region (Ong 2011b).

But there still loom knotty questions. What are the conditions that have (re-)generated the construction boom in the region today? What sort of capital investment is tied up in city building? What kind of urban politics and governance is behind the production of space? In what ways do these construction projects generate a pattern of labour migration that is associated with construction? And what do these growing construction economies mean for the lives of people living under the physical transformation of the city? What might be their ecological consequences? Finally, how might we approach a city that recognises multiple and malleable dimensions in the production and governing of space?

1

This book responds to these questions through an examination of Jakarta in the last decades.

But first, how does all this concern me?

## I. Confession of a Cowboy Builder

In 1988, towards the end of my architectural training in Surabaya, East Java, my friend and I set up an informal construction firm (informal means without a licence). We renovated houses, designed the interiors of small offices and showrooms, and built garages mostly for our relatives and their friends. In Indonesian we were called *pemborong* (a wholesale service in construction). We went to the construction sites and worked with a *mandor* (head of construction workers). Little did I realise that in the two–three years spent running my own construction enterprise, we were engaged in the whole circuit (or should I say circus) of what we in the academic world today called practices of "informality". First of all, we were still students, we had no licence, so we never paid any tax. And our relationships with clients and workers were based on mutual understanding. Except for drawings to communicate ideas, nothing was presented on paper. There were no contracts for any work in any of our construction projects. We never applied for any building permits partly because it was expected that we should "go ahead" so that the field officer (*pengawas lapangan*) from the district or municipality would come and we would settle the account on the site (again without paper). I also learned how to pay local thugs to unload building materials; I learned how to "donate" bricks, cement and tiles to a local headman or district officer as a "social contribution" (to upgrade his private residence). Especially, I learned how to ensure the security of the construction site. I did not learn all this from my architectural school. They were all acquired in the field. I also soon learned that there was one man I feared most. That was our *mandor*, not because he was physically tall and rarely smiled but because he had access to the world of (informal) labour.

The *mandor* is a central figure in the Indonesian construction industry.[1] We can't work without him (always a man). He holds the key to the world of construction workers. More specifically, he controls the labour supply side. He knows where to find workers who have been segmented by specialisation, such as the mason, the carpenter, the blacksmith, the *pembuat batako* (precast brick maker), the *penggali tanah* (person who digs the hole, the excavator) and so on. He seemed to know all of them, including their families. We sub-contracted him to recruit workers from his various villages (or other places) to work on an urban construction site. He thus was a pivotal figure who mediated between the company and the workers, but not a broker (*calo*) whose job is only making connections but who is not involved in the actual work. The *mandor* not only organises the workers, allocates or distributes them to their work places according to their skills, but he works with them as a head labourer on the construction site till the end of the project. He is responsible for everything, from paying and retaining to firing workers. We, middle-class professionals, were simply unequipped to carry out such a task. For workers the, *mandor* is not only their source of work and income, but also their leader (but not their "boss") whom they respect. We often saw on the construction site workers who voluntarily took care of our *mandor*'s children and family who lived there. He is a figure whom construction workers recognise as a "brother" or even a "father" who possesses a certain moral authority to take care of them. (We had such a great *mandor*, but we also had others who got an abusive one.) The world of the *mandor* and the workers is thus filled with local relations of power, trust and debt which co-exist with the formal world of architects and construction companies.

This seemingly patron-client relationship between the *mandor* and the construction workers shaped the culture of the construction site. Another important contribution of the *mandor* is the linkage he made between the city and the countryside from which the majority of workers came (Firman 1989; Sjahrir 1995). Construction industries have shaped the social relations of a village where the *mandor* recruited his workers. The *mandor* and the workers mostly came from the same village, and they would return there when they were no longer needed on the construction site. The relationship is close and mutual with labourers going to the city and returning to the village following the working period that the *mandor* has organised for them. Workers from other villages or outside the circle of the *mandor* and his sphere of influence would therefore have difficulty in entering the labour market of that *mandor*. But once a worker is in, he would have no difficulty in keeping his occupation even though he could be transferred from one *mandor* to another.

The labour supply is thus constructed within the relation between the rural and the urban. The *mandor* and the construction industry play a major role in integrating rural households into the urban economy. They co-produce the city; many workers stay and build for themselves settlements known as *kampung* through which they then become urban subjects (see **Chapter 1**). The rural–urban relationship is also sustained by a cultural ideology that values the rural less, a conception that is translated into a lower valuation of their labour, especially for the unskilled. And yet the remittance from a family member working on the urban construction sites still contributes meaningfully to the income pool of a rural household. In short, the issues of labour in the construction of the Indonesian/Asian city cannot be separated from the construction of the relation between the urban and the rural.

This construction culture which I experienced in the 1980s is certainly not unique to Indonesia, and I believe it has continued until today. *Mandors* continue to play a major role in mediating between the formal profession of architect/contractor and the informal construction workers. Or could we say that they play a significant role in the production of migrant workers? A study of the *mandor* and its socio-political ecology is still needed, especially since the end of the New Order (1998 to the present) which I assume has entailed a formalisation of construction work forces as more and more workers are urbanised, professionalised, if not unionised. Such a study would also need to locate the *mandor* in a historical context of which they form a part.

## Capital

I stopped working as *pemborong* in 1990 as I moved to Jakarta to live with my family who had moved there a few years earlier. With no network of friends in the capital city, I couldn't do what I had done in Surabaya. I therefore settled myself in a formal construction firm in Jakarta. It was not just an average firm. It was the Jakarta design office of Shimizu Corporation, a giant globalised Japanese construction company which had opened a representative office in Jakarta to work on major projects in Indonesia.

I was hired as a fulltime employee (working from 8 am often to 8 pm) in an air-conditioned office building at Jakarta's "Golden Triangle". We were in a building called Setiabudi Internasional. This is owned by Jan Darmadi, a major developer with several tourist-related projects in Bali, the island which was by then considered a colony of Jakarta (Aditjondro 1995). Mr. Darmadi once said that "Jakarta Setiabudi International (JSI) and Shimizu have a long history of positive cooperation – Shimizu constructed one of our flagship hotels, the Grand Hyatt Bali...".[2] Hotels and office buildings were indeed on my drawing board (though a lot of my time was devoted to designing some patterns for the tiling of an office lobby, and countless timber joints for a resort hotel in Bali). The real pleasure was when, riding in a family car to the central part of Jakarta, I was able to impress my family with the landmark buildings that were being designed and built by Shimizu.

Little did I realise that soon Jakarta would be filled with many more landmark towers, all designed by architects and firms that I had once known only from architectural magazines in my school's library. By the mid-1990s in the city's business hub, New York architects Kohn Pederson Fox were completing the Jakarta Headquarters of Bank Niaga. The architect provided a mosque for this 27-story office tower. In a 1993 article, Naomi Pollock wrote of this mosque: "Inspired by North African minarets, the mosque sits amid a roof-top garden above a 900-car garage". Of the tower, she commented: "clad in Italian granite-and-glass curtain wall, the office tower commands views of the city but is shielded from the equatorial sun by coated-aluminium brise-soleil" (Pollock 1993).[3] Brennan Beer Gorman was in the middle of building the Jakarta Stock Exchange Tower; Pei Cob Freed's twin granite towers at Bank Danamon Square were preparing to compete with Paul Rudolph's just completed spectacular Wisma Dharmala Tower. Behind them were Murphy/Jahn Architects who had just submitted a design portfolio for three skyscrapers: Kuningan Persada Tower, Djakarta Tower, and Jakarta Communications Tower, the last presented in the manner of what James Scott (1998) would call a panoptic "seeing like a state". A 1995 article described the impression:

> a holographic work of art that represents the five Indonesian principles of philosophy [Pancasila]. Visible throughout the day and night and from numerous locations within the city, this elegant feature will locate the tower physically and symbolically in the country's psyche... It was to be initiated on the 17 August 1995, marking the 50th Anniversary of the Republic of Indonesia, and signaling, through its innovative design, the country's entry into the 21st century ("Murphy/Jahn" 1995).

All these famous North American architectural firms had come to Jakarta in the late 1980s to rebrand the city. Where the financing was coming from is a complex story that needs to be told through a political economic history of Suharto's New Order (see **Chapter 5**). As for Japanese capital, although Shimizu's Jakarta office was established in 1980 (for reasons I will discuss below), it was clear that by the end of the 1980s, when I was about to join Shimizu, Japan's own construction-based "bubble economy" had just burst and much of the air was out. The only way to re-pump the air was to stretch its already established passage to Southeast Asia. My Shimizu of the early 1990s thus belonged to this era of overseas expansion.

The history of Japanese and Indonesian relations in urban construction however goes well back to the era of early decolonisation. Soon after the transfer of sovereignty in 1950, Japan (which had occupied Indonesia between 1942 and 1945) came up with a financial package, known as the funds for war compensation, to help rebuild Indonesia, particularly Jakarta (Kusno 2018). The package came from attempts to secure construction deals for Japanese construction companies. President Sukarno immediately grasped the funds he badly needed and he also embraced Ms. Nemoto Naoko (who became Dewi Sukarno Putri, his sixth wife) and who was sent by a construction company to win a building contract (Miyake 2006). As is now well known, Sukarno used a large portion of the funds to build the skyline of Jakarta along Thamrin-Sudirman street. The President had long wished to build what he called "three dimensional buildings" in Jakarta to remind Indonesians of its glorious past in construction skills as demonstrated by the 8th century monumental Borobudur in Central Java. Japanese war compensation funds supported these "prestige projects" of Sukarno which included the 29-storey Wisma Nusantara, then the tallest office building in Indonesia, the 14-storey Sarinah Department Store and the 14-storey Hotel Indonesia, among other hotels. The support of Japan soon took the form of capital investments, continued through the 1970s and 1980s, as Japan became the largest foreign investor in Jakarta and Indonesia. The opening of Shimizu's Jakarta Design Office in the 1980s, I suspect, is inseparable from this earlier post-war history of Jakarta–Tokyo relations.

But by the 1990s, as indicated above, Japan was no longer alone in its building of Jakarta's skyline. American architects especially were hunting for jobs overseas; as Philip Langdon commented at the time: "opportunities in the United States have left some 15 to 20 per cent of the country's architects unemployed or underemployed" (Langdon 1995). The downturn in domestic construction in Japan and the US was considered a catching up time for Indonesia (as well as for other Southeast Asian countries and China). This was the postcolonial era of a construction boom and the globalisation of architecture replacing the earlier imperialism which had produced the colonial architecture of Batavia, Georgetown and Hanoi. But if optimism among North American architects prevailed in the 1990s, such that, in Christopher Choa's words, it was the time when "you can do things over there that you would never get to do back home",[4] this kind of feeling in fact was not new. In the age of colonialism, French Indochina for instance was optimistically seen by French architects and planners as a site of experimentation in contrast with "a growing pessimism about the possibilities of urban planning in France itself" (Rabinow 1989: 318). The globalisation of architecture thus cut across colonial and postcolonial times, but there is a significant difference. The globalisation of architecture today is no longer just between the designated metropole and its colony.[5] Instead, it is carried out now with "Hong Kong money, Japanese contractors, Thai construction workers, Korean-American architects, and North American building products [as they] are turning up at job sites from Selangor to Seoul" (Pearson 1993: 3).

## Transnational Construction Workers

As Asia was experiencing a construction boom, most noticeably in the 1990s (before the 1997 financial crisis), a globally oriented but profoundly unequal regional integration was taking place between capital and labour. The *Far Eastern Economic Review* (FEER) reported in 1995 that "in most of the sizzling economies of East and Southeast Asia, armies of migrant laborers are building the glistening skyscrapers and the throbbing expressways, airports and transit systems of the region's boom towns" (Hiebert 1995: 54). Some countries served as suppliers of labour, others as hosts, while a few both gave and took foreign labourers (or workers). Through a graphic and accompanying detail, the FEER shows for instance that Thailand, in 1994, "supplied more than 400,000 workers; three quarters of whom went to Singapore, Hong Kong, Malaysia, Taiwan and Brunei. The lion's share worked at construction projects" (Hiebert 1995: 55). Meanwhile, a local Thai official acknowledged that "without the Shans (workers from Myanmar) we could never have built the stadium in time for the Southeast Asian Games".[6] Unlike the Thai official, the government of Qatar and the architect of Doha Stadium (Zaha Hadid) find it hard to acknowledge the death of over 800 workers on the World Cup's Doha stadium which has been constructed to bolster the nationalist agenda of the Middle Eastern state (Riach 2014). In any case, capital expansion, global-nationalist cultural events and liberalised economies are the driving forces of urban development in Asia, but the rise of cities in the region is due in no small measure to the muscle of the labourers from neighbouring countries.

Migrant workers were often paid far lower than the minimum wage of the country they worked for. And yet what they earn is still higher than what they could make in their own country. Indonesian workers, without whom many projects in Malaysia, Singapore and Japan would remain a blueprint, would prefer to stay as long as the construction company lets them, even though many of them arrived illegally by boat at night. According to the FEER, many governments have no idea how many foreign workers are working on domestic building sites because many are illegal. In any case, as a professor of construction economies in a Japanese university pointed out in the mid-1990s, "foreign workers (legal or illegal) are now set as part of Japan's construction industry" (qtd. in Hiebert 1995: 55). If we stretch this a bit to cover the expanded geography of Japan's construction industry, we can say that those foreign workers (legal or illegal) were my co-workers except that I worked (legally but perhaps less well paid) in the air-conditioned office not in Tokyo, but in Jakarta.

For me, working in Shimizu's office was probably just as hard as working on the construction site. It was no longer clear to me which one was harder: moving around in and out of construction sites (as I did in Surabaya) or sitting at the drawing board in an air-conditioned office for a whole day. A scholarship for graduate study in upstate New York finally solved my dilemma. I still remember the day I informed my manager. The very kind Hanado-san took out his business card and wrote on it a message in Japanese to his colleague in Manhattan. He asked me to show the card to the people in Shimizu's New York office in case I decided to give up my graduate study. What a backup plan! So, I left my architectural practice in 1991.

## Auto-Constructions

I returned to construction only ten years later, but this time, in another informal setting. In 2001, after a series of devastating floods (see **Chapter 4**), my parents decided to evacuate and build for themselves a house on a piece of land, right next to my sister's house. The land was bought together (cheaper by two, after a deal) from a real estate company which was not supposed to be making business out of selling and buying land from their land bank. By the 1990s, Jakarta traffic had grown to the point where visiting a family member who lived in the same city could be an ordeal (see **Chapter 3**). That is the materiality of Jakarta. It has thus become more and more desirable for the elderly to live closer to their children and grandchildren, so that it would be easier for everyone to take care of each other. This idea was immediately put into practice. It is certainly cheaper to build on your own, especially if other family members can be mobilised.

For my parents, everything was about family. So the house would be built by my brother-in-law (who has a degree in civil engineering and ran a small construction company which has made him look like a *mandor*) and overseen by me. I had no problem with this arrangement, but what troubled me was that my parents' house would look exactly like the house of my sister which itself was copied from a real estate promotional brochure. It is not a sin for houses to look alike, but my architect's instincts found it hard to accept this. I spent a good few weeks altering the floor plan (while following the foundation which was already laid out) and the façade to make it less imitative, so that the two houses that stand together would not look like a mirror image. Then there was the fence. Unable to design it myself, I decided to let Henrik, the mason, build according to his taste. Henrik, from Central Java, did a great job but he built a fence with a style that is hard to describe. I told my parents that this was a Hindu-Islamic Javanese style. For sure, it looks different from the modernist fence of my sister's and the Renaissance style of our neighbour. If I could theorise this family affair, I would probably suggest that auto-construction involves many cultural agencies and the informality associated with it is a practice that cuts across different classes and cultures. It can be seen all over Jakarta, mostly under the radar, and it constitutes huge construction economies of its own (see **Chapter 2**).

Henrik lived not far from the house of my parents. He too owned a little house in a nearby *kampung* neighbourhood which he said was a house-in-progress as he continued to build and upgrade the house each time he could get hold of some building materials. From building my parents' house, he got an extra bonus of an Asian toilet, a sink and all the remaining new tiles for roofs and floors plus various construction tools. He had also collected some other building materials for his incremental method of house construction. He would use them gradually when more resources and time became available, but a few years later he was no longer sure about his plan of "completing" his house. Some other ambition had inspired him. Only later did I realise that he was thinking of building, on his small plot of land, some rooms for rent. The *kampung* where Henrik lived exists like a pocket within a real estate complex. It has survived largely because the real estate developer went bankrupt before he was able to acquire all the plots in the area. The *kampung* has grown informally in the middle of formal real estate housing. And the occupants of that *kampung* have shifted to people who have found work in households and commercial enterprises associated with the growth of real estate housing. And they demand rental spaces from that *kampung*.

The *kampung* has grown with people busy with all kinds of small home industries and services. The physical environment thus is marked by a variety of building styles with a great mix of building materials (recycled and new). Constructions are part of everyday life as houses are always in a state of work-in-progress. The emerging building type is a two–three storey brick building with rooms for rent. This new type of building is what inspired Henrik who wishes to retire from masonry work and run a room rental business. There are a lot of demands for rooms, Henrik once told me. My sister's family driver, who is a single man, in fact just moved into one of these rental units. He shared the building and toilets with other drivers, vendors and cleaners who work for families at the real estate housing and at nearby shops and department stores (such as Korean H-Mart and Indomaret). Henrik told me that he had been involved in constructing some of these buildings whose owners are not from the *kampung*. There are many more irregular "auto-constructions" of rental buildings by people outside the *kampung* to accommodate, not the *kampung* folks, but people from various places who are working in the surrounding real estate residential and commercial properties.

Henrik has noticed that his *kampung* is undergoing a major change, both socially and materially. This is a *kampung* where the numbers of children are decreasing. It is hard to say that "*gotong royong*" (mutual help) is as important as before. It is not clear if everyone knows each other. There are more institutionalised professionals and uniformed staff living there by renting, so they would be in their room only at night time. The *kampung* where Henrik lived is just one among many surviving *kampung*s in Jakarta today which are undergoing a change of status. First, many urban *kampung*s, as Henrik's, have been reconstructed so that there are rentals to accommodate a working middle-class population who are employed in the nearby residential and commercial establishments. Second, many *kampung*s' land has been formally titled (through a land certification programme promoted by the World Bank), so their value has gone up (as predicted by Hernando de Soto) to the point where many original inhabitants have sold their certified lands to wealthier owners or to small property developers who were not from the *kampung.* Third, the *kampung* can no longer be associated with the urban poor who have either been relocated to high-rise rental apartments or displaced to the outskirts of the city.

And, as far as we are concerned, the *kampung* is receiving investment, albeit in an incremental way. It has become one of the most active sites of "auto-construction" in Asian cities. As in the view of the British *Building* magazine cited at the beginning of this chapter, we have often associated city building in Asia with mega-urban projects, new towns and iconic high-rise towers and have seen them as a symptom of the urbanising landscape or "Manhattan transfer". Such focus however has overlooked the intensity of auto-constructions which have been marking the cities of Southeast Asia. It is this opportunity for not only auto-constructions but also for making money through a new building type for rent that the *kampung*s have survived. The last time I visited that *kampung*, Henrik was no longer living there. His "house-in-progress" had been replaced by a two-storey brick rental building. Did he build it? It is also not clear to me who owns this new building. There are cars now parking in his *kampung*'s alleyway. The streetless *kampung* has been adapted to allow cars to slowly move in and out. Or perhaps it is the car that adapts to the narrow alleyway?

## Back to the Future of Capital?

Moving forward in time, today, as the British *Building* informed us, the Indonesian construction sector ranks in the top ten in the world, but we are not sure if the construction in the *kampung* where Henrik used to live, or in any *kampung*, was included in the estimation. For sure the UK's global construction firms would be welcomed by the country, but they would find competition from regional contractors as national developers such as the Sinar Mas Land Group, Lippo Group and Ciputra Group are approaching investors from Japan, Singapore, South Korea and China as strategic partners to share both profits and risks (see **Chapter 5**). As the *Jakarta Post* reported:

> Pollux Properties Indonesia is collaborating with the Singapore-based Qingjian Group Co. Ltd as its investor for the 5,000 square meters Pollux Mega Kuningan project in Jakarta. The two companies recently signed an investment and construction cooperation agreement. Qingjian Group Co. Ltd is also the main contractor for the development of the 2.1 hectare Pollux Mega Superblock Encore in Bekasi. Next to these two projects, they are preparing to cooperate on more projects in the near future.[7]

The Qingjian Group is just one among many Singaporean property developers and contractors interested in Jakarta's "lucrative nature for property development".[8]

The list includes Pacific Star, Keppel Land and CapitaLand. And their interests are broad, ranging "from residential projects such as apartments and commercial ones, including shopping malls, and industrial estates".[9] Since foreign companies more often prefer to hire labourers locally, the Indonesian government is contributing to the labour market by making attempts to certify construction workers. This poses a big challenge; as of 2010, a report indicated that "there were 5,592,897 construction workers in Indonesia, but only 35,000 were certified".[10] I am not sure if Henrik or my *mandor* would make it to the short list. And I am also wondering if they would even worry about certifying their skills. After all, can the city be actually measured and built by certain (international) qualifications, standards or dimensions? And this also reminds me of what Indonesian writer, Seno Gumira Ajidarma, once said about Jakarta: It is "a city of a thousand dimensions".

## II. The City of a Thousand Dimensions

Seno once indicated that Jakarta consists of many conceptions and perceptions of space that often go beyond the materiality of the built environment. The city is formed by many dimensional layers, but since they are not always relationally organised, the order of things is not only messy but also absurd. And this seems to have produced people with different ways of relating to the materiality of space. Seno thus told a story about his friend who watched a couple who lived in a house made for a *warung* (food stall). They already lived there when they were quite young. And as time passed "by 1980 they already had 11 children, but the stall— the only space available—has not grown. How do they solve the space problem? It is a mystery. For sure 13 people have been sleeping in the only available space which during day time functions as a *warung*!" (Seno 2004a: 213).

And in another story:

> Twenty years ago, I borrowed a house of a vagabond to shoot a film for my school assignment. The house is so small that I had to lift the roof so that my camera could catch a view of the interior of the house. The house is exactly the size of a person lying down. It fits for a bum who doesn't have anything or need anything.... I can conclude that his house is a mental house. It can't be understood in terms of its physicality. It is to be approached mentally. Comfort is determined not by the size of the space or the number of occupants, but by the mentality of the inhabitants.... Jakarta is just such a mental house... Large space feels small and little space seems huge. (Seno 2004a: 214)

Thousands of millions of dollars have been invested to build Jakarta so that the city could get the right "three dimensions" Sukarno had in mind. Yet, many years have passed, and many "development" programmes have been initiated by both local and international agencies, by national developers and inhabitants themselves through constructions of new towns and *Kampung* Improvement Projects, and still the couple with 11 children continues to live in their *warung* and the vagrant suits himself in a one person "sleeping-only" space as if time has stood still.

Towards the end of the story, Seno reconstructs the city by indicating that while there are gaps and incommensurability between the different dimensional layers in spatial practices as inspiring as they are absurd, what lies beneath the layers is the order of capitalism. Seno puts a lot of weight on capitalist modernisation as the basis of the chaotic superstructure, but he also argues that capitalism doesn't constitute a totality as those layers, in their co-existence, never quite connect with each other.

Capital indeed has permeated every urban space of the city. As indicated above, it produces spectacular towers and gives the centre, following the wish of President Sukarno, "three dimensional" (read: monumental) buildings to symbolise the great construction culture of the nation. Capital has also penetrated the *kampung*, dissolving the duality of land markets. Following the wish of Hernando de Soto, the recent programme of land certification has created the security of tenure via land ownership, at once turning "dead capital" into a valuable asset that can be easily used for investment. All the different dimensions of space have finally met in the (single) capitalist market. And yet the integrated market economy, while changing the material space, does not seem to transform the spatial practices of people living in it. This may all be due to the material conditions of the people who have not changed, and in response they produce a city of a thousand dimensions.

Seno coined the term "kota seribu dimensi" ("city of a thousand dimensions") to characterise the spatiality anomalies of Jakarta. For him, Jakarta cannot be measured (and therefore understood) unless we approach it psychically. The city of a thousand dimensions is a city with absurd contradictions that doesn't follow the logic of dimensional ranking or order. In such a logic, a greater space is equated with increased freedom; Jakarta, for Seno, is a city of voluminous space but with so little space for freedom, and yet in the tiny space one can find in the city, boundless dynamics thrive. I was inspired by Seno's urban psyche, but I cannot write with his great idiosyncratic method. I was also more interested in looking at the city of a thousand dimensions as a construct of a political rationality that evolves over time to become normal in its absurdity, or formal in its informality.

My affinity with Seno's provocation of Jakarta as "the city of a thousand dimensions" has to do with our shared historical subjectivities. We were products of Suharto's milieu and our view of urban changes in the post-reformasi era is necessarily tied to or haunted by that era. We see more continuity (which could take mnemonic forms) behind the dramatic urban changes taking place in the post-Suharto era. Suharto's repressive order has produced not only silences or self-censorship but also (as for Seno) non-realist or surreal micro narratives that nevertheless represent realities of state violence, including the structural and symbolic ones. Jakarta is clearly a product of authoritarianism and capitalist modernisation. It is however hard to take the measure of the space that has been produced as people rework the space instantly on overtime to accommodate their different spatial practices. Hence Seno calls it the city of a thousand dimensions.

## A Thousand Plateaus / A Thousand Dimensions

According to Andy Fuller (2004) (Seno's foremost commentator), Seno uses a "postmodernist style" that is at once popular and avant garde to critically engage with power as it is invested in Indonesian politics and culture. Such a style, we could add, developed out of the pressure to respond quickly to daily events which, if not acknowledged immediately, could disappear into dust. Writing for him is a medium for a quick and uncontrollable discharge. It is just like farting, a smelly gas that can't be hidden even though the causes or sources are not always known. Undetectable but powerful, farting is a form of communication under a repressive regime. But Seno continues to "fart" even after Suharto had stepped down. Today Seno (2008) "farts" with pride. He even calls his post-reformasi's work "Kentut Metropolitan" (Metropolitan Farting) and he encourages people to "fart" naturally if not proudly. Naturally too then Seno's urban commentaries are necessarily fragmented and incomplete. They are however consistently critical but not to the point of calling for an urban revolt. Like farting, his call is never too loud and generally implicit. In exposing injustices in this way, Seno appreciates the human capacity to rework the existing condition to the point of stretching a space to an unmeasurable extent. The result is a city of a thousand dimensions, constructed by a thousand subjectivities, governed by a thousand rules. Together they have produced a thousand ways of ordering as well as messing up the city.

I believe that Seno's depiction of Jakarta as a city of a thousand dimensions is figurative, an attempt to both appreciate and criticise the multiplicity or irreducibility of a city that seeks to stabilise itself through a never-ending state of becoming. His "thousand dimensions" recalls Deleuze and Guattari's "thousand plateaus", a never-ending process of assemblage. I am not sure if Seno had these two French thinkers in mind, but he reads widely, and he embraces social theories from the West as well as from the East. I attended one of his seminars which was organised around some European critical thinkers. We were both interested in a wide range of critical theories which we feel free to appropriate without a commitment to stay firmly with any certain one. I had read some pages of *A Thousand Plateaus* for inspiration before I discovered Seno's work, so my identification with Seno's "thousand dimensions" might have stemmed from my discursive curiosity towards the Deleuze and Guattari volume. These two works may have shared some similar ideas, but they also could not have been more different.

Seno's "thousand dimensions" is an attempt to intervene *from within* a repressive regime's production of space. It doesn't stand outside the system within which it is embedded, nor does it constitute any resistance against the city and the regime that produces it.

The *Thousand Plateaus* volume, while exploring "ways of being which are always open to multiplicity and the becoming of the world" (Shaw 2015: 158), takes as its mission the traversal to a totally different mode of thinking against the unity of European representation of identity (Adkins 2015). Deleuze and Guattari tried to problematise the dominant Western system of thought by theorising a different knowledge and, as I will indicate below, to do so from sources outside the geographical West. They conceptualised each of the thousand plateaus as an assemblage that exists only temporarily as part of a rhizomatic network with other plateaus. In such a configuration, there is neither a foundation to anchor a movement nor a progression to an ending point. There is no core, no peak, and no climax in the thousand plateaus. There are only relations held together by the middling of the rhizome (Shaw 2015). We thus see a range of names for the plateaus which indicate an anti-foundational philosophy of non-progression, for instance, the "Rhizome", the "Body without Organs" and "Nomadology" among others (Deleuze and Guattari 1987).

Deleuze and Guattari conceptualised a thousand plateaus to represent a radically different system of thought. And they drew inspirations from outside Europe—most notably from an anthropological study of Bali—as if only through a reworking of other cultures "out there" could a solution be found for Europe to stand *outside* its a priori position. They asked: "Isn't there in the East, notably in Oceania, a kind of rhizomatic model that contrasts in every respect with the Western model of the tree?" (cp. Deleuze and Guattari 1987: 18). *Thousand Plateaus* thus was inspired by the study of the Orientalised "other". It owes much to the study of Bali by Artaud for concepts leading to the Body without Organs and Bateson for plateaus (Shaw 2015). We have an instance of anthropological imagination of the other as an antidote to Western problems (Rahn 2008). Yet Bateson and other anthropologists and artists who lived and worked in Bali in the 1930s observed and theorised Bali within the optic of colonial fantasy of a harmonious and apolitical Bali. They showed very little interest in considering the political and historical conditions of Dutch colonial power within which both their subjectivities and Balinese society existed (Robinson 1995: 7). It is quite ironical that while *Thousand Plateaus* was a work of political desire to produce a new mode of (European) life, it drew its theoretical concepts or inspirations from the ahistorical and apolitical works of colonial anthropologists on Bali.

As "the city of a thousand dimensions" and "the thousand plateaus" belong to quite different social contexts, they are connected through what Edward Said (1983) called "traveling theory" and colonial modes of knowledge production. Such a connection has made the question of origin obsolete, and it is equally problematic to say that the East is offering a different thought model to Europe. I do not know what *A Thousand Plateaus* and "A Thousand Dimensions" have or could have done for each other, but for this book, I simply take the liberty of appropriating them loosely to organize my own method, story and argument. I evoke terms such the "middling" for chapter 1, the "rhizome" for chapter 3, the "way of water" for chapter 4, the "assemblage" for chapter 5 and the "multitude" for the epilogue, but I use them to describe neither resistance nor an alternative model of thought. Instead, I use these terms to depict a form of governance, a statecraft that rules the city through a rhizomic structure. *Thousand Plateaus* is an anti-foundational work that values movement and becoming over establishment or government. Its anti-mathematical axiomatics seem compatible with the schizoanalysis of Seno's city of a thousand dimensions, but Seno is not interested in seeking resistance or a position outside the power system. For Seno, there is no outside from which to stand. This is where I find Seno's position closer to mine, but unlike Seno who emphasises the idiosyncratic city, I seek to present the political rationale or the governmentality of the city of a thousand dimensions.

This book therefore takes shape from extrapolating from three-dimensional architectonic form. It consists of socio-political analyses across a range of topics, divergent sites, a range of actors and their discourses. The chapters could be read as presenting a series of historically determined contemporary events that seek to reach out towards one another but cannot always quite touch, even as they figuratively intersect. The chapters could thus be read separately, but together they form an assemblage of fragments. There are connections between the chapters even as they do not amount to a detectable pattern or a well-known type or a theory. I came to choose the topics represented in each chapter because there were news items and conversations about them.

Those who know Jakarta would immediately recognise the familiar features that make up a typical conversation: *kampung*, *macet* (traffic jam), *banjir* (flooding), urban politics, public space, new town, and, now, the yearning for a new capital city. These topics are often in the news with varying intensities, but they have also become so familiar that they enter a conversation not as news, but as everyday talk. This book however addresses these familiar features of the city with a makeshift method to slowly connect them with vast arrays of life and history, sometimes by way of mobilising gigantic forces, statecraft and ambitious or localised responses to detect some phenomenon emerging out of confusing interactions. I hope readers will see that the topics presented in the chapters are not only familiar facts, but also "matters of concern" (Latour 2004). What interested me was the call (by a range of actors) for a change in a city that doesn't offer a unity that might tie diverse domains of practice into a coherent whole. I approach this call as a matter of concern.

Bruno Latour (2004) has indicated that matters of concern can be everything, from ideas to material conditions of production and the social context that mutually produce what is misunderstood as "matters of fact". Latour's method inspires me to consider how a variety of aligned and divided actors, from professionals and businessmen to political figures and the interested public, along with their associated discursive and non-discursive materials have entangled, co-produced, or reassembled a city which seems to have taken a thousand dimensions. It is a matter of concern for me because such an assemblage is not only political, but it has also become normal or normalised as a "matter of fact".

## Approaching the City

It will have become clear, so I hope, that my way of reading the city was informed by disparate thinkers, such as Seno, who offered inspirations. This book, as most books on urbanism, often represents the subjectivity of the author more than the realities of the city, realities which we can never fully grasp. While not always explicitly, I have benefitted from a mix of theoretical insights to help coordinate my understanding. They range from urban political economy and critical infrastructure studies to topological analyses. If we free ourselves to learn from them without too much commitment and desire for consistency, and tolerate differences and contradictions among them, we can be led to think that heterogenous elements can have a relational order and that a structure can have incommensurable dimensions. I can no longer be clear how they helped me assemble parts into a relation and how they entered discursively into my narrative. I benefitted from them but in the end, considering the amorphous field of urban studies and the debates between scholars in the humanities and the social sciences, there is no way for me to add up the book's stories into a singular logic of urban change. I can propose only a series of intentions and understandings that have contributed to the book's method.

*The desire for a change is pertinent to the project at hand.* It represents once again the theme of movement or moving forwards, which, as I first indicated in *The Appearances of Memory*, "has been a crucial concept and problem for modern Indonesia for much of the last century" (Kusno 2010: 3). Over the last century the problematics of *gerak* (moving) have taken multiple configurations, from the state-generated idea of "development" through "order and stability" (of the Suharto regime) to the calls from the multitudes for *pergerakan, reformasi* and *revolusi* especially after the fall of Suharto. This book focuses on the latest interest in the new and in acceleration, as the marker of motion, which gives legitimacy to those who are in power, who seek modernity and who want to be urban, once more, in a post-authoritarian context.

*The older and newer elements are mutually constitutive.* To study the ethos of becoming urban, contemporary or modern, is to be attentive not only to the new but also to the old, for they co-exist. The book shows how the new and the old work together in multiple configurations constituting spatial practices that are rhizomatic in their relations with each other. To study Jakarta thus is to carry out a historicist work that shows the contingency, the possibility and the heterogeneity of incoherent spatial practices that constitute nevertheless a provisional movement that seeks to mark a new time.

*The "post-" era demands a method beyond binary opposition.* While the new shares a similar ethos with the old, Jakarta's residents are no longer living under Suharto's authoritarian regime. Some have said that the city and the nation are undergoing democratic transition. Others have said that we are getting democracy now. While the images of the Suharto regime may have merged into a background with those of the colonial or pre-colonial past, I believe they are still the living ghosts of the present. For instance, evictions by force have become unsustainable and politically costly (even for the powerful), but evictions continue more and more on paper and through the market. Such a change still carries a problematic layering of the older urban political cultures. But still, we are after all in the social domain of the post-Suharto era. Given the "post-" as a condition with the mixed characteristics of those "who had freed themselves on one level but who remained victims of their past on another" (Said 1989: 207), we have lost some common historical adversaries associated with the Suharto regime. While society or culture reproduces itself in the time of change, we can no longer rely on a binary oppositional framework, as between the (authoritarian) state on the one hand and (the hopefully democratic) civil society on the other hand engaging in the struggle to maintain or improve their place in power relations. The current milieu is criss-crossed by mutually constitutive power relations, where subjects and objects are beneficially and problematically intermingled with no apparent order and hierarchy. The dominant force could be simultaneously a force of resistance, and the emergent could be embroiled in the restoration of the old adversary. The order of things is uncertain, and it can't be stabilised through a binary taxonomy.

*The global is often subjected to localisation.* One of the most productive methods in analysing globalisation has been the focus on the "complex negotiations between globality and locality" (Huyssen 2008: 11). The narratives of such a method are still often based on how the local, e.g. the place-based city, confronts the unbounded global world. On one side, there is power, and on the other, resistance; the global is transforming the local. Such a formulation is productive, but, considering the unevenness of power and influence between cities, it often doesn't take us deep enough into an understanding of the ways in which postcolonial modernity or capitalism and globalisation have evolved, the kind of urban form it created and what it might mean in for the urban life today. A shared global picture could be co-constructed by attending to localised practices. In this book I follow the suggestion formulated by Ong Aihwa in the book co-edited with Ananya Roy, *Worlding Cities*, to grasp the heterogenous practices of worlding (i.e. spatialising practices) in the city:

> The starting point of analysis is thus not how singular principles define a city environment, but rather the array of problem-solving and spatializing practices that are in play in shaping an urban field... Spatializing practices thus form the urban as a problem-space in which a cast of disparate actors – the state, capitalists, NGOs, foreign experts, and ordinary people – define what is problematic, uncertain, or in need of mediation, and then go about solving these now-identified problems such as urban planning, class politics, and human capital. (Ong 2011a: 10)

Each chapter in this book thus represents an array of spatialising practices which involve a cast of disparate actors. Each in their own way articulates a technique of urban transformation that helps shape societal relations.

I have put them together in this book to articulate Ong's call for understanding "situated experiments" as an "art of being global" (Ong 2011a: 4) to refine statecraft, to exploit the potentiality of social and environmental crises and to imagine futurity. The chapters, individually and collectively, represent an approach to "the city of a thousand dimensions" where practices rule over policies, disasters multiply opportunities and the lack of planning could become a craft of governing. I seek to tease out the contexts of such production, and to describe how people from different positions reproduce it, take advantage of it or seek to change it. I agree with Seno that the city has become more multidimensional as a result of uneven capitalist modernisation, and that people normalise the space that has been produced by adapting their life to it. I would add that over time an unplanned planning culture has developed into an art of governing an urban population, but that such a culture, as this book intends to show, can also be contested, transformed, or ignored.

The following is an outline of the chapters, with each carrying a primary concern, but when they are pieced-together, they give a sense of the overlap in a conjunction that illuminates a dimension of existence, its profound disruption and the emergence of multiple crises.

## Outline and Structure of the Book

**Chapter 1**, "Middling Urbanism", takes up the theme of gaps and incommensurability of the city's different dimensions especially between the formal city and its informal settlements, but it seeks to track systematically the order that has nevertheless given Jakarta a relational structure. It shows how the irregular settlements (known as *kampung*) are constitutive parts of urban development in Jakarta as well as in the city's extended peri-urban areas. I outline the condition, connection and the contexts that have contributed to such an urban relation which include the state's politics and the order of the international division of labour and investment. I argue that the persistence, location and functionality of *kampung* constitute a milieu for "middling urbanism".

**Chapter 2**, "The Rule of Many Orders", outlines the political ecologies of urban housing in Indonesia. It offers a sketch of the politics behind the lack of state capacity to deliver mass housing as a historically determined art of governing through uneven power-sharing. I argue that the lack of universal access to decent shelter is due in large measure to power being shared between the state, capital and civil society both before the "Era Reformasi" (era of reform [1998]) and after it. The lack of housing provision is arguably a most explicit representation of Indonesian statecraft where the state, local administrators, business groups, leaders, dealers and residents mutually constitute and shape land markets for their beneficially problematic deals.

**Chapter 3**, "Roads, Rhizomes and Regimes", discusses the multitude of Jakarta's transportation flows and its political economy from a historical perspective. I show how the city continues to flow under traffic congestion and how politics, businesses and cultures intersect in giving rise to a rhizomic system of "para-transportation" which, while serving as an antidote to the pain of urban breakdown, has developed a regime of differential infrastructural modes.

**Chapter 4**, "Where Will the Water Go?", examines how annual flooding in Jakarta is perceived and responded to by different social actors in the city. The objective is to make sense of how flooding has led to both disaster and opportunities as well as modes of governing society; how different understandings of flooding are implicated in knowledge and power and how flooding becomes a form of governmentality and source of speculation among policy makers, planners, developers and residents of the city in developing their own politics of infrastructure.

**Chapter 5**, "A New Assemblage City", tells a story of a property developer involved in building a new city. It shows how the attempt to transcend the old city by incorporating the "best" from "global cities" in both the East and the West revealed only or contributed yet another layered sediment of contradictory spatiality. The case contributes to the current discussion of spaces of "post-suburbia" and deepens our understanding of the complexity of building a new city in a social formation that is marked intrinsically by a system of power relation as is characteristic of Indonesian political culture.

**Chapter 6**, "Urban Politics", looks into a new configuration of urban political practices following the rise of populism in Indonesian politics. I examine how the Governors of Jakarta, Jokowi and Ahok respectively, sought to undermine traditions of multi-dimensional power established since the early 1970s under the authoritarian New Order government of Suharto. Against this systemic informalisation of power, the new tradition of Jokowi and Ahok has emphasised the formalisation of civil, political and economic relations which however has also alienated some forms of the local tradition of autonomy and anonymity on which the urban poor depend for survival.

**Chapter 7**, "Islamist Urbanism", explores the recent Islamist ascendency and its articulation in urban space in Jakarta and Bandung, the two major cities of West Java. I look at how the democratic social order and the quest for religious self inform each other in shaping urban form and space. Practices associated with neoliberal reforms as represented by transparency, objectivity and self-help are reworked in and through the built environment as a medium for the articulation of conservative Islamist identity and concerns.

**Chapter 8**, "Escape from Jakarta: The Future Redux", takes President Jokowi's proposal to build a new capital city elsewhere and contextualises it through the issues covered in the book: the complex problems facing Jakarta, from flooding, subsidence and traffic to inequality and the rise of identity politics. It then considers if the new idea of a new capital city offers a plausible way out of a crisis of governability or if it is a case of elites abandoning responsibility for the city.

Chapters Nine and Ten are a collective work or a work that came out of a conversation with a group of scholars working on Jakarta. **Chapter 9**, "Jakarta: A Conversation", discusses the intersections of politics and culture in urban governance and the ways in which the formal and informal traditions of urban politics operate in the contested spaces of Jakarta. It also covers issues from the rise and fall of a governor to the emergence of an Islamist movement in the pressured spaces of Jakarta. This conversational piece with scholars from different disciplines covers several themes discussed in the book while seeking to understand the undercurrents of Jakarta politics and the extent to which these can be understood through conventional concepts from the social sciences.

**Chapter 10**, "Our Streets: Reflections on a Pandemic City", stemmed from a series of conversations via Zoom with Suryono Herlambang and Wahyu Astuti in Jakarta and Frans Prasetyo in Bandung. The surge of COVID-19 cases and deaths in the summer of 2021 heightened our concerns for safety which added gravity to other factors that were already weighing against the social life of the city. Out of our regular conversations, we decided to organise some notes into an essay about roads as experienced during the pandemic situation, how roads embodied nationalist utopia, streetlife, speed, barricades and revolution. We show how, while COVID-19 is global in character, the response to it reveals some local specificity in Indonesian urbanism.

The **Afterword**, "On 'Multitude' and the Urban Question", reflects on the asymmetries of power and influence between cities at the level of both theories and practices. I consider how the concepts of the multitude (as formulated by Antonio Negri and Michael Hardt) and the urban question (a Marxist critique of urban studies formulated by Manuel Castells) are linked and how (after the book's narratives) they might be relevant or not for thinking about Jakarta and its struggle for urban change.

## Notes

[1] Very few studies have been done on *mandor*. See Firman 1989.
[2] A similar summary is given in JSI's 2021 Company Report: "Known for service excellence and product innovation, JSI has managed to gain the trust and respect of international business partners, including Hyatt International, Accor Asia Pacific, Itochu Corporation, Shimizu and Nomura" (https://en.jsi.co.id/assets/uploads/media/AR%20dan%20SR%20Tahun%20Buku%202021-JSPT-FINAL-SUBMIT%20OJKBEI.pdf).
[3] Pollock, "KPF Bank Complex Rises in Jakarta": 4.
[4] Christopher Choa, who led HLW's design work in Asia, cited in Langdon 1995.

[5] The model today is no longer the Euro-American urban centres or suburbs. Instead there is a city-state such as Singapore which, according to a report, has in recent years been ranked "the best place in the world to do business". The UK came in only at number 21, below Malaysia. See: Colin Cram, "Why Singapore is Building a New Indian City 10 Times its own Size", *The Guardian*, 7 Jan. 2015.

[6] Hiebert, 1995: 55. Hiebert also reported that in 1995, "Japan has some 160,000 foreign construction workers. But other estimates put the number closer to 270,000".

[7] Aulia R. Sungkar, "National Developers Looking to Team up with Foreign Investors", *The Jakarta Post*, 5 Nov. 2015.

[8] Wendra Ajistyatama, "Foreign Developers Eye Local Prospects", *The Jakarta Post*, 11 July 2014.

[9] Ibid.

[10] "Construction Workers to Get Certified", *The Jakarta Post*, 2 April 2011.

# Middling Urbanism

The urban form of cities in Southeast Asia has been associated with qualitative terms such as "messy urbanism", "incomplete urbanism", "incremental urbanism", and quantitative terms like "mega urban region" and "megacity" (Chalana and Hou 2016; Dovey 2014; Lim 2012; McGee and Robinson 1995; Rao 2012; Roy 2011). Such depictions stem from scholars who observed urban expansion in the Global South as a complex interface between the city and the country. In contrast to "suburbanisation", which suggests a more or less unidirectional "urban sprawl" phenomenon due to the expansion of serviced land, the urban transition in Southeast Asia is, according to scholars of the region, taking the shape of a hybrid space known as *desakota* (from the Indonesian words *desa* for village and *kota* for town) (Friedmann 2011; Leaf 2011; McGee 1991). Coined by Terry McGee, the term describes "a last zone of urbanisation, where non-agricultural activity is increasingly mixed with agriculture" (McGee 1991: 7). Such zones are "significant foci of industrialisation and rapid economic growth" which clusters "around the large urban cores of many Asian countries" (ibid.).

Most scholars working on Asian urbanisms support McGee's formulation, agreeing that these hybrid spaces are new, distinctive and even an enduring form of transitional urbanisation. Yet the primary concern of their studies is the geography of the peri-urban area, and they have therefore largely overlooked a similar hybrid formation in the urban core of the city. This chapter seeks to suggest that the kind of peri-urbanisation on the outskirts of the city may well have taken place first in the urban area.

This chapter, with a focus on Jakarta, argues that a series of urban and rural complementarities, as in *desakota*, continues to take place in the city in the form of an interaction between its formalised area and the irregular settlements known in Indonesia as the *kampung*. I use the term "irregular settlements" to designate *kampung* (instead of squatter settlements, illegal settlements or informal settlements), for in almost all cases they are acknowledged as *de facto* settlements. The aim of this chapter is to show that irregular settlements are constitutive parts of urban development in both Jakarta and the city's extended peri-urban areas. And the persistence, location and functionality of *kampung* on the outskirts of

Jakarta or in middle of the city constitute a phenomenon of what I would call a "middling urbanism". By this term, I seek to contribute to the discussion on the nature of urbanisation and suburbanisation in the Global South. Instead of a unidirectional transition to a normative urbanisation or suburbanisation, cities in Southeast Asia (with very few exceptions) have exhibited a phenomenon of middling urbanism in both their urban centres and the outskirts of the city. For the case of Jakarta, the phenomenon of "middling urbanism" is built on politico-economic calculations sustained by a particular culture of governance.

## Positioning Middling Urbanism

I define middling urbanism as an urban condition characterised by the existence of the *kampung* in formation of the urban centre or peri-urban areas. It follows that the *kampung* plays an important social, economic and political role in the functioning of the city. The *kampung* forms a mutually constitutive relation with the formalised city in the co-production of a distinctive urban norm and form that take a "middle" position if projected along various socio-economic and cultural axes. "Middle" or "middling" here connotes a dynamic spatial and temporal relation of sharing, the quality of which carries the meaning of "both–and", "the-same-but-not-quite" or "in-between" the city and the countryside. By using the term "middling" in a sense of neither at the front nor at the back to characterise the *kampung* neighbourhood, I do not mean to suggest the deficiency of the *kampung* or that the *kampung* lacks the capacity to urbanise and that it needs assistance and modernisation—a claim which has become an ideology of development (even though improvement in living conditions in some settlements is *de facto* required).

Spatially, the *kampung* is an intermediate space where recent migrants from the countryside first recognise themselves as urbanites, not just in the territorial sense, but also in socio-cultural practices. The *kampung*'s existence as an intermediate space is also necessary as a stabiliser of an increasingly polarised urban-rural system. It serves to moderate conflicts between the city and the countryside. Its complex *habitus* engages economically, politically and culturally with (instead of in opposition to) capitalism and the state. A middle stratum by definition, the *kampung* is neither opposed to nor outside of the normative urbanisation but mediates between the shared and conflicting interests and concerns of those living in the city.

The indefinite character of middling urbanism also acknowledges that the *kampung* has heterogeneous but distinctive features that it shares in contrast to the city. The *kampung* constitutes a different type of land market, distinctive neighbourhood, livelihoods and resources, in relation to developer-driven housing estates and the formal land market with which it co-exists. Consequently, the *kampung* (while socially considered to be peripheral if not marginal) needs to be centrally located, conceptually, in the interstices of the nation-state and global capital. It is neither simply a victim nor a survivor of capitalist modernisation as has often been (mis-)understood. Instead, it exists, persists and grows in and through contradictions of the capitalist mode of exchange. It operates in the context of uneven capitalist modernisation which demands a continuous and simultaneous destruction and construction of the *kampung*. In its entanglement with the state and capital, middling urbanism reflects on the labour relation and class mobility of *kampung* dwellers in relation to the formalised city. The members occupy various positions (in the middle of forces) that cut across the formal and informal sectors in their collective aspirations for upward mobility.

What follows is an attempt to construct a "provisional diagram of how to understand a city" (Amin and Thrift 2002). It is not an ethnographical account of the *kampung* which urban anthropologists have quite extensively presented (Guinness 2009; Jellinek 1991; Murray 1991; Newberry 2006; Peters 2013; Sullivan 1980, among others). I structure my argument in various sections, with each contributing to a conceptualisation of the *kampung* as a different space but one that is intertwined with the formalised city, the state's politics and the milieu of the international division of labour and investment. While most of my thinking for this chapter is based on my observations of Jakarta/Indonesia, I believe some of the issues addressed are relevant for thinking comparatively about other places (McFarlane 2010; Roy 2009; Simone 2010).

## The Banality of the *Kampung*

In "Provisional Notes on the Postcolony", African philosopher Achille Mbembe describes "banality" in terms of "those elements of the obscene and the grotesque that Mikhail Bakhtin claims to have located in 'non-official' cultures but which in fact are intrinsic to all systems of domination and to the means by which those systems are confirmed or deconstructed" (Mbembe 1992:3). Such a definition fits the place of the *kampung* in an urban system which is characterised by unequal and yet mutual exchanges between the state, capital and labour. Typologically, a *kampung* is a densely populated irregular urban neighbourhood the residents of which, for the most part, are not rich if not relatively poor, although occasionally some have become wealthy but still prefer to live in the *kampung*. The houses and the people tend to be crowded together, thus giving an atmosphere of *ramai* (a sense of many things occurring at once) (Figure 1.1).

The *kampung* is also viewed by the state as representing "non-official" cultures of self-reliance which partly stem from a social environment that is not sustained by adequate infrastructural services. In poorer *kampung*, buildings are often constructed incrementally with substandard materials, which makes the neighbourhood vulnerable to fire, floods (for those by the riverbank) and epidemics. Building construction in a *kampung* often does not follow building codes, so the built environment does not reflect planning regulations. Zoning in planning would work against the spatial practices of *kampung* dwellers because in the *kampung* the land is flexibly used. The land on which the buildings stand (which I will discuss later) may lack legal status, but this does not mean that the settlement is illegal. Land values are often negotiable and usually follow a different tier that is lower than the market rate. The characteristic of the *kampung* is such that its domain can be considered as different from the formally planned parts of Jakarta, yet it is also tied to "all systems of domination", both confirming and deconstructing power.

**Figure 1.1.** Street scene in *Kampung* Pulo (author's photo).

Being connected to all systems of domination means that the *kampung* takes many dimensions. It has its own legal status that stems from the moral economy of the state. It has a rhythm of *kampung* life sustained by the sedimented cultural memories and social practices of the neighbourhood. It also exists within an international division of labour and investment where it supplies labour from its semi-proletarian households to keep wages low. The time of capital thus co-exists with that of the *kampung*, as people in the neighbourhood reproduce their condition of existence in and through capital and the state's strategy of rule. This web of power relations between the state, capital and the *kampung* explains why urbanisation, i.e. the "modernisation" of the city (and its concomitant eradication of *kampung*), has been in fact slow despite the claims of rapid urban transformation. The *kampung* continues to exist and grow in many different forms, despite instances of eviction and relocation.

## Intersectional Binarism

Students of urban geography, sociology and anthropology have noticed the profound physical contrast between the *kampung* neighbourhood (where houses are constructed with walls made from a combination of cement and braided bamboo) and the *kota* (represented by street-side "brick" buildings) in the major cities of Indonesia. Jeff Dreyfuss for instance, has depicted Jakarta as a city with "two personae—'the big village' and 'rock city'" (Dreyfuss 1990). Alison Murray has noticed the difference in cultural lifestyles (produced mostly out of constraints though sometimes by choice) and indicated that *kampung* residents communally construct their lifestyles in contrast to "the metropolitan superstructure and its structure of power and policy" (Murray 1991: 15). Cowherd and I, among others, have also emphasised the contrast between the automobile-dependent middle-class real estate housing complex and the *kampung*'s narrow alleyways (Cowherd 2002b; Kusno 2000). Such a contrast, as we argued, formed part of the state's narrative of modernisation. It enables members of the upper-middle class to distance themselves from the *kampung*, which they see as "backward" or "belonging to the past". We set up this binary trope of the (relatively modernising and individualistic) urban middle class versus the (communitarian) masses (known as *rakyat*) in order to understand the city as a site of domination, marginalisation and contestation (see also Mahasin 1992).

It is important to note, however, that the binary opposition between the *kota* and the *kampung* is not only a scholar's construct. Indonesian commoners (including those who live in the *kampung*) also recognise such binary categories of the *kampung* and the *kota*, as are often described in their own speech through notions such as *gedongan* (those of the wall) and *kampungan* (rural-like). Such a binary framework seems important for them to make sense of their surrounding world as they locate themselves in the course of urban development. The persistent use of *binary* frameworks such as the *kampung* versus the *kota* has also been noticed by Erik Harms in his *Saigon's Edge* (2011). Harms shows how Vietnamese reliance on binary schemes has produced (instead of constraining) "stories that are full of dreams and unspeakable silences" (Harms 2011: 221). Harms aptly uses the word "edge" to suggest that the binary framework that makes up the edge is actually quite flexible as one side can cut into the other: "Like the double-edged blade of a knife, edginess cuts both ways, sometimes cutting back against structures of power and sometimes cutting the very social agents who wield it" (ibid.: 4). This sense of cutting across different spheres is less a resistance than an incision from inside a power system.

An example of such a "cut" could take the form of how *kampung* dwellers and private property developers mutually and literally cut through a wall that separated them so that the two worlds of the *kampung* and the *kota* could be connected by a gateway (Figure 1.2).

**Figure 1.2 (a and b):** A cut in the wall (left-side); entrance from a *kampung* to condominiums and mega-commercial superblocks in Jakarta's CBD (right) (author's photos 2016)

The cut through the wall is necessary for the *kampung* dwellers to enter the formal complexes of condominiums, offices and shopping malls where they work as drivers, maids, gardeners, handymen, security personnel and vendors. Likewise, the property developer who built the wall in order to increase the value of the property also took advantage of the cut. The food stalls, vendors and rental places provided by the *kampung* on the other side of the wall serve as "facilities" for the low wage workers employed in the formal establishment. This relationship between the *kampung* and the *kota* is clearly uneven but it is also mutually beneficial. For the private developer, the breach in the wall is an act of cost saving as it serves to externalise costs associated with labour and services; for the *kampung* dwellers, the cut allows access to a livelihood beyond their neighbourhood.

The urban spaces of Jakarta are thus filled with cuts in the walls where the two worlds are linked symbiotically as well as pathologically. The existence of *kampungs* is often "off the map". The pockets of urban *kampung* (shaded areas of the map in Figure 1.3) continue to exist in the city like (hidden) organs in its body. They are scattered and fragmented but each one plays the role of an "edge" *within* the city.

These pockets of the *kampung* accommodate and supply workers, staff, shopkeepers and janitors for nearby establishments. They cluster around areas with concentrations of high-rise office buildings and shopping malls. They are often divided by a wall into which a doorway is cut for access. The symbiotic or pathological cross-network between the *kampung* and the city could be seen as a manifestation of middling urbanism which produces an urban form that is at once *kampung*-like. The *kampung* and the *kota* are living together apart, so the two are actually one (or the one is actually two). We could put them together as in the notion of "*kampungkota*" (after McGee's *desakota* which refers exclusively to the extended region) to represent a symbiotic urban process that relies on *both* division *and* collaboration (unevenly) between the two entities. For Josef Gugler, who uses the categories of the formal and the informal to depict the *kota* and the *kampung* dynamism, "the informal sector can be argued to be subsidising the formal sector" (Gilbert and Gugler 1992: 97–8). Such a formation of a *Kampungkota* city, however, is neither "cultural" nor timeless. It is part of a historical formation of power related to colonial and postcolonial forms of governance.

## The Invulnerability of the Informal: A Genealogy

The *kampung* has often been associated with the informal economy. The study of this economy has a long history, and yet few scholars are aware that the concept of the "informal sector" was first inspired by a study of the Indonesian economy during the colonial era. In the 1910s, studying the Indonesian economy, Dutch scholar Julius Herman Boeke teased out a sector of the colonial economy that resisted the incorporation of the colonial state. Boeke saw small traders, craftsmen and farmers dominating the sector, all of whom were supported by family labour and managed with an "oriental mentality" (Boeke 1953 [1910]). He indicated that this sector stood in full contrast to large enterprises that operated on capitalist principles. These two systems, while divided by different levels of technology and patterns of development, lived side-by-side unevenly as one was dominating and expanding while the other held strongly to its values and resisted incorporation. Boeke's formulation was aimed at problematising the evolutionary narrative of the empire's capitalist project. He emphasised the irreconcilable difference between the two economic systems. His dual economy theory eventually developed (in the

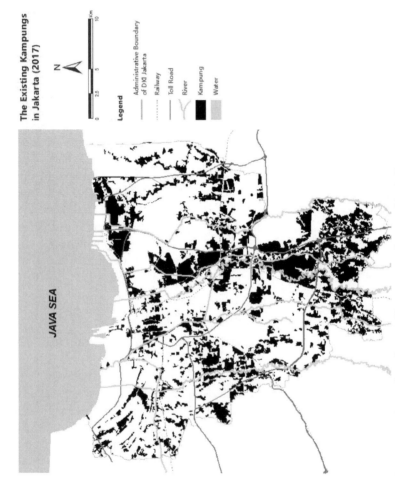

**Figure 1.3** An analytical map of *kampung* settlements (shaded)

*Source*: constructed 2018 by Prakoso, Saputra and Dewangga, based on aerial image data from Google Earth 2017; courtesy of Miya Irawati and Rita Padawangi.

postwar era) into a set of binary categories of the modern and the traditional, the formal and the informal, in the study of what is considered less-developed "third world" countries.

Postwar theorists, however, have given Boeke's formulation a new direction. In the mid-1950s W. Arthur Lewis developed an economic theory based on the dualism of industrial and non-industrial economies. Lewis indicated that the "unlimited supply of labor" in most developing countries could serve as the basis for the development of a modern industrial sector in both the core and peripheral countries. Lewis believed that poor countries would develop if they shifted labour from their informal economy into manufacturing (Hosseini 2012). In 1971, Keith Hart and labour economists at the International Labor Organization picked up Boeke's theory through elaborating the concept of the formal and informal sectors (Hart 1973). The informal economy remains an important category for analysing urban change, especially in developing countries. For urban anthropologists, the informal is characterised by "small-scale, family-type operations, with low capital, maximising family labour, operating in illegal or unregulated areas, marked sometimes by illicit operations, and with ease of entry and low skills" (Guinness 2009: 58). Guinness underlines the important characteristic of the informal, which is flexibility in time and space, as the key to survival, because it allows them to "conduct a number of different operations, even in the same day" (ibid.: 58–9). The flexibility attributed to the informal sector is specific, but it is also inseparable from the formal sector with which it co-exists.

Geographically, if the informal is accommodated in the *kampung*, its relations with the formal sector would necessarily locate the *kampung* in propinquity with the offices, shopping malls and formal residential areas. In short, the *kampung* is needed by the city even though the nation-building rhetoric of modernisation comes with a threat to the *kampung*'s existence. The *kampung* is central and yet peripheral at the same time. It is simultaneously in and out of place. It is geographically in the "middle" of the city, yet it is seen and unseen at the same time.

In the early 1990s, Soetjipto Wirosardjono, the Deputy Chairman of the Central Bureau of Statistics, described how the city of Jakarta relied on the "internal dynamics" of its urban society as well as the "external dynamics" of the economy (Wirosardjono 1991: 61). He did not use the notion of "periphery" and "core" to designate the relation between internal and external dynamics, but he used the notion of the "informal sector" (while acknowledging the term's gross simplification of realities) to indicate "the supporting element of the city". For Wirosardjono, the informal sector is crucial for the city to "fulfill its primary economic functions in the fields of manufacturing, export, import, trading" (ibid.). The "primary economic" which has brought "the city to the world" needs goods and services provided by "people operating in the informal sector, like hawkers, street vendors and so on" (ibid.). Street vendors supply food for wage labourers; informal mechanics maintain cars even though they are not involved in the manufacturing of cars. The "internal dynamics" enables the performance of the "external dynamics". Wirosardjono concluded:

> Without the informal sector the workers would simply be unable to survive on the level of salary they are receiving ... only because of this extremely low level of prices, the industrialists and the business sector can afford to pay such a low salary to the workers ... The living standard of the main part of the urban population, which includes lower rank civil servants and military, is such that the presence of the informal sector is inevitable. (Ibid.: 62)

From Wirosardjono we learn that the state, the industrialists and the workers are connected to one another through the informal sector. They constitute a power relation that ultimately shows how the capitalist world economy is based on the production of the "informal sector" and its army of "semi-formal workers" who do not depend exclusively on their wage income for their livelihood. Wirosardjono, however, was also perfectly aware that in this mutually constitutive relation between capital and labour, the informal sector "will never be able to uplift their condition towards entering the formal sector" (ibid.: 65). Wirosardjono proposed that the role of the informal sector be acknowledged and suggested some "transitional policies" that are "just and people-oriented" to support the informal sectors so that they could grow together with the rest of urban economy (ibid.).

## The Mystery of the Household

As indicated earlier, the Indonesian urban *kampung* has been extensively studied, especially by scholars from the fields of urban anthropology and sociology. It is fair to acknowledge, however, that while in most studies the *kampung* is seen as a crucial part of the city, its linkage to the dynamics of the world-capitalist system is still insufficiently addressed. In their studies of households in the world-capitalist system, Immanuel Wallerstein and others have pointed out that when enterprises move activities to the peripheries they look for conditions where labour costs can be kept low. They indicate, more importantly, that wages can be kept down if workers are coming from a "semiproletarian household" with multiple sources of income so that their survival would not depend on their low wage (Wallerstein 2004: 35; see also Tabak and Crichlow 2000).

For Wallerstein, a worker's survival should not be analysed in terms of his or her individual income. Instead a worker ought to be understood as a member of a household, which Wallerstein sees as an income pooling unit. Workers are held together by "some form of obligation to provide income for the group and to share in the consumption resulting from their [pooling of multiple sources of] income" (Wallerstein 2004: 32). Wallerstein's concept of household enables us to understand the *kampung* as a spatial domain for income pooling activities by workers living in a city. If one or two members of a *kampung* household work in the formal sector, such as in shopping malls, office buildings or factories, and contribute to a certain percentage of the family income while others make up the difference through additional work as street vendors and maids or in petty commodity production, they are, by definition, members of a semi-proletarian household. Meanwhile, the "reserve wage-labourers" are kept there, (temporarily) maintained as workers in the informal sectors. In this sense, the reserve labourers are not always coming from the countryside. Instead, they could come from within the city itself, i.e. the kampung.

Furthermore, as a space of arrival for migrants from the countryside, the work force in the *kampung* would not only be abundant but also migratory and transitory, in which case they would be unable to organise and to push for the increase in real income, for full proletarianisation. In this scenario, a *kampung* is not only a spatial medium for internal group survival but an informal household within capitalist forces capable of reducing labour costs for capital to maximise profits. In this sense, the *kampung* is part of a system of power that organises societal relations with capital and the state. One might consider that such production of the *kampung* is a form of subordination of the *kampung* to capital, but such a scenario also suggests that the eradication of *kampung*s would reduce capitalist accumulation.

This contradiction explains why *kampung*s persist and will continue to persist as long as they function as the spatial formation of the semi-proletarian households of capitalism. In this sense, the modernisation of a city would necessarily involve the preservation of the *kampung* along with the maintenance of the semi-proletarian household. The *kampung* phenomenon described so far also explains the anomaly that we find in both modernisation theory and in Marxist urban studies, which define capitalism in this regard in terms of the urbanisation or the proletarianisation of work forces, respectively. However, as indicated in this chapter, what we have in a capitalist city of Southeast Asia, such as Jakarta, is not proletarianisation or urbanisation, but semi-proletarianisation characterised by a middling urbanism. In this process the *kampung* plays an important role. In the following section, I outline how the state produces the *kampung* as a system of power that contributes to the formation of middling urbanism.

## The Governance of the *Kampung*

The "economic" logic that I have emphasised so far is, however, insufficient to understand the ways in which a *kampung* is governed culturally and politically. One much-remarked characteristic of the *kampung* is the culture of "helping one another" (*gotong royong*), which has enabled the community to be resilient and self-reliant when facing challenges. Some scholars, rather romantically, see the *kampung* as the embodiment of this "traditional" culture that has developed autonomously below the state. Others (for example Sullivan 1980) emphasise that such a tradition owes much to the state's invention of culture. From this perspective, the cohesive image of a *kampung* with its community formation could be seen as largely a construction of the state programme. This includes a whole set of cultural rituals and ceremonies to imagine a community in a *kampung*, such as the Independence Day festival (*17 Agustus-an*); the celebration of the Islamic New Year of *Idul Fitri*; all other community programmes and practices associated with "cleaning the environment" (*bersih kampung*); the rotational saving in the practice of *arisan*; the night watch routine of *ronda*; the youth organisations of *karang taruna*; the district organisation of *kelurahan*; and the education of family welfare of *Pendidikan Kesejahteraan Keluarga* (PKK) (invented in the early 1980s). The neighbourhood unit of the *kampung*, known as the *Rukun Tangga* (RT)/ *Rukun Warga* (RW) unit and inherited from the system of social control invented during the Japanese occupation of Indonesia, is nothing less than a state territorial governing of the urban population.

These two perspectives (*kampung* as popular tradition, and *kampung* as state invention), each emphasising one position over the other, do not have to be exclusive. The *kampung* not only organises itself from "inside-out" through its own community, but the space is also organised from the "outside-in" by the state. From existing studies, a *kampung* carries a double power of being governed by both the self-management of the community (from below) and the state (from above). How they mutually articulate their positions in relation to each other is what makes *kampung* at once social and political.

What this doubling also suggests, however, is that the state is involved in a transaction of power that is characterised by ambivalence and contradiction. On the one hand, the state seeks to "control" the *kampung* by promoting its integrity, wholeness and autonomous character. It encourages practices that constitute a communal bond (*kekerabatan*), such as through communal work (*kerja bakti*), traditional festivals (*acara adat istiadat*), *kampung* assemblies (*majelis kampung*), and consensus decision making (*musyawarah*). Yet on the other, the state also seeks to prevent the *kampung* from becoming a political block that could lead to resistance against the state. While the state casts its power territorially by what

James Scott (1998) calls "seeing like a state", it has never been quite able or willing to penetrate deep into local affairs. The state preserves a distance close enough to nurture state-affect but sufficiently distant to refrain from taking responsibility for the livelihood of the *kampung* dwellers. We could conceive of the distance as an indication of the state's inability to provide housing and other infrastructure for the poor, but, as I have tried to argue, it is also related to the state's strategy of governing just enough to minimise political challenges (Slater and Kim 2015).

The state's politics of distance is often translated into strategic but actually "reluctant" development packages for the *kampung* (from promoting the selective Kampung Improvement Project to rewarding practices of greening the *kampung*). And at a time of crisis (such as that of the late 1990s monetary crisis), for fear of unrest, the state would allow laid-off workers to occupy government-owned "unused land" (*tanah terlantar*) including space beside rivers and railways as well as under toll roads (Kusno 2013). In the *kampung* we thus see complex infrastructure that is neither formal nor entirely informal; it is a mix of both. The *kampung*'s inhabitants set up their own transport and utility systems, no matter how inadequate they are, but they are always in relation to formal institutions and public facilities that are minimally provided in a limited way by the state and private sector.

## The Middle Power

The state's limited strategy of rule in the *kampung* also finds expression in yet another form of power relation. Students of Indonesian politics would recognise the influence of the "middle" power in the *kampung* that serves to mediate between the state and the *kampung* (Barker 1998; Wilson 2011). The state subcontracts the middle power to ensure order and stability from below. The middle power takes many forms ranging from religious leaders to urban thugs, the latter being organised collectors of tributes, especially in public spaces. The best-known of the middle power are *preman* (thugs), and behind or above them are *oknum* ("shadowy" quasi state personnel) who are connected to (often behind the scenes but not always under the control of) the state apparatus or certain political parties. These relatively independent subcontracted powers occupy a grey area and constitute a "middle" regime that controls the small businesses and livelihoods of the *kampung*. They are often members of the *kampung* community who could be seen as the local ruling elites and their security apparatus, but their relatively autonomous connection to power outside the neighbourhood often makes them both heroes and villains for the community. As power brokers moving in and out of the *kampung*, they maintain order. The degree of their attachment to the state power or political parties depends on the degree of the looseness in the center.

In the post-Suharto era, when the state could not always hold its authority, the middle power splintered into pieces of competing localised powers each looking for business or influence and who were, in some cases, available for hire.

In this complex structure of collusion and contradiction between different agencies, the *kampung* has developed a form of socio-political organisation, at once top-down and bottom-up, within as well as outside the state. It is in this configuration of politics and culture that we can understand the statecraft of a postcolonial city, its relation to the *kampung* and capital accumulation, and how the *kampung*'s income-producing "pooling" activities are interwoven with the state invention of tradition and the influences of local leadership. The capitalists searching for semi-proletarian households to sustain their level of profit find strength in the *kampung*'s social institutions. The state, seeking order and stability, finds in the *kampung* a means to develop its statecraft of indirect rule. The urban poor struggling to keep their livelihood in the city find the *kampung* and its social network of mutual assistance as resources to deal with hardships. It is in this entanglement between the enterprises' capacities, the state, the middle power and the urban poor that the *kampung* is consistently produced and reproduced over time despite the rhetoric of modernisation and threats of its eradication. The persistence of *kampung* therefore is due to its role in sustaining (rather than challenging) the urban system of power and strategies of rule.

## Land Complicity

If self-management is the hallmark of the *kampung* and the source of support for capitalist modernisation and the statecraft of indirect rule, how is it sustained? In one sense, the answer has already been given: the culture of "helping one another" (*gotong royong*) sustained by practices of sociality and the sharing of space. Yet such sociality cannot be achieved by haphazard methods. Its attainment is possible only through a system of land legality which, as will be shown later, further supports the system of power that I have outlined so far.

Several insightful studies have highlighted the complex ambiguities of legal categories of land in Indonesia. Reerink and Van Gelder (2010) point out that in Indonesian cities there are three co-existing categories of land. The first is the land under "formal tenure", land registered under the National Land Agency and known as the "formal land market". The second category is the opposite of the first, which is the land under "informal tenure". This category applies to state land (or "abandoned" private lands) occasionally occupied by squatters with government "permission", but with no basis for tenure. The third category falls between the first and the second, referring to land under "semi-formal tenure" that is registered only by the local (not national) government. It includes customary lands as well as lands with inherited ownership rights. Most *kampung* land is in this third category.

Some scholars use the term *de jure* for the formal tenure to differentiate it from the informal and the semi-formal tenures that are recognised only as *de facto* (Leaf 1994a). This "land dualism" (of the formal and informal land markets) constitutes the socio-economic "division" of the city: the formal space of the *kota* and the informal space of the *kampung*. This dualism has recently been challenged by the land certification programme. Lands under the third category (semi-formal tenure) may advance to the status of formal tenure if the occupants register the title for their land individually with the National Land Agency. The inhabitants of semi-formal tenure have a choice to remain in the semi-status or "move up" by way of formalising the land they have occupied. Promoted by the World Bank, formalisation has widened the sphere of the formal land market and reduced the domain of the informal land market. After certification, many *kampung* dwellers have sold their lands to developers. Others have kept their land and become landlords who rent their strategically located properties to the higher-income managerial class who work in the Central Business Districts (Santoso and Irawati 2015).

Land certification, however, moves gradually and unevenly. It remains to be seen how the communality of the *kampung* changes as land becomes a formalised asset. To date, a significant number of *kampung* residents have retained their lands under a semi-formal tenure status for two strategic reasons. First, formal tenure does not mean full security as the state could still repossess lands for national development projects. Second, keeping semi-formal tenure means that one does not have to follow the rules and pay the higher fees that would apply to formal tenure land ownership, and such non-compliance makes living in a *kampung* more affordable. Semi-formal tenure thus supports semi-proletarian households, which are the central apparatus for the functioning of the international division of labour and investment. The persistence of semi-formal tenure could be said to be contributing strongly to the preservation of the *kampung* and the character of middling urbanism.

## The End of Middling Urbanism? Possible? Desirable?

I have so far painted a picture of the *kampung* as a relational entity. As such, the *kampung* is also subjected to change most visibly by external forces, but often unnoticeably by enterprising individuals from within the *kampung*. By way of conclusion then, let me consider briefly a change in *kampung* today. If we walk around an inner city *kampung* behind a new large-scale commercial development in Jakarta, we find rapid growth of new economic activities that serve the needs

**Figure 1.4a, b:** The emergence of "middle-class" rental spaces in a *kampung* (author's photos 2016).

of the establishments in the new development. Those needs include "food, pre-paid card, photocopies; hair dressing, laundry and motorcycle taxi", as well as, most significantly, "rooms for rent" with AC (see also Simatupang, Irawati and Mardona 2015). There are also goods and services affordable only for those who are working in the nearby CBDs. The life rhythm of the *kampung* in such area has been transformed to serve the needs of the nearby large establishments. Owners of many *kampung* houses have sold their properties or converted them into rental spaces to accommodate staff working in the nearby CBDs (Figure 1.4a, b).

One could argue that what is happening in some of the inner city *kampung* is a form of "gentrification" by the *kampung* dwellers themselves (see chapter 2). The conversion of these *kampung* houses into "mid- and high-end" rental spaces tells us about the changes in the modality of the *kampung* as it develops into a service area for the core. Be that as it may, the urban *kampung* continues to adapt with some undergoing gentrification while others reproduce more irregular *kampung* such that the uneven "symbiotic" development between the *kampung* and the CBDs continues to take place in different parts of the city as well as in the peri-urban new towns.

In this chapter, I have shown not only the importance of locating the city in a core-periphery relation in accordance with the international division of labour and investment, but also how such a location is sustained and shaped by socio-cultural practices associated with the way society is governed. The kind of capitalist modernisation that operates in the peripheries, which relies on the semi-proletarian households, is sustained by the statecraft that has produced the culture and politics of the *kampung*. Perhaps historians of the future would be in a better position to tell us if middling urbanism would end with the demise of capitalist world-economy. Whether such an end is desirable needs further reflection, which is the subject of the next chapter.

Chapter

2 | The Rule of Many Orders

In Chapter One, I showed how the interests of the state, capital and workers intersect to produce a statecraft of spatial organisation in Jakarta and that this intersection constitutes a "middling urbanism" which is essentially a mutually constitutive rule of many orders. Middling urbanism enables the state to disregard social housing, and this disregard has in turn given rise to the self-management of *kampung* settlements and their informal land market at the local level. In effect, this art of governing enables the urban poor, to a certain extent, to find their own accommodation. Thus, the state is neither neglecting nor intervening through policies or programmes of housing for the poor but only letting people in the irregular settlements house themselves.

*Kampung* settlements not only save the state from the cost of housing its population, but also create a grey zone of governmentality bestowing on local administrators, community leaders, business entrepreneurs and land brokers a role in producing space and maintaining social order. Such a power arrangement relies not only on the capacity to keep the loyalty of sections of the political and business elites, but also on not governing the masses directly (a task left to the locally managed leadership), in so far as they do not pose a challenge to the state. It follows that since both the state and the local government have very little interest in housing the poor, their efforts to build low-cost housing (for instance as in the case after an eviction) are often marked by complex deals which involve many players (from business groups to land dealers) who often effect their transactions in extra-legal forms of bribery, payoffs and political maneuvers. Similarly, any "best practice" associated with housing provision proposed by international agencies would often find itself absorbed or recombined into this ensemble of various orders.

This chapter outlines the rule of many orders in the field of human settlements in a postcolonial context. It problematises the assumption dominant in the study of neoliberal urbanism: prior to market provision in the 1980s, the state did provide social housing for its population.[1] In the capitalist periphery, the government historically has never quite recognised state provision of social housing for the majority of its poor citizens. Instead, the state rules in and through the order of informality. What follows is a story of such an order as told through the field of housing, how housing evolved since decolonisation and eventually transformed in the post-Suharto era, and how the current drive for ground rent is leading to the demise of urban *kampung* settlement.

## Historicity

In the late 1990s, Manasse Malo and Peter Nas indicated that the Indonesian state (with the military support) and the business elites were the most powerful players in transforming the city of Jakarta (Malo and Nas 1996). Since the 1970s, the Indonesian government has chosen the path of laissez-faire capitalism as a fundamental tenet of economic growth, accompanied by marketisation and private housing development.

Such an urban development is carried out as a general government plan of "modernisation", but the specifics are left mainly in the hands of private developers with little or indirect control by the central government. The government makes plans and monitors development nationally through a national planning board (known as BAPPENAS), but it does not have a city planning board responsible for planning and developing Indonesian cities. This gap has bestowed complete power on private developers who are making maximum use of the relatively powerless urban government (Dorléans 2002; Firman 2000). For instance, the government of the Suharto era could make arrangements with connected developers (under the pretext of private/public partnership) to take over urban/local decisions for its own economic and political gains. This alignment, a manifestation of "public-private partnership" between the state and capital, has continued after the collapse of Suharto's centralised regime as it is integrated further into practices associated with neoliberalism (Robison and Hadiz 2004).

Indonesia's post-Suharto decentralisation policy has given power to the local or city governments, but it also continues to strengthen the position of private developers, especially those with strong capital investment portfolios. Thus, we see that the governors of the post-Suharto era continue to rely on private developers in their aspiration to put Jakarta on the map of world cities.[2] Yet, support for the urban poor in the form of housing has never been a priority. This is due in no small measure to the legacy of Suharto which followed a path that is different from the unrealised socialist "housing" intent associated with the Sukarno era.

During early Independence, Indonesian nationalism and its concomitant idea of revolution were organised around the notion of *rakyat* (the common folk—in Indonesia this generally means the poor). In 1950, immediately after the transfer of sovereignty from the Dutch to Indonesia, the government declared housing (*papan*) as one of the three primary needs besides clothing (*sandang*) and food (*pangan*). The identification of the newly independent state with adequate housing may be attributed to the historical neglect by the colonial government which made housing a symbol of both modernity and decolonisation. The first Congress on Housing was soon held to mark a commitment to achieving socialist modernity. The Congress declared that the new government should make housing available for people, especially the poor (Kusno 2013; Colombijn 2010). Several measures were immediately introduced such as standardisation of land status at the national level and establishment of housing agencies (Colombijn 2010).

However, due to political instability, limited resources and the flood of migrants into Jakarta, the government was forced to compromise on its socialist aspiration for universal housing. To deal with the housing shortage, it had to rely on resources from the *rakyat* who were encouraged or assisted (when possible) to build dwellings on their own through practices of "gotong royong" (mutual help) while leaving intact the variety of land status from the colonial time. The "legal dualism" of land (between the national and the local) continued to function in tandem with an informal land market which operated at the local level (Leaf 1993, 1994a; Bowen 1986). The poor were accommodated in such a market under a variety of land status governed by the local (instead of national) administration. This arrangement in effect compromised the aspiration of the socialist-oriented state for universal housing under a unified national land status.[3]

When Suharto took over the country with its New Order regime, he replaced the 1950 socialist-oriented housing aspiration with a privatisation scheme. In 1972, his administration organised the regime's first national workshop on housing. A set of important decisions were made which have left a large imprint on the spatial organisation of the city. Jakarta was the site of experimentation without concern for the implications on the social environment of the already divided city. Private developers were encouraged to acquire land (via the issuance of "Location Permits") to build upper middle-class housing (Cowherd 2002a; Dorléans 2002). Developers moved fast to consolidate their position by setting up a lobby organisation, Real Estate Indonesia in 1975. The government, on the other hand, established its own housing company called PERUMNAS (Perumahan Nasional or National Housing) to take care of the housing for the "lower income" population, although in practice the company largely targeted civil servants who were simultaneously members of the ruling party (Rosser 1983). Meanwhile, the majority of the urban poor were "permitted" to live on lands operated under informal land markets in *kampung* areas.

As soon as Suharto took over power and steered the path of "development" under the tutelage of Washington, the World Bank agreed to support the Kampung Improvement Programme (KIP) which started in 1968 and went to the late 1990s (near the end of Suharto's regime) (Silas 1984, 1987). The KIP was the first and the only state "upgrading" project of *kampung* (although the Dutch colonial government had already done some of this type of physical upgrading in the 1920s). The KIP focused on physical and infrastructural upgrading such as pathway paving, drainage provision and communal washrooms. It was however limited to *kampung*s considered as potentially exemplary as the inhabitants, after KIP, would invest in homeownership (Irawaty 2018: 25–41). Such a scenario however has led to the possibility of gentrification, as after upgrading, the land price of the neighborhood would increase and occupants of the upgraded areas find it desirable to have their land certified in order to maximise the value of their property. Nancy Kwak, in her study of the hegemony of homeownership, indicates that the KIP in Jakarta and Surabaya was meant to encourage personal investment in homeownership via tenure security (Kwak 2015: 219–20). KIP sought to enable the *kampung* population to upgrade their status. As such its reach and impact were limited. The poorer population who had no choice but to live in areas considered unfavourable continued to rely on "gotong royong" assisted by an assemblage of religious leaders, headmen and later on members of NGOs (Tunas and Peresthu 2010; Winayanti and Lang 2004).[4]

By the 1980s the state put firmly in place a social structure of relations that governed various local and global participants in the housing industry. All the three housing sectors—the upper middle class in the domain of private developers (Real Estate Indonesia), the civil servants under the state housing company (PERUMNAS) and the lower income population in the sphere of *kampung*—are connected to the state via various forms of patronage. For instance, the acquisition of land by private developers was backed by the state and its military apparatus especially for projects that involved partnerships with Suharto's family. The accessibility of PERUMNAS state housing was tied to the status of the civil servants who were members of the ruling party. The inclusion of a *kampung* in the Kampung Improvement Programme (KIP) was subjected to the *kampung*'s environment and the prospect of its inhabitants owning their own homes. The membership of the self-help *kampung* was controlled by local leaders and thugs with ties to the government's security apparatus to ensure order and harmony in the neighbourhood. This set of orders was sustained by differentiated infrastructures (official and improvised) and variegated land markets (formal and informal), making housing by definition "available" to everyone. It has created a rule of many orders for a city that on the surface appears quite "messy".

Suharto's statecraft was not without contradictions, but he occasionally made remarks such as that the aim of his government was to harness capital (and not be enslaved by it) for the development of society at large. He found no contradiction in acknowledging the right to adequate housing while leaving the majority of the urban poor to struggle to find accommodations in the informal land market. He saw no opposition between the domains of the state, capital and civil society, as they were all supposed to collaborate even as they were treated unevenly in their respective domains. They were all related as "one" under the state's rule of many orders.

## After the New Order

What has changed after the end of Suharto's regime? What might have happened to the order of housing since then? The collapse of the Suharto regime shifted the *kampung* from what was understood as a low-income settlement into a property asset (Firman 2002; Bunnell and Miller 2011). The IMF's view of Suharto's regime is that the oligarchic state had distorted the market, so a more committed pro-market arrangement should be installed under the premise of decentralisation. If we look at the subsequent Indonesian Presidents' economic teams in the past 20 years we can say that the neo-liberal—pro-market—force has been largely at work. However, we can also say that what is going on is a new development in the New Order's political tradition.

As far as the *kampung* question is concerned, the most profound effect of decentralisation is the expansion of capital's sphere of operation through the World Bank's supported project of "formalising the informal land market" (Hoek-Smit 2002; Kusno 2013). Nancy Kwak indicates that

> the Bank argued that the complex, four-part *hak milik* (right of ownership), *hak guna bangunan* (right to build), *hak sewa* (tenant rights), and *hak pakai* (right of use) confused residents and took away potential benefits of ownership. In its place, the Bank urged a single legal system of government-managed paper certificates that replicated the US system of titling. . . . By streamlining titling procedures and improving amenities (as well as funding for those amenities), the Bank hoped residents would naturally recognise the benefits of homeownership. (Kwak 2015: 219–20)

The World Bank's rule is not new as this has been the idea behind the KIP, but land titling seems to have carried more weight after the influence of Hernando de Soto who argues that such a measure could transform irregular settlements and their informal land market into valuable assets. For de Soto, the "dead capital" of *kampung* land is waiting to be awakened and incorporated into the formal financial market (De Soto 2000). What needs to be done is land certification, as this will allow *kampung* to be financialised. If more and more lands of *kampung*s are certified, more and more opportunities will become available for *kampung* to be gentrified through what David Harvey called "ground rent"—a property value attributed to the mere circumstance of having a location in the city (Harvey 2010).

The project of "land certification" was introduced in the late 1990s, but it was fully mobilised only after the financial crisis to help restore the real estate industry. The upgrading on paper of *kampung* essentially replaces the physical upgrading of KIP. It has become a new way of "improving" the *kampung*. By upgrading the "right to build" obtained through the informal land market to the "right of ownership" (by way of land tilting), a *kampung* occupant can trade the certificate in the formal market. Yet through such financialisation, the *kampung* dweller could participate in the gentrification of *kampung*, leading, in many cases, to self-eviction, or "eviction by paper" (Harms 2016).

The classic definition of gentrification foregrounds the renewal of what is seen as deteriorating or unproductive areas to attract upper middle-income people to move in, often with the consequence of displacing poorer residents. But gentrification can also take place through land certification as the signifier of property ownership. Land certification offers security only to property owners and credit-worthy citizens, and it opens wide the possibility of *kampung* takeover by a higher income population. Land certification is often followed by an increase in rents as land owners need to pay tax following the property rules—a burden which they would now share with their tenants. This is happening in many strategically located *kampung* in Jakarta. Walking through *kampung* in the central parts of Jakarta today, we see more and more advertisements for rooms for rent which are affordable only by the managerial class or higher income workers employed in nearby offices and shopping malls.

The dissolution of "legal dualism" and its associated informal land market on which *kampung* stood have in effect decreased the availability of spaces for the poor in the city. A broader space is opened for financial capital to penetrate *kampung*, but there has also been a change in the power structure of housing that had been in place since decolonisation. While the governments (both national and local) continue to give public housing low priority, the low-income population is facing the threat of higher rent displacement under the new scheme.

## Conclusion

As in Chapter One, I have here argued that *kampung* was historically established out of a negotiated relation between capitalism, the state and civil society. Yet the restructuring of capital in the late 1990s (following the collapse of the Suharto regime) has transformed the relation. This chapter outlines historically how various actors were involved in matters concerning housing with an uneven division of tasks to cover the diversity of grounds. Private developers targeted the upper middle-class group; the state-owned housing company PERUMNAS prioritised civil servants; workers from informal sectors took care of their precarious *kampung*. The central and local governments (often in partnership with private developers) filled up some holes, when needed, by providing (less than adequate) low-cost rental apartments for evictees. These actors work with a constellation of informal power brokers consisting of local leaders, land brokers, dealers and thugs. Together they have constituted a rule of many orders in housing provision. Such a rule is to prevent political challenges to the failed effort to establish social housing for the majority of the urban poor.

Yet this order that underlies middling urbanism is today undergoing a challenge. *Kampung* has increasingly become a site for accommodating only the higher-paid working class who can afford higher rent. Low-income workers who cannot afford such rents are now forced to move to the outskirts of Jakarta, to the regions of Bekasi, Bogor and Depok. With so little government policy to help them economically, they are simply priced out to a new location. The diminishing informal land market (due to the individualised land certification) is transforming the sociality of *kampung* and has displaced the poor farther away from the city.[5]

With this change, future analysis of *kampung* as part of urban development would need to ask how resilient the urban *kampung* as housing may be in the urban future for the lower-class population. Do members of the urban poor living in Jakarta see the transformation from within *kampung*? For sure, they are seeing the changing landscape of *kampung*. They not only see more upgrading in some of their *kampung*s, but they also know that the informal land market, which has sustained their *kampung* for a very long time, is disappearing due to the expansion of land certification. They also see more inequality as the government seems to have no control over the urban development that is taking place, as the wild forces of capital continue to assert pressure on the city. They are probably aware that the power-sharing system which has kept the order of things is reaching a limit, as speculation targeted at *kampung* lands has entered everyday life. Perhaps as many more are displaced by higher rents or selling off their certificates and move farther and farther away from the city, a political challenge to the city and the nation may emerge.

For much of Jakarta history, the relation between the city and the nation has been beneficially problematic, and with decentralisation, it is increasingly contradictory. What they have done to each other will be explored in the subsequent chapters, starting with traffic and road conditions.

# Notes

[1] According to the dominant narrative, influenced by neo-liberal ideas, the state is expected to withdraw from providing housing, and it would play the role only of "enabling" housing markets to operate. This dominant narrative is important for an understanding of the neo-liberal forces, but it also tends to homogenise the specific conditions of cities in the Global South. For a discussion of the privatisation of infrastructure, see Graham and Marvin 2001. For a reflection on the housing sector in Southeast Asia, see Porio 1997 and Pugh 1994.

[2] Private developers' strategy of going "back to the city" continues to transform urban space in the image of a global city, the aspiration of which would strain the ecology of the city itself. This has forced the government to play only a catch-up role with proposed infrastructure development (such as toll roads, MRT, deep tunnel, seawall).

[3] This situation is described by some scholars as *de facto* tenure security, which despite being informal is recognised even if it does not carry legal status. For a discussion of *de facto* and *de jure* security, see Leaf 1994a.

[4] For an assessment of post-World Bank-supported KIP in Surabaya, see Das 2006.

[5] For some cases in the CBDs of Jakarta, see Leitner and Sheppard 2018.

Chapter

3 | Roads, Rhizomes and Regimes

"Anya indeed has decided to sell fritters (*gorengan*) in the afternoon
at the road side in front of her rented house. Located in *kampung*,
the road is crowded because it is often used as *jalan tikus*
(rat run, or a narrow short-cut lane)."
(Latifah 2019: 252)

The notion of *jalan tikus* (rat runs) refers to narrow lanes that drivers often use to avoid the traffic on main roads. They are known only to locals and are often associated with laneways in the *kampung*. Off the map, the routes are hard to describe. Knowledge of *jalan tikus* however, is essential as it may help avoid being stuck in traffic congestion on the main roads. People like to discover *jalan tikus*, but no one can be clear how they were formed. What is clear nevertheless is that their existence is tied to the city that is regularly rated as one with the worst traffic and congestion in general. Jakarta is also perhaps one of the mega-cities with the highest growth rate of private vehicle ownership. Looking from a bird-eye's view, a reporter declared in 2016 that: "Jakarta was named the world city with the worst traffic in one index last year based on satellite navigation data, which found the average driver starting and stopping more than 33,000 times in a year. An estimated 70% of the city's air pollution comes from vehicles" (Van Mead 2016). But this is not a recent phenomenon.

Since the early 2000s, Seno Gumira Ajidarma, Indonesian writer and great observer of *"manusia Jakarta"* (Jakartans) has his own calculation. "For someone who uses the car to get to work, one third of life would have been spent inside the car. So, if he started working at the age of 25 and retired at the age of 55, he would have spent not less than 10 years of his career in traffic" (Seno 2004b).

This chapter focuses on some aspects of Jakarta's transportation by considering the interface of politics, economics and culture in the shaping of both the city's traffic congestion and its flows. It discusses some of the conditions that have caused traffic congestion, including governmental engagement with the problem, and the multiple ways by which people move around the city through a "para-transportation" system, "para" in the Greek sense: "beside", "alongside" or "subsidiary". It is like a *jalan tikus* which constitutes an alternative way of going around the city. I use "para" here to refer to a privately constituted transport system that not only complements but also challenges or corrects the unplanned system of the city. In a city where investment in public transport is low, the private sector takes over the flow of the street and creates for everyone a transport system that is characterised by multiplicity, a relation in multiple dimensions or a rhizome that is embedded in a political and economic regime.

First it is important to acknowledge that phase one of the Jakarta MRT was officially opened only in 2019. It adds to a great variety of existing publicly and privately run transport. This variety of vehicles is reflected in the many different terms for vehicle types, which range from electric trains and various kinds of buses to 3-wheel *bemo* (a traditional form of public transport influenced by *jitney* of Indian origin) (Figure 3.1) and *becak* (pedicab, introduced by ethnic Chinese in the early 1950s) as well as *ojek* (freelance motorbike taxi). They are owned by different agencies: some are individuals, others are connected to the municipality, but most are private companies with no connection to the government. They are regulated differently, so (in Jakarta) some are not allowed to operate on certain streets, while others, such as *becak* (since the 1980s) and *bemo* (recently) have been banished from the capital city.

**Figure 3.1.** *Bemo*: A traditional means of public transportation influenced by the *jitney* of Indian origin (author's photo 2017).

Roads in Jakarta also have a hierarchy which structures the use of different types of vehicles even though such rules are not always enforced and are occasionally violated. The variety of transport and the inconsistency of regulations contribute to the haphazard development of Jakarta's road network, since many roads are not located on the map. Discursive as they are, the transport stories of Jakarta can be narrated in a way that points to the larger spatial transformation and power relations of different political regimes.

Transport is inseparable from the roads on which it depends. A road, like a vehicle, nevertheless connects places, as it negotiates spatial separation. A road however can also reinforce division. A highway that cuts through a field to connect two towns often separates a community. Jakarta is made up of series of roads that cut and link places with very little concern over planning—a term that many argue may not apply to the fast-growing, haphazard urbanisation of the city. Some of the roads are constructed by the government, while others are built by private developers, and many more by anonymous communities in narrow alleys which have become *jalan tikus*, but all of them have contributed to making Jakarta a gigantic maze. The roads, like the various forms of transport, thus have many networks which co-exist but are not necessarily interconnected. Jakarta's traffic (*lalulintas*), according to researcher Hermawan Sulistyo (2006), resembles tangled threads (*benang kusut*).

This chapter seeks to tease out some dimensions of Jakarta's transportation and road system which have been formed discursively and fragmentarily over time with little coordination among stakeholders. The aim is to problematise a technocratic reading of the city as assumed by planning where parts are (to be) organised under an integrated system. Instead, as this chapter will show, Jakarta displays a hybridised assemblage of different roads and transport modes which make up a politically charged rhizomatic regime of urbanism.

## Order and Disorder from a Colonial Time

Urban public transport during Dutch colonial times was marked by the fixed and limited route of the electric tram of the *Bataviasche Electrische Tramweg* which linked the city to the suburban train services of the state railways (Dick 1981). The North-South electric tram (which emerged in 1899 out of the horse-tram lines) linked the old Batavia in the North and the new centre in the South. The tram's route along Molenvliet (today's Gajah Mada Street) and Harmonie was featured like a promenade in colonial tour guide books and postcards. The asphalt road that flanked the Ciliwung River was an emblem of modernity and it was often sprayed with water to maintain cleanliness (Mrázek 2008: 26).

Some postcards from the past show speeding cars, trams, motorcycles, carts, bicycles and pedestrians on the roads, creating an environment of diverse mobility. The tram, not unlike the road, was a melting pot as people from different ethnic backgrounds were allowed to take it. Both the road and the tram introduced the concept of time, technology and mobility that seemed to be new then and were available for everyone to use even as the city, characteristic of the colonial era, was divided along racial lines (Mrázek 2008: 8–10). We can say that the concept of the public evolved in connection with the emergence of trams as a means of urban transport even as the lines were limited to places considered important in the colonial context.

The regular route of the tram was complemented by door-to-door taxi services for the colonial elite and pony carts (*dokar*) for the Indonesians (Dick 1981). Despite this arrangement, the road traffic was chaotic with many reported traffic accidents (Khusyairi 2011). Many different kinds of vehicles apparently co-existed with pedestrians, but they did not always agree on the rules of priority and order of circulation. Sources from colonial times provide many accounts of the "chaotic" street scenes of colonial cities. Partly in response to this, Thomas Karsten, the most famous Dutch architect and town planner in colonial Indonesia, considered roads as one of the most important components in the design of Indonesian towns. In *Indiese Stedebouw*, he laid out his theoretical treatise for urban designers and policy makers. Karsten indicated, in the words of planning historian Pauline Roosmalen, that

> roads should have a clear and intuitive hierarchy, so road users would not be confused about the function and the course of every road in a town. To indicate and differentiate main roads, local roads, etc., Karsten stressed the need to apply unambiguous visual distinctions of trajectories and profiles. Main roads, for example, should be long, wide and straight, whereas local roads should be shorter, narrower and curving. If designed this way, their use and appearance would facilitate the flow of traffic and communications with the city. (Roosmalen 2017: 279–80)

The context of Karsten's proposal is nothing other than what, in Karsten's view, was the disorderliness (*rommeligheid*) of urban space in the colony.

## The Mosquito Fleet

In the late 1950s, Sukarno, the first president of postcolonial Indonesia, ordered the removal of trams from Jakarta's streets. Seeing the tram as a remnant of colonialism, people cheered as the tracks were removed in 1960. The disappearance of the trams left the city with no fixed and dedicated routes, but only buses operated by the

*Perusahaan Pengangkutan Djakarta* (PPD), a state company which, as it evolved over time, suffered a series of financial crises and mismanagement. In 1967, due to poor maintenance, only 40 out of 370 buses were operational. As a result, as H.W. Dick reports, the city

> was filled largely by a 'mosquito fleet' of many thousands of privately owned *opelet* [the post war wooden cabin automobile for 6-8 passengers] and *bemo* operating discursively on and off former tram routes. Meanwhile door-to-door services were provided by tens of thousands of *becak*, which since the Japanese occupation had almost entirely displaced the once ubiquitous pony carts from the colonial era. (Dick 1981: 74–5)

This "unincorporated system" (Dick's term) nevertheless provided direct jobs for many drivers, but it also served as a background for the new regime of Suharto (who ascended to power after a bloody coup in 1965) to "incorporate and modernize" the post war urban transport systems. Dick and Rimmer define "incorporation" as a taking over by state enterprises of the traditional, non-corporate sector, which then operates under the influence of capitalist development (Dick and Rimmer 1998). The incorporation resulted in the displacement of informal transports which gave way to the domination of capital-intensive technologies of transportation, such as taxis, stage buses and railways. Dick and Rimmer also indicate that this process of "incorporation and modernization" stemmed from the Structural Adjustment Programme of the World Bank to assist with the development of "third world cities".

## The New Order's Coordination

The rise of Suharto's regime in 1966 is synonymous with what Richard Robison called "the rise of capital" (Robison 1986) which came in tandem with the belief in "stages of development" as prescribed by modernisation theory. Guided by "Pancasila" (the philosophy of the state) to prevent the return of Communism, Suharto declared the New Order as the time for political stability and economic development. He gave the New Order an image that was in contrast to what he called the "Old Order" of the Sukarno era. His new time represented order, stability and economic progress in which foreign capital investment would play a major role. The urban regime of the Suharto era followed the idea of "incorporation and modernization" where the government worked with capital in developing the city. For this mission, Suharto was considered lucky to have had inherited a Governor appointed by Sukarno, the mighty Ali Sadikin.

When Ali Sadikin took over as Governor of Jakarta in 1966, he was determined to reverse the unincorporated transport systems and turned them into an integrated whole (Ramadhan 1992 [rpt. 2012]). While he did not bring back trams, he instead revitalised the PPD bus system by setting up several bus terminals and increasing the number of buses. He worked together with the U.S. Agency for International Development (USAID) programme which first allocated loans to new private bus companies, leading to monopolies on certain routes.

The PPD eventually took over the management of eight of the twelve private companies (Dick 1981). Prior to the end of his tenure in 1977, Sadikin ordered the replacement of *opelet* and installed a minibus fleet which gradually developed into *mikrolet* (a short form of "micro-opelet", buses supplied by Mitsubishi Colt [Figure 3.2]) to cover secondary routes and roads too narrow for buses.

**Figure 3.2.** *Mikrolet* (author's photo 2016).

The expansion of *mikrolet* and buses was a manifestation of modernisation as it at once displaced the much smaller *opelet*, *bemo* and the slow *becak* to the peripheries and thus away from the main streets of Jakarta. The city would be served by only "modern" and motorised vehicles. In the early 1970s, attempts were made (unsuccessfully) to motorise *becak* in order to increase their speed. Meanwhile, taxis (which used to serve only tourists and diplomats) were promoted as a popular means of transport. By the end of Sadikin's tenure in 1977, "modernization and incorporation" of urban public transport had generally been achieved.

Central to the integration was the downgrading of the role of *becak*, the most popular informal means of public transport. It took, however, many more years after Sadikin to completely clear *becak* from the main roads. A study sponsored by the World Bank indicated that "various types of transport range from the three-wheeled *bejak* [*sic*] (similar to the rickshaw), 60,000 of which were estimated to have been on Jakarta streets in 1979, to overcrowded trains and to private luxury automobiles. These vehicles compete with each other and with the pedestrian and hawker for the limited road space in the city" (Clarke 1985: 39). A census taken in 1983 showed there were still almost 40,000 *becak* operating in the city (of which fewer than 8,000 were legal), though unofficial estimates suggest that there were close to 65,000 (Specter 1984). The displacement of *becak* to the outskirts and to only night time service before eliminating them altogether reflects the general policy of the government to speed up development associated with increasing traffic flows. *Becak* were considered too slow, non-modern, and inappropriate for the era of development. It reminded the state of Indonesia's underdevelopment. The term *becak* is from "bo-ciak" the Hokkien phrase for "haven't eaten" which implies a lack of money to buy food. *Becak* thus is associated with being poor: one is assumed to have been forced to become a pedicab driver. And, perhaps more importantly, *becak* represented the anarchic world of *rakyat* (poor commoners) who needed to be protected and yet were difficult to bring under governmental control.

The speed of progress mattered in the New Order era, and this was symbolised most notably by the provision of motorised vehicles. The authority of the government was conveyed through the exercise of regulations (including subsidised tariffs) for motorised transport, all in order to eliminate non-motorised vehicles, such as bicycles and *becak* as a condition for ensuring speedy traffic flows. One might well discern a strategy of control and the desire to implement the ideology of development sustained by "order and stability" in the redeployment of urban public transport in the Suharto era.[1] The motorisation of urban transport, however, not only served the centralisation of power (and thus could be used as a spectacle of the state's authority in controlling the streets), but also served to facilitate the flow of capital. By the 1980s, the motorisation of urban transport had taken the form of spatial expansion and highways for peri-urban settlements, shopping malls and industrial landscapes in the extended metropolis.

Yet, as this chapter will demonstrate, the control over public transport (including its eventual neglect and lack of investment by the state) served simultaneously the policy to encourage private car ownership and the building of toll roads, an enterprise that involved companies owned by members of Suharto's family. By the second decade of Suharto's rule, between 1975 and 1985, road construction for motorised vehicles absorbed a large portion of loans from international institutions such as the Asia Development Bank, the Japan International Cooperation Agency (JICA) and USAID. The assistance from these agencies came in tandem with the promotion of private car ownership. For that to work, however, space had to be extended and land acquired beyond the administrative territory of the city.

## *Desakota*

Terry McGee describes the linkage between land transport and the creation of the extended metropolitan region in Indonesia. In his reflection on roads, he indicates how

> the creation of the extended metropolitan region has depended upon a massive investment in land transport systems. The first element in this development has been the creation of national road systems... [(such as) the freeways from Jakarta to Surabaya and Bandung] which funnel goods and people to and from the national centers.... They have become major elements in the arterial networks that service the extended metropolitan regions (EMRs). A second component is the introduction of main freeway access between the city cores and the international airport... There is also a secondary network of roads that service industrial estates and new townships in the EMRs. These arterial routes are invariably serviced by para-transportation systems such as motorbikes and lorries that convey the poorer people. (McGee 2002: 647–8)

As indicated in Chapter One, McGee further notes that the development of the extended mega-region is nothing like the sprawl of North American planned suburbia. Instead it expands by 'leap-frogging' existing land uses, forming a particular hybridised landscape in the region that McGee has labelled *desakota*: a mix of urban (*kota*) and rural (*desa*) landscapes and lifestyles with *kampung* (lower class neighbourhoods) within and around residential and industrial estates (McGee 1991). At the intervals of these different urban forms are pathways (often unplanned) that both separate and connect different communities and where "para-transportation systems", or "subsidiary" means of transportation such as motorcycles develop. I will discuss motorcycles a little more in closing. It is sufficient for now to indicate that through the subterranean pathways and para-transportation systems, such as motorbikes and lorries, workers are sent out from their *kampung* to serve the surrounding industrial estates and new townships.

McGee's analysis emphasises the gradual integration of various formal and informal transportation systems in response to the formation of freeways. The freeway, however, was a crucial component of the eventual restructuring of capitalist modernisation in the 1980s, one that was associated with the New Order's developmentalism. The first toll road in Indonesia was the *Jagorawi* toll road which links areas connected to Jakarta, Bogor and Ciawi (hence the acronym *Ja-gor-awi*). It generated a *desakota* region. Constructed in 1973 and opened in 1978 by President Suharto, the road is three lanes wide in each direction and links Jakarta to the West Javanese cities of Bogor and Ciawi. It launched the long and lucrative career of the state-owned toll road operator, *Jasa Marga*, which collaborated with private investors in toll roads, including Suharto's daughter, Siti Hardiyanti Rukmana, known as "Mbak Tutut". *Jagorawi* was crucial for the new town development of peri-urban Jakarta, which by the 1980s began to mushroom along the toll road.

Consequently, the villagers along the *Jagorawi* corridor were either displaced overnight as they were forced off their land or suddenly found themselves next door to new developments. Such a scale of landscape change was possible only under the authoritarian rule of Suharto. The toll road opened up the opportunity for property developers and industrialists to hunt for land accessible to the freeway. With *Jagorawi* cutting through the area, developers acquired land with the assumption of the road's accessibility with no consideration of the burden automobiles would place on the surrounding areas. How lands were acquired along *Jagorawi* and eventually developed has been studied;[2] what I would like to emphasise here is the dramatic change of the landscape as seen by people driving along the toll road. The straight-line linking Jakarta to Bogor was a shock of the new considering the tangled threads of Jakarta streets. It symbolises the acceleration of New Order time, but the use of *Jagorawi*—and what it stands for—is not without criticism. Fuad Hassan, once Minister of Culture and Education (1985–93), recollected in 1995, that:

> Before, between Jakarta and Bogor, there was only one noticeable billboard announcing that 'here will be built an Islamic Center'. The notice is still there today, but it is not the only one. Now, *Jagorawi* is not only a name for a toll road. It is associated with new residential areas. Along *Jagorawi* are billboards of new towns with promises of a modern life style. The main attraction is the golf courses which are watered all through the dry season to keep the areas green, leaving the patchworks of agricultural fields drying out. Soon, along *Jagorawi* one will see patches of 'foreign' lands... The villagers will learn the meaning of [the English words] 'river', 'lake,' 'hills' and 'valley' as they are attached to the names of the modern residential clusters. (Hassan 1995: 76–8)

Hassan observed *Jagorawi* from a ride on the freeway. The automobile was seemingly the only means of transport that enhanced the new spatial experience.

Yet it was an experience that visualised not only modernity, but also the violence of displacement. In 1978, when *Jagorawi* was officially opened, Gunawan Mohamad, an Indonesian poet and writer, published a story titled *Jagorawi*. His protagonist, Ronggur, is a fellow who has just returned to Jakarta (from five years of living in a deep forest in Irian Jaya). Ronggur took a ride on the new corridor. He was amazed (ironically, we might think, in the light of future congestion; and see Figure 3.3):

> 'Five years ago, there was no such road, now it is like in America!' Hambali, who sat beside him, smiled. He understood Ronggur's feeling. He had driven through three times, and still *Jagorawi* is sensational. 'We don't feel we are in the chaotic and suffocating Java'... There is only an almost perfect sense of tranquility which could only be experienced inside a car, the transport that gives a sense of distance from everything else outside the compartment. 'You are not the only one who is stunned [*terpesona*], there are people out there who are also stunned'. There are villagers on each side of the road watching *Jagorawi* and the speeding cars. They too are stunned, but perhaps they just realised that it is no longer possible to go from their side of the road to the other side.... *Jagorawi* connects the three cities but it also divides their village. (Gunawan 1979: 460–1)

## Automobiles and the Business of Toll Roads

Prior to *Jagorawi* and the new town developments, debates were common over the position of public transport in Jakarta. In the 1970s, proposals were made by a team that included Dutch planners to counter the development of automobile-based transport systems in the city with particular emphasis on the expansion of the railway (Cowherd 2005: 165–92). This progressive effort to encourage public transport as the embodiment of planning, however, was dismantled by the "growth coalition" in the 1980s who favoured urban and suburban transformation. And central to the growth coalition is the automobilisation of city and suburb.

The eventual campaign for privatisation and deregulation in the 1990s left planning almost wholly in the hands of private developers. It is worth noting, however, that the 1990s also witnessed, ironically, a proliferation of ideas on planning regulations, such as land use, environment and transport, but it is also widely known that the urban development of Jakarta at that time largely worked against such ideas. The disjuncture between planning and deregulation was due in large measure to the shift in the political economy of transport, from a commitment to public transport in the 1970s, to encouraging private car ownership; from the metropolis of the street, urban monumentality and promenade which characterised Sukarno's era, to the horizontal sprawl of suburbs and greater territorial units enabled by the commodification of land from the 1980s on. Central to this shift is a new relation that emerged out of an interaction between the highway, the automobile and the image of the American suburb favoured by developers (Cowherd 2005).

As automobile hegemony began to take root with more freeways and flyovers in Jakarta and new towns in the greater region, in 1992, the government stopped subsidising PPD buses, which reduced the number of big buses from 238 fleets per year between 1985 to 1992 to only 36 fleets per year between 1993 and 2000.[3] Thus by 1995, a metropolitan newspaper reported that "during busy hours, an average of at least 20,000 cars pass Jalan Sudirman (a major thoroughfare in the city) alone. What exacerbates the problem is that 86 per cent of all those vehicles are private cars and a mere 2.6 percent are public transportation vehicles".[4] The lack of investment in public transport had a huge consequence for the services provided by the PPD. The state bus company was basically left alone to suffer or die, as people too had abandoned them "for reasons that must be obvious to anyone who ever boarded a bus in Jakarta during peak hours. Anyone who can afford it would certainly prefer to drive a private car, jams or no jams".[5]

**Figure 3.3.** Traffic congestion and billboards advertising cars and promoting the war on drugs (left side) and the MCU "Civil Wars" movie (right) (author's photo 2016).

With planning by private real estate developers and freeways in the hands of the President's family, automobiles became the kings of the roads, an ascendency that was to the detriment of public transport. Traffic jams and the lack of reliable public transport became an ideal condition for the proliferation of cars (see Figure 3.3). Newspapers at the time discussed extensively the stress on Jakarta streets, and while it was clear to everyone that "the logic of opting for either an elevated, or underground, mass rapid transit system is evident... the problem is that the authorities have so far been unable to decide which system to adopt".[6] Such indecisiveness arose not only because the understanding of the need for a dedicated mass transportation system was absent, but also because there was an unwillingness to confront automobile industries, the toll road corporation and ultimately the businesses of Suharto's family.

## The New Town

As indicated above, the relation between the highway, the automobile and the new town is crucial in the establishment of Jakarta's transport regime. When *Jagorawi* was constructed, deals had been worked out between the "growth coalition" of government and private developers to organise transport infrastructure around the interests of capitalist modernisation plans. Concomitant to *Jagorawi* was the issuance of the Location Permit to help developers to acquire large-scale tracts of land to create new towns. Freeways, car industries and the expansion of the property market are thus interconnected in the production of space, lifestyles and "middle class" subjects, and this relation is often depicted consciously or unconsciously in property market advertisements. Marketing material of new towns was filled with the images of automobiles, American lifestyles and the new Indonesian "middle class". Inextricably intertwined with this package of capitalist modernisation is the market liberalisation promoted by the WTO, the IMF and the World Bank, which affected a variety of industries from banking to automobile and toll road construction, a large portion of which was awarded to companies affiliated with Suharto's family and their cronies. This automobile coalition reached its most perfect form in the early 1990s, when the connection between Jakarta and the new towns was so badly disrupted by traffic jams that Ciputra, a major developer (working with Jasa Marga), built a toll road to link five of his company's properties scattered around Jakarta, including Bumi Serpong Damai in the South West of the city and Pantai Indah Kapuk in the North. Urban planner Haryo Winarso points out that "this was a road that had never been considered in the government's master plan for Jakarta" (Winarso 2006: 667).

Developers tend to find locations close to existing freeways, thus taking advantage of the government's limited road infrastructure. If a special toll road was built by developers to boost more sales of new towns, as in the case of Ciputra indicated above, it was ultimately to encourage greater usage of cars. Ciputra is known for his leadership in real estate development. He is promoted by his own peers as a visionary developer, but little is known about how his vision of neighbourhood has contributed to the disappearance of street life and neglect of sidewalks and ultimately to the formation of automobile culture. As far as this chapter is concerned, Ciputra knew perfectly well that for a property to stay marketable, the street in front of the house had to be accessible by two cars passing side by side no matter how small the house. His automobile-based design paradigm has marginalised other approaches that sought to promote sidewalks or pathways not intended for cars. It has also contributed to the formation of a new urban form that stands in contrast to the surrounding *kampung* neighbourhood.

## The Will to Own Cars

The connection between the large-scale development of new towns and the promotion of private car ownership is relatively clear. The contribution of this connection to the growth of automobile industries is pretty straightforward. What has not been sufficiently commented on is how the correlation marginalises public transport and contributes to Jakarta's infamous traffic jams. By the 1980s, the automobile industries, based largely on dealerships of foreign cars, had become one of the most important sectors in Indonesia's story of economic growth. The government clearly supported the automobile industry, which was sustained by the increased number of middle-income earners who sought car ownership as a symbol of their status.

The monetary crisis of 1998 and the concomitant collapse of the Suharto regime did not dismantle the automobile industries. Instead, the sense of insecurity among the upper-middle class was translated into even more usage of private cars. After the fall of Suharto, in the time of crisis, car sales magically jumped to an all-time high. Meanwhile, in the 2000s, developers, in response to traffic jams and the diminishing available land in the outskirts of Jakarta, formed a new paradigm of "back to the city" with the creation of superblocks, mixed-use luxurious condominiums, offices, hotels, shopping malls and entertainment centres all in one complex. This return to the city has increased not only the number of upper-middle class city dwellers but also automobiles in the urban centre.

There is thus a connection between the transformation of the urban form, the growing automobile industries, the failure of public transport and the chronic traffic jams in Jakarta. Needless to say, but more difficult to research, is the weakening of urban governance by systemic and entrenched corruption, cronyism and collusion at many government levels. The decline of the urban environment came in tandem with the deterioration of public transport. The automobile industry clearly benefits from frustrations with the public transport system as people opt for private vehicles and know that the city buses are old and poorly maintained and that many are owned and operated by unregulated private companies. Many buses do not have proper braking systems or speedometers, and many drivers have no driving licence. In 2005, about five years into the era of post-authoritarian Jakarta, Rustam Effendy, the Head of the city's Department of Transport (*Dinas Perhubungan*), pointed out the stark contrast between public and private transport. Fewer than ten per cent of people in Jakarta used public transport; according to Effendy, this is due to the poor level of service, while just a year before, car ownership applications reached 269 every day (as cited in Santosa 2005). Meanwhile, in the first few years of the busway (operated since 2003), the only mass transportation system then in existence and built after the end of Suharto era, the bus was able to attract only 14 per cent of commuters (Santosa 2005; see also Kusno 2010: 49–70).

As Jakarta entered the era of President Bambang Soesilo Yudhoyono (SBY) (2004–14), the traffic in Jakarta had so deteriorated that the President had to raise his voice to the Governor of Jakarta for the first time. The President seemed to be mad at Governor Fauzi "Foker" Bowo and instructed him that "traffic congestion has to be solved before 2020".[7] However, this seemed an impossible mission to accomplish, as according to the Head of the city's Transport Agency, and as mentioned above, on average, 269 cars and 1,235 motorcycles are sold each day in the capital, with vehicle numbers rising by 10 per cent on average each year. Meanwhile, Jakarta's roadways can accommodate in the city only 0.01 per cent of the total number of cars at any time.[8] The city continued to favour cars all through the SBY and Foker era and the differing treatment received by private and public transport respectively continued as can be seen in the tax for private vehicles, which is pegged at 6 to 10 per cent whereas that for public transportation vehicles is pegged at 16 to 20 per cent.[9] Due to lack of investment, public transportation has been downgraded to the point of being generally considered a strictly lower class mode of transport. While the need for public transport among the lower class remains high, public transport accounts for less than two per cent of total vehicles on the road. As I will show below, the lower class has found their own solution to traffic issues: resorting to motorcycles which have flooded the roads of Jakarta, especially since the 2000s when financial capitalism expanded to the households of the urban poor through credits for motorcycles.

## Traces of Resistance, *Macet* and Road Culture

As new towns and highways continue to supply automobiles, and with public transport services remaining at an all time low, car owners easily sustain and strengthen the hegemony of automobile culture. They even develop a resistance to public transport. For instance, when the governor sought to extend Jakarta's busway lanes to upper middle-class neighbourhoods, such as Pluit, Pondok Indah and Kelapa Gading, residents there protested by hanging banners in their neighbourhoods. For them, the busway would eliminate one car lane and palm trees on the median strip. Since then, every effort to deal with traffic congestion by way of curbing the use of cars has encountered a challenge. When lawmakers designated several main arteries as "3-in-1 zones" where during the morning and afternoon rush hours, a car can drive through these arteries only if it has three people on board, such measures also failed to push commuters into buses and carpools. Instead, it has created job opportunities for people to serve as jockeys. Near the entrances to the zones, men, women and children line up on the street, raising their index finger offering themselves as the second or third passenger to commuters in a hurry. They rarely get caught for jockeying is technically legal. Lawmakers are aware of this, and they have sought to introduce Electronic Road Pricing to discourage car driving, but the plan is still stuck in bureaucratic deadlock.

It seems *macet* (traffic congestion) can't be solved easily. Instead it has produced a distinctive culture of the congested road. During *macet*, vendors approach vehicles trapped in the jam. In the event of extreme *macet* or "*macet total*", drivers expect them to be around to provide refreshment even though their presence contributes further to the congestion. The longer the jam, the more crowded the road becomes as vendors move around cars, trucks and buses offering refreshments, toys and newspapers. *Macet* has also created entrepreneurial informal traffic controllers who direct cars for small change. Meanwhile, it has also allowed street singers, musicians and poets to 'serve' passengers more entertainingly on the bus. Indonesian literary scholar, Iwan Gunadi observed most vividly this phenomenon on his regular city bus trip:

> Since 1999, it has been common to see poets performing in Jakarta's buses, not only in the big ones, but also smaller ones as well such as *metro-mini*. Since 2001, almost every day I saw poetry reading in my city bus. Sometimes, they read the poetry of Rendra, Taufik Ismail, Emha Ainun Najib, and so on. Most of the time, they read their own poems or those composed by their friends. A few perform really well and are full of commitment, but most of them just follow the trend of reading poetry in the bus in order to get small change from passengers. (Gunadi 2003: 68–9)

Meanwhile, in the post-Suharto democratic era, roads are often blocked not only for repairs, but also for marches, rallies and protests against the political authorities. In the history of Jakarta, streets have remained largely uncontrollable spaces.

## The Agency of Everyday Life

We have discussed the relations between the growth of automobile ownership and the construction of new towns. It is now appropriate to zoom in to look anecdotally at how residents of the new towns respond to the urban transport regime of Jakarta. As indicated above, if we follow the advertisements for new towns, it is clear that these towns would be served by private automobiles linked to a freeway. Yet, it is also clear to the most naïve home buyers of the new town property that the toll road's existence does not make Jakarta any closer. A majority of middle-class residents still work in Jakarta, and they continue to rely on their cars to get to work, a commute that can take two hours. The residents are perfectly aware of the problem and have responded by creating diverse strategies that combine formal and informal transport to move around.

To illustrate: my cousin, who lives in a new town, has been able to make her boss agree on letting her leave her work place before 2 pm but she has to be in the office by 6 am. This allows her to avoid the peak traffic hours. However, this only works for her because she is a long-time employee of a small family business and she lives with her parents who handle the household's morning chores. Others, like my sister, organise a car pool with neighbours in the early morning to a nearby train station where they can take a train to reach the city centre where they work. My sister's car then returns to her house to give rides to her young daughters to their schools and after-school programmes. My nieces' days are filled with activities, in part to keep them busy outside the house till the end of the day when my sister or her husband comes home. The families of my two sisters rely not only on cars, but also on drivers, which include my father and brother who works from home. Three households of our family are fortunate enough to live in the same "new town" neighbourhood so they can easily practise "mutual help" (*gotong royong*) and make their own transport arrangements, from sharing drivers to carpooling. Yet, still they rely on cars. Cars have become an unspoken necessity as there is virtually no public transport within the new town.

The challenge of driving on roads with heavy traffic has also generated the need to hire a driver. One can say that the car, the driver and the new town are a package of middle-class daily life (not to mention a domestic helper). But how does a driver manage his own transport to work? One of my sister's drivers (who has a family) lives outside the area so he comes to work by a combination of *mikrolet* and *ojek* (motorbike taxi). Another driver goes to work on his motorbike. He lives nearby in a *kampung* located in an interstitial space between two new towns. He rents a room in this *kampung*, a significant part of which has undergone *in situ* transformation into rental units (*kos*). Many drivers working in the area live in his *kampung*.

This phenomenon is quite widespread as *kampung* continue to survive through various adaptations to accommodate workers. *Kampung* are often off the official map, but, as discussed in Chapter 1, they are located both at the "heart" and on the "margins" of planned middle-class neighbourhoods. These leftover spaces, often hidden behind the wall or a mosque that defines the territory of a real estate property, are places where service workers (such as drivers, maids, vendors, shopkeepers, gardeners and small suppliers) of the new town live. Countless *kampung* still have a vibrant existence beyond the official map of Jakarta and the new towns. From *kampung*, all kinds of informal transport such as motorbikes, lorries, minivans and bicycles are discharged daily in and through the holes and pathways, the *jalan tikus*, that connect them to the city and the new towns. While these para-transport systems are crucial for the daily life of residents of new towns, they are never represented in the promotional material depicting life in new towns.

## The Growth of Para-Transport Systems

The majority of workers, like my sisters' drivers, come to work by a combination of *mikrolet* and motorbike taxi, and increasingly by their own motorcycle. The government's lack of investment in public transport has prompted a multitude of privately-owned public transportation possibilities which has grown like a rhizome. By the 2000s, Jakarta's streets were plied by a great mix of unreliable yet functioning public transport modes, including the old *mikrolet* and all kinds of minivans and minibuses competing for passengers. The tight competition among drivers, who are required to pay a sum of money (*setoran*) to the operators each day and take home only the surplus, has prompted drivers to set up their own traffic rules. They can pick up or drop off passengers anywhere they like. They can block traffic or idle their vehicles to wait for passengers. Since there is no standardised service norm set up by the government, the different companies have no interest in talking to or coordinating with each other. The city government has no control over the routes, quality, pricing, or safety of the nearly 100,000 transportation vehicles (65 per cent of which are thought to be over 10 years old) operating in the city as a "mosquito fleet".

Although unreliable, this para-transportation system that grew out of the ruins of public transport plays a major role in moving people without cars around the city. In the end, Jakarta's residents in fact are not starved for choice when it comes to transport, as a newspaper reports: "The city's streets are clogged with *ojek* [motorbike taxi], *bajaj* [three-wheel taxis], minivans, buses, taxis and private cars. Until recently *becak* still operated in parts of the city. Some hardy individuals ride bicycles. *Ojek* are popular for their ability to weave in and around traffic, but sometimes a jam is too much even for them..."[10] (see Figure 3.4).

**Figure 3.4.** *Ojek* and their makeshift terminal (author's photo 2016).

The term *ojek* comes from "ngobjek" which means "looking for a livelihood" in order to survive difficult times. It emerged in the 1980s after *becak* were banned from operating in major streets. One can see *ojek* as a reincarnation of *becak*. Some believe that *ojek* first appeared in Jakarta in 1969–70 in the form of bicycle taxis. Many *becak* drivers (re-)turned to bicycle *ojek* when they lost their *becak* in the 1980s. *Ojek* grew rapidly following the Asian Financial Crisis in 1997 when several million workers were unemployed. Yadi, an *ojek* driver, tells his story: "I used to work in a printing shop, but was fired after the [1998] riot... There are not enough jobs in Jakarta, so we think being an *ojek* driver is not bad".[11] From the driver's account, we can say that *ojek* is a backbone of the informal economy for it provides employment, especially in a time of crisis. It however grows as an alternative means of transport which improves urban mobility when the formal transportation system is never reliable.

*Ojek* drivers are part of the para-transport rhizome. They often lack licences and their motorbikes are often unregistered. *Ojek* can reach almost everywhere in the city, especially areas not covered by formal public transportation networks. Just like taxis, they are flexible and adaptive as they tailor to the needs of their customers. The pickup places are undesignated. But unlike the taxi industry (before the Uber regime), driving an *ojek* is an individual enterprise. It has its own order within a largely unregulated environment. Yet *ojek* are not isolated from the formal sector. They serve established business owners and staff, workers and shoppers as well as school children. The existence of *ojek* thus intersects or overlaps with formal public places: stations, malls, markets, bus stops, offices and residential gates. Today *ojek*'s mode of circulation has inspired a series of corporate entrepreneurs who set up transport businesses (in fierce competition with *ojek*), such as Gojek, BribBike, Jeger, LadyJek and BluJek. The para-transport rhizome continues to grow across the boundary of the formal and informal.

## The Sea of Motorcycles

The most phenomenal form of para-transport today is the motorcycle. As indicated, it stemmed from a crisis of 1998 and the need to expand the domain of self-employment, but it is also largely generated by the poor public transport system which has pushed the urban majority, the lower-middle income people, to find their own solution. Motorbikes grew phenomenally in the 2000s when inexpensive models that could be bought on affordable credit schemes became widely available. The growth continues to this day. Dahlan Iskan, former Minister of State-Owned Enterprises, added another layer of meaning to the use of motorcycles. He once indicated that "motorcycles give an opportunity for common folks (*rakyat kecil*) to catch up. It is a medium for them to become middle-class citizens".[12] The popularity of motorcycles has enabled the lower-class population to move around and they have become as mobile as the upper-class. A 19-year-old man says: "I can go everywhere with the motorbike, because the public transportation here sucks. It's not comfortable, it's not fast, and it's very cheap when you buy a motorbike" (qtd. in Bainbridge 2013). Such mobility applies to both men and women.

In Indonesia, mobility carries a class status. It is common to see young people in their *kampung* sitting on their motorbikes chit-chatting while holding their cell phones. Motorbikes and cellphones are two symbols of modernity. Motorbikes have also become a favourite gift-item from parents to their children and grandchildren or relatives in the countryside. On the other hand, the motorcycle is the medium by which the lower class can easily take on the automobile class on the street.

Motorcycles seem to have broken apart the class division that has been built into the city. Furthermore, as indicated by Iskan, the lower classes have become more productive subjects as they can also use their motorcycles to earn income, such as by working as *ojek* drivers. While Iskan may have been over optimistic, I Dewa Made Susila, the chief officer of Adira Finance, Indonesia's biggest motorcycle

**Figure 3.5.** Motorcycles vs. cars: Motorbikes use forbidden busway lane to escape traffic (author's photo 2016).

finance company which (in 2013) employed a staff of 28,000, confirmed that half of those who bought a motorcycle are self-employed: "Half of them are using the motorcycles to earn money for living" (qtd. in Bainbridge 2013).

Be that as it may, today, Indonesia has the third largest motorcycle population in the world after China and India. Jakarta is the major contributor

**Figure 3.6.** "Ini Loh Jalanku!" [This is *my* road!]
*Note*: The text reads: Mang Somat and his beloved motor, Gustap. Everyone knows Jakarta is *macet* [congested]. The best alternative is the motorbike. It is slim, agile, and practical. It can be anywhere... on crossover bridges, on zebra crossings, on sidewalks, and can fly over cars".
*Source*: Ferdinandus Benny Rieky, in *Kolantas: Koplak Berlalu Lintas*, by Taupik, Wisnu, Kasmiyanto dkk ["and friends"]. Jakarta: Visimedia Pustaka (2014): 49.

to this ranking due the various factors outlined above, but in large measure to its traffic congestion: motorcycles are capable of filtering through traffic. Today over 18 million motorbikes are moving around the city. If the number of motorcycles is considered along with the number of traffic violations, Jakarta may be on the top of the list for motorcycle accidents. Motorists tend to ignore traffic signs, police patrols, sanctions and road safety rules. In 2013, Tom Hundley, a journalist at the Pulitzer Center, reported in *the Washington Post* on the frequency of traffic accidents in Jakarta: "the number of road deaths [rose] from just over 8,000 a year in 2002 to more than 16,500 five years later and doubling again three years later. Sixty per cent of the fatalities were riders of two- or three-wheelers".[13] Meanwhile, from his office in a tower high above the busy streets of Jakarta, Mustapha Benmaamar, a transport specialist with the World Bank, estimated that "Each day an average of 120 people die in accidents on Indonesia's roads".[14] In 2014, Jakarta municipality's transportation agency reported that in the city "as many as 3,000 people have died in the past five years due to accidents involving motorcycles".[15]

This chapter shows how urban transport contributes to the formation of disjointed dimensions of the city. Formed by a multitude of agencies, each with its self-interest as they benefit from the grief of others, urban transport has become an everyday sign of contradiction. While toll roads, motorists and the new urban form are signifiers of national progress, they are subjected to the political interest of the state and local government (as conflicting as they always have been). Developers are concerned only with the marketability of their housing properties and they see only automobiles and freeways. The automobile industries are interested in selling more cars and see only benefits in keeping public transportation inadequate. The middle class and the subaltern multitudes create for themselves, often through the gaps and cracks of the system, a space to move around. This includes *Jalan Tikus* which grew out of small winding alleys of *kampung* "beneath" the city. Like rhizomes, *Jalan Tikus* are not obvious, but they are an important part of the road map of Jakarta that changes almost every year. Each actant adds a dimension to the city, but they also contribute to the mutilation of urban space in such a way that while roads and transport continue to represent fantasies of unity and modernity, they also represent a dystopian breakdown. Yet if they represent today a broken promise or a road not taken, all the ideas of integrated public transport of the past, and the future imagining of green urbanism and a new jam-free city constitute only a list of desires that nevertheless provides antidotes to the pain of urban breakdown. The desire for a traffic-jam free city matches the desire for a flood-proof city, a subject of the next chapter.

## Notes

1. The Director General of Land Communications on the inauguration of the city bus project in mid-1978: "... urban public transport... is carried out by the government because [it] is a vital form of transport due to the need for a guarantee of continuity, order and reliability" (as cited in Dick 1981: 74).
2. For instance, by Cowherd 2002a; Firman 1998; Firman 2004; Leaf 1991 and Winarso 2006.
3. "Kondisi Perum PPD Kritis", *Kompas*, 20 July 2000.
4. "Jakarta Badly Needs Modern Transit System", *Jakarta Post*, 8 Jan. 1995.
5. Ibid.
6. Ibid.
7. Didi Purwadi, "SBY Perintahkan Foke Perbaiki Transportasi Jakarta", *Republika*, 22 Feb. 2011.
8. "More Stress Lies Ahead on Jakarta's Streets", *Jakarta Post*, 23 Jan. 2008.
9. Rudy Setiawan, "Fixing Indonesia's Public Transport Woes", *Jakarta Globe*, 4 Nov. 2013.
10. Alvin Soedarjo, "Busway Maintenance Needed, Say Passengers", *Jakarta Post*, 14 Aug. 2006.
11. Prodita Sabarini, "Avoiding the Traffic with Jakarta's Favorite Public Transportation", *Jakarta Post*, 14 July 2006.
12. Dahlan Iskan, "2012 Revolusi Ekonomi Sepeda Motor", *Pontianak Post*, 1 Jan. 2012.

[13] Tom Hundley, "A Deadly Cycle-Drama on the Streets of Jakarta", *The Washington Post*, 12 August 2013, at https://pulitzercenter.org/stories/deadly-cycle-drama-streets-jakarta (accessed 17 Dec. 2022).

[14] Ibid.

[15] "Motorcycle Accident Fatalities Reach 3,000", *Jakarta Post*, 17 Nov. 2014, at https://www.thejakartapost.com/news/2014/11/17/motorcycle-accident-fatalities-reach-3000.html (accessed 17 Dec. 2022).

Chapter

4    Where Will the Water Go?

"I just need them to answer my question: Where will the water go?"[1]

The governor of Jakarta (2014–17), Basuki Tjahaja Purnama ("Ahok"), was often puzzled by the persisting recurrence of stagnant water, along with rampant flooding (*banjir*), during almost every rainfall, which often included the business district along Thamrin and Sudirman protocol streets. Ahok believed that he had done all he could to eliminate *banjir*, but as the chapter epigraph indicates, nothing in *banjir* seems clear and straightforward.[2] Ahok took *banjir* seriously, and he wanted solving the flooding problem to be his signature accomplishment during his tenure as governor. Yet *banjir* continues to be a challenge—it was not as easily managed as he thought it would be, despite consuming a lot of his time and energy. Indeed, under Ahok, *banjir* signified continuing transformation or development of the city, as many projects were planned and initiated to rein it in, and yet *banjir* never failed to return as it had done in the past, or by surprise, leaving the many preventative projects nowhere in particular (Figure 4.1). *Banjir* seems to belong to an uncanny world, where its root causes are difficult to trace. Its appearance can be strange (*aneh*) and seemingly nonsensical (*nggak masuk akal*).

The issues of *banjir* have increasingly received attention in a variety of fields, and Jakarta has been a primary case study (Caljouw, Nas and Pratiwo 2005; Douglass 2010; Firman et al. 2010; Gunawan 2010; Padawangi and Douglass 2015; Simanjuntak et al. 2012; Texier 2008 and Dickson et al. 2012). Existing studies have significantly contributed to our understanding of the inadequate institutional, organisational and individual capacities for flood management in a city that is expanding rapidly. They also point to universal forces, such as urbanisation and climate change, which exacerbate flooding. It is fair to acknowledge, however, that, with a few exceptions,[3] existing studies on environmental problems tend to be technocratic and limited, as they do not take politics and culture as the primary focus of their investigation.

**Figure 4.1.**  *Banjir* Jakarta (author's photo).

This chapter attempts to complement these existing studies by exploring the multifaceted dimensions of flooding, such as how it is culturally perceived, understood and managed; how it is implicated in knowledge and power, and how it becomes a form of "governmentality" that nevertheless produces a critical consciousness among the public about the environmental crisis.[4] It also seeks to contribute to the recent literature, adding to works dealing with what Brian Larkin calls "the politics and poetics of infrastructure" (Larkin 2013). Recent works, as Larkin points out, have moved away from analysing the technical functioning of technology to considering how it constitutes both the rationality of governance and political imagination of both the ruler and the ruled (see, for Indonesia, Mrázek 2008; Kooy and Bakker 2008). This chapter builds on the insights of current scholarship from critical geography and anthropology of infrastructure to make sense of a social formation (such as Jakarta) in which *banjir* is associated with both disaster and opportunities. It seeks to contribute to works that emphasise the productive failure of technology that shapes a particular form of governmentality where, as in the words of Nikhil Anand, "leakages are more than just losses. They are uncontrolled, unknown flows of water that structure the lives and states formed by the city's water supply infrastructure" (see Anand 2015: 307).

This chapter is not about water supply, but water surplus as it floods the city. The focus is the absence (or inadequacy) of an integrated infrastructure and the presence of the discursive infrastructures that structure the city's unevenly shared power and hierarchy. In the uncoordinated "absent presence" of infrastructure, *banjir* allows for the possibility of exchange among people, power and money. It also allows the question of agency (who and what is behind *banjir*, for instance) to occupy an unsettling position that is open to interpretation. Infrastructure, in this context, gives *banjir* a truly fluid existence.

If infrastructure, like a slippery, unpredictable *banjir*, can be nowhere and everywhere at the same time, how should we approach the issue that is both real and imagined? It seems to me that a possible approach to slippery objects is to look for materials that are equally discursive, ranging from news reports, official publications, popular culture and social media, and advertisements to field observations, overheard remarks, and conversations, as well as our feelings about the city as we have experienced it over time. Methodologically, I seek to organise those discursive materials around the use of certain vocabulary terms seen as representing the meaning of *banjir* and its associated infrastructure. These are notions of *banjir* as *bencana* (disaster), as *bocor* (leakage), as *berkah* (blessing) and as *budaya* (culture), which structure the political meaning and practices of the infrastructure. Such an approach may be attributed to Jakarta's unique character (but not so unlike other postcolonial cities) as a city divided by infrastructure, a condition which undermines the conventional understanding of infrastructure as carrying an integrative purpose of serving the public as a whole.

It may be useful, therefore, to remember that, historically, Jakarta has never implemented a unitary infrastructural ideal aimed at benefiting the wider public (as was attempted in most Western cities, such as late nineteenth century London and twentieth-century US suburbs).[5] Instead, Jakarta, from the beginning, has represented a series of fragmented, privately-funded infrastructure projects, constructed to benefit only certain stakeholders. In the absence of providing a universal public good, multiple infrastructures built by different groups divide people, but also create an imagined community, as people have a shared sense of uncertainty and anticipation around, for example, *banjir* (see Barker and Gibbings 2018). The various programmes and facilities operate like an infrastructure of difference as communities are both united by *banjir* and yet divided by their responses to it due to the variety of solutions they have built for themselves. The fragmented infrastructures nevertheless serve as mediators between different communities. As people experience flooding, they imagine themselves in and through these diverse infrastructures that worked (or failed to work) for them.

## An Infrastructure to Unify the City?

Towards the end of 2012, Ahok, then Jakarta's vice-governor, rushed to see his superior, Governor Jokowi, at his office. It was a few weeks before marking their first one hundred days of governing Jakarta. Ahok wanted to report, after weeks of extraordinary work, that he had managed to tidy up the annual city budget and discovered an excess of US$750 million from the past year's budget—an unbelievable amount. Jokowi was happily shocked. He told his vice-governor that he had never seen such an amount of money when he served as the mayor of Solo. Ahok, in turn, replied, "especially in East Belitung, Pak" (referring to his former role as *bupati* ["district regent"] there) (qtd. in Agustina et al. 2013: 32). They were also astonished to find in the files that previous administrations had put forth twenty-two projects to resolve traffic jams and flooding, but none of those projects had been carried out or completed for the reason of "lack of funds" (ibid.). This reason was clearly nonsense for the new leaders.

Jokowi and Ahok had no time to investigate why, if there was so much surplus money, worthwhile projects went unfunded, but they felt empowered. They were pleased that they had almost everything they needed at their disposal: a stock of ideas and an excess of money to execute some of the projects. What they didn't quite have, however, was time, as they had to demonstrate to everyone in a relatively short period of time (ideally, during their tenure) that they were capable of accomplishing something really substantial to mark their campaign-promise ideal of a *"Jakarta baru"* (new Jakarta).

Jokowi and Ahok were quick enough to learn that traffic jams and flooding were the two most strategic public issues, as everyone was affected by these perennial problems. Imagine if they could solve them once and for all. After looking through the existing collection of ideas, they chose "deep tunnel", a project that was first floated in 2007 by Governor Sutiyoso at the end of his term (a bit too late to save his image). The idea was based on Kuala Lumpur's Stormwater Management and Road Tunnel (SMART) project. The main attraction for Jokowi and Ahok was that "the deep tunnel can deal with flood and traffic jams at the same time. In addition, it can also function as a channel for telephone and electric cables, gas pipelines, and sewage drains".[6] Such a multifunctional tunnel would integrate for the first time the city's diverse, uncoordinated utility network, which would all be sharing a single underground pathway. For Jokowi, "this is a breakthrough".[7] All-in-one, it would represent the city's first integrated infrastructural ideal. Jokowi and Ahok were told that the tunnel could be constructed rather quickly, in just four years, which was soon enough to represent the core achievement of their administration's first term. And above all, it could be done quite easily, as the project is underground, deep enough to avoid land-ownership issues or any trouble with authorities outside the territory of Jakarta. Jokowi and Ahok were enthusiastic. They could use the excess funds that Ahok had found in the budget "so that the deep tunnel [could] immediately start" the following year (Agustina et al. 2013: 32), along with what are known as conventional methods of flood mitigation in the city, such as the World Bank-sponsored river-dredging, well-drilling and normalising of reservoirs and rivers. Since the tunnel would be more effective than all of those "surface" treatments, Jokowi launched "deep tunnel" as his first infrastructure project. But, alas, the project would not be carried out.

In January 2013, a few weeks after the announcement, a massive flood hit Jakarta. So devastating was the flood that the media used the phrase *alam mengamuk* (nature is furious/mad)![8] *Banjir* showed its true nature and washed away Jokowi's dream project. Referring to the massive flood, the Ministry of Public Works determined that a deep tunnel would, as a practical matter, be inefficient and ineffective. The capacity of the deep tunnel was considered too small to handle the madness of *alam*. Since then this "immediate" technological fix has received very little support, and over time even Ahok himself, after becoming governor in 2014, doubted that the deep tunnel would ever solve the flooding problem. In 2015, after being approached again by a developer/investor and the persistent engineer who initiated the project, Ahok reported: "I just need them to answer my question, 'Where will the water go?' Neither of them can answer this question, so of course, I am doubtful".[9]

## Where Will the Water Go?

The matter of "where will the water go" ("*airnya mau dibuang kemana*") is, apparently, a haunting question.[10] Ahok was not the first to ask such a question. According to him, the question was also put forward by Sutiyoso when he first proposed the tunnel project in 2007, after a massive flood. It is not clear what response he got, but apparently there has never been a good answer to the question. That seems to indicate, nevertheless, how difficult it is to understand the flow of water in Jakarta. For sure, many cities and municipalities have constructed deep tunnels quite successfully, but apparently Jakarta is considered to be different. Maybe it has something to do with the city sinking. Maybe there *is* something different about the way water flows in Jakarta. Ahok felt such a difference. As governor, he increasingly expressed his frustration and confusion over the logic of Jakarta's *banjir*. He could not understand how inundation could occur on roads that had never been flood-prone in the past: "It is odd that inundation moves from one area to another. Yesterday, Jl. Tunojoyo was inundated. The road had never been inundated before".[11]

Ahok, however, learned that issues accompanying flooding are not just technical. Instead, they carry a dimension that is social, if not political. And they often led to the discovery of unruly things or uncanny happenings. "It is strange [*tak masuk akal*] that Gembrong was flooded, because it has never been before. Civil servants in East Jakarta initially said that the pump in Gembrong was broken because a cable was bitten by a rat, but when I checked, the cable was fine, but was not installed properly". Meanwhile, "in Dukuh Atas, the pump's cable was cut ... Jalan Fatmawati was crazier [*lebih gila lagi*]. There is no way Fatmawati could sink. It turned out there are tires and traffic lights inside the drainage ... I suspect sabotage".[12]

"I am not sure", Ahok mused, "is this a game or not, but I was then asked to issue emergency funds in the amount of 50 *miliar rupiah* (US$3.8 million)".[13] For Ahok, *banjir* points not only to disaster, but also to excess and leaks, terms that in turn are associated with corruption and collusion. The excesses of *banjir*, apparently, can be channelled into someone's pocket.

On the other hand, *banjir*'s unpredictability and impartiality also connote some kind of unidentified behind-the-scenes agency—that is, the work of an extraterrestrial being. As noted previously, *banjir* is often described (in the media) as nature being angry. In this understanding, it would be too much to fight *banjir*. The notion of *banjir mengamuk* might have come from the belief in supra-natural power. Historian Restu Gunawan points out that in 1932, when a massive flood hit Batavia, some people believed that it was "Nyi Loro Kidul *mengamuk*" (rampage of the Sea Goddess).[14] News circulated then that the *banjir* was sent by the Queen of the South Sea, who was furious that the colonial state had detained Sukarno in 1931. Such understanding is, in itself, interesting when read in the context of resistance against colonial rule, but it can also be understood in terms of a traditional belief in the power of supra-natural forces. Restu Gunawan refers to how *banjir* was perceived almost 100 years ago, but such an understanding still resonates today if people still think *banjir* is natural or there is nothing to be done about it.

So does this mean that water makes its own decision about where it will go? Perhaps *banjir* is capable of making a deal, too? When Jokowi became the governor, a cartoonist showed an animated *banjir* introducing itself by reaching out its hand politely (as well as creepily) to shake the governor's hand (Figure 4.2):

This "meeting" between human and nonhuman symbolises a variety of things, one of which is perhaps a deal being made for mutual benefit. The question "Where will the water go?" could also suggest that agency can lie in objects or processes that are nonhuman if not supra-human. A month later Jokowi told a reporter, as if in answer to this cartoon: "I just started my term a few months ago. I am not a superman, a god, or a magician who can just turn his hand to eliminate *banjir*";[15] perhaps the statement was to assure *banjir* that together they can work something out. Or perhaps Jokowi was saying that he needed more time to understand not only the nature of *banjir*, but also what was so unnatural about it. Meanwhile, the diverse residents of Jakarta daily must face the question of "where will the water go?"

Such a question must have shaped the imaginations, actions and choices of individuals, and some of the answers and attempted solutions are unravelled in the city's discursive infrastructures. What follows are some instances that allow us to observe here and there the imagining of *banjir* in and through infrastructure and the implication for the formation of communities divided as well as united by flooding.

**Figure 4.2.** The flood greets Jokowi.
*Note*: The text translates as: "Hello Sir, just want to introduce myself. My name is *Banjir* Jakarta".
*Source*: Benny Rachmadi, "Jokowi Hadapi Banjir" (Jokowi confronts/approaches the flood), 28 Nov. 2012 (from Kontan, http://images.kontan.co.id/main/kartun_benny/302).

## Communities of Infrastructures

The unevenness of Jakarta's topography is widely acknowledged. It can be seen in the urban form. It also often finds expression in maps that represent the city's flooding patterns. Excess water goes to the *lokasi rawan banjir* (flood prone locations), and those areas, while not always synonymous with places where most of the urban poor live, indicate the social inequality of the city. Such mapping initially served to establish where the water will go and to prepare for flooding, but such maps turn out to be unreliable, if not misleading, over time. It is difficult to predict if the same area, or indeed any area, will be inundated or stay dry the following year. In 2007, when a massive *banjir* hit Jakarta, inundating 70 per cent of the city, killing 55 people, and displacing over 350,000 people from their homes, Pluit, a vulnerable flood-prone area located below sea level in North Jakarta, was "magically" unaffected. Some residents of the district (mostly ethnic Chinese) attributed this miracle to *hoki* ("good luck" in Hokkien) that had protected the "abode of the dragon" (i.e. Pluit's location, according to Chinese beliefs) (Widyanto 2007: 40).

Such *hoki*, however, was not determined by the power of the dragon some residents believed lived there. Instead, it was due to the extra efforts of the communities living in Pluit's housing estate to raise the wall of their levee (ibid.). After 1996 and 2002, when Pluit was flooded at an average height of one metre, residents independently formed the *Forum Masyarakat Peduli Lingkungan Pluit* (Communities that Care for Pluit's Environment) to work together whenever a nearby levee broke. Each neighbourhood sent ten capable men to work with security personnel to mend the levee. Pluit covers an area where both the rich and the poor live. They have long lived together collaboratively, though not always comfortably, but *banjir* has brought them together as a community. "The rich and the poor worked together arm-in-arm", a community organiser reported (ibid.).

Tjhi Fat Khiong, then head of RW 07,[16] indicated to me that the Pluit communities were united by previous *banjir*; in 2007, through a system of water pumps, they created for themselves a localised infrastructure of flood control. He pointed out that the communities collectively bought sixty water pumps and a set of generators to pump water out of the area. They also hired three workers to watch over the six huge pumps that operate around the clock. As a result, today Pluit comprises communities of water pumps and residents know perfectly well where the water should go. Water is pumped over the levee out into the river and sea.

Kelurahan Pluit (a ward located at Penjaringan subdistrict) sits on 7.7 square kilometres (three square miles) of land that is lower than the adjacent sea. Residents must feel as if all of Jakarta is dependent on their pumps. The Pluit Dam (constructed in 1965) contains the Cideng River and nine others before that water is pumped out to the sea. Tjhi told me that he appreciated the pumps and private guards. The pump stations are placed strategically along the Pluit Dam and the canal and river embankments. It feels safe when all the communities cooperate and pray together to the dragon and for the pumps and the guards. Residents long ago lost confidence in the developer who is supposed to manage their district. They consider that the developer is interested only in new business, not the quality of life. For example, throughout Tjhi's time living in Pluit, he has seen that many green areas were converted into commercial establishments such as shopping malls. Residents also did not want to bother the municipality's Public Works Unit (Dinas Pekerjaan Umum), as that apparatus was not always reliable, given the vast challenges the city was facing.[17]

**Figure 4.3.** Community-funded extra pumps and pipes in North Jakarta (author's photo).

## Where Might the Water be Coming From?

The communities of water pumps that Tjhi organised are only a part of a larger, but not so well-coordinated, network of dams and embankments that loosely form Jakarta's urban system of flood management. Pluit thus can never quite develop a securely self-contained infrastructure, no matter how many pumps are installed. Its fate depends on the management of water flowing from elsewhere in Jakarta. For other parts of the city, the answer to the question "where will the water go?" is rather clear: it goes to Pluit, where it is pumped out to sea. As such, Pluit is always in need of *hoki*, but *hoki* being *hoki*, it is not always present, no matter how much incense is burned. Tjhi, like most people in the city, knows where the water should go, but he has little idea about the source of that water or the volume that will be received from other parts of Jakarta. His feeling is that water can come from anywhere and at any time. Pluit residents fear *banjir kiriman* (flooding water from outside their areas). Thus, they need *hoki* to secure their place.

There were times when *hoki* was not around, however. In late January 2013, six years after Pluit was spared from 2007's massive, historic flooding, a part of the West Flood Canal embankment, near the Menteng area of Central Jakarta, collapsed. The levee in that area suddenly broke, as water was filling the West Flood Canal after a floodgate at nearby Manggarai in South Jakarta was opened. The overflow went behind Pluit Dam, and the water put too much stress on the dam. *Tempo* reported on the catastrophe as it was experienced by a guard who watched over Pluit's water pumps:

> Joko, who had stood watch over the dam's water pumps for 32 years, was astounded that the seven pumps, which he had been operating since that morning, were outpaced by conditions at the dam that afternoon. The water level quickly rose to 25 centimeters. "The pumps were running at full capacity, but the water kept rising". Continuing to rise, the water level finally overflowed. In fact, this time the water at the Pluit Dam rose to 275 centimeters. This broke the previous record, namely, 135 centimeters in 2007. (Widyanto et al. 2013: 45)

As a result, more than 4,500 Pluit homes, belonging to the rich and the poor alike, were inundated with floodwater one to two metres deep. A week after the initial flooding, Tjhi had to ride in an amphibious vehicle belonging to the Indonesian Red Cross to move around the housing complexes still under water. He lamented, "the good prospects of the area had been washed away" (qtd. in Widyanto et al. 2013: 47). As Pak RW, Tjhi had done well for some years to keep his district dry, but in 2013 Pluit became the area hit by the worst *banjir*. Tjhi blamed the flooding on the change of land use over several years in his district. When he moved to Pluit in 1982, "Mega Mal[-l] Pluit, Mal[-l] Emporium Pluit, and Pluit Junction had not been built, and there had not been a land reclamation project to build the Pantai Mutiara residential area" (ibid.). These complexes reduced further the amount of open, green areas, and contributed to land subsidence in Pluit, which was once (during Dutch colonial times) swampland and a water catchment zone.

Tjhi blamed the municipality's property developer, Pembangunan Pluit Jaya Company, which, after 2000, became a corporate entity called Jakarta Propertindo Group. Its management company, Estatindo, expanded its real-estate holdings by encroaching on areas reserved for environmental conservation. For Tjhi, in the long run, those violations brought floods into Pluit. Yet, according to Jakarta's Zoning Office and its Geospatial Information Agency, the flooding in Pluit was caused simply by damaged water pumps. For them, what was needed was better maintenance of the pumps. But for Joko, the hardworking pump operator on duty at Pluit Dam: "The pumps are strong enough for pumping out rainwater. But water does not only come from the sky" (William, Supriadin and Istman 2013: 50). The technician in Jakarta's Office of Public Works, who believed in a technological fix, replied: "If the embankment of the West Flood Canal had not collapsed, Pluit would have been safe" (ibid.) . Governor Jokowi, after personally inspecting the drains, concluded that the collapse of the embankment was "due to a weak control management" (qtd. in Widyanto et al. 2013: 47). Jokowi and Tjhi ultimately believed that the *banjir* was caused by human error. It was due to government failure and developers' greed. Little did they realise, perhaps, that their perspectives, which focused on what could have been done, represented a different consciousness in Jakarta's history of *banjir,* as most residents believe that *banjir* is *bencana alam* (a natural disaster).

## *Banjir* as *Bencana* (Disaster)

During Jakarta's massive flooding in 2007, Governor Sutiyoso defended himself by saying that flooding was part of a natural cycle and there was nothing he could have done about it (Mydan 2007: A 11). "There is no point in throwing abuse around", he said, adding, "what is important to know is ... I was up till 3:00 AM trying to handle the refugees" (ibid.). Such an answer is typical. Almost all governors would say the same thing. His successor, Fauzi Bowo, is known for repeatedly asking people to understand (*maklum*) that "because *banjir* is a natural factor [*factor alam*] that is difficult to handle".[18] *Banjir* has long been understood as a supra-human force. The term *bencana* might be linked to a belief in the working of "natural"—nonhuman—forces. When *banjir* is understood as a *bencana*, it gives an impression that no particular human or any agency or institution is to be blamed. Some *kampung* residents living on riverbanks also believed that "the flood is only a natural disaster which could happen at any time; I don't see any connection between the location of our houses and the worsening floods ... it could be a message from God; perhaps he was punishing us for our sins".[19]

Governors of Jakarta have often exploited the idea of *bencana* as stemming from natural forces to wash their hands of any responsibility. Their position could be seen as drawing from a framework that separates the environmental from the social and the political, as if they occupied different domains. Such a position is often also shared by scientific communities that emphasise Jakarta's geo-environment to explain *banjir*. The city's government officials have often cited the scientific reasoning that *banjir* is inevitable, because 40 per cent (some 26,000 hectares) of the city's territory (which is about 65,000 hectares, or 251 square miles) is "low land", which means below sea level. The explanation continues with more geographical facts, including that the city is crossed by as many as thirteen rivers—each carrying, unequally, massive amounts of water from the nearby mountains to the sea. In addition, Jakarta sits in a shallow delta, so during the rainy season, much of the city can be filled with water very easily, especially during heavy rainfalls. Furthermore, the fate of the city is also determined by full moons and tides. When ocean tides reach their peak, they tend to overwhelm the shoreline and cover the north end of the city. Those explanations are not exhaustive, but may suffice to highlight how and why *banjir* is clearly a natural phenomenon, and thus it is not fair to just keep pointing a finger at the city government. There is even a statement in the municipality's official publication about *banjir*'s intractability: "elements of nature are far more powerful than the limited (territorial) sovereignty of the municipality".[20]

This geo-environmental argument is drawn from a belief that *banjir* is caused by atmospheric (cosmic) forces, and thus flooding is somehow a "natural" event—or, oddly, a supra-natural phenomenon. This, then, also suggests that one can't really avoid it, get rid of it, or fight it, especially when it is "mad", but one can still try to minimise or mitigate its impact. One can also learn to live with it, as well as escape from it. Victims can flee the disaster caused by the "cosmic force" to emergency accommodations (at schools, mosques and relatives' houses), and return once the flood has receded. Adaptation and accommodation are behind such thinking, which, ironically, also assumes that *banjir* is a "normal", natural phenomenon. This assumption has served as a paradigm for flood management since colonial times, if not before.

## Engineering the Waterways

That Jakarta is a city of rivers and canals is something that is known but not always obvious to everyone. Thirteen rivers, large and small, flow one into another before they all flow into Jakarta Bay. Consequently, Jakarta is secured, thanks to the colonial government and its engineers, by a complex system of dams, dikes, embankments, floodgates, and, in recent years, water pumps. This dike-and-dam system can be said to stem from the colonial Dutch belief that even if *banjir* is *bencana alam*, its impact can be minimised by technology (e.g. dams and floodgates). Such a belief survives till today. The infrastructure, however, is quite old, and is relatively ignored and only reluctantly maintained, as signified by the piles of garbage that continue to choke the floodgates. That neglect, some believe, is due to the city government's overall poor "maintenance culture". Others believe that the anti-flooding system is obsolete, and the city should not bother to keep investing in it.

Governor Ahok considered the colonial system of flood management not only outdated, but even somewhat responsible for *banjir,* partly because the floodgates that are central to the system rely too much on human decision-making that is often irresponsible, if not *tak masuk akal* (nonsensical). For instance, during the 2016 annual flood, Ahok asked, "why did Angke River so overflow that it inundated West Jakarta? I immediately suspect that you guys [floodgate operators] flushed all the water [*buang airnya*] to West Flood Canal".[21] He noticed that several areas in proximity to the West were all dry. How could that happen?

> This means you guys closed the floodgates [in certain areas]. Why did you do that when you knew that a huge volume of water was coming down from the hills? Why did you close the gates? Just for *iseng* [fun]? If you close the gates, the water will accumulate there, and when the level reaches *siaga 1* [alert level 1] you guys will suddenly open them [and] Jakarta of course will be inundated. I have told you guys since 2014, don't ever close floodgates anymore [during the rainy season]. Let the gates stay open, all of them, but you guys never listened … How could you still say that [gate closing] is a *protop* [old permanent procedure] from the Dutch era … *Emang Belanda negara lu sekarang* [so is your country today Dutch]?[22]

Despite these complaints, Ahok knew well that the Dutch floodgate system was meant to control water so that it could be flushed to the sea during the rainy season and stored during the dry season. There is some logic behind the original design of that floodgate system—in the sense that if a balance between water in and water out could be maintained, Jakarta would neither flood during the rainy season nor be without water at other times. Ahok, however, had in mind a strategy to manage both *alam* and people at the same time. Unlike the Dutch who showed no interest in preventing the formation of *kampung* settlements along the riverside,[23] Ahok sought to use the floodgate system exactly for that purpose. For him, floodgates should always be open during the rainy season, because now there are reservoirs and water pumps downstream, but the gates should be closed during the dry season so that the water level would reach a point where it prevented people from building houses on the riverbanks.[24] The governor had his own way of appropriating Dutch engineering and reworking it to fit with his method of flood mitigation. While following the Dutch logic of releasing water during the rains and holding it during the dry season, he used it to prevent the formation of *kampung* settlements along the riverside.

Mark Caljouw, Peter Nas, Pratiwo, Restu Gunawan and A.R. Soehoed, among others, have informed us of the great works of Dutch engineers, especially Ir. Herman van Breen, who worked for Batavia's BOW (Burgerlijke Openbare Werken, city public works) and served, beginning in 1919, as a member of Batavia's

Gemeenteraad (local council).[25] Van Breen's system of canals and floodgates was a significant sign of modernity, a symbol of humanity's capacity to exert control (to a certain degree) over the natural environment. In 1918 Van Breen designed a flood-control system to channel the flow and regulate the volume of water that goes through the city. The aim was to allocate floodwater so that it could be distributed here and there. The task was to balance water distribution in such a way that, when *banjir* occurred, not a single place would be fully inundated.

Van Breen's main focus then was the Ciliwung River, the largest river that cuts through the middle of the city. His idea was to reduce the river's volume by distributing its excess water to other rivers through one main conduit. He thus sought to create a series of canal and sluice gates that would intercept the Ciliwung River's flow so that, when its volume increased to flood level, the excess could be distributed to other rivers. His geographical imagination was active, too. By 1918, Van Breen had already projected that the city's territory would expand from its 15 square kilometres to 23 in 1949 (from less than six to almost nine square miles).

Van Breen's 1917 map (Figure 4.4) shows the attention he paid to the southwestern part of Batavia. He gave particular attention to the protection of the Menteng and Gondangdia areas (where most elite Europeans were living) and assigned to the grand Manggarai floodgate the special task of distributing water through different channels (*saluran—hoofdaanvoerleiding*) to adjacent rivers. The Manggarai floodgate thus has three gates, each with its own function. One gate is for distributing water from the Ciliwung River to the West Flood Canal, another for maintaining the water volume of the Ciliwung River and the third gate is for flushing.

Not surprisingly, the Manggarai floodgates were guarded by security personnel during the colonial era, especially after reports that other areas of Batavia started to suffer from flooding once the Manggarai floodgates began operating. Van Breen's solution involved the differentiated distribution of risks, which, in the colonial situation, basically involved reducing risks for those living in the Menteng area (predominantly Europeans), while increasing risks for others elsewhere. In other words, the practice of spatial differentiation through the use of infrastructure development has been in place since colonial times.

## Engineered Flooding

The system of flood control thus intertwines with the power relations embedded in the city. As *banjir* has become more frequent and has worsened, the floodgate has shifted from being a tool for risk prevention to becoming an instrument for risk distribution. Its function has transformed from moving water to moving risks.

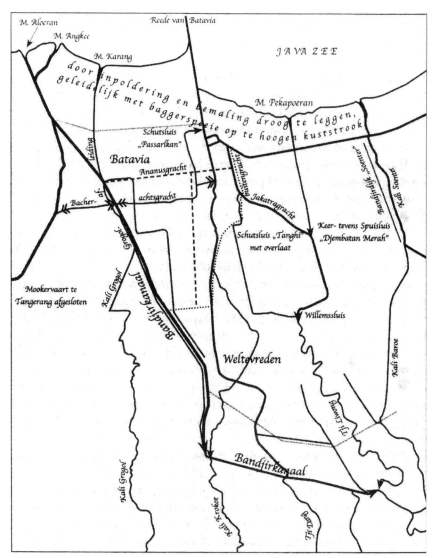

**Figure 4.4.** Van Breen's 1917 map.[26]
*Source*: Caljouw, Nas and Pratiwo (2005); courtesy of *Bijdragen tot de Taal-, Land- en Volkenkunde* [BKI]; see also Van Breen 1917.

Individuals who control the gates have to decide which areas can absorb more risks and which areas can be sacrificed as a way to control flooding elsewhere. This raises questions such as: what is the principle of, and what are the assumptions behind, the risk distribution embedded in the floodgate system? Is the principle negotiable? Does the floodgate actually control where the water will go?

**Figure 4.5.** Flood Alert: Disaster Response Post—*Siaga Banjir: Posko Tanggap Bencana* (author's photo).

Jakarta has over fifty floodgates of various sizes on its thirteen rivers.[27] The water level at the upstream floodgate determines whether the gates downstream should be lifted or closed. This also means that all of the floodgate controllers have to coordinate and decide which gates should not be opened until it is absolutely necessary. So we can say that the decision is subject to a variety of conditions, ranging from one that is objective—measurable by numerical indicators of water level—to those that are calculated by economic and political stakeholders with a biased interest in protecting elite neighbourhoods and the presidential palace. Flood risk may thus be externalised to areas of low economic and political significance to protect urban elites and their space in the city. At this level of operation, floodgates serve as a medium for the differentiation and rearrangement of an urban hierarchy.

The floodgate operators, all sufficiently trained and with high school diplomas, are supposed to work together by sharing information (through two-way radio communication) to manage the flood-control system. Each floodgate is supervised around the clock. The large floodgates are watched by four to eight operators, while smaller gates are normally run by two people. Operators have a huge responsibility to carry out decisions based on the reports they receive about other gates, but often they have to use their instincts. Edhi Widodo, a gatekeeper, noted: "We have to be extremely careful in observing the water volume, especially during the rainy season. While there is a procedure we must follow, we still often need to rely on our instincts in our decision to open and close the floodgates".[28]

Yet, while the gatekeepers follow their calculations and instincts, they have higher masters who are responsible for making the ultimate decision. Responsibility is hierarchically allocated between units in the Municipality's Office of Public Works (Dinas Pekerjaan Umum) and between the city and the national governments according to the level of warning. For instance, within the Municipality, different heads of the Office of Water Management (Tata Air) are assigned different levels of responsibility in response to the degree of warning. The Kepala Seksi (section chief) is responsible for the less alarming Siaga [alert] IV; the Kepala Suku Dinas (department head) for Siaga III; the Kepala Dinas Pekerjaan Umum (the head of Public Works) for Siaga II; and, when the water level at Manggarai floodgate reaches nine and a half metres, Jakarta's governor is responsible for Siaga I. It makes sense that Ahok was particularly attentive to the Manggarai floodgates, which were under his authority. Meanwhile, some rivers and canals as well as sluice gates are controlled only by the central government. Floodgates, like the waterways, are divided among stakeholders.

For instance, during the 2013 flooding, President Soesilo Bambang Yudhoyono (SBY) gave permission to open the gate that protected the presidential palace. This kind of decision is needed to moderate flooding in other areas. The president said: "I ask that every effort be made. The center will help" (qtd. in Agustina et al. 2013: 32). The decision to open the floodgate so that the presidential palace shared the burden of flooding is highly symbolic, as it served to register the idea that flooding is a shared problem and that both the elite and the poor are equally at risk. When flood water finally reached the palace, perhaps SBY was pleased that the image of him standing in knee-high water talking on his cellphone was widely circulated in metropolitan newspapers. After all, didn't the photo prove that Pak SBY was suffering, too?

## *Banjir* as *Bocor* (Leaking)

By the time that SBY gave permission to open the floodgate that protected the palace, water was already everywhere else in the city. Pluit, as we have seen, was already submerged. The business district along the protocol streets of Jalan Sudirman and Jalan Thamrin was paralysed. In some areas, the flow of water was deadly. At the United Overseas Bank Plaza (where my sister works), off Sudirman Avenue, two workers were killed by water that quickly filled basements. In all, eleven people died and nearly twenty thousand were displaced, and Governor Jokowi declared a state of emergency for the city. At that time a spectacular image circulated on social media that showed, from a bird's-eye view, the inundation of the Hotel Indonesia Roundabout.

The Hotel Indonesia Roundabout is the centre of governmental pride, the symbol of national progress, the site of major shopping malls and the CBD of Jakarta that conveys a sense of perfection and control. It is supposed to be resistant to flood water. Yet in 2013, it revealed most visibly the public secret that Jakarta is, after all, full of leaks. It represents the city as, in Rudolf Mrázek's phrase, a broken flushing toilet (Mrázek 2013: 294).

As such, *banjir* can be associated with *bocor* (leaking). And when *banjir* is seen in this way, it can no longer be seen as *bencana*. If *banjir* as *bencana* focuses on where the water is coming from (sent by god or the angry *alam*), *banjir* as *bocor* shifts attention to where the water will go. *Banjir* as *bocor* involves human intentionality and the capacity to allow leaks or make leaks go undetected. *Bocor* has made *banjir* more slippery, as it becomes more difficult to know where the water will go. When *banjir* is understood as *bocor*, it also suggests that something has gone wrong and humans are responsible for it. How *banjir* is eventually understood as *bocor* represents an important shift of power and knowledge.

I should, however, note that the understanding of *banjir* as *bocor* is as old as constructing the idea of *banjir* as *bencana*. In 1918, a massive flood hit Batavia. It overwhelmed Van Breen's flood canal. Historian Gunawan indicated that illegal extortion by unscrupulous opportunists took place during the flood:

> When their houses were inundated, a number of indigenous [*boemi poetra*] workers of Toko Kolff went to see their boss. They intended to borrow money to buy food, as prices went up following the flood. The boss said yes, but he demanded that a letter of reference from their *kampung* head be provided so that he could determine that his workers actually needed money. So the workers went to meet their *kampung* head (who is also a *boemi poetra*), but to their dismay, the head charged twenty-five cents for each document. This was not only expensive, especially during difficult times, but it was also illegal. The workers had no choice but to pay. (Gunawan 2010: 119)

That kind of illegal extortion, already taking place in colonial times, is an example of *bocor*—an instance of how *banjir* is reworked by opportunists for personal benefit. The *kampung* head cared less about *banjir* as *bencana*. He was more interested in the excess he could gain from *banjir*. By extorting money, he turned *banjir* into a *bocor*. This has prolonged the cyclical life of *banjir* in the sense that it allows people to benefit every year by, for example, extolling rescue fees, flood relief political campaigns and the economy of cleaning up after flooding, as well as the whole business of repairing potholes.

People in Jakarta are often sceptical about the city government's attempts to end *banjir*, perhaps because without *banjir* there will be no *bocor*. And can one live without *bocor* in a place like Jakarta? There is money to be made by maintaining (rather than eliminating) *banjir*, as every "project" (known more as *ngobjek*—money-making opportunity) to deal with *banjir* carries opportunities for "*bocor*-ing" money into pockets. In this sense, *banjir* brings not only misery, but also money. Thus, building infrastructure to get rid of *banjir* once and for all is probably too ambitious and almost a utopian enterprise, as it means closing down the opportunity for the city to leak.

## *Banjir* as *Berkah* (Blessing)

If *bencana* can be caused by and lead to *bocor*, then it can also become *berkah*. As a worker, Ari Syarifuddin had a relatively steady income due to the amount of trash that accumulated at sluice gates. He worked almost daily to push the debris off the gates. He told a reporter that "you may look at this as trash, but I see it as money".[29] Syarifuddin's livelihood depended on *banjir*, as the functioning of the gates depended on his management of the trash dumped into the river. His world was organised around the relations between the river, the readiness of the gates, and *banjir*, which together constituted his system for living in the city. But there are other instances where *banjir* is not so much about the amount of trash, but more a "blessing" (*berkah*) in ways that serve as a social infrastructure.

When infrastructure failed to mediate, what brought people together was *banjir*, which has become an object that cuts across different social domains, creating not only shared miseries but also opportunities for different social groups to work together. For *banjir* to become *berkah* (blessing), it needs to bring forth a condition for people to assemble, to carry out mutual help (*gotong royong*), to "thank", which literally means to give and to take (*terima-kasih*). *Banjir* causes different social, political and business groups to meet even though they have different agendas. They meet due to the absence or the lack of infrastructure. Or, for better or worse, they meet because they *are* the infrastructure. When people are coming together, they make *banjir* social, which in turn allows *banjir* and humans to work together to sustain the presence of each other.

Out of *banjir* and the breakdown of viable infrastructure, different types of people emerged and formed a temporary assemblage, which in turn produced a kind of sociality across different agencies. Gunawan grouped them based on their activities.[30] Those whose houses were flooded reached out to government and politicians for help; as victims, they transformed themselves as legitimate subjects to be accommodated. Those who survived *banjir* felt an obligation to help the poor who were living in high-risk areas. And, I should add, those who wished to make some money set up make-shift water taxis and charged those they considered wealthy to transport them out of the flooded area. In a nutshell, while business is involved in providing mutual help, there is an enactment of moral obligation to help people suffering from *banjir*. In this instance, individuals serve as a form of infrastructure (Simone 2004), and through their embodied mediation, a community of *banjir* (due to the lack of infrastructure) develops. When people (more than infrastructure) are relied on, *banjir* gains an extra meaning. It constitutes a social life.

Such social formation evolves over time. Gunawan recorded a past practice, which he considers a kind of "best practice". During the 1918 flood, the historian narrates:

> Residents of Batavia shared their food. Batavia's philanthropic *smerofonds* distributed a few thousands in monetary aid. The Governor General visited inundated *kampung* and offered money. Residents offered spaces for refugees, especially along the east and west sides of the Molenvliet streets. Among them were Thalia buildings, the house of Tjie Eng Hok, the building of Tiong Hoa Oen Tong Hwee, Jamaiat Khair, Kong Boe Siang Hwee, and the verandahs of several houses owned by ethnic Chinese … *Thaliafonds* provided f300, Mr. Tjie Eng Hok tens of bags of rice. Mr. Lauw Soen Bak gave three boxes of salted fish … Chinese Kapitan Khow Kim An with his guards visited the flooded *kampung* and bought an entire stock of food from food stalls and distributed them to those who found refuge in different houses. (Gunawan 2010: 124, 125)

In this scenario, *banjir* produced shared subjectivities and it suspended the divisions of a colonial city even though the social hierarchy was enhanced through the relative positions of donors and recipients vis-à-vis aid. Gunawan's story has a contemporary resonance.

Today, politicians, corporations, enterprises and religious groups compete for a role in flood relief. The lack of infrastructure continues to produce opportunities for politicians and political parties to use *banjir* to gain electoral support. *Banjir* has become the occasion for political elites to meet the urban poor, and to promote themselves as advocates for them. Various emergency tents carrying logos and banners of organisations, political parties and corporations accompany every relief mission. Enterprises work hand in hand with multitudes of nongovernmental agencies, in part to satisfy social responsibility, in part to form bonds and gain influence. In this sense, disaster carries with it opportunities, and from the perspective of enterprises and political elites, *banjir* is thus something that is problematically desirable. In some ways, one could argue that the sociality formed around *banjir* and celebrations of solidarity and mutual help have prevented mass protests against mismanaged *banjir* and the urban spatial injustices associated with it. The result constitutes a culture of living with *banjir* as something that is acceptable. Such a cultural formation relies on a circularity of time, space and practices. It is in this sense that the question of "where will the water go?" suggests that the water will return, and for political-party stakeholders who seek to increase their influence, such reliable circularity allows for anticipation, including annual budget allowances and strategic planning.

Flood relief and mutual help during periods of *banjir* contribute to the restoration of a sense of normality. By thus helping people to return to a normal life, they make *banjir* liveable. By doing so, relief and aid also make the coming and going of *banjir* a normal, "social" phenomenon. When people (rather than things or institutions) can be relied on for relief, risks are internalised as part of one's subjectivity. In this human embodiment of infrastructure, risks become not so risky anymore. And there is something political about this mode of subjection. It naturalises the socio-political dimension of *banjir*. The temporary cooperation of people in times of *banjir* serves to overcome *banjir,* but without ending it. This ensures that *banjir* will return, and so will flood relief and mutual help, as well as maintenance of social relationships that, when they mutually constitute each other, are integrated into a whole system of what one would consider as a "cultural tradition"—a *budaya.*

## *Banjir* as *Budaya* (Culture)

In 2002, a newspaper reported that when it comes to issues of seasonal flooding, the answer is "no big deal, many folks are used to it", even though people, such as Lani, aged 35, will never forget how her fourteen-inch television, the most valuable item in the household, was carried away by the stream.[31] When floodwaters flow through the city and this is accepted as part of regular events in urban life, *banjir* is integrated into cultural practices. Such acceptance normalises *banjir* in yet another way. When *banjir* is perceived as a "normal" phenomenon, a culture of adaptation to live with *banjir* also develops in the social environment, from techniques of building construction—such as houses on stilts and flood relief through mutual assistance—to domesticating the effects of *banjir* through drawings, poems and songs. In this mode of living with *banjir*, flooding is often represented not only as a threat or a disaster that could bring misery, but also as an adventurous and even festive and humorous event. *Banjir* thus has constituted a tradition of living with it. It becomes a phenomenon that has been integrated into customs and generalisable memories. Thus, a culture that assembles human, nature and materiality is formed through *banjir*.

Zaenuddin H.M., a journalist, once observed that "every time *banjir* hits the capital city, everyone tends to be very engaged in the issues and debates, even though most is just talk, without solutions or any meaningful actions. But once *banjir* is over, everyone forgets instantly and no one really cares anymore" (Zaenuddin 2013: x). After the flood, most people resume their daily lives and *banjir* becomes just one more story among the many others in everyday life.

Over time, *banjir* is integrated as normalcy. People know that *banjir* will come back, and they also know that it will again go away. Soon, any particular *banjir* loses its specificity as memories of it merge with the fragmented images of a series of other *banjir* recorded by historians and journalists and lodged in personal and communal memories. In Zaenuddin's *Banjir Jakarta*, every *banjir* is listed in a manner such that one is hardly distinguishable from others. His book is a memory work that, ironically, invites an understanding of *banjir* as a living history of the city. *Banjir Jakarta* is organised chronologically, that is, according to the flow of *banjir* over time. Zaenuddin even mentions in his introduction that notable *banjir* already took place in the fifth century, long before the time of Batavia founder and VOC official J. P. Coen (1618–23) and all the way up to the Jokowi era (2012–14). The table of contents lists chronologically the following years: 1621, 1654, 1893, 1909, 1919, 1932, 1950, 1952, 1960, 1963, 1976, 1977, 1984, 1985, 1994, 1996, 1999, 2002, 2007 and 2013.[32]

Zaenuddin's book consists of a series of snapshots of *banjir* over time. It leaves us with the impression that *banjir* is an "annual" urban event, some more festive or disastrous than others. The time of its return is somewhat predictable, even as it has become more frequent today than before. Yet the manner of its arrival is always somewhat mysterious. The book also invites us to ask the question, how far back do we need to go to understand today's urban floods? *Banjir* in the area of today's Jakarta has already been recorded since the time of the Tarumanagara kingdom (358–669 CE). And what scale of analysis would make more sense—urban, regional, national, or global? Can it be analysed in terms of who is (most) responsible for *banjir*? Who suffered and benefitted the most? Should climate change be blamed? Or is it easier and more action-oriented to blame riverbank-dwelling poor people?

Zaenuddin's book, however, is not meant to centre on policy. Instead, it seeks to show the recurrence of *banjir* as *budaya* (culture). It starts with a lyric of a 1970 song by Benjamin Sueb, a Betawi comedian, which begins with *"Jakarta kebanjiran"* (Jakarta is flooded) and ends with a normalising acceptance of *banjir*: *"coba tenang jangan ribut; jangan pade kalang kabut"* (try to stay calm, don't fuss; don't, sir, be chaotic") (Zaenuddin 2013: vii). Considering the *longue durée* of *banjir*, one wonders whether, over time, *banjir* has not only sent water, but also produced culture. In other words, has *banjir* produced a "flood culture", that is a culture formed by disaster, by the perception or understanding of *banjir*, by the technique of managing floods, and by the opportunities *banjir* provides to reinvent tradition, to form community, to legitimise authority, to displace people, to make money and to renew the city?

## Displacing *Banjir*

Cultural aspects of *banjir* are often seen in terms of continuity, but there are ways to see *banjir* differently. For instance, what if the time of *banjir* is understood as linear (instead of cyclical), progressing towards a catastrophic end of the world? What if *banjir* is seen as getting worse and worse from year to year, so that it and the culture associated with it must be controlled or ended once and for all? A different perspective demands that we consider moments of shift and rupture against *budaya banjir*, but such a transition, as this section will show, leads only to the politics of blaming whoever is easily identified as the "agent" of *banjir*.

As indicated earlier, the scale and depth of the 2007 *banjir* put Governor Sutiyoso in a defensive position. While arguing that *banjir* is *bencana alam*, he understood that some actions were needed to minimise the impact of that natural disaster, especially when financial support was available for doing so. Iwan Gunawan, a senior disaster-management adviser at the World Bank in Jakarta, identified the *banjir* of 2007 as historic. It became "a wake-up call for decision makers"(qtd. in Cochrane 2016: A4). It started a negotiation between the Indonesian government and the World Bank that, after several years of deal-making, finally led to the first dredging programme in four decades. The World Bank agreed to support the "river normalisation" project with a focus on dredging with a US$189 million grant that, after some delays, started in 2012.[33] The government, for its part, is expected to maintain the city waterways to control sedimentation and to prevent the return of clogging problems.

As river normalisation started, the state began to turn its gaze to the "infra-" structure of the city: the hidden waterways behind shopping malls, apartment blocks and *kampung* houses along the riverbanks. By then, 70 per cent of the waterways were considered blocked by "garbage, debris, and utility cables" (Cochrane 2016: A4). The Asian Development Bank's country director for Indonesia described Jakarta's rivers as the "trash cans of the city" (Cochrane 2016: A4).[34] Such a finding demands action. Sutopo Purwo Nugroho, head of information for Indonesia's National Disaster Mitigation Agency (Badan Nasional Penanggulangan Bencana, BNPB), explained in 2012 that:

> The scope and problems of flooding in Jakarta continue to increase. Aside from the natural factors, it is anthropogenic [man-made] factors ... Nature used to be the dominant factor before the '70s. After that, the causes of floods became more complex. The combination of natural and anthropogenic [factors] is what makes the floods happen.[35]

Shifting the gaze from nonhuman forces to human activity, BNPB has named the dumping of household garbage and industrial waste into Jakarta's rivers as contributory anthropogenic forces.[36] And just as society itself is structured unevenly, the blame is quickly directed predominantly at the most vulnerable citizens: those people who occupy the riverbank. The focus on people who live on the riverbanks has contributed to a fixation on their habitual practice of throwing household garbage into the Ciliwung River. As one resident indicated, "We do not know where else to throw our household garbage because there is no garbage dump in this area. We throw it onto the riverbank so it will be washed away"[37] (Figure 4.6).

**Figure 4.6.** Publicity campaign linking *banjir*, garbage and the river during the time of Governor Jokowi. The banner reads: "Dumping of rubbish into rivers invites *banjir*" (author's photo).

The focus on human behaviour and the concomitant river normalisation project have led to a belief that riverside dwellers are the main cause of *banjir*. They are the perpetrators. They are the problem that has caused the city to leak. However, everyone also knows that riverside dwellers are flood victims themselves. So, as both victims and perpetrators, dwellers of irregular settlements are subjected to what Foucault would call a "regulatory discipline".[38] And they become "docile subjects", open for transformation. They get from the government this message (and this is what Governor Ahok would say to justify the eviction of riverside *kampung* dwellers and relocating them to high rises): "Move away permanently from the riverbank; it is dangerous for you and, furthermore, it is actually causing floods in the city". The river normalisation project thus serves as a prelude to displacement without which, according to this narrative, the river flooding cannot be managed.

The critique of anthropogenic forces entails an identification of problems that, in turn, have led to the eviction and relocation of *kampung* dwellers. As *Kompas* (3 Feb. 2014) put it, "the normalisation of the river requires the removal of *kampung* settlements on riverbanks".[39] Riverside dwellers became the subject of disciplinary practices, and relocating their settlements was considered a "more realistic approach than creating new reservoirs". As a result, according to *Kompas*, about seventy thousand Jakarta households along the Ciliwung River would need to be relocated so that the river could be widened to accommodate more water and to allow for an inspection path on both sides.[40]

**Figure 4.7.** River scene in *Kampung* Pulo (author's photo).

The *Kompas* article was accompanied by a map of settlements along the Ciliwung River in the central part of Jakarta. The map also provided the names of the areas and the numbers of people targeted for relocation. It also calculated the number of apartment units needed to resettle those being evicted. Governor Jokowi instructed that both sides of the river should be kept free of any structure to allow for an "inspection path" and "this year we start from Kampung Pulo and Kalibata". The mayor of Central Jakarta confirmed that in one year, "there will be no settlement from Karet floodgate to Tanah Abang bridge"; the city government declared that "river normalisation will start from its territorial boundary at Depok down to Manggarai. However, our priority for now is Kampung Pulo".[41]

*Kampung* Pulo (Figure 4.7) was identified as the most vulnerable area during the rainy season, as it retained water from upstream areas that flowed into the Ciliwung River. In August 2015, the city government determined to seize *Kampung* Pulo's occupied land from its residents in order to expand the river's capacity. The eviction was marred by a clash between officials from the Public Order Agency and residents who fought to stay along the river. Almost one thousand households were evicted, and some of those were relocated to the two newly built sixteen-storey low-cost apartment towers, about a kilometre from the *kampung*. Governor Ahok claimed that the eviction was meant to "save the residents from flooding, so that Kampung Pulo will never *banjir* again".[42]

The dissolution of one infrastructure thus has led to another. In this sense, the raging floodwater is not only destructive but also transformative. The old world of *Kampung* Pulo cannot be retained, according to city officials, if a new world is to be born. Apartment buildings, as symbols of urban modernity, are built at different places to accommodate the relocated *kampung* dwellers. Yet all of those who are "saved" remain attached to their old world: they are still poor, and now are even more dependent, for sure, on an infrastructure that was built solely to justify their displacement and over which they have no control.

## The New Urban Form

In 2005, ten years before the eviction of *Kampung* Pulo's residents, I was involved in a one-week training workshop for members of the Urban Poor Consortium, a community-activism organisation. One of the issues concerned the relationship between *banjir* and the disappearance of the city's green open spaces and water catchment areas. The discussion led to questions about *kampung*, its dwellers and their relationships to the river. The community organisers indicated that the urban poor were perfectly aware how they were perceived by the middle class and city government officials. In 2005, a community leader said something like this to me (reproduced from my field notes):

We know that there is a tradition of blaming the urban poor—that they have narrowed the river, and they throw garbage into the river, and so on. But this charge is no longer new to us. We have heard this kind of charge very often to the point that the people who charged them are also getting tired of this understanding. The scale of *banjir* today is just too big to be caused solely by the irregular settlements on the riverbank! There must be other practices that have also caused *banjir*, such as the deforestation up- and downstream; and the disappearance of green spaces in the city caused, not so much by houses [built] along the river, but by the development of commercial enterprises, such as shopping malls and condominiums, many of which violated land use [regulations]. And a substantial area for water catchment [was] converted to commercial complexes.

Accordingly, from the perspective of the Urban Poor Consortium, the elites, too, contributed to *banjir*. They, too, violated land-use rules. Developers were involved in backdoor deals with government officers to obtain permits for development in green areas. Members of the consortium were perfectly aware that the business elites who built superblocks, new towns and housing by taking up green spaces are the main contributors of *banjir*.[43]

In the history of Jakarta, the 1990s were the height of city zoning infringements.[44] Since the 1980s, upstream areas have taken massive advantage of the weak spatial zoning in greater Jakarta. "As a result", as Rita Padawangi and Mike Douglass point out, "Jakarta's open green area was reduced from 40 per cent in 1985 to 9 per cent by 2002" (Padawangi and Douglass 2015: 531). Many villas, hotels and shopping centres were built during this period by kicking aside zoning rules. Meanwhile, downstream areas had already started violating zoning in the 1970s, with water-collection areas transformed into commercial opportunities for housing compounds, industrial complexes, recreation sites and shopping centres. Bunyamin Ramto, Jakarta's vice governor (1984–88), confessed that half of the twelve-hundred hectares (4.6 square miles) of North Jakarta's off-limit areas was filled in and used to build residential areas.[45] Developers knew that their properties were being built in a known flood area, but houses were still built and sold rapidly.

Buyers seemed to believe that flood control infrastructure, such as canals and pumps, would reduce the risk of flooding, so why not buy those houses? I related earlier the stories from Tjhi Fat Khiong about how his area, Pluit, was constructed by Endang Wijaya (Acai) in the 1970s, with a blessing from Ali Sadikin. Over the years, with the city government, the residents there set up three pumping stations, which they named after planets—Mars, Venus and Jupiter.[46] They also built a 100-metre-long embankment three metres high and ten metres thick, on which stood some additional pumping stations. The height of the embankment has been raised three times in the course of twelve years, all to prevent the area from becoming a total flood zone.[47] Such engineering support is predicated on the assumption that technology (and _hoki_) can control _banjir_. But, alas, as we have also seen, Pluit was inundated in 2013.

Today's developers nevertheless continue the brave legacy of Pluit by engineering their built environment to beat _banjir_ with their own systems of flood mitigation. In most property development today, we see the grading and levelling of open land so that water will flow out of the space to the surrounding lower areas. This privatised and localised (and uncoordinated) method of flood mitigation has compromised the old flood-gate canal system. It has made obsolete van Breen's invention. We do not know much yet about the impact of the haphazardly built, private systems of flood control, but we know that today's _banjir_ is more unpredictable than ever. The flow of water is more difficult to control because the contours of the city are changing due to the uncoordinated levelling of ground by individuals and developers who care only about their own property. They don't care where the water goes provided it goes outside their property lines. This approach has motivated even more self-styled methods of flood mitigation throughout different neighbourhoods, especially among those property owners who have been left alone to find their own solution. This includes middle-class neighbourhoods in Northwest Jakarta, where my parents are living (Figure 4.8). Everyone (including those who live in the _kampung_) raises the floor inside their houses to reach the high water line and, consequently, the sidewalk outside follows the individually designed flood-mitigation path. Such elevation (_peninggian_) requires no permit. It is a pure, bottom-up approach to flood mitigation with no need for an environmental impact assessment.

For individual households, _peninggian_ is costly, and there is a limit to how high one may go by raising an existing floor or adding a new one above the old floor. Property developers know this very well. They thus offer a much grander and yet simpler "solution": just leave the sinking neighbourhoods and move to a new city. The historic 2013 _banjir_ in Pluit thus has not prevented developers from developing property in coastal areas. Right after the great deluge in Pluit, PT Agung Podomoro Land Tbk, a major real estate company (which at one point branded itself using the motto "back to the city", with superblocks in Jakarta), started to promote a mega project called the New Pluit City. The notion of "new" gained substance after the flood, which sank the property values of the now "old" Pluit. New Pluit City will be located on reclaimed land surrounded by sea, away from Jakarta. It will be like an unsinkable ship leaving behind the drowning mainland Jakarta. The company's "New City" brochure declares with little sense of irony:

The City is located [on] an open-water Jakarta Bay which provides you a memorable waterfront living experience. The ocean will no longer be a stranger to you as it is a part of your everyday life. Surrounded by water, the city is opening up new business opportunities that use the sea as the main commodity. Balance plays an important role in Pluit City.

**Figure 4.8.** Raising the house entryway (*kaki lima*) (author's photo).

**Figure 4.9.** "Pluit City: A World Class Waterfront City—The New City in North of Jakarta". *Source*: Meikarta's promotional brochure.

There are here all kinds of metaphors and allusions to water and ocean as not being a threat, but as giving a new life (even as it is valued more as a commodity), and *banjir* Jakarta would no longer be part of everyday life. Here we see again an instance of how the breaking down of one infrastructure has led to another. Property goes, property comes—just as normal as *banjir* that goes and comes regularly—but New Pluit City won't be relying on the water pumps of Tjhi Fat Khiong's generation. New Pluit City is yet another "Jakarta Baru". Unlike that of Jokowi and Ahok, this one will not be in Jakarta. It will be on an island of its own, where the ocean will become a friend, and the "old" Jakarta will be a stranger. PT Agung Podomoro is doing its best to make consumers feel safe. The company brought in Boskalis and Van Oord, the Dutch contractors who built Palm Jumeirah and the World in Dubai, and which claim a history of building the port city of Surabaya in 1911. And perhaps more importantly, so the promotion continues, the New Pluit City will be protected by the Giant Sea Wall, in the shape of the mighty bird Garuda (see the following section) in case nature ever dares again to strike back (*alam mengamuk*).

But New Pluit City's construction did not get underway without controversy and challenge. Protests took place in Lontar village, Banten province, where Boskalis and Van Oord were mining sand. Meanwhile, bribery and corruption charges against those trying to take advantage of sketchy law enforcement led to the imprisonment of Agung Podomoro Land's CEO. But by then, according to the Save Jakarta Bay Coalition (Koalisi Selamatkan Teluk Jakarta), "in 2015 alone there were 113 cases of forced evictions that occurred in Jakarta affecting 8,145 families and 6,283 micro businesses".[48]

## The Great Sea Wall

Since the great flood of 2007 (considered to be a different kind of flood, for it included the rushing through of sea water), Dutch and Indonesian experts have been discussing a coastal development plan, but it was only in 2014 (at the end of SBY's term) that the project gained recognition. In November 2013, Mark Rutte, prime minister of the Netherlands, brought 150 business people from 106 companies, the "biggest ever Dutch delegation to visit Indonesia" (and including Van Oord, who was just awarded the contract for New Pluit City), to Indonesia to stimulate trade and development.[49] That visit was followed by one by Melanie Schultz van Haegen, the Dutch Minister of Infrastructure and the Environment, in April 2014. By then, the master plan of National Capital Integrated Coastal Development (NCICD), declared a joint project of the Indonesian and Dutch governments, was officially presented. The artist's rendering shows how the master plan's infrastructure could take the shape of Indonesia's national symbol, the mighty Garuda bird of Hindu-Javanese mythology.

On April 1 and 2, during Minister Haegen's visit, a high-level roundtable meeting was held in Jakarta, involving the Coordinating Ministry for Economic Affairs, National Development Planning Agency, Ministry of Public Works and the City Government of Jakarta. It was attended by 150 experts (consisting of academics, government officials, private-sector representatives and twenty young professionals) from Indonesia, South Korea, Japan, China and the Netherlands. The presentation revealed that the master plan is ...

> ... truly Indonesian in its design, reflecting Indonesian culture and matching Indonesia's rising status, as the Garuda will protect the city and will bring safety and prosperity to the National Capital. It will offer Greater Jakarta a new image clearly visible and recognisable from the sky ... It is the first image of Indonesia which foreigners and Indonesian expats will see when landing over the Bay of Jakarta. It is shaped to provide space for growth and connectivity ... A capital ready for the 21st century. To be proud of and to be enjoyed by all ... This is more than just an ornament or a landmark. The Great Garuda protects the National Capital of Indonesia against the sea ... [At the ground level] the Great Garuda will be the prime location for investors. For new residents, it will be a new, modern place to live; and for Jakarta residents, the place to escape the crowded city without traveling for hours to spend some time on the waterfront with clean sea water and a fresh breeze.[50]

The series of presentations by experts from the different units was sustained by colourful statistics, maps, tables, graphs, diagrams, images, projections and predictions—all of which ultimately helped, in the words of NCICD's team, to "turn threats into opportunities". On the last slide of the second day's concluding panel, the audience read these encouraging words: "Action for protection is required *now*!! It is possible: *Ya kita harus bisa*! ("Yes we've gotta be able to do it!")".[51]

Infrastructure is an irresistible sign of the modern, ideally put in place by the government to symbolise that it still holds power in its hand. As indicated at the beginning of this chapter, Jokowi once dreamed of a deep tunnel as his infrastructural ideal. Two weeks after winning Indonesia's presidential election, Jokowi returned to his obsession with infrastructure for the city. He jump-started his leadership by endorsing the plan for a Giant Sea Wall to save Jakarta from drowning. But, just two weeks before Jokowi was sworn in, outgoing President SBY, wishing to register the project as the legacy of his own administration, had already signed off on this plan.[52] He instructed the coordinating minister for economic affairs, Chairul Tanjung, to perform the groundbreaking ceremony on October 9, just ten days before Jokowi took office.

While Indonesia's post-Suharto presidents all wish to register their legacy in and through the Giant Sea Wall, little have they cared that just such a project was first initiated in the 1990s under Suharto's regime of private enterprises. Thus, the basis of the Giant Sea Wall is actually a Presidential Decree from 1995, and it has been kept alive as the legal foundation for all the subsequent land reclamation projects. Little did these post-Suharto leaders realise, too, that Suharto's decree was not really intended to help the state save the city. Instead, it was meant to promote and protect another, perhaps final, round of capitalist accumulation for private developers, many of which were business partners of Suharto's family. After the city's creative destruction and peri-urbanisation that is beyond repair, the sea is the "last frontier" for everything that is new and hopeful. Yet, sitting uneasily between illegality and the desire for law enforcement and capitalist rationale, the status and governance of the Giant Sea Wall are just too complicated to clarify.[53] Thus, until today, no one seems to know what is justifiable with regard to the reclaimed land.[54]

Much of the sea wall's presumed justification resides in the prophetic language of counteracting the (inevitable) subsidence of the city. While capitalist logic has certainly made the design for such a mega project possible, *banjir* has made the project desirable. The city will sink without it, so the argument goes. This argument alone, however, releases many more aspirations, which often surpass the issues of *banjir*. Its technical fix will certainly surpass Van Breen's canal and floodgate system in function and symbolism, but its real power resides in establishing a new set of fantasies about the longevity of Jakarta: that a new life, a new city can be imagined and created again and again. Much like the annual return of the old *banjir* that eluded critical scrutiny, the idea of the Giant Sea Wall eclipses critiques of the conditions that have led to *banjir*.

Naomi Klein, after mentioning Jakarta's 2007 *banjir*, once wrote that "after each new disaster, it's tempting to imagine that the loss of life and productivity will finally serve as a wake-up call, provoking the political class to launch some kind of 'new New Deal'" (Klein 2007: 48). The sea wall that promises a new global city is just such a new New Deal, and this, for Klein, is a form of "disaster capitalism" with ties to economic reengineering. Be that as it may, this chapter suggests that resolving Jakarta's *banjir* requires much more than a wake-up call. Nor is it meant to be a silver bullet to resolve the city's flooding woes once and for all. Instead, more pervasively, it shows simply the expansive potential of *banjir*, how much political power and money can be generated by maintaining (instead of eliminating) the floodwaters' circuit of coming and going.[55] With *banjir*, there will always be another new New Deal to make.

Ironically, the new Giant Sea Wall cannot even be considered as a proper "new deal" project. As Koalisi Selamatkan Teluk Jakarta points out, "the land reclamation project didn't have any Strategic Environmental Assessment (SEA, or KLHS [Kajian Lingkungan Hidup Strategis]), has had no public participation in the process of the Environmental Impact Assessment (EIA), and there was no fulfilment of the rights to information on the potential threats of environmental damages and losses".[56] Coalition members also believe that with a focus on fighting the sea water, the sea wall will just "hinder the outlet of the thirteen rivers discharging in Jakarta Bay. The reclamation project will exacerbate, rather than solve, the floods which occur yearly during the rainy season".[57] As such, the Giant Sea Wall project brings us back to the question that continues to haunt Jakarta: where will the water go?

## In the End ...

This chapter suggests that the discursive nature of Jakarta's infrastructure has shaped multiple narratives of *banjir*. There are thus all sorts of readings, interpretations and subjectivities to come to terms with: *banjir* as *bencana*, *bocor*, *berkah*, *budaya* and so on. At different moments the Queen of the South Sea has been blamed, as has urbanisation, the urban poor, capitalist modernisation and property developers. At another time or simultaneously, blame has fallen on the contour and topography of the land, the typology and morphology of the built environment, the moon and climate change. All of those have been seen as the causes of flooding. Environmentalists, green activists and the urban middle class see the lack of green space as partly responsible for the floods, and the governor blamed those living in irregular riverside settlements for clogging the waterways. All of this just goes to show how people, at different times and under different circumstances, assign "agency" to human activity, nature, the supernatural and infrastructure. These different explanations and imaginations provoke anxieties, the responses to which have different effects—they cause evictions and new multi-million dollar projects; they give political legitimacy and social life to the divided city; they beget culture, which links *banjir* and everyday life with the cosmos; and they convey to project engineers and managers conflicting messages, as, after all, there are benefits to and profits to be made from keeping *banjir* alive.

Where will the water go? Water goes where it can be kept in the state of becoming, of always in-the-making by an assemblage of interests in which nature and culture, object and subject, past and present intersect. Like a body of water when touched, the manifold responses to flooding flow one into another, and leave the city in a state of flux. In the end, none is reliable to counter the thoroughgoing deterioration of the city's social, natural and built environments. Such a condition is a blessing in disguise for property developers to sell the promise of utopia by building new cities against the unacceptable condition of Jakarta. This is the story of the next chapter.

# Notes

[1] "Deep Tunnel Project Questionable: Ahok", *Jakarta Post*, 18 Feb. 2015, available at http://www.thejakartapost.com/news/2015/02/18/greater-jakarta-deep-tunnel-project-questionable-ahok.html (accessed 18 June 2017).

[2] "It doesn't make sense [*nggak masuk akal*] ... The main areas of Jakarta shouldn't have any reports of flooding [*banjir*] or stagnant water [*genangan air*]. As long as Pluit Dam is doing well, there shouldn't be any such thing as stagnant water in the areas, including the Palace ... Actually, water here is not stagnant, it is just clogged. How can Pasar Baru be inundated, even though the nearby river in Gunung Sahari is deep [after the dredging]? ... It turned out to be caused by the closing of a floodgate. So, open the gate please" (Ikbal, "Ahok: Nggak Masuk Akal Bundaran HI Banjir", Postkotanews.com, 31 Aug. 2016, at http://poskotanews.com/2016/08/31/ahok-nggak-masuk-akal-bundaran-hi-banjir [accessed 23 June 2017]).

[3] Works that take seriously the roles of culture and politics include Douglass 2010; Gunawan 2010; Padawangi and Douglass 2015; King and Idawati 2010; Silver 2008 and 2018, and Van Voorst 2016.

[4] Foucault's governmentality has been influential in transforming environmental studies to deal with neoliberal management of environmental crises; see for instance Brand 2007; Kooy and Bakker 2008 and Agrawal 2005. For a different take, see Peter Evans's conceptualisation of "governance" and "ecologies of agency" in Evans 2002; see also Boomgaard 2007.

[5] As Matthew Gandy points out, "in broad terms, we can conceive of the modernization of industrial cities as a shift from 'private city' to the 'public city,' whereby fragmentary, piecemeal, and highly localized solutions to the problems of water and sanitation were superseded by the promotion of more complex kinds of coordination between political and economic interests. This transition was in fact a double movement so that public activities such as washing were increasingly restricted to the private sphere whereas privately organized access to potable water or sanitation was gradually incorporated into a centralized, networked, and municipally controlled metropolitan form". Gandy, however, also indicates that such a universalist approach to the modernisation of urban infrastructure was never applied to colonial cities: "Yet, throughout much of the global South this last phase in the modernization of water infrastructure remains only partially completed: in many cities, for example, neither comprehensive sewer systems nor waste water treatment works were ever introduced ..." (Gandy 2006: 19–20).

[6] "Jokowi siapkan terowongan multifungsi", *Kompas*, 4 Jan. 2013.

[7] Ibid.

[8] The expression "alam mengamuk" in relation to *banjir* can be found in various reports at different times, e.g. Qur'anul Hidayat, "Derasnya terjangan banjir di Puncak, Bogor, Warga: Masya Allah air mengamuk", news.okezone.com, 5 Feb. 2018, at https://news.okezone.com/read/2018/02/05/338/1854750/derasnya-terjangan-banjir-di-puncak-bogor-warga-masya-allah-air-mengamuk (accessed 25 July 2018); Stevanus Subagijo, "Alam yang mengajarkan", Beritasatu.com, 15 Feb. 2014, at http://id.beritasatu.com/home/alam-yang-mengajarkan/78138 (accessed 20 June 2017).

[9] "Deep Tunnel Project Questionable: Ahok", *Jakarta Post*, 18 Feb. 2015.

[10] Wanda Indana, "Ditanya deep tunnel, Ahok: airnya mau dibuang kemana", metrotvnews.com, 17 Feb. 2017, at http://news.metrotvnews.com/read/2015/02/17/359346/ditanya-deep-tunnel-ahok-airnya-mau-dibuang-kemana (accessed 25 July 2018).

[11] "Ahok Confused by Flooding in South Jakarta", *Jakarta Post*, 5 Oct. 2016.

[12] Ahok, as reported in "Pumps Out of Order Ahead of Rainy Season, Flooding Likely", *Jakarta Post*, 2 Nov. 2016.

[13] Ahmad Romadoni, "Ahok Curiga Ada yang Sengaja Bikin Jakarta Banjir", news.liputan6. com, 9 Feb. 2016, at http://news.liputan6.com/read/2432060/ahok-curiga-ada-yang-sengaja-bikin-jakarta-banjir (accessed 21 June 2017).

[14] *Pandji Poestaka*, January 1932 issue, p. 92, as cited in Gunawan 2010: 133–4. For an exploration of the human and water relationships from social-anthropological perspectives, see Boomgaard 2007 and Pannell 2007.

[15] Randy Ferdi Firdaus, "Jokowi: Saya bukan Superman, dewa, pesulap untuk atasi banjir", www.merdeka.com, 25 Dec. 2012, at https://www.merdeka.com/peristiwa/jokowi-saya-bukan-superman-dewa-pesulap-untuk-atasi-banjir.html, (accessed 20 June 2017).

[16] A Rukun Warga (RW, community association) is an administrative territorial unit comprising six or so Rukun Tetangga (RT, neighbourhood association), where each RT comprises thirty to fifty households.

[17] *Tempo* reported that 40 per cent of the land area of Jakarta (24,000 hectares) is located under sea level. Those areas relied on pumps, but "only 9,000 hectares were protected by water pumps" (Widyanto 2007: 40).

[18] As cited in "Foke Minta Warga Maklumi Banjir", *Koran Jakarta*, 27 Oct. 2010, p. 6.

[19] Bambang Nurbianto, "Riverbank Squatters Ignorant of Environmental Destruction", *Jakarta Post*, 11 Feb. 2002.

[20] "Unsur-unsur alam ini jauh lebih berkuasa daripada wilayah administrasi yang diatur oleh manusia". Jakarta officials reported that *banjir* is related to natural phenomena and the power of the "natural elements" is larger than the managerial power of humans. See the official website of Jakarta Municipality, June 2012, at http://www.jakarta.go.id/v2/news/2012/06/persaingan-antara-manusia-dan-air-upaya-pengendalian-banjir-pemerintah-provinsi-dki-jakarta#. Vt3aV003Np8 (accessed 23 Nov. 2016).

[21] As cited in Ahmad Romadoni, "Ahok Kesal Petugas Pakai Aturan Zaman Belanda Malah Picu Genangan", news.liputan6.com, 2 March 2016, at http://news.liputan6.com/read/2449259/ahok-kesal-petugas-pakai-aturan-zaman-belanda-malah-picu-genangan (accessed 23 Nov. 2016).

[22] As cited in Romadoni, ibid.

[23] Restu Gunawan argues that the colonial municipality had never considered ways to prevent flooding in *kampung* (Gunawan 2010: 113).

[24] Ahmad Romadoni, "Ahok Perintahkan Pintu Air Manggarai Buka 24 Jam", news.liputan6. com, 2 March 2016, at https://www.liputan6.com/news/read/2449747/ahok-perintahkan-pintu-air-manggarai-buka-24-jam (accessed 2 Dec. 2022).

[25] Herman van Breen (in his capacity as vice-mayor of Batavia) published his works in different journals, most notably four articles in 1923 in *De Ingenieur in Nederlands,* issues 23, 26, 27, and 28. He also wrote about the history of water management in Batavia from 1610 to the 1900s. See Van Breen 1919 and Gunawan 2010.

[26] The map shows how the *bandjirkanaal* (flood canal) was constructed around Weltervreden (the garden city of Menteng and Gondangdia), where government buildings and European neighbourhoods were located. The *bandjirkanaal* serves as a main conduit to redirect water flowing from the TjiLiwong (Ciliwung) River to Kali Grogol, Kali Krekot, Kali, and Tjideng. The canal thus protected Weltervreden from potential flooding. The Manggarai floodgate (not shown) is located at the meeting point of the *bandjirkanaal* and the TjiLiwong [Ciliwung]

River. The map also shows how other canals connecting various rivers were constructed around the old coastal town of Batavia and along the *bandjirkanaal*.

[27] This information from a flood management technician in 2013 may not be accurate, as a newspaper already reported in 2007 that "some ninety-three sluice gates have been constructed in thirty-four locations throughout Jakarta's river network. Some gates were built in the 1920s by the Dutch administration". See "Sluice Gates Proving to Be Profitable", *Jakarta Post*, 14 Nov. 2007: 5.

[28] For a report on the management of floodgates, see "Managemen Pintu Air di Jakarta", kabarinews.com, 3 March 2008, at http://kabarinews.com/manajemen-pintu-air-di-jakarta/2638 (accessed 23 Nov. 2016).

[29] "Sluice Gates Proving to Be Profitable", *Jakarta Post*, 14 Nov. 2007, p. 5.

[30] See Restu Gunawan's discussion of philanthropic activities during *banjir* in Gunawan 2010, Chapter 3.

[31] See Bambang Nurbianto, "Seasonal Flooding? No Big Deal, Many Jakarta Folks are Used to It" and "Jakarta Squatters Unaware They are Part of the Problem", *Jakarta Post*, 13 Nov. 2002.

[32] Zaenuddin's book is not based on historical research, but it helps construct the idea of continuity or normality of *banjir*. The book mentions nothing about flooding between 1671 and 1893. A more reliable source is the work of Restu Gunawan (2010) which mentions years that were missing in Zaenuddin's book, such as between 1699, 1711, 1714, 1854, and 1872. There is a mismatch of the years of *banjir* between the account of Zaenuddin and that of Gunawan.

[33] The river-dredging project was initially called the Jakarta Urgent Flood Mitigation Project (JUFMP), for which the state and the municipality provided some matching funds. The project was only sporadically and marginally carried out during the term of Governor Fauzi Bowo (2007–12). It was delayed (*molor*) until the legal basis of the loan was established. "Perpres Pengerukan Sungai Keluar Akhir Oktober", *Koran Jakarta*, 17 Oct. 2010. About "river normalization", see also Ley 2018.

[34] Cochrane also indicates: "On a recent day, the pile of trapped trash bobbing on the surface [at Manggarai's floodgate] included a motorcycle helmet, sandals, soccer balls, styrofoam containers, a bicycle inner tube, and a pillow. There was some natural debris, too: banana trees and a dead rat. Jakarta's clogged waterways are not just a minor irritant and eyesore. They amount to a serious urban environmental problem that has killed dozens of people during flooding in recent years, caused countless illnesses, displaced more than one million people, and led to billions of dollars in losses".

[35] As cited in Rizki Saleh, "Banjir Tetap Intai Jakarta, Penyebabnya Lebih Kompleks", berita2bahasa.com, 23 Dec. 2012, at http://berita2bahasa.com/berita/01/1912312-banjir-tetap-intai-jakarta-penyebabnya-lebih-kompleks, (accessed 20 June 2017).

[36] See also Bambang Nurbianto, "Blue, Black, and Red Rivers Run through Jakarta", *Jakarta Post*, 13 Nov. 2002.

[37] "Residents Continue to Use Ciliwung as a Garbage Dump", *Jakarta Post*, 26 March 2008.

[38] Foucault discusses the relation between a docile body and disciplinary acts that seek to transform it in *Discipline and Punish* (1975; English trans. 1977).

[39] "Relokasi Warga, Syarat Normalisasi Sungai" (Relocation of residents is required for normalization of river), *Kompas*, 3 Feb. 2014, at http://megapolitan.kompas.com/read/2014/02/03/1340285/Relokasi.Warga.Syarat.Normalisasi.Sungai, (accessed 20 June 2017).

[40] Ibid.

[41] Ibid.

[42] Basuki Tjahaja Purnama (Ahok), "Mereka Ingin Mentahnya, Bos ...", *Tempo*, 6 Sept. 2015, p. 40.

[43] Developers' violation of land-use regulations recalls the practice of informality, which, according to Ananya Roy, applied to both the formal and the informal sectors. See Roy 2005.

[44] Major violations of land use regulations already started in the 1980s. Rio Tambunan, who was head of the City Administration Office (Dinas Tata Kota) from 1971 to 1975 revealed (in an interview in 2002) how "land use was changed following the wishes of property developers who were allowed to make profits from selling lands" (Rio Tambunan, "Tata ruang Jakarta diubah atas pesan sponsor", *Suara Pembaharuan*, 3 March 2002). For reports on violations in the 1980s and the 1990s, see: Dorléans 2002 and Douglass 2010.

[45] Mahardika Satria Hadi, "Kisah Tentang Rawa yang di Uruk", *Tempo*, 3 Feb. 2013, p. 54.

[46] "Diterjang Rob, Dientak Amblesan Tanah", *Tempo*, 3 Feb. 2013, p. 53.

[47] Ibid.

[48] See "Joint Letter of Concern on the Government of the Netherlands Support on Reclamation of 17 Artificial Islands and NCICD Project in Jakarta Bay", 28 Oct. 2016, at https://www.tni.org/files/article-downloads/concern_on_the_gov._of_the_netherlands_support_on_reclamation_of_17_artificial_islands_and_ncicd.pdf (accessed 21 June 2017).

[49] For a brief report by the Embassy of Indonesia at The Hague on Mark Rutte's visit, see http://new.indonesia.nl/index.php/en/all-category/84-asean-multilateral/532-dutch-prime-minister-visit-to-indonesia-version-2-0-of-the-bilateral-relationship (accessed 21 June 2017).

[50] Power Point presentation prepared by the team from National Capital Integrated Coastal Development for the high-level roundtable meeting, reporting on the master plan, its current status and implementation (Jakarta; 1 and 2 April 2014).

[51] Presentation of Dr. Ir. M. Basoeki Hadimoeljono, director general of spatial planning, Ministry of Public Works, "Key Messages from the Expert Meeting", National Capital Integrated Coastal Development's High-level Roundtable Meeting, Jakarta, 2 April 2014.

[52] Bill Tarrant, "The Great Wall of Jakarta", *Reuters Asia*, 22 Dec. 2014, at http://www.reuters.com/article/us-environment-jakarta-seawall-idUSKBN0K017420141222 (accessed 21 June 2017).

[53] For a critical discussion of the NCICD, see Thompson 2018 and Silver 2018.

[54] For some reports on the controversy, see: "Arguments For, Against Reclamation", *Jakarta Post*, 6 Nov. 2015; "Reklamasi Teluk Jakarta: Berharap Solusi Menuai Kontroversi", *Properti Indonesia* 24, 274 (special report, May 2016): 20–33; and interview with Rizal Ramli, coordinating Minister for Maritime Affairs, "Jangan Semua Dibawa ke Presiden", *Tempo*, 18–24 July 2016, pp. 100–3.

[55] In a study of flooding in Semarang, Lukas Ley uses the term "borrowed time" to describe the politics of maintenance in the neoliberal time. See Ley 2017.

[56] Koalisi Selamatkan Teluk Jakarta, "Joint Letter of Concern on the Government of the Netherlands Support on Reclamation of 17 Artificial Islands and NC1CD Project in Jakarta Bay", 28 Oct. 2016. See: https://www.tni.org/files/article-downloads/concern_on_the_gov._of_the_netherlands_support_on_reclamation_of_17_artificial_islands_and_ncicd.pdf. (accessed 21 June 2017).

[57] Ibid.

Chapter

5

# A New Assemblage City

"To chase a horse one must ride on a horse (骑马追马)."
(Mochtar Riady, 2016)

"Meikarta surpasses anything this country has ever seen, epic in its scale and vision as a truly integrated city of the future. Not only does Meikarta redefine what a modern city should look like and feel like. It sets the new standard for a world city in Southeast Asia and beyond."
(Lippo Homes 2018)

On 17 August 2017, on the 72nd anniversary of Indonesian Independence, the Lippo Group, a family-run conglomerate and one of the largest property developers in Indonesia, launched its "largest project ever". The project, called "Meikarta" (named after Li-Mei, the wife of the group's founder, Mochtar Riady), is located in Cikarang, Bekasi, about thirty-four kilometres east of Jakarta. The Lippo Group promises to develop here an area of 5,400 hectares, making it the "Shenzhen of Indonesia" (Figure 5.1).

The first phase of development, with a value exceeding US$21.11 billion, involves 500 hectares (with 100 hectares of open green space), 250,000 units of prime residential property and 1,500,000 square metres of prime commercial space. James Riady, the CEO of Lippo Group and son of the group's founder, told media that "we foresee that the future of the Indonesian economy is on the outskirts of Jakarta. Together with the government's massive infrastructure development plans—which aim to connect the capital with the Greater Jakarta area—we believe our project can create jobs for at least 6 to 8 million people in the near future" (qtd. in Soegiarto 2017). James Riady also suggested that Meikarta would outcompete Jakarta and become the country's new economic centre. The timing of the launch coinciding with Indonesia's Independence Day, the allusion to the future, and the CEO's remark about reviving the national economy all suggest that the Lippo Group is leading the nation through a production of a new mega-city. The new city is not intended to be a suburb of either Jakarta or Bandung, the two closest major postcolonial cities. Instead, it is to be a new "world city".

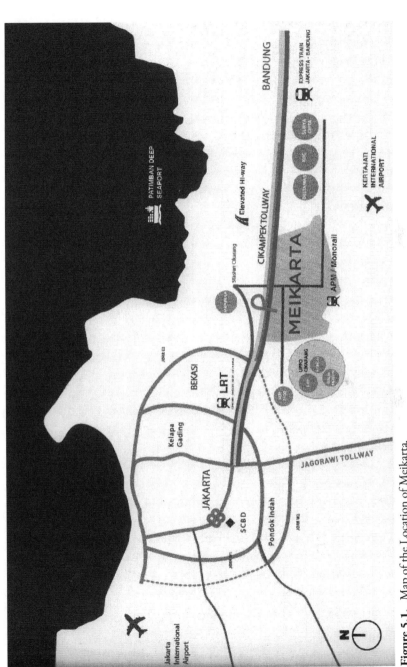

**Figure 5.1.** Map of the Location of Meikarta.
*Source:* Meikarta's promotional brochure.

The Meikarta project, however, carries with it known malpractices. Before the necessary permits were obtained, the Lippo Group was already selling the property to buyers. To fast track the project, its executive directors bribed officers of the Bekasi Regency to issue licences.[1] Considering the unclear regulatory framework of local government in the country, however, such a strategy is not unusual for any group pioneering development projects. It is understood that developers of major projects require good networks within government institutions to help ease or speed up the completion of their projects. Roy refers to such spatial-economic transactions between the state and developers as a legitimised, informal practice even though it is a violation of planning and land use regulations (Roy 2005). Yet today this tradition of "elite informality" is being undermined by the law enforcement of the Indonesian Corruption Eradication Commission. Meikarta has thus been under a legal spotlight since the arrest of the Bekasi Regent and certain directors of Lippo Cikarang for their roles in the bribery connected with the issuance of property permits for the project. There is much to unpack here in considering this largest ever project for the Lippo Group.

This chapter seeks to contribute to the discussion around the idea of "after suburbia" by teasing out components, discourses and forces that constitute the property development of the Lippo Group, of which Meikarta is a part. It begins with a brief history of Indonesian property development amidst the Asian financial crisis in the late 1990s, and how such a history has shaped the Lippo Group and its production of space. The narrative is organised around the agency of the Group, especially its founder, Mochtar Riady, and his family. It shows the interface of business, culture and politics in the production of space "after suburbia".

## (After) Suburbia

The concept of "suburbia" has undergone a series of changes over time. Its earlier reference to only residential development is now considered by many to be too narrow. Urban scholars, especially in the United States, have recently identified new or different developments in the suburbs. The sprawling of Los Angeles, for instance, with its multiple centres includes not only residential areas but also spaces for commercial and economic activities—spaces that have come to be called "post-suburbia" (Phelps et al. 2006). Others have developed other terms to refer to the same idea, such as "edge cities", "edgeless cities", "post-metropolis", "exurbia" and "technoburbs" (Garreau 1991; Lang 2003; Soja 2000; Fishman 1987).

Concomitant to the "LA School" is a formulation by scholars working on the extended metropoles of Asia. Led by Terry McGee, they have observed a more diffuse and scattered form of urbanisation characterised by a profound mix of urban and rural land uses in the expanding urban fabric of metropolitan areas such as of Jakarta and its surrounding region, known then as *Jabotabek* (Jakarta and its surrounding Bogor, Tangerang and Bekasi) (McGee 1991). From the urban-rural transactions at the fringes of major Southeast Asian cities, terminological innovations ensued, including "desakota" (McGee 1991), "extended metropolitan region" and "mega-urban regions" (Douglass 2000). All these terms share an agreement that the concept of "suburb" as a residential development has failed to capture the complexity or multiplicity of urbanisation. They have also generated interesting debates on whether Asian suburbanisation is different from its American counterparts (Dick and Rimmer 1998; Friedmann and Sorensen 2019).

In this chapter, I choose not to enter into a debate about whether Asian and American post-suburbias are converging. I will simply show how the spaces that the Lippo Group produced cut across different cultures while being tied to the political economy of the place of which they are a part. By doing so, I seek to contribute to the discussion on the "layered sediment of contradictory temporalities and spatialities" of our suburban planet (Keil 2018). I argue that the Lippo Group sought to build a private city (or town) but that its value is derived essentially from the ideology of suburbia. And yet, the group seeks to transcend the dependency of the suburb on the city by tapping into the ideology of autonomy, centrality and (exclusive) community. What follows is a story of the Lippo Group and the forces, processes and agents that shaped its production of an Indonesian post-suburbia.

## The World of Lippo

The Meikarta mega-project stemmed in some ways from the period of the Suharto regime when financial investment was increasingly shifted to the real estate sector.[2] Lippo, however, had a distinctive experience during that era. But first, let us get acquainted with this family-run conglomerate. The Lippo Group owns a number of companies in different industries under the control of a single developer—Mochtar Riady (and his family). The group's promoter refers to the conglomerate as the server (if not saviour) of one's lifetime, from cradle to casket. The Lippo Group has a hospital in which to give birth or to recover when sick and it has a cemetery park for the dead to rest. In between this circle of life, the group provides education from junior kindergarten to university, offices for working, malls for shopping, venues for businesses, lifestyle and entertainment as well as residential housing for living with family. The group also runs high-tech communication and media industries to connect the whole community. In short, Lippo's diversified businesses promise a total environment for a generation and beyond. Much of this totality is represented by the group's slogans that seek to control both time and space—"The World of Ours" and "The Future is Here Today".

"Today", however, is inseparable from the past. And Lippo's past is best understood through its founder, Mochtar Riady, born Lie Mo Tie (Li Wen Zheng 李文正]) in Malang, East Java, who turned 93 in 2022. Like many early wealthy Chinese Indonesians, Mochtar worked his way from poverty to undreamed riches, mostly through instinct, timing, connections and, no less importantly, patronage. Yet unlike other early wealthy ethnic Chinese businessmen, Mochtar Riady commands Indonesian, English and Chinese languages and possesses a degree from Nanjing University. These language skills and later formed connections to China and the US proved beneficial in building his business empire in Indonesia.

Mochtar started his career by running a trading service office (which he called Lippo [力宝] to mean "the treasure of power") in Hong Kong to help Indonesian importers obtain letters of credit (Riady 2018b). He then built his fortune at home as a banker in the 1960s. After a few years of successfully fixing and upgrading some small local banks in Java, he accepted an offer in 1975 to run Bank Central Asia (BCA), which was owned by Liem Sioe Liong, also called Sudono Salim, a close friend of President Suharto who was also an indirect bank shareholder. It is known that Salim and Suharto helped each other become immensely rich. By 1997, a year before the collapse of the Suharto regime, the Salim Group was reportedly "the world's largest Chinese owned conglomerate, with US$20 billion in assets and some 500 companies" (Harvey 2005: 34). And the Suharto family, by the time the president was forced to resign, was the largest landowner in Indonesia: they were estimated to have controlled over 3.5 million hectares of land with a value close to US$57.3 billion.[3]

Yet, despite his closeness to the oligarchs, Mochtar always considered himself a "professional" as he worked to expand BCA from one office to become the largest "private" bank in Indonesia with 600 branches by 1991. As he recalls, the asset value of BCA under his management "surged from $1 million to $3 billion in 1990" (Riady 2018c). While Mochtar was credited for the BCA, much of its success was due in no small measure to the bank's connection with Suharto, who had the power to funnel government or semi-government business through the bank. Backed by Suharto, BCA was perhaps more powerful than the state bank, as it was almost free from any regulatory constraints.

Only towards the end of the 1980s, during what Mochtar called the "new era" of deregulation and privatisation of banks, did he begin to think of owning his own bank (Riady 2018c). By then, the government allowed foreign and domestic joint-banking ventures and encouraged the opening of branches by Indonesian banks. Mochtar took the opportunity to merge his trading office of Lippo with other local banks, but he did not forget to include Sudono Salim in his enterprise. This was how "Lippo Bank" was born. By the end of the 1980s, Mochtar recalls that he "had come to effectively oversee the management of two banks—BCA and Lippo Bank" (Riady 2018b). Both were related in a complex way and they co-produced diversified conglomerates: "Sudono and I had become co-owners of many financial institutions through mergers and acquisitions" (Riady 2018c). Mochtar (having also a share in BCA) can be seen as pioneering in Indonesia the fusion of ownership and management, which contribute to what Harvey understood as an arrangement for "the restoration of economic power to the same people" (Harvey 2005: 31).

The "new era" of the deregulation and privatisation of banks that started in 1988 made the property industry a golden business. By 1995, Salim and Mochtar were co-listed in some major landownerships (*Indonesia Property Report* 1995: 20). Before we move on to discuss the shift of Lippo from banking to land development, however, it will be instructive to reveal a little bit more about Lippo's elite informality, which seems to be practicable everywhere in various forms. Elite informality also left a mark in the US as the Riady family ventured to America and lived in a Los Angeles suburb.

## The American Adventure

As a businessman in a developing country, as Mochtar would "lament", a privileged relationship to state power could be very beneficial, from getting protection to special treatment and bailout in a crisis. Without such elite informality, it is hard to imagine how Lippo could do business in China where government ministries own companies that are Lippo's partners. Yet, as in Indonesia, Mochtar was also aware of the danger of getting too close to the source of power. In his memoir, he indicates his discomfort with Suharto's patronage: "I felt that Sudono and Suharto were too friendly with each other. Their personal relationship made me uneasy" (Riady 2018c). This uneasiness, as real as it might be, was perhaps also compounded by the sense that while considered "successful" as executive director of BCA, Riady's share in the bank was smaller than that of Salim and the Suharto children (Lee 2009a). The uneasiness was perhaps also prompted by the opportunity of the new era in finance wherein Lippo Bank would be better off as an independent bank.

Riady decided to leave BCA even though, as he claimed in his memoir, both Salim and Suharto objected to his resignation: "Seeing that I was determined to strike out on my own, Sudono finally agreed to let me go my own way. I exchanged my shares in BCA for Sudono's shares in Lippo Bank under a deal designed to make Lippo an independent bank" (Riady 2018d). After that, Mochtar took steps to turn Lippo Bank into an international financial conglomerate. He partnered with groups beyond his usual Sino-sphere, which include Japanese and French counterparts, and opened a branch for Lippo Bank in California.

In the US, as early as the mid-1980s, Mochtar bought two banks.[4] One was a small Chinese-owned bank in San Francisco, which he later renamed "Lippo Bank" (Lee 2009a). The second was the Worthen Bank in Arkansas. Through the Worthen Bank, he befriended a young and ambitious politician named Bill Clinton who wanted to become president of the United States.[5] Mochtar immediately took part in financing Clinton's campaign. This proved to be a good move, and Mochtar and his son James (who was sent to the US "to hone his management skills" by managing the two banks) were frequent visitors at the White House (LaFraniere, Pomfret and Sun 1997), and it was reported that a key Lippo official worked in the Clinton administration (ibid.).[6] Through their contacts with Clinton, the Riadys set themselves up as lobbyists for both China and Indonesia, the two places where they located their major businesses. For China, they sought to please their Chinese partners by urging Clinton to renew China's trading privileges and reminding the US president that trade and human rights are two separate issues. For Indonesia, the Riadys sought to improve Indonesia–US ties at a time when the relation was strained by Indonesia's treatment of workers and human rights abuses (ibid.). In this role, the Riadys proved themselves to be Indonesian nationalists (with a structure of feeling towards China). Certainly, they sought to impress upon Suharto that they were not only businessmen, but also nationalists who worked to connect Suharto to the White House (something that none of Suharto's business cronies would be able to do). Other than that, it was all for their business so that it could grow or be rescued by the government when needed. As declared by the US court that charged James Riady for illegal contributions to 1996 Democratic campaign finances: "Defendant James Riady generally believed campaign contributions to be good for the reputation and business of the Lippo Group and various Lippo entities, including defendant Lippo Bank California".[7]

Despite this bittersweet time with Clinton, Riady's banks in the US were caught several times for violating regulations due to the Riadys' funnelling the bank money to their private enterprises (LaFraniere, Pomfret and Sun 1997). This was common in Indonesia during that time (as exemplified by BCA) where banks provide a ready pool of cash for their owners to finance their private businesses, but such a practice was untenable as seen by US regulators. Not long after the 1997 Asian financial crisis, the Lippo Banks (in the US and various places in Asia, including those in Indonesia) were sold to partners.

Recalling the 1997 Asian financial crisis, Mochtar believes that it was created "by a combination of speculative investments by US funds and rumours of a looming currency crisis" (Riady 2018e). For him "in 1997, Indonesia was in a relatively good economic shape" (ibid.). He blamed the rumours that had weakened the rupiah and crashed the currency. He acknowledges, nevertheless, that "Indonesian banks were left with mountains of bad loans as one corporate borrower after another defaulted" (ibid.). Almost all private banks were nationalised and put under state control. Some were listed for liquidation under a state-appointed asset management agency, others were taken over by the state. BCA, the Salim Group bank, that was too big to fail, received an injection of public funds. Lippo Bank, according to Mochtar, was only "shaken" thanks to Lippo's diverse interests in China and Hong Kong. "Lippo Bank managed to avoid this [fate of nationalisation]", but it too entered the Indonesian Bank Restructuring Agency (IBRA) for the recapitalisation of its assets. The state still had to inject about US$430 million and took over 59 per cent of the shares in Lippo Bank before the bank could be sold to an investment agency called Swissasia Global for about US$90 million.[8]

Since then, Lippo Bank has moved from one hand to another, but it never returned to Mochtar. The shock seemed to have discouraged Mochtar from relying on the banking industries. As Mochtar recalls, by the end of 2004, "I had sold not only Lippo Bank but also most of my bank related businesses in Macau, Hong Kong and the US. I decided to focus Lippo's operation on two areas: land development, and information and telecommunications" (Riady 2018e).

In the end, Mochtar considered the banking business "onerous" and "stressful", and not worth passing to his children and grandchildren. He had seen how, after the financial crisis, "Lippo Bank was under the strict supervision of the Bank of Indonesia, the central bank, and we had to obtain permission for every new business activity. We were a commercial bank, yet we had no freedom to make management decisions" (ibid.). Yet he also acknowledges the role of the state as Lippo Bank "needed funds to deal with its huge pile of bad loans" (ibid.). Many of these non-performing loans came out of the bank's engagement in the speculative property business. In addition, his bank problems were also related to cash flow issues tied to his property projects (Lee 2019a).

## Phoenix from the Ashes: The Birth of a Post-Suburbia

With Lippo Bank gone, it seemed that a treasure had been lost. But also gone were all the endless troubles related to the banking business, the ordeal of bad loans and the stress of elite informality under the Suharto regime. Indeed, the loss of the Lippo Bank turned out to be a blessing in disguise. Mochtar explains that in the early 1990s, when loans and land were easy to give and take, one of Lippo Bank's corporate borrowers got into trouble due to an unexpected surge in interest rates

(Riady 2018d). As a result, the borrowers left Lippo Bank with three tracts of land that were used as collateral for the loan. "These tracts of land, totaling 70 square kilometres in area, were located between 25 km and 59 km from central Jakarta" (ibid.). They were too far from the city, he thought, for any investors to be interested in the plots. Furthermore, "it was a wasteland with no trees" (ibid.). Be that as it may, the land came at the right moment, as it enabled Lippo to expand and switch its operations from finance to the development of land resources.

The "wasteland" also came early enough in the 1990s for the Riadys to turn it into a major asset. Lippo Bank was still around then to support the Riadys' newfound property projects. There was also more going on in the Riadys' existential life during that time: the Riadys became Christian. James once said that God spoke to him personally: "I thought I was a good man. God said, 'You're a horrible man'. I cried and cried and cried. Since then I try to be a better person, and my life has changed" (qtd. in Lee 2009a). As for Mochtar Riady (who by then had turned sixty), after a period of some reluctance, a pastor's sermon (in a church where attendees were top corporate executives) on how "all humans were born with a sinful nature", affected him deeply. He started to realise that all his good deeds, from building Buddhist temples, Muslim mosques and Christian churches to giving jobs to many people and making countless donations were not enough. "Who had never cheated the government?" the pastor asked. "I found that I could not swear that I had never done so". And "who among you has never lied to your wife at some point?" came the second question. "Tears flooded my eyes. I realised that I was indeed a sinful person" (Riady 2018f).

The seized "wasteland" could then be seen as a blessing, divinely speaking, a chance to redeem the Riadys' sinful souls through the space they sought to build for a new community. But while Mochtar had accepted the lands as his and was determined to carry out the mission of developing them himself, he could not find any model to follow. These tracts of land were so far away from Jakarta; they could not be planned as a suburb. Mochtar went to different places to learn about suburbs and townships, but true inspiration came only when he travelled to Shenzhen. He was impressed with how this special economic zone, which is some distance away from both Hong Kong island and Guangzhou, could become a metropolis of its own with manufacturing jobs and housing for millions. So came Mochtar's master plan, which he revealed in his memoir:

> One of three plots of land in Lippo's possession was in Karawaci, 25 km west of Jakarta. There were many plants operated by foreign companies in the area, but few houses suitable for foreigners. I decided to transform the land in Karawaci into a new housing area. I started building a new town complete with a school, hospital, supermarket and golf course. On the eastern wasteland of Cikarang, I decided to build an industrial park. This

industrial park was divided into four areas for manufacturers from four Asian economies—Japan, South Korea, Taiwan and Indonesia. A housing area was also developed for the workers at these factories. The last plot of land, in the hilly Karawang area, was the biggest development challenge. It was too far from central Jakarta even for an industrial park, so I turned the land into a sprawling cemetery.[9] These projects transformed three tracts of wasteland into valuable assets. (Riady 2018d)

These three tracts of land, seized as collateral from a defaulted debt in the early 1990s, became what is today the biggest asset of the Riady family. After merging its eight different companies in 2004, a business empire was thus born, the "Lippo Group". It was principally organised around these tracts of land, which were used for business while fulfilling the family's heart and soul. By the 2000s, with the tightening of rules, banking was no longer the most effective way to generate cash to support property development. There were other more productive financial instruments, such as real estate investment trusts (REITs), which had just entered Singapore in 2002. The Riadys decided to monetarise their properties in Indonesia via this property trust in Singapore. Backed initially by their successful shopping malls in Greater Jakarta, the Riadys' illiquid properties were effectively turned into cash to fund their property projects thanks to the REITs. Lee reported that "Lippo was among the most enthusiastic sponsors" i.e. owners who incorporate their properties in this form of trust (Lee 2009b: 39).

By 2012, ten years into REITs, Lippo, having built up a huge portfolio of properties in Indonesia, was considered "the largest property developer in Indonesia as measured by assets, land bank, revenue and net profit".[10] From the Lippo Group's base in Indonesia, Mochtar also set up property development headquarters in Singapore and put one of his sons, Stephen Riady, in charge of Lippo Group's overseas operations. He appointed James Riady to the Indonesian operation, and James became CEO of the Lippo Group.

Today, it is all hands on deck for the family to develop Meikarta, the US$21.11 billion investment and the biggest project in the history of the family-run conglomerate. As Mochtar reminds everyone, "I am pouring my heart and soul into creating a new city in Indonesia. Meikarta will integrate residential areas with academic research facilities to create a new kind of community" (Riady 2018a). It is where the "future is here today", but as we have discussed so far, such a "today" is all due in no small measure to taking advantage of the climate of the Suharto era. Before Lippo left banking, a huge chunk of Lippo's money had already been invested in the property business. So before the Meikarta period, there is perhaps something to learn from Lippo's first two post-suburban projects in the 1990s: Lippo Village and Lippo's Orange County.

## The World Lippo Seeks to Create

The development of Lippo Karawaci (formerly called Lippo Village) started in 1992 with the construction on a central 500 hectares of a total 2,800 hectares. Supported by Lippo Bank and aided by Hong Kong business magnate Li Ka-shing as a shareholder, Mochtar's vision of a new community was already crystallised there with the construction of as many "public" facilities as possible at the outset in the central area—a symbol of Lippo's dedication to serve the new community. By 1997, Riady already declared its 220,000 square metre "Super Mall" to be the largest in Indonesia. From an adjacent toll road, towers for offices and condominiums could already be seen. Lined up around the main entrance were an international hospital, a five-star international hotel, a fifty-two storey and a forty-two-storey residential tower, rows of shophouses, and a very expensive private school and university. All these register the idea of world-class facilities. Lippo's residents live on a site organised hierarchically around a 6.5 hectare, 18-hole golf course, called Imperial Golf, planned by English-born, American golf course designer Desmond Muirhead, and a lake that serves as the centre of the residential complex. But with the home of James Riady and his family on an island, accessible only by private helicopter, the lake is more like a moat. Hogan and Houston think that the site of Riady's mansion (with soaring French windows and Greco-Roman columns), echoes "the traditional symbolism of Javanese Sultanate and Chinese emperor systems of authority" (Hogan and Houston 2002: 249). Houses on and around the golf course are the most expensive and secured. Each cluster of houses is called *taman* (garden) and all are gated with only one entrance for each cluster. Each *taman* refers to a place in the world (such as Taman Holland, Taman Boston, Taman Mediterranean, Taman Osaka, Taman Paris as well as (the less expensive choice) Taman Ubud, Bali. The houses in each *taman* are built according to the stereotypical architectural style of the place after which it is named. All the residents (including expatriates) are housed in an array of such thematised estates.

Lippo Karawaci also offers complete infrastructure and assumes a self-sustained governmental power. It is proud to provide its own town management. It has a town manager of its own, so there is no need for city governor or local government to get involved. According to Gordon Benton, the town manager and planner of Lippo Karawaci, "it is the only township throughout the nation to have drinking water from the tap, municipally-treated central sewage system, all services underground, hierarchical and traffic-calmed [*sic*] street designs, and ... a Town Management Division" (qtd. in Hogan and Houston 2002: 249). The Town Management Division is effectively the city government. It promises full security for its residents who are not involved in the governance of their environment, as represented by the town's motto: "We take greater care of YOU!" (qtd. in Leisch

2002: 346). This seems to follow Mochtar's vision of a new community, but it also embodies the consolidated diverse interests of the conglomerate. It represents all eight elements of life that Mochtar has sought to coordinate (Riady 2018d). For him, the space of Lippo Karawaci is an inside-out of the Lippo Group:

> We placed a high priority on ensuring that the town would be able to provide residents with all of the services that are essential for daily life. A residential area must have the facilities to meet these needs. We thought that eight types of facilities were essential: shopping malls with various specialty stores, supermarkets, movie theaters, play areas for children, hotels and schools. This meant that Lippo had to expand its operations into these eight areas. I decided to operate these businesses (through acquisitions or partnerships) as independent companies and grow them into nationwide chains. (Riady 2018d)

And these eight areas are sustained by yet another eight qualities, for after all the members of this new town are "business elites" who want Karawaci to:

1.  Be a benchmark for one's social status. That is why the land price cannot be cheap.
2.  Be a most beautiful, safe, and enjoyable environment.
3.  Have education facilities of first-class quality (*kualitas wahid*).
4.  Have a modern hospital of international standard.
5.  Have Golf facilities of international standard.
6.  Have a complete set of sports club facilities.
7.  Have complete and comfortable shopping centers.
8.  Have offices that are grand (*megah*) and luxurious (*mewah*). (Riady 2016: 195)

## California Transfer

The second property, about 3,000 hectares in Cikarang, Bekasi has a different quality. It is about 34 kilometres east of Jakarta, way too far to lure Jakarta's upper class to it. It is, however, near the official industrial zone designated by the central government for multinational companies (largely from East Asia) as they moved to Indonesia for cheaper labour (Arai 2011). In this context, it was logical for Lippo Cikarang to develop properties that would attract foreign and local managers, as well as workers who could afford to buy houses.

Taking advantage of its proximity to private industrial estates, Mochtar thus established in the 1990s a subsidiary of Lippo Karawaci called "Lippo Cikarang Tbk" with a focus on finding support and developing partnerships to build an urban centre that would integrate real estate and industrial estate with the development of infrastructure. Planned by a "Master Planner" called Meng Ta-cheang, the aim was for Lippo Cikarang "to develop into a viable city of its own, serving as a new center to the surrounding industrial and suburban housing".[11]

Two zones were set up: "Delta Silicon Industrial Park" to accommodate the working needs of different manufacturing and trading enterprises and "Orange County", a residential zone with a variety of themed housing styles (resembling those of Lippo Karawaci) and luxurious condominiums. Both zones were organised around a city centre that boasted a complete set of facilities such as a twelve-storey office tower, a seven-storey global trade centre, a four-star international hotel, a shopping mall and "water world" park, a hospital, schools and a golf course with club facilities.

Names such as "Delta Silicon" and "Orange County" recall California, where James Riady once lived. Despite all the bitter memories of the banking business in California and his US campaign contributions which cost him a fine, two years probation, 400 hours of community service (to be performed in Indonesia), and being banned from entering the US, James Riady could not forget Californian suburban locations such as Orange County (Irvine, Newport Beach) and Beverly Hills. He arranged for Lippo's directors and planners to visit these places (Cowherd and Heikkila 2002) and went on to hire architectural design firms from Orange County. As a result, as Hogan and Houston indicate, what has been produced (in both Lippo Karawaci and Orange County) were nothing short of "direct clones of Southern California housing styles and estate themes with minor modifications to allow for different climatic conditions". (Hogan and Houston 2002: 258). Yet, while Californian in spirit, Orange County was in reality a project in partnership with Japanese trading company, Mitsubishi Corporation (Tani 2018). Japanese scholar Kenichiro Arai goes as far as pointing out that Lippo Cikarang was essentially built by East Asian investors, such as Sumitomo (Japan) and Hyundai (Korea). "These foreign partners provided a large part of the capital and the actual construction work and Lippo itself functioned more as a facilitator for various permits, land consolidation and marketing" (Arai 2015: 486).

## The Eastern Connection

Despite all the extraordinary efforts to connect East and West, Orange County produced only partial results. Orange County was relatively sleepy from the beginning. There is a relatively well-patronised shopping mall and a few other facilities, but other than these, most of the area in Orange County is still vacant. Initially, Riady targeted expats working for foreign companies in the Indonesian industrial estate, but there is not enough demand from the estate, even though it is home to more than 1,000 plants of mostly East Asian manufacturers, including giants such as Toyota Motor, Honda Motor and South Korea's Hankook Tire. After some years, it was clear that foreign expats and foreign workers alone were not enough to populate Orange County. Bartholomeus Toto, the director of Orange County, did what he could for the development. In 2016, Toto even declared Orange County to be a trendsetter for urban development and proposed a new master plan based on transit-oriented development (TOD). The plan was to take advantage of recent government's plans to build a toll road and railway to link Jakarta and Bandung. Located between these two cities, the area of Orange County would immediately benefit from this future infrastructure development. In collaboration with Mitsubishi Jisho Sekkei Inc., Toto invited renowned Japanese architect, Kengo Kuma, who designed Japan's National Stadium for the 2020 Tokyo Olympics, to serve as design advisor for the first phase of a new masterplan. According to Toto, "Kuma is an expert in combining expressions of traditional culture with modern materials and technology in a design that is artistic and phenomenal".[12]

Koki Miyachi, general manager of the architectural design department of Mitsubishi Jisho Sekkei Inc., confirmed in 2016 that the plan would be based on the concept of the "liveable city" to "improve the quality of life of everyone" there. It would apply "green architecture" supported by an artistic "pedestrian way". The city would be known for its "unique and impressive skyline". Through this collaboration with Japan, Lippo's Orange County is expected to become a "new California city" supported by "32-in-1 super complete facilities" ["fasilitas super lengkap 32-in-1"].[13]

Toto's timing seemed to be right. Just five years earlier, in 2011, the then president of Indonesia, Susilo Bambang Yudhoyono, launched an ambitious Master Plan for the Acceleration of the Expansion of Indonesian Economic Development. The idea was to use infrastructure to "debottleneck" the flow of investment to Indonesia. Soon, forty-four regulations concerning investment were revised to accelerate the flow of capital. Such a flow relies on physical infrastructure, which is itself an object for investment (Ridha 2018). Moving on, in 2012, a high-level meeting between Indonesia and Japan was held in Tokyo. A consensus was reached to carry out a programme called Metropolitan Priority Areas, which was to bring connectivity to the scattered property developments in *Jabodetabek* (the Jakarta Metropolitan Area) through a coordinated transport infrastructure. The close to US$30 billion project would be carried out with a public-private partnership (PPP) deal.

Due to Orange County's location, this government initiative was a big deal for Lippo. The state had created an opportunity for capital to flow in and through infrastructure. But the support of Japan, the older brother, alone would not be sufficient to boost and stretch Orange County so that it could take full advantage of the government's infrastructural plan. Fortunately, stars were in alignment for Lippo. In 2016, a business delegation from China's Shenzhen came to visit the Lippo Group. An ambitious deal with a value of US$14.5 billion was struck.[14] The Shenzhen Yantian Port Group and Country Garden Holdings agreed to develop two wings of Lippo Cikarang: the industrial zone and the commercial property projects. This Chinese entry was big, bigger than its Japanese counterpart. With this Chinese deal, Orange County would no longer be the same. Toto's career too was immediately transformed. He was soon asked to cover a larger scale project by serving as executive director of Lippo Cikarang. The aim was to fold Orange County into the new ambitious project which was planned to kickstart in 2017. The time had come for Orange County to be rebranded. Japan's "new California city" would be recalibrated by a new marriage with China. Meikarta was thus born. The child was to be raised in Orange County, but she would look like Manhattan.

## Meikarta: The World of Ours

**Figure 5.2.** Meikarta showroom in a shopping mall (author's photo 2018).

In 2017, Meikarta was launched with the idea that Cikarang would be surrounded by a high-speed train route linking Jakarta-Bekasi-Cikarang-Bandung, the Patimban Deep Sea Port, the Jakarta-Cikampek Elevated Highway, the Automated People Mover (APM) monorail and Kertajati International Airport. It proposes an urban form that recalls Manhattan and its famous Central Park. But unlike Manhattan, Meikarta is to be the largest manufacturing hub in Indonesia and at once a smart metropolis with a most sophisticated infrastructure to house, serve and employ one million people. It will have "distinctive architecture for each residential tower with different styles from various eras and cultures", such as towers in an "Asian style", "European style", "American style" and "Modernist style".

The boss of Meikarta, James Riady, expected that Meikarta would immediately boost Orange County as "the CBD of Meikarta".[15] Together with Delta Silicon, the "Silicon Valley of Indonesia", Orange County is expected to spur economic growth in the region, making Lippo Cikarang the centre of the Indonesian economy. There are already ten global institutions on board: "Columbia University Medical Center, University College London, the University of North Carolina, Genesis Rehab Services, the World Trade Center, HTC Corporation, China Telecom Global, JM Eagle, Zhong Ying Finance, and Lausanne Hotel Management Institute". Together, they constitute "the truly integrated city of the future", which would set a new standard for a world city in Asia and beyond, or so the Meikarta brochure read. In the months leading up to the 2017 launch, Meikarta's advertising and promotional materials were everywhere in the media and malls owned by Lippo (Figure 5.2). Much of the success of the campaign was due to spending US$107 million, but it was also owing to a negative campaign blitz against the urban condition of Jakarta.

In *Bourgeois Utopias*, Fishman argued that "suburbia can never be understood solely in its own terms. It must always be defined in negative relation to its rejected opposite: the metropolis" (Fishman 1987: 27). All the Lippo projects have been defined in negative relation to Jakarta. In particular, the advertising of Meikarta has made Jakarta essentially a city of garbage with flooding, pollution, poverty, crimes and traffic jams all depicted as part of daily life. The unruly streets of Jakarta are contrasted with an interior of a condominium, surrounded by glass walls, and which is equipped with interactive informational panels. The glass walls open, not to the street but to a new skyline of technopoles as if all units are interconnected in a "milieu of innovation" by advanced informational and communication technology (Castells 2010: 62). Such a presentation devalues Jakarta and by extension, the state. Yet, while Meikarta can be seen as a prime example of a new informational global city above the state, its values are explicitly linked to the provision of transport infrastructure supported by the state.

In any case, the Meikarta launch was a hit, and pre-construction sales targets were through the roof. Boosted a few months later by the topping-off ceremony of the first towers, which was attended by a powerful cabinet minister and former military officer, General Luhut Panjaitan, a top gun of President Jokowi, the success of Meikarta seemed to be all guaranteed. Yet soon after that, a series of unfortunate events unfolded, and everything went downhill. Allegations that construction began before permits had been obtained were followed by Meikarta employee and contractor protests over unpaid salaries and bills due to a dwindling flow of Chinese funds (Tani 2019). Then news circulated that China's tighter capital controls had led to the pulling out of Chinese partners including Shenzhen Yantian Port and Country Garden Holdings. Finally, there were arrests of top Lippo executives, including Bartholomeus Toto, by Indonesia's anti-graft agency for paying off city officials to obtain building permits for Meikarta. These events, along with a raid of James Riady's home, caused Lippo's shares to plunge and panic soon ensued, causing condo buyers to start demanding full refunds.

The future of Meikarta is no longer looking so bright. It must surely be hard for Mochtar to believe that Meikarta, a project of his heart and soul, built to accommodate the middle class' need for "affordable" world-class condos (unlike Lippo's other high-end projects) and a signification of his good deeds, would suffer from such a misfortune. But empowered by his talent for survival and his faith in Christianity, Mochtar has been quick to respond. After some deep thinking for one-two weeks, and another "three-four months to put together a transformation plan to make sure it was a plan that was fully funded and can succeed", he expects to see "no more hiccups" ("Riady Scion" 2019).

To restore Lippo's scandal-tainted image, Mochtar approached his thirty-three year old grandson, John Riady, an MBA of the Wharton School of the University of Pennsylvania and a *juris doctor* of Columbia Law School. John recalls that "it was just at home, we're quite casual about things", when Mochtar spoke with him followed then by his uncle Stephen and finally his father James (qtd. in Tani 2019). The elders made a pitch for him to serve as the CEO of the Lippo Group, replacing his father. After thinking about the offer over New Year's, John agreed to take the job.

John was not a fresh graduate with no working experience. He had headed Lippo's effort to go digital by venturing into e-money enterprises. He was quite successful initially in e-commerce even though his platform was behind rival companies and he had made some missteps for which Mochtar offered a lesson: "I told John, 'You made a big mistake, because you always think about buyers, but you never think of sellers... that was your mistake'" (qtd. in Tani 2019).

Despite this, the hope of Lippo's Meikarta lies in John. He is of the post-Suharto generation and a symbol of the future. If the wrongdoings of those from the Suharto era were just too many and unpardonable, then John, having grown up in a new era, should be able to redeem the family and save the project. After all, it seems fitting that the new community of Meikarta be led by the next generation. The young CEO wants Lippo and the place it created to be where young people would say "It is place where I am challenged, where I grow, where I'm taken care of" (qtd. in Tani 2019). These words from the new CEO are meant to shore up confidence among investors and customers and, most importantly perhaps, members of the family. For John, after all, "it's a big role. So I don't take it lightly... You have a responsibility not only to the family but to the minority shareholders at large. That's real" ("Riady Scion" 2019).

Squeezed between the family bosses who established lofty goals and visions and the demands of shareholders for tangible results, John had no choice but to get ahead. He inherited a project not of his own making, one that continues to face troubles, the most recent (December 2022) of which include a lawsuit for postponing debt payment and demonstrations of buyers demanding refunds due to delays in handing over units.[16] Tasked with the unforeseen and the anxiety of not falling behind, John explained that "if you put aside the noise around Meikarta, and I think there is a lot of misunderstanding there, the fundamental business case (for the company and shareholders) is very strong" (quoted in Tani 2019). Those misunderstandings include "Transparency and governance, I think this will be very important going forward... we also need to do a better job of communicating our vision, about serving that Indonesian middle class and allowing them to have a better life because of what we do" (qtd. in Tani 2019). Without wasting too much time skipping back and forth to connect the dots, the new CEO is reassembling the pieces into a whole to make people believe that "Meikarta, in some sense, is a proof of concept and we look forward to replicating that across different parts of Indonesia" (qtd. in Tani 2019).

Transparency and governance are not only the key terms for getting ahead but they are also the terms of contestation in the urban politics of Jakarta today, as will be discussed in the next chapter.

## Notes

[1] Kharishar Kahfi, "Lippo Group Executive Arrested in Meikarta Bribery Case", *Jakarta Post*, 16 Oct. 2018.

[2] For accounts of this crucial period, see Arai 2015; Cowherd 2002a; Dorléans 2002; Firman 2000; Kusno 2013; Leaf 1994a and Shatkin 2017.

[3] "Nilai Tanah Keluarga Cendana Hampir Rp. 800 Triliun", *Properti Indonesia*, Jan. 1999, pp. 34–5.

[4] In his autobiography, *Mochtar Riady* (2016: 99-101), Mochtar indicates that in 1980, via Jack Stephens (a broker who owns Stephens Inc. Bank in Arkansas), he bought stock in the Union

Planters Bank in Memphis which had made him the largest shareholder of the bank. In 1984, with Liem Sioe Liong, he bought 30 per cent of the shares of the Worthen Bank in Arkansas. He then appointed James Riady as the President Director of the Worthen Bank.

[5] Mochtar's connection with Clinton was established via Jack[son] Stephens, a broker who owned Stephens Inc. Bank in Arkansas. Stephens introduced Worthen Bank (the largest bank in Arkansas) to Mochtar. Stephens knew Clinton (who was then Governor of Arkansas) very well. There was a story in Mochtar's autobiography how Stephens asked Mochtar if he would like to meet the Governor during the welcome party for Mochtar following the acquisition of Worthen Bank. Stephens then immediately called Clinton who showed up in just 15 minutes. Mochtar said to Clinton that "one day, you would be number one person in America" (Riady 2016: 123).

[6] Mochtar envisaged that "it was due to the intensive working relations between James as Worthen Bank's Principal Director and Clinton as Arkansas' Governor" that when Clinton became President, "James was appointed President's economic advisor, whereas Mr. Oey Kian An, the President Director of LippoBank was appointed U.S. Vice Minister [*sic*] of Commerce. Oey later became a vice chair of Clinton's campaign team" (Riady 2016: 101).

[7] Robert Jackson, "Clinton Donor Riady Pleads Guilty to Conspiracy Charge", *Los Angeles Times*, 12 Jan. 2001.

[8] Nurul Qomariyah Pramisti, "Bangkitnya Kerajaan Bisnis Perbankan Mochtar Riady", *Tirto. id*, 10 Oct. 2016, available at https://tirto.id/bangkitnya-kerajaan-bisnis-perbankan-mochtar-riady-bSGZ (accessed 25 Oct. 2022)

[9] The cemetery is called San Diego Hills. It is inspired by or modelled on Rose Hill and Forest Lawn in LA. "To promote harmony in the worldly life", Mochtar indicates, "the Hills is organized around four cemetery zones, each representing a religion: for the Muslim; for the Christian, for the Catholic and for the Buddhist/Confucian" (Riady 2016: 201).

[10] Oxford Business Group, "On the Market: Several Developers are Listed on the Indonesia Stock Exchange", *The Report: Indonesia 2012*, p. 185.

[11] Lippo City Masterplan, as cited in Hogan and Houston 2002: 251.

[12] Qtd. in Adhitya Himawan, "Lippo Cikarang Gandeng Kengo Kuma untuk Design Orange County", *Suara.com.*, 17 Nov. 2016, available at https://www.suara.com/bisnis/2016/11/17/131300/lippo-cikarang-gandeng-kengo-kuma-untuk-design-orange-county (accessed 25 Oct. 2022).

[13] Ibid. "32-in-1", in English in the article, represents the idea of a super complete (*super lengkap*) amenity where 32 facilities are in one area:
"Sky Park, Lippo Mall, Luxurious Residential, Shopping Street, Lippo 61 Plaza, lippo 5* Hotel, Service Apartement, Lippo Tower Office Building, Sky Lounge, Roof Top Bar, Zu Private Membership Club, Convention Center kapasitas 7000 orang, Dali Hotel 400 kamar, Fine Dining, Bioskop Cinemaxx 10 studio, X-zone, Wellness Center, Grand Chapel 3000m2, Soho, Japanese Cultural Center, Korean Cultural Center, Senior Homes, Condontel, Green Belt Outdoor Recreation Area, Home Furnishing Center, Helicopter Service, Dormitory, SPH International, YPPH School, Universitas Pelita Harapan, Japan College dan Health City" ("Ini Dia Fasilitas Kondominium Mewah 'IRVINE SUITES' Lippo Cikarang," *Beritabekasi.co.ed*. 21 November, 2014, at https://beritabekasi.co.id/2014/11/21/ini-dia-fasilitas-kondominium-mewah-irvine-suites-lippo-cikarang/).

[14] Ratri Siniwi, "Lippo Group Welcome Shenzhen Business Delegation to Jointly Develop Industrial Estate in Cikarang", *Jakarta Globe*, 25 May 2016.

[15] As cited in Danang Sugianto, "Ada Apartemen Mewah di Cikarang, Orange County atau Meikarta?" *detikFinance*, 21 March 2018.

[16] For a chronology of the troubles of Meikarta, see a report in "Kronologi Lengkap Kisruh Meikarta Hingga Didemo Pembeli," at ekonomi.bisnis.com, 13 Dec. 2022, available at https://ekonomi.bisnis.com/read/20221213/47/1607990/kronologi-lengkap-kisruh-meikarta-hingga-didemo-pembeli/3 (accessed 20 Jan. 2023).

# Chapter 6 | Urban Politics

Urban politics are a familiar element in Western societies, but the phenomenon has not historically been present everywhere, especially in Indonesia. Indeed, the Indonesian term for urban politics, *politik kota*, emerged only after the collapse of Suharto's authoritarian rule in 1998, because it was only then that the central government granted cities the power to determine their own policies and promote public participation through, finally, the election of governors and local councils. This point was made by Suryono Herlambang , a researcher of urban planning, in his introduction to *Politik Kota dan Hak Warga Kota* [*Urban Politics and the Rights of Urban Citizens*], a collection of newspaper essays from 2000 to 2006. With new laws guaranteeing regional autonomy, the direct election of local council members and governors, and a proliferation of critical commentary about daily life in the metropolitan press (*Kompas*), Suryono asked, "[Has] urban politics . . . returned to the city?" (Herlambang 2006: ix).

Since decolonisation, a hierarchical tradition of central government prevented municipalities in Indonesia from gaining power over their own affairs.[1] Decentralisation in the postcolonial era, however, now means that local/city governments may make decisions that affect urban form and life. The new policy has also allowed local elections for the head of local government. With this, a new style of local politics has emerged where an unexpected individual outside the circle of the political elites could be elected governor. It has allowed for instance Joko Widodo (Jokowi) and Basuki Tjahaja Purnama (Ahok) (from a Christian-Chinese minority) who had no previous connection to Jakarta, to become Governors of the city. The new policy has also given new civic and democratic values which are often translated into populist politics and programmes such as "good governance", the practice of which ranges from transparency and accountability to free bus, education and health care, as well as to certain degree, public participation. Urban politics thus has become more popular than national politics as the city has replaced the state as the arena for the representation of popular values. While it may still be difficult to separate the effects of municipal from national decision-making (especially in the capital Jakarta), as disputes surface regularly over authorities, jurisdictions and competencies, urban politics nevertheless is now an essential part of life in Indonesia and has come to play an increasing role in the production and contestation of space.

Any new configuration of political practices, however, also entails an invention of tradition, as well as disputes over *whose* tradition. To explore these issues, I will focus on a particular period in the history of Jakarta: the Jokowi-Ahok era. This began when Joko "Jokowi" Widodo was elected governor in 2012, and it continued through the term of his successor, Basuki "Ahok" Purnama.[2] Yet, while I use the policies of Jokowi and Ahok as a main frame of reference, the chapter's focus (including its temporal frame) is not intended to limit discussion. Indeed, I hope to raise the issue of how a new agent of social order may create entirely new claims to tradition of governance in the production of the built environment (in this case, in a place where most important economic and political decisions were once made at a national, or even an international level). As urban politics becomes a new site for the production of cultural hegemony and physical form in the region, there is much to learn from the way Jokowi and Ahok sought to constitute a new tradition of urban politics. In particular, I will show how the two men had legitimised their rule through a "politics of time", which problematised previous political practices (while revealing the difficulties in overcoming them); and yet at the end this politics is being displaced by the urban politics of Anies Baswedan, the current governor of Jakarta (2017–22).

## Mental Revolution

On May 10, 2014, the then-presidential candidate Jokowi outlined a vision of his leadership of the country in the following years, if elected:

> The reforms implemented in Indonesia since the fall of Suharto's New Order regime in 1998 were merely directed towards an institutional revamp. None has yet focused on the paradigm, mindset, or the culture of politics in Indonesia in the context of nation-building. In order for a meaningful and sustainable change to take effect, and in accordance with Indonesia's Proclamation of Independence, just and prosperous, a mental revolution is much required . . . there is still a large number of traditions [*tradisi*] or a kind of culture [*budaya*] that is evolving and growing rapidly, creating repression as in the New Order. These range from corruption, intolerance of differences, greed, selfishness, a tendency to use violence in problem solving, legal harassment and opportunism. These are still going on, with some growing more rampant. . . . It is time for Indonesia to take corrective action . . . by imposing a mental revolution which creates a new paradigm, political culture, and nation-building approach which is more humane, suitable to the Nusantara cultural traits, easy and coherent. . . .

The use of the term "revolution" is not excessive. This is because Indonesia needs a breakthrough in its political culture to thoroughly put an end to all the bad practices that have long been left to spread since the era of the New Order till the present. . . . I have started this movement when leading Surakarta and since 2012 as the Governor of Jakarta. . . . *Insya Allah* [God willing], this effort will develop further and expand to become a truly national movement as mandated by Bung Karno [a reference to Sukarno, the first president of Indonesia], as the revolution itself has not ended. The Indonesian Mental Revolution has just begun.[3]

I quote this statement at length because it indicates how the term "mental revolution" became a manifesto for Jokowi's presidential campaign. It also shows clearly how the need for such a "mental revolution" was defined by the practices of its enemies—by those who profited from traditions that flourished during the repressive era of the New Order (and which still remain). Jokowi was suggesting that only after Indonesians combated these traditions could they restore "the original character of the nation", which he defined as *"santun, berbudi pekerti, ramah dan bergotong royong"*.[4] These words are impossible to translate accurately, but they suggest everything that is good: "grace", "kindness" and "mutual help". Of course, Indonesians intrinsically know that if one can be all these things, one will have no enemies. But what is important here is that these are terms for human relations which, in the language of governance, refer to an ideal relation between the ruler and the ruled.

During his campaign, Jokowi also occasionally used the term "corruption", and related it to mentality and traditions. While it is not easy to unravel the relation between *tradisi* and *sikap mental* [mental attitude], Jokowi has argued that a corrupt work ethic evolved under the former regime into a *tradisi* [tradition] and *budaya* [culture]. Any Indonesian bureaucrat would likely acknowledge that corruption is wrong, and that it is often caused by a wrong *sikap mental* (Server 1996; Smith 1977). But Jokowi was in effect explaining that corruption, collusion and nepotism had taken root in the nation because they had grown into a tradition and culture.[5] For Jokowi, a tradition may be formed over time, and when it is allowed to run as deep as in Indonesia under the New Order, a *"revolusi mental"* is needed to uproot it.

Jokowi has thus sought to combat the New Order's traditions—the whole practice associated broadly with corruption. It may be useful here to note that Jokowi's vision, or mission, is consistent with the populism that has marked the politics of Southeast Asia since the financial crisis of the late 1990s and the collapse of authoritarian regimes in many parts of the region (Mizuno and Phongpaichit 2009).

"Populist politics"—as one can learn, for instance, via Ernesto Laclau—is based on two propositions (Laclau 2005; Anderson 2009). First is the sense that a society ought to be based on the principle of equality—a concept formative of that of the nation. For Jokowi, this is represented by the "original character" of the nation, attained through a quest for what he understands as "balanced development". Second, the force of a populist movement is based on its opposition to an enemy, which, in the case of Jokowi, is represented by the former New Order regime. Jokowi's war against the legacy of Suharto, then, must be understood as taking place not only at the level of performance but, more substantially, at the level of mentality—of culture and traditions. The question of whose tradition is thus pivotal and lies at the centre of politics in Jakarta and Indonesia today.

It is further useful to recognise that the traditions Jokowi seeks to combat so that the nation's mentality can be restored are associated with conditions of "informality" developed in both state and civil society. Ananya Roy and Nezar AlSayyad conceptualised informality as a "mode", a "modality", a "method", and a "way of being" that govern the life of cities in both developed countries and the global South (AlSayyad 2004; Roy 2005). In so doing, they raised two important points. First, they called attention to informality as a practice involving both the ruler and the ruled, the elite and the underclass. In terms of the built environment, informality thus covers both shanty towns and upper-class compounds, for both are based on violations or irregular deals, such as of land-use regulations. This means the relevant conceptual divide needs to be revised as "not between formality and informality but rather [as] a differentiation *within* informality" (Roy 2005: 149).

Second, Roy and AlSayyad claimed that informality may be produced by the state. And in this sense, the range of informality can be stretched to include the list of terms identified by Jokowi as *traditions* of Suharto's regime: "corruption, intolerance of differences, greed, selfishness, a tendency to use violence in problem solving, legal harassment, and opportunism". Jokowi's "mental revolution" thus is a call for a direction opposite to, or different from, the traditions of informality of the Suharto era.

For the sake of analysis, I have repacked the list Jokowi has identified as traditions of the Suharto era (which continue today) in the following section as five urban traditions of informality — each of which is governed and performed by different social groups.

## The Five Traditions of Urban Politics

### *The Oligarchic Tradition*

In one of the very few works on urban governance in Jakarta, Manasse Malo and Peter Nas described (at the height of Suharto's authoritarian regime) the workings of power in the city as follows:

The most important groups operating in the Jakarta urban arena are central and local administration, the military, the business community, and the common people. The military and the administration form one governmental strategic group that is very dominant in administrative affairs and urban planning. The business community, including the banks, industry, and large developers, also has strategic resources at its disposal, and in co-operation with the government strategic group it effectively determines the development of Jakarta by the construction of offices, malls and houses (Malo and Nas 1996: 130).

Malo and Nas indicated that these three elements—business groups, the state and the military—determined the development of Jakarta, because they possessed the power to shape the city. The city, then, was not run simply by business groups, because the military colluded with the head of state to make sure there were businesses and assets to share. It should therefore be possible to understand much of the city's history during this period by researching the actions (or collaborations) of these three groups (see e.g. Cowherd 2002a; Dorléans 2002; Firman 1998; Leaf 1994a). Such an investigation (as represented in Chapter 5) would surely also uncover a story of urban informality as conducted by the elites. This is the very tradition that Jokowi wishes to overcome, because corruption, legal harassment and the use of force to settle matters are clearly products of this elite alliance. Jokowi and Ahok tried to harness them to help achieve their urban agenda, and yet in some instances, the military and the police were used to support evictions.

This emphasis on the power of the elites in the work of Malo and Nas is understandable, as the object of their analysis is the authoritarian state.[6] They thus assume that power operates only top-down. Yet, by focusing only on an elite coalition behind the transformation of space in the city, they overlook a peculiar (or not so peculiar?) tradition of Indonesian politics: the role of middlemen, often operating as thugs [*preman*], shadowy officials [*oknum*] and brokers [*perantara*]. These individuals or groups operate as a hinge between the top and the bottom, and their authority in many cases is "subcontracted" to them by the powerful to manage the common people at the local level (Onghokham 2003).

## The Subcontracted Tradition

Contrary to dominant perception (as represented by Malo and Nas), however, the city of Jakarta has never been completely run from the top. Such a perception typically relies on an obsession with the central power of the state to integrate the urban population to achieve unity [*manunggal*] (a concept I will discuss later). But it is equally important to note (as indicated in Chapters 1 and 2) that power in Jakarta is commonly subcontracted to civilian organisations, civilian militias, local leaders, or headmen (Barker 1999; Lindsey 2011; Ryter 1998; Wilson 2011). Indeed, these micro-powers are a "necessary component in the maintenance of state power and the collection of taxes" (Barker 1999: 122). Subcontracted power moves within the structure of governance and may take many forms—as in the middlemen mentioned above. Such figures may appear to act with relative autonomy, even though they are tied to or harnessed by powerful groups and the ruling elite. Just such a situation was reported in a newspaper story from the time of Suharto describing a land deal case that involved developers, state agencies, local *oknum* and independent *preman* brokers:

> It appears that brokers have established a very close working relationship with local officials. In addition to supplying information, such officials help establish the "legitimacy" of the broker. . . . In the case of disputes or uncertainty about ownership, these same officials are called upon to resolve the problem. They are not uninterested parties in such matters, since the fees and commissions they receive for witnessing land transactions and other services are a significant part of their income. (*Jakarta Post* 1990)

Local elements thus operate as contractors or subcontractors to the ruling groups, maintaining and shaping order at the local level. Yet they do not necessarily work together, as each has its own discursive domain. And they may further subcontract their tasks to even more local organisations, to the point that the originating centre of power may have little idea what is going on at the local level. The city, then, may accommodate many players, many brokers and many deals with or without direct acknowledgement by the central government. This may be seen as an example of the decentralised "patron-client" political tradition of Southeast Asia (Scott 1972), or the "one-and-the-many" authority of Indonesia (Reid 1998).

This form of decentralised tradition can be traced back to the precolonial era (Onghokham 2003). Indeed, as a "tradition", it was appropriated and nurtured by the colonial administration, which had run into problems governing the societies it had conquered. Under the Suharto regime, patron-client relationships took a more direct form. It was thus quite common for the Suharto government to subcontract to thugs or civilian militias the control of the *rakyat* [common people]. The government also subcontracted to loosely organised civilian and youth groups, such as Pemuda Pancasila (shown in the documentary *The Act of Killing*), to terrorise specific communities for political and commercial gain (Ryter 1998). These organisations appeared to be both inside and outside the military; they were civilians, yet they were also connected to the state apparatus to form the "New Order Racket state" (Wilson 2011).

To sum up, a "tradition" of decentralised power developed in Jakarta and Indonesia over a long period of time, continually being reinvented as a mode of governance. This tradition survived the collapse of the Suharto regime, yet its many layers have now splintered into fragments. The paramilitary civil organisations of the Suharto era, for instance, have become freelancers looking for new contracts, while new groups have been invented. Along with other mass organisations (*organisasi masyarakat* [*ormas*]), they have constituted new socio-political forces from below while forming a complex alliance with political parties. The *ormas,* each with its own ideology, seek influence in neighbourhoods often on the basis of ethnic or religious identity. Some are Islamist by orientation, some are ethnic, some are violent and destructive, some are more tolerant and peaceful.

**Figure 6.1.**  A banner of Forum Betawi Rempug (FBR), Jakarta.
*Note*: The banner says "#2019FBR - taking care of kampung" (*jagain kampung*) (author's photo 2019).[7]

These groups have clashed with each other in moral policing or in a contestation for support and followers, lending the impression of an urban "turf war", but they are all engaged in some forms of political participation (Noor 2012). They came out of the process of decentralisation of power which has given rise to local politics. When local elections were introduced in the mid-2000s, political entrepreneurs soon realised that they could increase their chances to win election by gaining support from the *ormas* who have influence at the community level.

There are thus many more subcontractors today, who continue to control the streets, by, for example, providing security for *kampung* neighborhoods and street vendors (Figure 6.1). Such figures can operate independently, or they can be supported by politicians and business groups. Yet it is this tradition of power sharing, strategic alliances and subcontracting that has emerged out of and continued to sustain the oligarchic tradition.

Connected to this tradition of subcontracted power is another tradition, located in the bureaucracy, known as *pungli*, a short term for *pungutan liar* [illegal fee extortion] or *korupsi* [corruption].

## The Bureaucratic Tradition

"Corruption" has long been considered a tradition of Indonesian bureaucracy.[8] Historians have traced it back through the colonial and precolonial eras to what is known as the era of kingdoms (for Java, this would include the Hindu-Buddhist Majapahit, the Islamic Mataram and other sultanates).[9] During this time, no civil servant of the kingdom (of any rank, from minister to district head to guard) received a salary. Instead, their income was derived from their right to collect taxes and receive tribute from the common people.[10] This practice of making commoners cover the living expenses of civil servants prevailed down to the level of local government and the household. Thus, the staff or servants of a district head would accept "fees", or a certain percentage (*persenan*), from those who needed their services. As far as the *rakyat* were concerned, every man in the bureaucracy was a tax collector, and they were much disliked. In modern times, such dislike has been expressed by the term *pungli* [extortion].

One consequence of this tradition within the contemporary bureaucracy is that it costs almost nothing to appoint new staff, because individual positions have no (or few) salary implications. In fact, it may be beneficial to appoint new staff, because each such position may be sold to its new occupant. For individual bureaucrats, the ultimate goal is to buy a position with good prospects for receiving tributes or fees. "Money politics"—to buy access and position—is thus recognised as a tradition.[11] To the extent that corruption continues today, then, it has much to do with the fact that civil servant salaries are too low. But the continuance of such practices also relies on the assumption of corruption as a tradition.

This is certainly not a tradition that is popular among the common people. How do they react to it?

## The Rakyat Tradition

As a capital city, Jakarta concentrates many things, including wealth, power and jobs; it is precisely this quality that continues to make it attractive to migrants. A large percentage of Jakarta's contemporary population belongs to a social group Malo and Nas identified as the *rakyat* [common people] or *wong cilik* [common people with little connection to wealth or power]. Yet, they rightly described this group as powerless, because "migrants who settle on empty space are not organised and do not promote common plans" (Malo and Nas 1996). Nonetheless, the *rakyat* are important because they are a majority, and because they are simply too numerous and diverse to effectively control. Governments, from precolonial through colonial to postcolonial times, have had a hard time administering this "urban majority" (Simone 2014). Such efforts are further hampered by unresolved issues of who the *rakyat* are, where they come from and what they are doing—all of which translate into questions of control.

The *rakyat* are further important because their relationship with the ruler is supposed to embody a particular and historically important ideology, referred to in the Javanese language as *kawula gusti*. The *rakyat*, too, are the foundation of Indonesian nationalism. The ideal of any Indonesian government is thus to achieve *manunggaling kawula gusti*: the "union of the one and the many" (or the ruler and the ruled). In practice, this means the submission of the subjects to the ruler, who, in turn, must commit himself to advancing their interests. Failure to achieve this relation would result in the ruler losing the divine authority [*wahyu*] that underlies sovereign power.

All Indonesian governments have sought to achieve union with the *rakyat*. Consider, for example, Sukarno's *"penyambung lidah rakyat"* ["the tongue of people"] or Suharto's *"dwi tunggal"* ["two and yet one"]. The populist "pro-*rakyat*" programmes of the post-Suharto era are essentially another attempt to bring the government and the *rakyat* back into a *kawula–gusti* relation. Thus, as Jokowi has said, "Fixing the life of the marginal will give a positive atmosphere to the life in the center" (Endah 2012: 189–90). All leadership concepts include the *rakyat*, as attending to it constitutes the moral economy of the state.

The moral economy of the state—a concept Jokowi has distilled as "the poor should be helped"—has been a notion widely shared by previous rulers, but it has gained new prominence in the era of populist politics. The *rakyat* share this understanding and know (or at least the elites fear they *might* know) when power is being abused. Signs of disintegrating power can take many forms, from economic to environmental to political crises, but they are all read as a general cultural crisis (often understood as *zaman edan* [a time of madness]).[12] As an essentially powerless group, the *rakyat* had few options when confronted with such a situation. But historically (and arguably also today), the *rakyat* simply fled when they felt oppressed, making flight a form of protest.[13] Alternatively, the *rakyat* could resist by not listening to a ruler's order, or they could pretend either not to understand, or to misrecognise, his commands.

Ignoring power is a familiar action of the *rakyat*, often associated with a particular vocabulary. The intent here is to give authority a headache, and its articulation is associated with words such as *nekat* [taking risks], *keras kepala* [stubborn, lit. "hard-headed"], *anarkis* [anarchic] and *tunggal* [autonomous or singular, i.e. not dependent on any power]. These are all terms used by the ruling class to describe situations in which the subaltern expresses a desire not to be governed. Here, the performance of informality (as a violation of law) by the underclass is conditioned by the *rakyat's* idea about themselves, about the nature of power and its applications. The *rakyat* thus invents a tradition of resistance within its own perception of power.[14] Thus, in a period of political transition such as during a power vacuum or an economic crisis, the *rakyat* may form its own *mobokrasi:* anarchistic, disregarding governmental norms.[15] The reciprocal view, however, is that the state is irresponsible and that it has failed in its obligation to improve the life of *rakyat*.[16]

## *The Kampung Tradition*

The fifth tradition (more directly related to the study of the built environment) involves the vast area of the city called the *kampung* which (as discussed in Chapters 1 and 2), may be seen as an expression of the informality of the life of the *rakyat*, but it may also be conceptualised as a product of the state and capital in externalising the cost of housing. In other words, the *kampung* can be seen as the spatial expression of informality that involves the state, capital and the community. In the *kampung* there is a great mix of land tenure which has made untenable or contestable the definition of the "illegal". There is also informal leadership (the platform for exercising subcontracted power) which has made *kampung* relatively self-managed. And there is a mix of urban and rural cultural practices and an ambiguous sense of belonging that have complicated the idea of urban citizenship (*warga kota*). *Kampung* is also understood inadequately as a "space of tradition" and often misinterpreted as a "space of transition". Thus, the complex presence of the *kampung* has routinely been dismissed by policy-makers as something that will eventually disappear or become gentrified (by way of gradual land certification) into formalised housing. Yet some scholars argue that the *kampung* is a permanent feature of Indonesian cities, one that existed prior to colonialism and that will continue to exist even after the end of the capitalist world-economy. Whatever the case, the *kampung* challenges both modernisers and urban theorists.

Consider for a moment Georg Simmel's "Metropolis and the Mental Life" (Simmel 1903) and Louis Wirth's "Urbanism as a Way of Life" (Wirth 1938). These two classic essays characterised the city in terms of its density, heterogeneity and anonymity—qualities the authors saw as offering the experience, simultaneously, of individual liberation and alienation. In a place like Jakarta, however, the contrast between city and countryside is not as clear. Jakarta is filled with a variety of *kampungs*, where rural traditions are still found, and where the dominant cultural attitudes and socialisation patterns are associated with the countryside. Indeed, one can say that migrants to Jakarta may find in the urban *kampung* components of their former rural lives.[17]

The *kampung* thus serves to moderate alienation and conflict, as well as to gradually socialise rural folk to urban conditions. Thus, while the state and the capital may seem to want to demolish the *kampung*, they are really more intent on maintaining it as a space of exception (to a certain point)—at least, as far as it (still) benefits them. All governments see the *kampung* ambiguously, for they see in it the *rakyat* (or the labour) they need. And they see a space in which to resolve housing problems (through the residents' own cheap labour) and other urban conflicts—even as they (very slowly) try to modernise it.

## Overcoming Traditions?

I have spent much of this chapter attempting to describe some of the informal urban political traditions of Jakarta—both those of the elite and those of the common people. These five traditions have a long history as a modality of life, and the first three became well developed under the oligarchic regime of Suharto. Jokowi and Ahok's urban programmes can be seen as a critical response to these traditions. I will next outline some of the urban programmes (associated with the idea of "mental revolution") that they have advocated as part of their response to these urban political traditions.[18]

Prior to the tenure of Jokowi and Ahok as governors of Jakarta, City Hall was seen as the embodiment of an old, bureaucratic apparatus operated behind closed doors by the elite. Under Governor Ahok, it was seen as a place open to public scrutiny. This is largely due to initiatives of Ahok (who took over from Jokowi in 2014 after Jokowi was appointed President of Indonesia). As governor,

Ahok brought a performance-based managerial style to the municipality and insisted that city governance be conducted in public. To enhance transparency and accountability, he occasionally recorded and uploaded videos of meetings with staff and city council members to YouTube—a decision applauded by the public. He transformed the municipality from being a haven for corrupt and lazy staff through a new emphasis on competitive performance; he cut the number of middle-ranking officials by 20 per cent and streamlined departments for efficiency; instituted an open-recruitment process that required civil servants to compete for the limited positions in each office; and rewarded the meritorious while firing unproductive department heads and staff. Such bureaucratic downsizing had already saved millions of dollars, which Ahok then used to raise allowances for productive officials. He also eliminated budget mark-ups and ineffective programmes and streamlined project proposals and reports. And he replaced cash transactions with bank transfers, to ensure proper accounting. Together, such reforms (influenced by a neoliberal work ethic) had minimised the practices of extortion and corruption that were part of the old bureaucratic tradition. Under Ahok and Jokowi it had become increasingly difficult for City Hall to continue the tradition of "business as usual". Their reformation had placed municipal government *under the public gaze*, where it could serve as an agent of change and a site for the invention of a new tradition. The governor thus retained strong popular support especially among the middle class—in large measure because of his anti-corruption stance and his ability to reform bureaucratic culture.

This drama of bureaucratic reform was regularly reported on by the media, making City Hall one of the most interesting spectacles in Jakarta. Residents followed the disciplining of public servants and became fascinated by stories of resistance from among the old guard. City Hall was thus seen as embodying a kind of hope, precisely because its bureaucratic tradition was being shaken, scrutinised and reformed. Thus, although Ahok and Jokowi's reforms may primarily be explained as an anti-corruption drive and an exercise of "mental revolution", they had also created a new image for City Hall. Such a measure had slighted some senior bureaucrats and politicians as well as business groups who had been benefitting from the old tradition. It is reasonable to imagine that they wished that Ahok would not be reelected so that the old tradition could be restored.

The new administration likewise registered its presence on the street. Ahok and Jokowi targeted the much disliked *preman* and challenged their domination of the streets. The power of the *preman*, as discussed above, embodies the tradition of subcontracting on which oligarchic power has relied in many instances. Like bureaucratic culture, it has a long history and is not easily discarded; nevertheless, city government must deal with it if it is to register its influence on the *rakyat*. Toward this end, Ahok sought to remove patronage control over street vendors by relocating them to proper buildings and marketplaces. The municipality also planned to build more shopping malls for vendors and revitalise traditional markets. In these efforts, the city government tried to make clear that its enemy was the *preman* bosses, not the vendors themselves. Following the humane approach Jokowi introduced when he served as mayor of Solo, the Jakarta administration attempted to befriend vendors. The municipality arranged the reparation of vendors' carts (or offered vendors new ones), while providing, at no cost, permits to operate. Ahok developed a permit card with an ATM function so reimbursement collection from vendors could go directly to the municipality. He knew too that this would serve to disrupt the domination of *preman* who used to receive cash deposits (*setoran*) directly from vendors. To the *preman*, Ahok said, "ladies and gentlemen (*bapak dan ibu*) don't ever try again to play with small change. Repent please for the era of *preman* is over. Today is the era of the Italian mafia, the Godfather. The government is now the official *preman* that brings retribution to government's treasury" (qtd. in Kurnia Sari Aziza 2015). "Let us now be the new *preman*, the new Godfather", Ahok declared (qtd. in Alsadad Rudi 2014). He also installed a new system for pay parking that would take over the role of parking *preman*. He offered them a job instead as official government parking attendants, with a salary twice what they were making, to help his administration monitor the parking meters. By doing so, Ahok staged a war against the parking *preman* bosses. He declared: "Go ahead [*preman*], if you want to fight fiercely against us. We are ready, because we are also thugs, but official thugs" (qtd. in *Coconuts Jakarta* 2015).

By removing the influence of the *preman*, and thus undermining the subcontracting tradition, Jokowi and Ahok sought to bring the *rakyat* back into the government fold. This may be seen as populist politics, but it may also be interpreted as a necessary step to achieve *kemanunggalan kawula gusti* [unification of the ruler and the ruled]. The *kawula gusti* relations were further strengthened by a tradition of meeting directly with the governor at the city hall's *pendopo* every morning, and by installing Qlue (a crowd sourcing smartphone app) through which people could report directly and problems they face as Jakarta residents.

Finally, to win the hearts of *kampung* folk, Jokowi and Ahok launched a number of other programmes. Among these was the issuance in November and December 2012 respectively of Jakarta Health Cards [*Kartu Jakarta Sehat* (KJS)] and Jakarta Education Cards [*Kartu Jakarta Pintar* (KJP)] to enable access by the poor to health care and education. And since the beginning of the Jokowi–Ahok tenure, some 38 *kampung* locations had been designated as sites for the construction of new, decent *per-kampung-an* [settlements with a *kampung* environment]. The

Kampung Deret Program, as it is called, envisions a wide-ranging reconstruction and renovation of existing low-income settlements. In Jokowi's words:

> The *kampung* residents should have a clean public space. Their neighborhoods should have good sanitation, good septic tank system, good streets, and good green space. . . . How beautiful it would be if in the slum-like *kampung* of Cilincing, we could build centers for the arts, spaces for IT, small libraries and parks, among others. (Endah 2012: 189, 191)

This may sound like a middle-class dream for the underclass. Furthermore, as part of the effort, the governor also said he was willing to give tenure and certification to some lands informally occupied by *kampung* dwellers. Yet, as part of the modernisation effort, *kampung* traditions will be both assumed and simultaneously transformed. Thus, while the reenactment of traditions may give a sense of continuity and improvement, it also makes possible the relocation of the urban poor (including the violence associated with the eviction of communities in Kampung Pulo for instance) to new low-rise *kampung deret* [row villages], *kampung susun* [elevated villages], and high-rise rental apartments.

Ultimately, the new *kampung* programme was set up in favour of change—but not without limit. For example, it required the city to classify *kampung* into different categories. According to a report in the *Jakarta Post*, the Jakarta Housing and Administrative Buildings Agency identified "392 community units across the capital . . . [as] slum areas", and estimated that "50 per cent of the capital's population of 10 million are . . . low income or poor". Yet it also cautioned that "houses built on riverbanks or public roads" would not be eligible for renovation funding (Dewi 2014).

Categories come with the power to exclude, but those who were eligible for *kampung*-upgrading initiatives would have no choice but to reckon with the governor's desire to formalise and transform existing *kampung*. In keeping with Ahok and Jokowi's aspiration to modernise and formalise housing in Jakarta (a consistent policy among all governors to date), the same news report cited a gubernatorial decree that every private developer acquiring a plot larger than 5,000 square metres must allocate 20 per cent of new building space for affordable housing. Meanwhile, it reported that the Housing and Administrative Buildings Agency was compiling a list of city properties that could be developed into low-cost apartments (even though such accommodation may be unsuitable to *kampung* traditions). With such property listing came the territorial logic of violence. Dian Tri Irawaty recorded instances of evictions under both Jokowi and Ahok's tenures as Governor of Jakarta.[19] While arrangements were made for dialogue, and these resembled a participatory approach (Jokowi's style) so that the urban poor could voice their concerns and aspirations and a consensus could be reached, the result did not translate into a systematic pro-*kampung* programme. Instead, under Ahok's administration, forced evictions were supported by the military and the police which ended in open contestations on the streets.

Ultimately, by the end of Ahok's term in 2017, the city administration's aim had become no less than to achieve "Jakarta without slums". On the one hand, this can be seen as reflecting the UN Habitat "Cities without Slums" campaign. But it is also inseparable from Ahok's desire to transform Suharto's traditions of urban politics, within which the *kampung* played an important part. From eradicating corruption in local government to integrating the *rakyat* through formal rental apartments, the new municipal programmes seek to dissolve the legacy of informality that characterised Jakarta during the previous era.

This rationale likewise underpinned Ahok's obsession with rules, permissions and the formal registration of all Jakarta residents. The ultimate representation of this is shown in plans for a Jakarta One Card, which would contain comprehensive information about its holder, from family ties to work and financial status. Through this single card, Ahok would not only ensure legibility for workers in the informal sector but also resolve questions of who the *rakyat* are, where they come from, what they are doing and how to control them. And while this move can be interpreted as creating urban citizens, it can also be seen as seeking to overturn the *rakyat* tradition of fleeing from power.

The populist policies of the Jokowi–Ahok administration were intended to show how the poor were mistreated or poorly served in the past, not because they were less fortunate, but because they formerly lived according to unjust traditions created in part by the government. They also intended to show that no one need be marginalised within a new tradition that seeks to distribute the fruits of development to all (even as some have been forcibly evicted from *kampung* along the riverside). The administration similarly believes that when the lower class is cared for, and when its needs are assumed to be not that different from those of the middle class, Jakarta will be freed from anxiety over the possibility of class rage and envy.

## Politics of Time

The question of "whose traditions" is intimately related to a politics of time. Much of the politics sketched out thus far is, at bottom, criticism of certain practices of Indonesian political culture reified under the previous regime of Suharto. Yet we should also note that the time of Jokowi and Ahok is also the time of neoliberal populism in which moving fast with their programmes was crucial to legitimising their election. This performative time, while it differs from the time of "order and stability" characteristic of the previous regime, delineates the priority of the new administration which emphasises projects strategically identified as capable of speedy completion and quick results even as they might not be the solution to the problem.

The administrations of Jokowi and Ahok came to power at a time when the city was highly divided and the nation was in the grip of powerful oligarchs. They arrived at the height of urban informality, when city government, political parties, private developers, urban residents and bureaucratic elites ruled by means of corruption, greed, selfishness, law violations and opportunism. Had the city continued on this course, it could have exploded into violent conflict. Even the old forces seemed to know that new leadership and a different urban imaginary were needed (at least temporarily or symbolically) to stabilise conditions in the city. It was in this context that Jokowi and Ahok—neither with previous ties to big business, the military, or elite families—sought to relieve pressures and articulate a new urban agenda. Thus, while Jokowi and Ahok sought to combat Suharto-era traditions and pursue a path of genuine reform, they also played a stabilising role.

Considering this situation, one could claim that the city's traditions of informality (especially the oligarchic and militaristic ones) are simply too deep to uproot, and that all Jokowi and Ahok did was to innovate *within* the reach of the old order. For instance, Ahok made a great deal of effort to harness private developers to put aside a certain percentage of their assets and profits for the city government to build low-cost apartments and public facilities. He was willing to issue permits, as in the case of the land reclamation project in North Jakarta, as long as the developers were willing to share their profits with the city even though such a project was considered ecologically unsustainable. His view that capitalism should be allowed to prosper in Jakarta as long as profits were shared with the city recalls a legacy of Suharto's regime. To defend the North Jakarta land reclamation project, Ahok thus referred to the legal document set up by Suharto's 1995 Presidential Decree regardless of the fact that such a decree was established with the explicit purpose of accumulating capital for Suharto's own families and cronies.

Furthermore, Ahok's aspiration for a "Jakarta without slums" is only part of a larger urban "beautification" agenda which includes not only efforts to prevent flooding but also to relocate the urban poor to what he considers proper housing (i.e. non-*kampung* low-cost apartments). And in pursuit of these goals, Ahok has shown no hesitation to forcibly evict residents from riverbank neighbourhoods and relocate them to highrise apartments. Indeed, the manner in which evictions were conducted—with a thousand-strong security force armed with tear gas, water cannons and riot gear—recalls only the era of authoritarianism.

So what appears new has soon become old; the "new traditions" established under Jokowi and Ahok have been negated, displaced, or crushed as much as by traditional forces. Ahok's tenure ended in October 2017, and by then there had been more than murmurs that his legacy was fragile. The massive protest by Islamic hardliners against Ahok (for what they saw as insulting a Quranic verse in his stump speech), is an indication just how vulnerable Ahok's position can be. The incident was an opportunity for politicians vying against Ahok's new urban politics. It was clear to many at the time that should Ahok fail to be reelected, Jakarta's next governor would no doubt once again raise the question of "whose tradition?". The arrival of a new administration could lead to a retrieval of New Order-like traditions of urban politics.

Ahok indeed failed to be re-elected. In what is considered the most politically problematic regional election in Indonesia's history, Ahok was defeated by Anies Baswedan. A very astute politician, Anies capitalised on anti-Ahok sentiments, especially on the blasphemy allegation, and won the race after seeking the support of Islamist groups including hardliners such as the Islamic Defenders Front (*Front Pembela Islam*). To this date, mainly for political gains, Anies maintains a close relationship with conservative and hardline Islamic groups and has an alliance with Rizieq Shihab, a controversial religious leader of the 212 rallies against Ahok (see Chapter 7). An Indonesian of Arab descend, Anies however shows no hesitation to express his populist "nativism" by evoking anti-Chinese sentiments. In his inaugural speech he stated that:

> In the past, all of us, the *pribumi* [natives], were oppressed and defeated. Now we are independent. It is time for us to become the hosts in our own country. Do not let Jakarta be like what is written in the Madurese saying: *etek se bertelor, ajam se rameh* [The duck (representing Indigenous Indonesians) lays the eggs, but the chicken (as Indonesian of Chinese descends) broods].[20]

Three years into his term, Anies however was considered "still missing mark" and creating only a "setback" (Sausan Atika 2020). Some critics believe his poor performance is due to incompetency. Others noted his political ambition, including his interest in bidding for the 2024 presidential election (Burhani 2020). The Jakarta public would not fail to remember his gimmick projects which include covering polluted rivers with a screen during the ASEAN Games and planting plastic trees along the main roads while destroying a large part of the green area in the National Square for the expensive Formula E electric motorsport championship. Meanwhile Anies broke his promise to stop Jakarta Bay reclamation, did nothing to mitigate flooding or improve mass transportation, and regularly came under fire for irregularities in budget proposals. His flagship programmes such as One District One Entrepreneurship (OK OCE) to generate new entrepreneurs and the zero down-payment housing programmes remain unclear. And his populist ideas to upgrade *kampungs* and legalise sidewalk vending as well as creating bike lanes on the city's toll roads are deemed by urban planners as violating land-use regulations (Sausan Atika 2020).

The responses from pro-*kampung* urban activists to Anies' administration have been mixed. Some believe that Governor Baswedan could be amenable to supporting programmes for *kampung* and the urban poor as he has been legally bound by a political contract which he had signed to help win the election against Ahok. Others are sceptical about the sustainability of the programmes, as the Governor hadn't shown a political will to build an integrated system to consolidate them and to systematically coordinate their implementation.[21] Such lack of political will, one could argue, is a politics of time. To establish a coordinated approach to the programmes would require the support of the state which means he must first win the presidential election.

The deeper implication of Anies' lack of leadership in substantive development is the undoing of some progressive practices and policies initiated under the administration of Jokowi and Ahok, those which concern transparency and accountability. For example, Anies decided to dispense with accountability reports at the two lowest levels of local administration in the city. The neighborhood chief (ketua RT) and hamlet chief (ketua RW) will no longer be required to submit budgetary accountability reports to the provincial government (Nugroho 2017). Instead the governor sought to set an example of what he considered as a social trust which was the basis of the working relationship prior to the reform introduced by Jokowi and Ahok. This regressive move has been welcomed by local chiefs who are exempted from making themselves accountable to the people. Meanwhile the e-budgeting system implemented under Ahok's administration was blamed as less-than-optimal when irregularities were found in the municipality's budgeting (Andriyanto and Tambun 2019).

Nothing is more explicit than Anies' last public presentation as Governor of Jakarta, in September 2022. Presenting Jakarta spatial plan (titled: The Acceleration of Transformation of Jakarta as a Global City),[22] Anies juxtaposed maps and images (in black-and-white) from "before" his tenure with the colourful scenes from "after" his administration. The dark and gritty atmosphere of the "before" seems to suggest that everything went wrong in the past, in contrast to the vibrancy and joy of the colourful present. Such a contrast serves populist politics in that Anies is not only different, but he has successfully worked for the people today against the time of Ahok, their "common enemy".

During his final weeks as governor, Anies reminded people that he had expanded access to public spaces whereas Ahok forbade motorcycles from entering the main street of Sudirman-Thamrin. "*That must not happen!*" Anies said.[23] He also added "keadilan" (justice) into his speeches. At the time when he declared his willingness to be nominated to run as the next President of Indonesia, he portrayed himself as the unifier of people of Jakarta, in contrast to Ahok whose policy, according to Anies, had deepened the divide in the city. We see the expressions of yet another round of populist politics in Anies Baswedan's speeches, which, according to Laclau (2005), is based on popular subjects such as "equality" and "justice", and the construction of a "common enemy".

Anies' administration raised once again the question of by whose tradition Jakarta should be governed, a question that would lead to a retrieval of more pre-Jokowi-Ahok traditions of urban politics. Lining up behind the supporters of Anies during his election campaign are prominent businessmen and military officers with a history of ties to the former regime of Suharto.[24] On the front line are new supporters, the Islamists who are eager to launch with the governor a version of Islamist urbanism in the capital. A new icon of Jakarta in the form of a floating mosque and "the biggest museum for the prophet outside Saudi Arabia", on reclaimed land are currently under construction (qtd. in Paat 2020).

## Notes

[1] For a discussion on the formation of Indonesian municipalities in early twentieth century colonial Indonesia, especially that of Batavia (established in 1905), see the works of Peter Nas (1990) and Susan Abeyasekere (1987). The Decentralization Act, decreed in 1903 by the colonial state, opened the path for the local government to make plans for the territory under their jurisdiction, but far too little support was provided by the central government to implement them. See also Roosmalen (2015).

[2] Joko Widodo served two years as governor of Jakarta before becoming president of Indonesia in 2014. When he departed, he was replaced by the vice governor, Basuki "Ahok" Purnama, whose term ended in 2017.

[3] Joko Widodo, "Indonesian Mental Revolution", first published in *Kompas*, 10 May 2014, as "Revolusi Mental", at http://nasional.kompas.com/read/2014/05/10/1603015/revolusi. mental (accessed 5 Dec. 2022). The English version was posted on 20 May 2014. See http://www.establishmentpost.com/indonesia-mental-revolution/.

[4] "Jokowi dan arti 'Revolusi Mental'", *Kompas*, 17 Oct. 2014, http://nasional.kompas.com/read/2014/10/17/22373441/Jokowi.dan.Arti.Revolusi.Mental.

[5] Joko Widodo: "Korupsi, kolusi, nepotisme, etos kerja tidak baik, bobroknya birokrasi, hingga ketidaksiplinan. Kondisi itu dibiarkan selama bertahun-tahun dan pada akhirnya hadir di setiap sendi bangsa" ( qtd. in "Jokowi dan arti 'Revolusi Mental'").

[6] Malo and Nas (1996) do not mention the "middle class" and they do not see much difference between the central and local government. They were just teasing out a tradition of urban governance peculiar (or maybe not so peculiar) to a city like Jakarta.

[7] FBR was sub-contracted by Governor Sutiyoso in the early 2000s to help restore order during evictions from *kampung*. Otherwise it is a relatively tolerant ethnic Betawi solidarity movement.

[8] *Pungli* and *korupsi* [extortion and corruption] are major keywords in Indonesia today. Indonesians all remember that the stepping down of Suharto was accompanied by rallies against

KKN (*kolusi, korupsi, dan nepotisme*) [collusion, corruption, and nepotism], which refer to the oligarchic tradition of the government.

⁹ This section is drawn from Onghokham 2003.

¹⁰ If a particular servant impressed the king, he might be paid with lands and farmers. But the kingdom did not generally seek to control how its agents generated income as long as they continued to produce tribute for the king. This system of low salary but high income through extortion sustained the kingdom. See Onghokham 2003.

¹¹ When the colonial state was established in the nineteenth century, its first governor-general instituted a salary system based on rank. However, in practice, illegal extortion continued, especially by local chiefs, because their salaries were not high enough to cover the need to maintain extended patron–client networks. Below the level of the regents [*bupati*], extortion thus continued. However, the small-time corrupt and their petty corruptions/extortions (below the *bupati* level) were often caught and punished by the colonial state. See Onghokham 2003.

¹² One can think of how people in Jakarta, or in Indonesia generally, have learned to doubt the power of the state to fairly distribute the necessities of life. They may even have learned to doubt the location of power if experience has told them that local chieftains and thugs [*preman*] are more important to their daily lives than the government is. Thus, historically, they may have learned that the government is powerless without the help of local chieftains or civil leaders—including the thugs who often appear to rule without supervision or control. Knowing that the government was unreliable and that they couldn't trust thugs, they informally and continuously set up their own (temporary) networks to cope with the conditions of uncertainty—a condition that often found expression in the built environment.

¹³ Malo and Nas (1996: 130) describe the *rakyat* as "the common people . . . the migrants who settle on empty space [and] . . . are not organized and do not promote common plans". But they do not describe why they were not organised and have no common plan. It is also generally accepted that organised protests and rallies on the streets or in front of government buildings have not been part of the *rakyat* tradition—even as NGOs and middle-class activists have hailed the importance of street protests, especially since the fall of Suharto. Instead, street protests or riots, organised under the name of the *rakyat*, are understood to represent cases of the *rakyat* being used, bought, or appropriated by powerful groups for political gain. In any case, the politics of the *rakyat* cannot be formalised under the concept of a "right to the city". This doesn't mean that the *rakyat* do not care about the context of their struggle to work and live in the city, but they have their own way of doing politics.

¹⁴ The *rakyat* seem to invent their traditions of action in relation to the "looseness in the centre", or the disappearance of the state—a condition in which the face of the state is not clear, or in which its political culture cannot be grasped. The other condition in which action by the *rakyat* may arise is when the state (to make itself present or to legitimise its power) oppresses the *rakyat* through evictions and violence. These two conditions—emphasising alternatively the absence or presence of the state—may find responses in anarchy and disobedience.

¹⁵ *Mobokrasi* [mobocracy] is a term used by the established ruling class to refer to a form of government ruled by *rakyat* who knew nothing about governmental rules. For a dictionary definition for the Indonesian context, see https://www.kamusbesar.com/mobokrasi.

¹⁶ But what kind of situation is likely to stimulate such behaviour? The context for it, one could speculate, may be a recognition that the moral economy of the state (since independence) has been based on an aspiration to achieve social justice for all Indonesians (*keadilan sosial bagi seluruh rakyat Indonesia*), and that any deviation from this mission would result in resistance. Related to this is a sense of uncertainty. AbdouMaliq Simone in *Jakarta* (2014) described this

condition of uncertainty as a stage for acts that give at least a sense of certainty: building a house on occupied land, building a mosque, forming an identity-based group and so on. One could add the restoration of selfhood, which often takes on a condition of not being governed.

[17] The city's connection to the village also takes place in the practice of *mudik*, an annual returning to the village during the Ramadhan New Year. *Mudik* combines the words *mulih* [healing] and *udik* [village], implying a return to the village for healing, before moving back to the city. The notion of healing here suggests a recovery and acceptance of one's rural roots after a whole year of struggling in a city characterised by density, heterogeneity and (relative) anonymity (yet a place that offers opportunities for progress). *Mudik* is an important annual event, invented by migrants (ie as we might call a mentalité) and it has become a central way to register the presence of the village in the minds of urban folk. *Mudik* has replaced circular (or seasonal) migration (*perantauan musiman*), which was more common in the past when farmers went to the city to work while waiting for the planting and harvest season in the village. The current condition therefore does not suggest a world of linear time and space, as suggested by the term "urbanisation". The city of Jakarta has a great mix of rural and urban patterns of tradition.

[18] Data from the section below are based on a variety of "middle-class" metropolitan newspapers and journal reports.

[19] For a comparison of *kampung* evictions under different governors of Jakarta, see Irawaty 2018: 47–57. Evictions occurred under almost every governor, though the methods by which they were carried out were different from time to time. Irawaty indicates that while Ahok mobilised the support of the military and police, Sutiyoso (being closest to the Suharto New Order) used both the military and *preman* to carry out evictions. All used the pretext of defending public safety or "public interest" and carrying out "development projects" or expanding the "green environment". See Irawaty: 55.

[20] "Dulu kita semua pribumi ditindas dan dikalahkan. Kini telah merdeka, kini saatnya menjadi tuan rumah di negeri sendiri. Jangan sampai Jakarta ini seperti yang dituliskan pepatah Madura. etek se bertelor, ajam se rameh. Itik yang bertelor, ayam yang mengerami". The full speech of Anies Baswedan can be found in *Rizqo* 2017. The longer translation can be found in Pepinsky 2017.

[21] This concerns the Governor's Decree on the Task Force on the Kampung and Community Planning Program which came out of the "political contract" with urban community activists in their struggle to defend *kampung* in the aftermath of evictions under Ahok's administration. See Irawaty 2018: 69. For a discussion of a range of strategies urban activists mobilised in their contestation for the right of the urban poor to live and work in the city, see Irawaty 2018: 57–72.

[22] Anies Baswedan, "Rencana Detail Tata Ruang 2022: Mengakselerasi Transformasi Jakarta sebagai Kota Global", 21 Sept. 2022 <power point presentation>.

[23] Silvia Ng, "Anies Bicara Keadilan, Singgung Pembatasan Motor di Era Ahok", 27 Sept. 2022, at https://news.detik.com/berita/d-6315697/anies-bicara-keadilan-singgung-pembatasan-pemotor-di-era-ahok (accessed 28 Sept. 2022).

[24] The list includes business moguls Aburizal Bakrie, Hashim Djojohadikusumo, Hary Tanoesoedibjo and Prabowo Subianto. See Al Azhari, Muhamad and Eko Prasetyo 2017.

# Chapter 7 | Islamist Urbanism

In the previous chapter we saw how the city serves as a site for the formation and contestation of urban politics and how, in parallel, it struggles for new traditions. In this chapter we look at how Islamist groups wrestle for hegemony by investing meaning in the built environment. The relationship between Islamism and the built environment raises the question of religion in the public space as the two may not be immediately linked. Such a secular preconception would presuppose a framework that religion (e.g. in the current context, Islam) has been outside the public space; the question thus relates to the ways in which religion can enter this space. If this assumption is granted, we must also ask how Islam has been relegated to the private sphere, and what kinds of values operate in the public space.

In Indonesia, such questions recall the discussions in 1945 among the ruling elites who had to define citizenship on the basis of religious or national belonging. As members of the Preparatory Committee for Independence, they had to decide whether in the Jakarta Charter (before it became the Constitution of Indonesia) they could plant the seeds of an Islamic state by obliging Muslims to obey Islamic law (*sharia*) (Elson 2009). Nationalist leaders (who were also Muslims), such as Sukarno and Mohammad Hatta, managed to persuade members of the Committee to drop the question as it would alienate Hindu- and Christian-dominated regions of the country. Assumed in the final Constitution of Indonesia is the belief in God without reference to a specific religion. This is a form of acknowledgement of the religious pluralism of Indonesian society. While such a consensus was reached at that time, the tension between the "nationalists" and the "Islamists" has never been resolved and continues to disturb Indonesian society to the present day. The tension has over time developed into an Islam-based political movement (known by Indonesians as "Islamist"—by definition a hard-line Muslim organisation to be discussed in this chapter) versus a position that champions a pluralistic multi-faith nation-state (known as "nationalist").

After the fall of the Suharto regime, which repressed Islamists for fear of their threat to the president's power, a band of hard-line Muslim organisations sought to pressure the state to adopt *sharia* as a basis for representing Indonesia as the world's largest Muslim country. However, hard-line Muslim organisations constitute neither a singular position nor a shared strategy. Instead, they have evolved into various positions in their relation to the state. Some of them (such as *Partai Keadilan Sejahtera* [PKS; The Justice and Prosperity Party—discussed below]) formed political parties seeking influence within the structure of the nationalist state (Noor 2011); others preferred to be freelancers, opportunistically moving between the nationalist and the Islamist, and a number preferred to dominate the streets by rallying for Indonesia to be an Islamic state. These latter groups organised themselves around an opposition to what they considered a democratic sphere of secular liberalism. The *Front Pembela Islam* (FPI or Islamic Defence Front—discussed below), for example, registered their presence through vigilante violence and the imposition of moral conduct in areas under their control. Others, such as the Salafi-modernist network and Hizbut Tahrir, dream of an Islamist Caliphate. All of these movements (with different degrees of legitimacy), along with older Islamic organisations represent the multiplicity of Islamic politics and religious movements and are seeking accommodation in the current Indonesian public sphere. Central to the rising tide of Islamism in post-Suharto Indonesia, therefore, is the question of how public space might accommodate Islam as a matrix of both subject formation and of social-political practices.

In this chapter, I seek to contribute to the ongoing discussion of the mutuality of religious practices and urban modernity by considering the rise of Islamism in Indonesia. I use the term "Islamist urbanism" to refer to the relationship between Islamism and the built environment (see also Batuman 2021). The term refers to the era of Islamist ascendency which followed the collapse of the repressive military regime of Suharto, and in which urban space or urban life plays a major role in registering the contemporary presence of Islam as a dominant (formal or informal) political force. While locating the story within the time frame of the current political formation, this chapter suggests that Indonesian Islamism (despite its regular anti-Western rhetoric) can be adequately understood historically only in relation to secular nationalism (represented by the state).

This chapter also acknowledges the multiplicity of Islamism, the plural Islamisms. The importance of plurality suggests attention to a broad range of positions that lie in between the antinomy of Islam and non-Islam (Hefner 2000). The term "plural Islamisms" suggests that individual and group identity is formed through an articulation of a position out of a series of relational practices that are situational and contextual. Religious identities, which some may claim are non-political, are always engaging with politics and are formed relationally through a construction of "distinction" that often involves calculated decisions concerning opportunities. There are also shifting positions as a member of an Islamist group can move on to become a member of a different Islamist group. Consequently, there are also Islamist groups that are more open to neoliberal ideas because of their ethnic, class or gender position, and there are those who embrace free speech and demonstration while rejecting democracy. Alliances between different Islamists thus cannot be formed on the basis of merely sharing an Islamic identity, but an alliance can be formed (as this chapter will show) by way of constructing a shared oppositional other, under the sub-text of "defending Islam".

This chapter explores the spatial mediation of ideology and political communication in Islamism. But we must first acknowledge the fluidity and ephemerality of spatial representations and practices. The language of space and the relation of form and content in spatial form are more salient and more ambiguous than in direct or printed speech. The significance of a built environment and the meaning invested in it can shift or drain away with time. Their audiences too are anonymous, fleeting and multiple. The built environment nevertheless throws light on and helps to construct the subject of Islam and the subjectivity of Islamists. In Indonesian studies, through the work of Clifford Geertz, we learn about the theatricality of power—the idea that acting in concert (as in an assembly or a rally) could powerfully convey a dominant political position (Kusno 2019). Urban or architectural space here could serve as a stage or setting (intentionally or unintentionally) to help create a believable scenario for identity formation. People could portray themselves to others performatively through space regardless of whether the space is designed for or without theatricality, and for liberation or repression. As such, architectural space participates in or engages with the question of ideological interpellation, of constituting an individual as a subject— in the context of this chapter, as an Islamist (Batuman 2021).

In this chapter the relationship between Islamism and the built environment is shown to have tended to function in three ways, according to three different though interdependent forms of usage. The first is by way of spatial representation that incorporates Islamic signifiers such as the mosque into themes of greening public space as part of city branding in Bandung, the former cradle of Islamic student movements. The second one is by opposition through mass rallies organised by Islamist groups calling for an "act to defend Islam"—at once an "interpellative performative statement" (Butler 2018)—in the National Monument Square (*Lapangan Monas*) in Jakarta. It also concerns the spill over effect of the opposition to the regulation of the everyday life of Muslim populations. The third concerns the discursive appearances of *mushollas* (prayer houses) in various lower income neighbourhoods of the everyday urban world of *kampung*. Together, they show the ways in which politics and space intersect in the representation of Islamism, and the centrality of taking control over the meaning and use of space for both political and religious expression.

**Scene I:** **The Avant Garde, the Political Party and the Greening of Religious Public Space**

In May 2017, Ridwan Kamil, then Mayor of Bandung (2013–18), opened a new mosque called Masjid Al Safar (a mosque for travellers) at the rest area of a toll road linking Bandung to Jakarta. It was an extraordinary event for the Mayor as he is the mosque's designer. Before becoming a politician, Kamil, a graduate of the Institute of Technology of Bandung (ITB) and the University of California Berkeley, had already established a reputation for himself as an avant-garde architect. He won the British Council Young Creative Entrepreneur Award and *Elle Décor* magazine selected him as Architect of the Year in 2009. The architectural firm he co-founded was listed for several years as part of the BCI Asia Top 10 Awards. The mosque was his contribution, in Kamil's words, "to the progress of Islamic art and architecture" (qtd. in Nur Yasmin 2019). Noticing that "Islamic aesthetics are very strong in geometry", he thus tried "a new, different geometry" (qtd. in Nur Yasmin 2019). There is no easy way to describe the shape of Al Safar. However, we can learn more from how it has been perceived formalistically.

A newspaper reporter wrote that it was conceived as a sculpture crafted out of a big rock. Another reporter called it *masjid origami* (origami-style mosque). The toll operator thought that the mosque was designed to look like a traditional Sundanese hat. An *Ustad* (Islamic preacher) argued that the mosque's main praying area resembles an Anti-Christ symbol, as of the "Illuminati" (ibid.). He tweeted his opinion in a video to his followers in a manner of a symbologist: "This is the entrance, see all these triangles. Almost all triangles. Even when you go inside, a triangle, an eye. So, when we pray, who are we facing? God, or this one-eyed triangle?" (qtd. in Nur Yasmin 2019). The Ustad refers to *Dajjal*, a one-eyed devil in Islamic mythology. This reference became a subject of heated debate in social media for several weeks. Architect-Mayor Ridwan Kamil had to intervene. First, the accusation was simply wrong, he said, for it carried a motive of defaming him in the political arena (as he was by then moving on to run for a governor position in West Java, the most populous province in Indonesia and a hotbed of intolerant Islamic groups).

Kamil then revealed that Masjid Al Safar is a result of a design experiment in applying the theoretical concept of "folding architecture" (influenced by French philosopher, Giles Deleuze). Accordingly, such an approach referred to nothing but a geometrical formula. Furthermore, Kamil continued, "the mosque was highly appreciated in Saudi Arabia since it was nominated for 2019 Abullatif Al Fozan Award for best architecture".[1]

Kamil forgave the Ustad and he believed that God was on his side. He vowed to never stop working "to bring progress which is the mission that God has given to him in this world" (qtd. in Nur Yasmin 2019). Referring to Allah's mandate and Deleuze's folding, the Mayor of Bandung simultaneously revealed himself as an avant-garde architect and a devout Muslim. Had Indonesia continued to be under Suharto's rule, it is unlikely that Kamil would have felt the need to mobilise his Islamic identity. Such a performative role makes sense only in the context of the rise of Islamists in West Java.

**Figure 7.1.** Masjid Al Safar, Bandung (photo courtesy of Frans Prasetyo).

Kamil's political aesthetic reveals the power of the religious landscape in which he is currently embedded. Kamil launched his political career in large measure thanks to the support of leaders of the Islamic political party, *Partai Keadilan Sejahtera* (PKS). In exchange for the party's support, Kamil must accept a running mate from within the PKS cadre. Kamil's deputy, the vice Mayor, was Mr. Muhammad Oded (who became the Mayor of Bandung in 2018).[2] The PKS knew perfectly well that while Oded had gone through rigorous training to become a senior member of the party, his path to the City Hall would not be easy without riding on Kamil's popularity (Prasetyo 2019a). On the other hand, to build his political career, Kamil understood that he must capitalise on his Muslim identity while maintaining his image of being an "independent" populist creative leader of Bandung. Between the avant-garde impulse of Kamil and the religious devotion of Oded, a form of middle-class oriented Islamist urbanism came to be formed in Bandung, the capital city of West Java. Such a blend of public personas demands a political organisation of space.

In an insightful piece about the transformation of Bandung from being a "creative city" to a "religious city", Frans Prasetyo, a scholar activist and visual ethnographer, indicates that as soon as Kamil came to power, he took on a project of beautifying the iconic *alun-alun* (the town square) of Bandung by strengthening its link with the nearby Grand Mosque (Prasetyo 2019a). The Governor closed the street off from traffic so that the *alun-alun* became the extended space or the verandah of the mosque. He then covered the 22,000-metre open square with synthetic lawn. Thus the *alun-alun* soon appeared to be *green*. The plastic lawn enhanced the appearance of the Grand Mosque, as green happens to be the colour used by most Islamic parties. The religious assembly is now facilitated by the new, clean "green" lawn. Furthermore, as Prasetyo points out, as an extended space of the mosque, visitors visiting *alun-alun* were asked to take off their shoes. With the beautification of the *alun-alun* came disciplinary tasks drawn from religious practices. Space follows time, and since the integration of the *alun-alun* into the space of the Grand Mosque, the most crowded time for the space is also the most crowded time for the mosque: around noon time during *sholat dzuhur*, 3pm during *sholat azhar* and 6pm during *sholat magrib* (Prasetyo 2019a).

The middle class of Bandung nevertheless welcomed the synthetisation of the square. The *alun-alun* became a place for both religious pilgrimage and tourism. Muslim visitors in particular like to take selfies with the Grand Mosque. For the non-Muslims who rarely spend very much time in the *alun-alun*, the object of their selfies is the lawn (which looks real in photographs) and the giant sign of *Bandung Juara* (Bandung Champion) that decorates the square. Through Kamil's beautification of the *alun-alun*, the new Islamists found a way to articulate themselves as simultaneously religious, modern and popular.

For Prasetyo, the design of the *alun-alun* facilitates the crossover between religion and public space, a routinisation of religious transgression onto what was once a relatively "neutral" public space. We could add that such "Islamisation" of the *alun-alun* is in line with the disciplinary cadre training of the PKS. The *alun-alun* serves not only as an extension of the Grand Mosque to accommodate its ritual and religious ceremonies but also as a public spectacle of training to be self-disciplined and to stay clean, like the lawn of the new *alun-alun*. The green *alun-alun* represents something of the internal character of the party's cadres who are mainly middle class and highly educated.

Kamil believes that design can give style to a person's character. After all, design for him is more about desire than anything else. Such a desire produced a form of religious assembly in a most iconic public space in Bandung and focused less on the condition that enables the production of space itself. The Lippo Group, through its corporate social responsibility fund, paid for the revamping of the *alun-alun* (Prasetyo 2019a and 2019b). The Group (as indicated in Chapter 5) is owned by an Evangelical Christian family in Jakarta whose support, according to Prasetyo, was in exchange for a building permit to construct a multi-purpose commercial complex in a strategic location. Such an arrangement did not seem to compromise the plenitude of Islamic religiosity (Prasetyo 2019b). After all, the design of the green space advances a new kind of appearance for all Bandung residents even though it works more for the Islamists. For Kamil's critics, it also advances a new kind of urban politics that is all based on image—a "gimmick" form of urban development (Prasetyo 2017).

**Figure 7.2.** *Alun-alun* Bandung (photo courtesy of Frans Prasetyo).

Following the *alun-alun*, in the other parks that Kamil succeeded in beautifying, he set up large signs with terms that served to bring religiosity into city branding. At least they have commercial legs to match the previous logos of Bandung such as the "Paris van Java" or the location of the 1955 "Asia-Africa Conference". They include slogans such as "Bandung Champion", "Bandung Smart City", "Bandung Creative City" and the other conduits that have entered the lexicon of city competition. Kamil's arousing slogans belong to the cultural industry of city branding, but they were made to work with religiosity as the brand. They were performative utterances that were constantly repeated to register the appearance of an Islamist urbanism. By the time M. Oded, the PKS's cadre, moved on to run for Mayor of Bandung, his campaign slogans, thick with religious atmosphere such "Bandung Unggul dan Agamais" (Bandung Champion and Religious), were assumed to be at once normal, desirable and marketable.

The green branding continued throughout the city in a series of park renovations. After the "success" of transforming the *alun-alun* Bandung to benefit the pious public, the city also revamped many of its *Taman* (an Indonesian term for park and garden). Prasetyo provides a detailed list of *Taman* that received Kamil's design touch (in the form of statues, signs and decorative ornaments): "Taman Lansia, Taman Musik, Taman Persib, Taman Film, Taman Pustaka Bunga, Taman Fotografi, Taman Vanda, Taman Labrin, Taman Cikapayang Dago, Taman Gesit, Taman Superhero,[3] Taman Sejarah, Taman Veteran, Taman Pet Perak, Taman Badak, Taman Dewi Sartika, and Taman Jomblo"; the last, being located under a flyover, had no trees (Prasetyo 2019a). So impressive were the numbers that the Mayor earned a nickname—*wagiman* (*walikota gila taman*) or "park maniac Mayor" (ibid.). While most of these parks have no religious content, they nevertheless constitute the image that Kamil sought to build, that is Bandung as a regulated green-looking city. And this achievement was communicated not only in physical space and on signboards, but also in virtual space.

Kamil is a Twitter fan, and has made his online presence truly felt in the city (Rachmatunisa 2015). Residents noticed how much the Mayor tweeted—everything from trivial notions to details of the city's creative programmes, to his working motivation, to sharing his version of good governance. His Twitter followers are important witnesses to his work. He even earned a Social Media Award in 2015 (ibid.). Kamil's tweets represent his impulses for performance, transparency and accountability. He wants everyone to know that he is personable and that the city looks smart, clean and Islamic. For example, in defence of his success in making Bandung more Islamic, Kamil tweeted that "Bandung is the most Islamic city in Indonesia, according to a survey conducted by the Maarif Institute. Please just google to find out! I have encouraged Quran recitation (*mengaji*) during Magrib; asked youth to pray in congregation (*shalat berjamah*) at dawn; meanwhile *zakat* has increased five times due to the online system, so have mosque-based credits without interest and so on. *Nuhun!* [thank you in Sundanese]".[4] The networked city and the mayor thus become an integrated brand. And in the business of branding, there is no difference between marketing and receiving criticism. Both would enhance his presence.

This emphasis on performance recalls values familiar to the neoliberal technique of individual self-cultivation. While Kamil is not a cadre of the PKS, this political party that supported him encourages self-management for its cadres, such as keeping points in a "score book". It rewards its cadres who perform extra religiously-oriented tasks with promotion to the higher level of leadership (Noor 2011). Such a practice would ensure the production of a devout subject who at the same time could be audited and accounted for. The deeper aim of this is "to lay the foundation for the creation of a transparent, corruption-free, and pious nation before God" (Ibrahim 2018: 29). The quest for religiosity through self-discipline, transparency and objectivity represents the PKS's "democratic impulses" and matches the Twitter world of Kamil.

The image that Kamil crafted for himself was one of a modern, smart, creative, hip, cosmopolitan and elite intellectual. In addition, he is a Muslim, perhaps too classy for many poor Muslims, but still a Muslim cheered by the middle class. Before pursuing his political career, his subjectivity was that of an urban designer seeking to take back public space. He made reference approvingly of cultural theorists from Roland Barthes and Charles Baudelaire to Manuel Castells, Jürgen Habermas and Henri Lefebvre (Kamil 2008). He liked to cite "city air makes you free" to suggest his cosmopolitanism. Over time, however, a shift in context provoked a shift in thinking. By the time he declared "Bandung Champion" thanks to his make-believe park revitalisation series, he spoke less of spatial injustices, and more of harmony and happiness. He banned *kaki lima* (vendors who use food carts) from main thoroughfares and oversaw a series of violent evictions of dwellers of *kampung* (lower income neighbourhoods characterised by irregular settlements) in order to register the idea of a "creative city" and to improve the urban "connectivity" of Bandung (Prasetyo 2017). With the ambition to build his political career and concomitant pressure to win the support of the Muslim majority, Kamil showed just how the stylisation of the *alun-alun* and calculated marketing gimmicks to brand Bandung could at once naturalise Islamism and keep the public happy. This is thus a story of how the branding of Bandung as a "creative city" and "green city" intersects with Islamist urbanism.

## Scene II: Defending Islam, the 212 Movement, and the National Site of Interpellation

Bandung is less than a hundred miles from Jakarta. The PKS has long been interested in commanding the capital city through its cadres' control of the Governor's office. It has not been easy. The PKS has made attempts since the first gubernatorial election in 2007, but their supported candidates were never successful until 2017 when Anies Baswedan stepped up to run against the then incumbent Governor of Jakarta, Basuki "Ahok" Tjahaja Purnama, a Christian of Chinese descent (whom we have met in a previous chapter). The fall of Jakarta to the PKS-supported Governor can be perceived as an illustration of the rise of Islamist influence in the city's and nation's politics.

The office of the Governor of Jakarta has traditionally been staffed by personnel from the pro-ruling national government circles. When Ahok became Governor in 2012, the disparate Islamist groups (mostly hardliners led by Islamic Defenders Front [FPI], the Salafi-modernist network, the Hizbut Tahrir Indonesia

[HTI], the Wahdah Islamiyah and the Indonesian Muslim Forum [FUI]) saw the opportunity to rise up together against him under the banner of *aksi bela Islam* (act of defending Islam).[5] On 2 December [two-one-two] 2016, the multitude of Islamist groups, who are not always in agreement and between whom there is sometimes antagonism and competition, held a massive rally to demand Governor Ahok's imprisonment; he was accused of blasphemy against the *Quran*. Since then, the rally and its participants have become known as "the 212 movement" (referring to the date of the major rally). In May 2017, after losing the election, Ahok was sentenced to two years in jail.

Every year since that early December protest, the 212 groups that make up the "aksi bela Islam" return to the streets in large numbers, gathering around Jakarta's National Monument Square for a "reunion" to mark the success of their 2016 anti-Ahok rally. When Ahok was Governor, he banned religious events from taking place in the Square. The new Islamist Governor, Anies Baswedan (who received co-support from the PKS and the "aksi bela Islam" groups) overturned the ban soon after he came to power and gave permission for the reunion anti-Ahok rally to take place on the square.[6] He also spoke at the 2017 reunion rally celebrating the openness of the National Monument to religious events (Yen 2017).

To galvanise the otherwise disparate communities for a show of force, the Islamist groups organised themselves around various signifiers, such as "anti-Ahok rally", the "212 Rally" or the "212 Movement" and the "212 Reunion" or the "212 alumni". They also set up the National Movement to Safeguard Ulema Fatwas (GNPF), whose members would not hesitate to take to the streets in order to "defend Islam". The "return to the streets" is perhaps the achievement of the 212 Movement. Yet such a movement is nothing but a theatrical performance to produce the appearance of substance, a discourse that shows simultaneously the power of Islam and the need to keep defending it. While the rally claimed to have no political interests, the return to the streets was opened to such interests. After Ahok went to jail, the street became the site for opposing what Ahok represented. But what Ahok represented is hard to describe even by the Islamist groups. Ahok is, after all, acknowledged by the urban majority to be a reformist, promoter of accountability and a major uncompromising force for anti-corruption, but also considered to be part of the establishment because of his closeness to President Joko "Jokowi" Widodo with whom the opposition camp and the Islamist groups have long had a troubled relationship (Institute for Policy Analysis 2019). Unlike the PKS, which prefers to work within the structure of the Indonesian Constitution, some Islamists of the 212 Movement consider the Indonesian state to be their enemy while others (such as HT Indonesia) seek to establish a caliphate.

**Figure 7.3.** Reunion of the anti-Ahok rally at the National Monument, Jakarta, 2 Dec. 2017 (photo courtesy of Yen Tzu-Chien).

For all the 212 Islamist groups, Ahok (despite his Chinese Christian background) is a signifier of a dominant system centred around a Jakarta sustained by the president, business groups, political parties and the police. The Islamist groups thus see themselves as representing the politically- and economically-marginalised Muslim majority. One of the groups' intellectuals, Adnin Armas, considers the 212 Movement to be a defence mechanism, an expression of Muslims' collective consciousness of being weak and marginalised (Armas 2016/17). He expects that this consciousness of being at the margin (in a country where the majority are Muslims) would constitute an Islamic subjectivity that would lead to a change in the Indonesian socio-political and economic systems. The 212 Movement has thus produced "212 aspirations" aimed at awakening the spirit of defending Islam. Practically, they are translated into socio-economic discourses using "212" as a brand, such as setting up Bank 212, TV 212, Minimarket 212 and so on (Armas 2016/17).

The "212 brand" refers not only to the registration of time and memory, but also demands an organisation of space. In turn, the space-time coordination would contribute to subject formation. For example, in May 2017, the Sharia minimarket cooperative set up the "212 Mart". In the course of one year, it opened almost 200 branches, over half of which are in Greater Jakarta.[7] As a profit-sharing cooperative, 212 Mart relies on community building. To open a branch, prospective investors need to receive support from at least 100 people in their vicinity. The supporting individuals in turn would become members of the larger 212 cooperative. The 212 Mart is not just an economic space, it is also a space for Islamic pedagogy. The store pauses operations four times a day to follow *adzan,* the Islamic call to prayer. The store takes care to stock what is appropriate for a Muslim family: "if parents give money to their children to shop, they do not need to worry, as we do not sell alcoholic beverages, non-halal foods or cigarettes".[8] Furthermore, all the products in the store have received *halal* certifications from the Indonesian Ulema Council (MUI). For Muslim investors, the 212 Mart is part of an "economic jihad" understood to be striving for Muslims' economic independence and a business-oriented meritorious struggle that sides more with Muslims. The new term "economic jihad" represents not only a business strategy of competitiveness in the face of economic inequality, but also a quest for a pious religious subjectivity (Maulia 2020). The term already implies strands of Islam which are unlike local traditional Islamic practices, considered to be leading towards Middle Eastern strands of puritanism.

**Figure 7.4.**   212 Mart (photo courtesy of Frans Prasetyo).

The leader of the 212 Movement is Mr. Rizieg Shihab, who is also the co-founder and head of the *Front Pembela Islam* (Islamic Defenders Front or FPI), one of Indonesia's largest hardline Muslim groups. He has been living in self-imposed exile in Saudi Arabia since 2017. He claimed his travel to the Middle East was fulfilling his promise to God to celebrate the defeat of Ahok in the 2017 Jakarta Gubernatorial Election. But at other moments he said that he is "exiled by the ruling regime".[9] In any case, he fled a month before he was named as a suspect implicated in a pornography case. Shihab's followers consider his flight to Mecca as a performance of *hijrah*. In his own words, "hijrah for a strategy, hijrah to rise again".[10] *Hijrah*, like economic jihad, is a term that has only recently gained popularity. For the 212 group, *hijrah* means leaving behind secular and hedonistic lifestyles to adhere to Islam. At its core, an Indonesian Muslim writer explains, "the *hijrah* movement calls upon fellow Muslims to abandon their less Islamic way of life.... An opportunity to change into better versions of themselves, versions that are closer to God".[11] In any case, it is a term for self-transformation, for identity formation after an interpellation into a religious norm.

*Hijrah* indeed could be used to illustrate the subject formation of FPI members. The FPI is a vigilante group that emerged after 1998 following the collapse of Suharto's New Order. Its origins, however, are inseparable from the institutional history of Suharto's paramilitary state and youth organisations. When in power, the New Order state "raised" them to help maintain the regime's order and stability (Wilson 2008). After the regime's collapse and in the new climate of freedom of the post-Suharto era, the paramilitary youth organisations and their associated *preman* (street thugs) gained autonomous power. They were quick to adapt to the new socio-political environment; they have reappeared in various forms and in different justifications such as that of "defending Islam". We could say that with the shift of context, the *preman* of the Suharto regime performed their own *hijrah* to become fighters for Islam. Discharged from the state's custody, many *preman* converted to the FPI after observing the opportunity to become Muslim and fight for Islam in the post-Suharto era. In his study of the FPI, Ian Wilson was told by a member that: "Now, in the *reformasi* era, nationalism, defending the state (*bela bangsa*) and all that shit don't cut it anymore. It's the groups that are about jihad and fighting vice (*maksiat*) that are the way to go" (qtd. in Wilson 2008: 193).

Released from the state's patronage and finding themselves in a climate of Islamic morality that has increasingly dominated the post-Suharto era, many *preman* joined the FPI to "carry out the Quranic edict of *amar ma'ruf nahi mungkar*—commanding good and preventing evil" (Wilson 2008: 199). The FPI's targets are not limited to liberal secularism. The Front also criticises what it identifies as liberal Islamic groups, moderate reformers as well as cosmopolitan traditionalists such as Abdurrachman Wahid (from Nahdlatul Ulama) and Nurcholish Madjid (once an intellectual leader of the PKS), as it considers them to be impure or polluted and seeks to cleanse or purify Islamic identity by reforming public morality. Such a mission has been carried out in the form of vigilante actions against what they consider to be signifiers of Western decadence, including bars, nightclubs and pool halls. Such targets clarify the identity of "us" against "them". Since they target public spaces, there is a quality of spatial performance in their expression of outrage. Wilson observes that "targets are chosen to maximise public exposure for the group and draw attention to its existence, and for this reason FPI's actions often appear to be almost scripted" (Wilson 2008: 203).

For members who used to be *preman*, such a spectacle of attack against certain buildings confirms their new identity as defenders of Islam. They are no longer a *preman* for the state apparatus or individuals, but a "fighter for Islam". In the past, as *preman* they often had to hide, but as fighters for Islam, they appear legitimate in public as a fully distinct subject in white robes. And, as one says, "instead of getting into fights over some little thing, now I fight for Islam" (qtd. in Wilson 2008: 207). The series of 212 anti-Ahok rallies was an opportunity for these men to grasp. The series of religiously-charged rallies at the National Monument Square registers the idea that publicly-exposed bodies acting in concert in white robes is at once a national assembly. At these rallies, leaders spoke from a platform, chanting religious phrases and, together with the masses, seeing themselves performing a "revolutionary" action. Meanwhile, the location of the rallies offers a grand setting for the media as well as for individuals with their cell phone cameras to transport the street scenes to multiple locations. The space, the assembly and the camera, regardless of the numbers pro- or anti-212, all contributed to making visible bodies of the Islamists who were "everywhere", pressuring the Indonesian government to defend Islam.

If the social world is constituted by meaning (regardless of its truth value), and its analysis necessarily is interpretative, what can we make of a demonstration that is claimed to be not an act of democracy, but an expression of religiosity? The rallies were in defence of Islam, and it was presented as a sacred ritual to defend the nation. The demonstrators wore white robes, praying and chanting the *Takbir* in the form of an assembly at National Monument Square, which for a time seemed to represent Mecca or Medina. Perhaps for the 212 Islamist groups, the formal Islamic-oriented political parties (such as the PKS discussed earlier) have all failed to represent them. They thus "take to the streets" through a public enactment of a rally, claiming that they defend Islam since the political parties have failed to do so.

### Scene III: Discursive Appearances: The Visibility of Invisible Islamic Motorcyclists and Alleyway Mushollas

So far, we have seen how Islamist political parties such as the PKS and mass organisations such as the Islamic Defenders Front (FPI) enacted Islamist urbanism in and through informal assembly and formal appropriation of public space, respectively. Through space, they wielded a great deal of influence over the city government, pressing their agenda for political outcomes. In this last section,[12] I consider the third form of spatial performance, one that is *everywhere and nowhere* but contributes equally to the formation of Islamist urbanism. The notion of everywhere and nowhere suggests the geography of everyday life, which is often overlooked because of its presumed banality and polysemy. It also refers to a marginalised neighbourhood that "unnoticeably" exists at the periphery of any urban centre. It is, however, not existentially marginal as it is part of the everyday-scape of everyone living in the city.

I have seen many such geographies in major cities of Islamic Indonesia, such as the alleyway neighbourhood or *kampung*, a densely populated urban neighbourhood that is not cognitively or socially marginal. It is an elementary urban form of Indonesia that continues to dominate the urbanscape of most cities in the country, including the capital global city of Jakarta. These neighbourhoods are characterised by irregular and unregulated settlements and zigzag alleyways, and exist in various parts of the city, often behind the high-rise condominiums and luxurious shopping malls or between new housing complexes. Situated on land dominated by the informal market, the existence of the *kampung* is precarious and filled with uncertainty as the city continues to renew itself by gentrifying these areas.

**Figure 7.5.** A *musholla* in the middle of a *kampung* near housing complexes in West Jakarta (author's photo).

Yet, while uncertainty serves as the condition of *kampung*, many *mushollas* (a small place of worship either freestanding or attached to a building) continue to be built in the alleyways of neighbourhoods. The scattered *mushollas*, with diverse architectural styles, are everywhere in the *kampung*. They are built with commitment and democratically (or better discursively) either by wealthy religious elites or by the neighbourhood community, often through *waqf* (charitable endowment) and other donations without any monitoring from, or coordination with, the government or any formal religious institution. They exist outside the state's gaze. Some were built under a patronage system that connects formal and informal organisations. One could say that they are supported by both elite and popular informality. But does such existence give the alleyway *mushollas* the power to keep eviction or gentrification of the *kampung* at bay? Or should we say that they are built to provide a sense of certainty or to render vulnerability liveable? The *mushollas* are built, in contrast to the surrounding dwellings, in a manner that would remind one of power, prosperity and permanence. They are in proximity to each other (some are as close as 50 metres apart), and each presumably has a story or history of its own. They seem to compete with each other for influence, but they continue to co-exist with, or without regard for, each other. Is it because there are so many of them that the building type and creatively fashioned repetitive form elude attention?

The geography of *mushollas* seems to move with the *kampung*, whose territoriality is always being redrawn following urban renewal. Their geographies could be said to be invisible, as most are not on official maps. Mapping the *mushollas* is thus as challenging as knowing the hidden sociocultural order of things, the political economy and power relations behind their circulation. Questions emerge about style, expression and semiotics of signs as well as each of their roles in the *kampung*. How do we account for the emergence of a *musholla* in the context of the current self-displacement of *kampung* dwellers, moving out after selling off their (newly certified) lands to individual owners and property developers? What is the relation between the continuing construction of *mushollas* and the displacement of the *kampung*? This contradiction between erasure of the *kampung* over time and the continuous production of *mushollas* is a story of Islamist urbanism that demands a shift from the usual analysis of the public square or the mosque as a state-sponsored monument to the analysis of civil societal politics and the political economies of urban transformation.

A *musholla* is a place where inhabitants gather to pray, to study or simply to rest. One could also add, for the "back-alleyway" *mushollas*, that it can be a place for critical discussions on social and political issues. A designated sacred space is by no means a requirement for belief, as daily prayers can take place anywhere. The spirit of "anywhere" is essential as it frees people from any attachment to a place.

This detachment, however, does not mean inattention to orientation (to *kab'a*) or to the geographical imagination of Mecca as the "centre". It simply means that the geography of praying can be mobile and thus invisible. There is a strong sense of mobility enacted here, which makes Islamic practices simultaneously everywhere and nowhere.

**Figure 7.6.** Plan to build a *musholla*. The text reads: "Help us build Musholla Nurul Amal" (author's photo).

Discussing a comparable sign of mobility, Aryo Danusari, an Indonesian anthropologist and filmmaker, has identified a phenomenon he calls "urban circularity" wherein the lower-middle class Islamic youth use motorbikes to move around the city's roadways to both register their presence and the religious practice of Islam that goes with them in urban spaces (Danusari 2013). They regularly take over streets, parks and other public spaces attached to commercial and public buildings, congregating there to discuss religious and other social issues that interest them. Such "performance" makes urban space a matter of theatrical expression of the individuality and collectivity of the group. An Islamic youth could write his own motorcycle diary in the context of riding together in a performative assembly. Furthermore, behind this performance, as Danusari points out, is a sense of marginalisation among the lower-middle class youth in the city of which they are a part (Danusari 2013). Some of these youth work during weekdays in formal establishments such as offices and shopping malls as lower-level service staff, while others are freelancers working for their own informal enterprises. They perform on Saturday evenings (the secular time for hanging out) to register their own sense of religiosity against the Saturday-night scenes of the city. Members of the Tariqa Alawiya Youth Movement, as it is called, make themselves visible not through any particular geography associated with Islam. Their circulation around the city and the temporary occupation of different spaces in it depend not on the monumentality of well-known religious structures, but rather on their mobility through the urbanscape (via motorbikes for example).

In this performance of space, mosques and monuments have become slightly irrelevant. Geography still matters (as they choose mainly public sites, not just anywhere), but only so that the performance can *take place*. They do not, however, intend to practise "place-making", as they disappear after the performance. So what is left when the urban spaces come undone? Perhaps only impressions, memories and reminiscences of something happening, but not a permanent trace of them being here or there. The visibility of Islamist urbanism relies on its performance of "invisible" geographies.

What seems to connect the Tariqa Alawiya's motorbike movements and the proliferation of *mushollas* in the *kampung* alleyways is the profound fragmentation of the city. The Tariqa Alawiya's youth movement seeks to connect the divided city temporarily by way of moving around the city on motorbikes, at once jamming the regular traffic and replacing it with yet another stream of vehicles. Similarly, the *mushollas* are expressions of fragments that nevertheless seek to reach out, through an invisible network, across the divided city radiating from the existence of the increasingly marginalised *kampung*. All of these illustrative materials point to yet another invisible force at work, that of capitalism, which is transforming *kampung* while giving context to the appearances of Islamist urbanism in Indonesian cities.

## Conclusion

In this chapter, I have teased out three different ways in which Islamists interact with the urban built environment in post-Suharto Indonesia. I first considered how the *alun-alun* in Bandung was remade by the city's Mayor under the influence of the PKS, a relatively powerful Islamist political party, and how the neoliberal ethos of inter-city competition for creativity, the concept of a smart city and green urban space (championed by the Mayor) were ushered into Islamist urbanism. If Bandung was remade through its populist architect-Mayor supported by an Islamist political party, in the second scene the National Monument Square in the capital of Jakarta, with endorsement from its city's populist Islamist Governor, was turned into a site of interpellation for Islamists by means of a series of rallies and assemblies to call for an act to defend Islam. Unlike the Islamists of the PKS who shaped space from the height of Bandung's City Hall, the assemblage of mass organisations (in the form of the 212 movement) in Jakarta at the national square relied on the spectacle of Islamic bodies and the concomitant production of a climate of moral judgement and of a conception of life that calls into question the nation's religious pluralism. I also showed how the discursive practice of assembly has produced a new type of convenience store in the form of a chain of shops under the brand "212". If the first and the second scenes rely on references to notable public spaces such as town squares or national parks and convenient stores, the third scene, centred on the proliferation of *mushollas* in *kampung* Jakarta, makes its appearance simultaneously everywhere and nowhere. It concerns the mushrooming of *mushollas* in lower income urban neighbourhoods in different parts of Jakarta that is traceable only cognitively by going in and through the scattered *kampung* neighbourhoods in the city. Thus, *mushollas* present another site of Islamic interpellation. Yet, unlike the symbolically charged public square, the *mushollas* in the *kampung* can be expected to be more inclusive of religious pluralism as each is located in a web of everyday urban *kampung* life that historically has been characterised by pluralist co-habitation.

These scenes are brought together to suggest a link between discursive and non-discursive institutional formations in the mutual articulations of Islamist urbanism. While the effects of spatial performance as a signifying method of identity formation are indeterminate and difficult to trace, it is fair enough to say that Indonesians are capable of recognising the emergence of Islamism, which is being triggered by its multiple appearances. This chapter shows just how the formation of grand events such as 212 rallies could generate microevents of 212 economic jihad in different locales; how the spectacle of public spaces and the beautification and regulation of their uses by design could catalyse political and popular support and lend credibility to Islamists' leadership in the City Hall; and how the rise of Islamism might have encouraged the construction of *mushollas* by unclear agencies more or less everywhere in the marginalised neighbourhood of the kampung. The spatial discourses presented here are assembled in a chained montage to gain a cognitive sense of Islamist urbanism. Whether they figure as threats or inspirations, it is clear that Islamists have both shaped and been shaped by the built environment of which they are a part.

The emergence of Islamist urbanism may be a result of the disjuncture between the city and the nation. Along with the twists and turns of socio-political and environmental crises, it seems logical to think that for Jokowi, Jakarta has gone beyond the point of no return. But the situation may not after all be so disastrous, for the wave after wave of "creative destruction" offers nevertheless an opportunity to imagine a new form of capital city somewhere nearer the geographical centre of the country, to begin or to complete the quest of nation-building.

# Notes

[1] As cited in Francisca Rosana, "Heboh Desain Masjid Al Safar, Ridwan Kamil: Diapresiasi di Arab", Tempo.co, 3 June 2019, at https://bisnis.tempo.co/read/1211846/heboh-desain-masjid-al-safar-ridwan-kamil-diapresiasi-di-arab (accessed 3 Oct. 2022).

[2] On 10 December 2021, prior to giving a Friday prayer sermon, Muhammad Oded collapsed suddenly and shortly afterwards he was pronounced dead at the hospital.

[3] The Superhero Park was built primarily for children. It includes a variety of Marvel and DC Comics heroes, such as Batman, Spiderman and Superman, some heroes from the Wayang world of Java, including the *Mahabharata*'s Gatotkaca, and local heroes such as Gundala Putra Petir [Gundala, the son of thunder].

[4] "Dialog Ridwan Kamil ke netizen soal Bandung yang dianggap kota maksiat", *Kumparan.com*, 6 Sept. 2018, at https://kumparan.com/kumparannews/dialog-ridwan-kamil-ke-netizen-soal-bandung-yang-dianggap-kota-maksiat-1536236983414930071/full.

[5] Sheany, "Understanding the 212 Movement", *Jakarta Globe*, 17 April 2018.

[6] "After Repeatedly Denying Responsibility, Governor Anies Admits to Permitting Anti-Ahok Protest Anniversary at Monas", *Coconuts Jakarta*, 30 Nov. 2017, available at https://coconuts.co/jakarta/news/repeatedly-denying-responsibility-gov-anies-admits-permitting-anti-ahok-protest-anniversary-monas/ (accessed 5 Oct. 2022).

[7] "212 Mart Gains Traction with 192 Branches in Past Year", *Jakarta Post*, 29 Aug. 2018.

[8] Sarah Yuniarni, "212 Mart: From Street Protests to Local Convenience Store", *Jakarta Globe*, 26 March 2018.

[9] As cited in "I Am 'Exiled by the Ruling Regime', Rizieq Claims as he Greets Anti-Ahok Rally Reunion Crowd", *Jakarta Post*, 2 Dec. 2019.

[10] Lalu Rahadian, "Rizieq Shihab klaim hijrah bukan lari dan sembunyi", *CNNIndonesia.com*, 19 Aug. 2017, available at https://www.cnnindonesia.com/nasional/20170819100615-20-235800/rizieq-shihab-klaim-hijrah-bukan-lari-dan-sembunyi (accessed 5 Oct. 2022).

[11] Hamdan Hamedan, "Hijrah Movement: A New Wave of Islamic Piety in Indonesia", *The Muslim500.com*, available in https://themuslim500.com/guest-contributions-2022/hijrah-movement-a-new-wave-of-islamic-piety-in-indonesia/ (accessed 14 Nov. 2022).

[12] The "third scene" is drawn from my earlier essay titled "Invisible Geographies in the Study of Islamic Architecture", *International Journal of Islamic Architecture* 5, 1 (2016).

Chapter

**8**

# Escape from Jakarta:
# The Future Redux

On 30 April 2019, soon after an election in which he won a second term, President Joko (Jokowi) Widodo announced a plan to move Indonesia's capital city away from Jakarta and the main island of Java to Kalimantan.[1] The reasons he gave were not surprising to anyone who has lived in Jakarta, and as indicated in the previous chapters, they include afflictions of flooding and subsidence (it is one of the fastest-sinking cities in the world), overcrowding, traffic congestion, environmental degradation, conflicts related to identity politics and other problems associated with governing such a megacity.

Other Southeast Asian countries have recently built new capitals: Myanmar's military regime relocated from Yangon to Naypyidaw in 2005, and Malaysia's administrative offices moved from Kuala Lumpur to Putrajaya in 1999. But Indonesia's vision of moving the capital has a longer history. We could ask: why did the four most-noted Javanese presidents—Sukarno, Suharto, Susilo Bambang Yudhoyono and now Jokowi—all consider the idea of moving the capital from Jakarta? Did their interest stem from perceived crises of their time and the need for a new "exemplary center" (Geertz) to restore their power? In any case, the idea of building a new capital city has long been an important part of Indonesian political culture, even if such plans rarely come to fruition.

## Turmoil in the Realm

Moving the capital city would hardly have been unprecedented in Javanese history. In 1745, a Javanese king called Pakubuwana II moved from his fallen palace of Kartasura to the nearby village of Surakarta. The old palace was in shambles as a result of internal royal conflict, rebellion, wars and political intrigues involving Javanese and Chinese populations and the Dutch East India Company (also known by the abbreviation "VOC", the Vereenigde Oostindische Compagnie).

The *Babad Giyanti*, an eighteenth-century chronicle, uses the term *daharuning praja* ("the turmoil in the realm") to refer to this time of disaster (Pemberton 1994: 30). It describes in detail the king's procession to the new capital.

The king brought with him not only his family, religious officials and servants, but also the Dutch company commandant and troops on horseback. Most important were the king's grand carriage, named Kyai Garuda after the mythical bird, his heirlooms and a banyan tree, all of which were believed to channel sacred forces that would strengthen the king's authority. Only then could he restore his position as "the nail of the universe" (the literal meaning of Pakubuwana).

The ritualistic move was needed to transform the reality of defeat into an expression of progress. Moving the capital elsewhere and leaving the old ruins behind were a means of overcoming the "turmoil in the realm". But this wasn't a revolutionary attempt to construct a new society. It was a restoration of an old, declining kingdom that was forced to accommodate the rising power of Dutch colonialism.

In Indonesian studies, Pakubuwana's procession is known as an enactment of what the anthropologist Clifford Geertz called an "exemplary center", a spectacle designed to provide reassurance that the universe was still in the king's hands. Today, this legendary move is considered the key to the establishment of Surakarta—which happens to be Jokowi's birthplace and the city where he served as mayor before moving up to Jakarta. For Jokowi's supporters and the Ministry of National Development Planning (Bappenas), today's reasons for moving the capital stem from constant "turmoil in the realm". In a May 2019 interview, Bambang Bodjonegoro, the head of Bappenas, proclaimed: "Java is overburdened, Jakarta is exhausted".[2]

Even if it would not be appropriate to connect the twenty-first-century experience of Jakarta with that of the eighteenth-century turmoil in the realm, the sense of the inevitable recurrence of disaster and renewal demands a reassembling of past instances especially in connection with the dream state of a nation. Jokowi would never wish to learn from any Pakubuwana, but he wouldn't mind finding inspiration from the first President, Sukarno. When asked to identify five figures who have inspired him, Jokowi said: "Bung Karno, Bung Karno, Bung Karno, Bung Karno, Bung Karno.... I always remember Bung Karno's *Trisakti* (the three magics): self reliance in politics, economy, and culture".[3] For Sukarno however the *Trisakti* demands material symbols:

> Man does not live by bread alone. Although Djakarta's alleys are muddy and we lack roads, I have erected a brick-and-glass apartment building, a clover-leaf bridge, and our superhighway, the Djakarta Bypass, and I renamed the streets after our heroes: Djalan Diponegoro, Djalan Thamrin, Djalan Tjokroaminoto. I consider money for material symbols well spent. I must make Indonesians proud of themselves (qtd. in Abeyasekere 1987: 210).

## Sukarno's Dream

Sukarno's call for building "Jakarta into the greatest city possible" so that it could be "an extraordinary place in the minds of the Indonesian people", is well known (ibid.: 168). What is rather less known however is that at around the same time, in 1957 and again in 1965, Sukarno formed a committee called *Panitia Agung* (the Grand Committee) to plan a future capital city on the island of Kalimantan, to be named Palangkaraya. The site, at the time of Sukarno's visit, was still a village called Pahandut populated by about 900 Dayak people in the middle of a wilderness (Van Klinken 2011). The President first launched the construction of Palangkaraya through an inauguration of a monument to mark its status as the provincial capital of Central Kalimantan. The new name was derived from a combination of the Dayak "palangka", meaning a sacred place or, in Sundanese, a throne, and the Sanskrit "raya", meaning great. Sukarno then proclaimed: "Let the city of Palangkaraya be the modal and model [for Indonesian cities]" (qtd. in Wijanarka 2006). The master plan and drawings of the new capital city however have never been found, and the political history of this city-building effort has yet to be written, but the idea of moving the capital city to Palangkaraya stemmed from Sukarno's chief advisor, Semaun, the first chairman of the Indonesian Communist Party (PKI), who suggested to the President that Jakarta was "genetically defective" for it was built by the Dutch in the interest of colonial power (Vltchek 2018).

Sukarno favored Palangkaraya for it is geographically located right in the centre of the Indonesian archipelago, symbolically fit as a site for a new exemplary centre of power. It would also become a "socialist city" given the involvement of Soviet engineers and funds. But Sukarno's aspiration was never fulfilled.

By the end of the 1950s, after securing funds from the United States and the Soviet Union, as well as a war reparations grant from Japan, he put aside his Palangkaraya dream and instead launched the construction of a series of monumental structures designed to make over Jakarta as a new "exemplary center" in time for hosting the 1962 Asian Games. Sukarno wanted Indonesia to be seen as modern now, not later. After hosting the 1955 Bandung Conference of Asian and African nations, he decided to "build up Jakarta as beautifully as possible . . . as spectacularly as possible" so that it would be "an inspiration and beacon to the whole of struggling mankind and to all the emerging forces" (Sukarno 1962a). Yet, while building up parts of Jakarta with modernist architecture and urban forms to overcome its colonial structure, he made a rather odd reference to Brasilia, as if haunted by his unfulfilled desire for the Palangkaraya project: "I referred to Brasilia, Brazil's capital city ... which used to be Rio de Janeiro, but the decision was made to relocate the capital city to be in the middle of the country... The land was empty. There were only trees, but it now has a grand city called Brasilia designed by famous architect: Lee Meyer [read: Niemeyer]'" (Sukarno 1962b).

Sukarno's plan was part of a nation-building project. It embodied the dream of a new future in a country devastated by years of colonial occupation, war and revolution. It expressed determination to overcome the colonial past, but it was also a response to the immediate political environment of the early independence period, in which Jakarta had become an arena of conflict between communists, Islamic groups and the US-backed military.

Sukarno's reconstruction of Jakarta thus was an attempt to quell turmoil in the realm in the context of decolonisation. But unlike the eighteenth-century restoration of Pakubuwana's kingdom, the refashioning of Jakarta was meant to be revolutionary. The city was conceived as the site for both the symbolic construction of the nation and the enactment of Third World liberation.

Sukarno believed that architecture was capable of revolutionising culture. The state also intended the spectacle of a new "exemplary center" to legitimise its power. Yet despite the effort to rebuild Jakarta as a beacon of modernity, by the time Sukarno was forced to resign in 1966, inflation, poverty and unplanned urbanisation had reached alarming levels.

## Marketing Fantasies

In the 1980s, proposals emerged to move the capital city to Jonggol, a subdistrict of Bogor Regency in West Java, 40 kilometres from Jakarta. President Suharto (who held power from 1966 to 1998) had dispatched his sons to work with private developers to acquire or grab some 30,000 hectares of land for building new towns in the area. He sought opportunities for expanding political patronage at the frontier.

By the mid-1990s, Jakarta was already showing explicit signs of an environmental crisis. It was nicknamed "the project city" in a nod to development driven by profitmaking calculations. Class disparity was increasingly visible in the cityscape. Devastating floods and paralysing daily traffic jams contributed to the deepening sense of trouble in the realm. While Jakartans recognised the threat of Jakarta's subsidence, it didn't lead them to voice their concerns or demand solutions through mass protest. They knew nevertheless that the city was unsafe, the streets dangerous and that anything could happen at anytime.

For their part, metropolitan media, such as (middle class) newspapers, depicted the city quite negatively. Most of their reports emphasised crime and disorder and showed no confidence in the ability of the city government to overcome the problems. This atmosphere of uncertainty and fear suited Suharto's military regime. Public and private security measures multiplied. Neighbourhoods were necessarily secured by *hansip* (security personnel), and community night watch. Businesses and new towns favoured gates, security guards and local *preman* (thugs). This security boom came in tandem with the privatisation of urban space. This has had a profound impact on the way people in Jakarta have lived their urban life and felt at home with a gated built environment.

By the time Suharto stepped down, the patterns of exploitative urban development had developed into environmental disaster and open conflicts. Social unrest has become more evident. There is no easy fix for Jakarta—it is probably too late. But it is still possible to squeeze every remaining opportunity, extracting profit from disaster.

The best indication of this practice of disaster-turned-opportunity is how the real-estate industry markets developments in greater Jakarta. Since the 2000s, advertising themes have been organised around the idea that Jakarta is deteriorating, and the only recourse is to "escape" from the city to privately run garden estates on the outskirts. They promise self-contained, gated new towns or "superblocks" built on elevated ground to avoid flooding.

This is not primarily about excluding the underclass (who can enter the enclaves as workers and service providers), but rather about creating an illusion of distance from environmental disaster. Superblocks are touted as having all the required facilities for upper-middle-class working and living, so residents will hardly need to leave the complex and confront the problems of the sinking city. In more extreme cases, this "anti-Jakarta" tendency takes the form of land reclamation projects off the coast, or visions of moving the capital elsewhere.

By the time of Yudhoyono's presidency (2004–14), it was clear that Jakarta had gone terribly wrong. With no real improvement on the horizon, the only easy way out was to imagine, once again, an escape from the city. Toward the end of 2010, he declared that the seat of government should be moved so that it could become "the real capital, the real government center, like Canberra, Brasilia, and Ankara".[4] The President favored Sukabumi and Purwakarta so that the new capital could be located in what would become Greater Jakarta.

A team of experts convened to explore the idea of moving the capital. Andrinof Chaniago, the most outspoken member (who later became the head of BAPPENAS during Jokowi's presidency), said Jakarta was carrying "too heavy a burden".[5] The team's plan, Vision Indonesia 2033, strongly favoured moving the capital to Kalimantan, a relatively underdeveloped region, but also degraded by resource exploitation. There, a "new epicentrum" could be built, which would help Kalimantan catch up with other regions.

We seem to have come full circle. Jokowi is proposing a similar idea that recalls the eras of Sukarno and Yudhoyono. While Jokowi's understanding of moving the capital perhaps could not escape the force-field of Sukarno's influence,

I am not sure if Jokowi's proposal stems from a wish to retrieve what is being lost to history. I would argue that Jokowi's proposal is embedded within the context of his relations with his "mental revolution", Jakarta and its urban politics. In the following sections, I build a web of connections between the urban political traditions against which Jokowi and Ahok defined their "new Jakarta" and the idea of moving the capital city.

## Gaming the Gap

Supporters of moving the capital city have pointed out that because Jakarta was built by the Dutch, it never had a visionary and comprehensive urban development plan. Indeed, Dutch colonialism produced only a fragmented spatial organisation. Batavia was never planned along the lines of Dutch ports like Amsterdam or Rotterdam. The colonial state was mainly interested in profits and lacked the political will to design a city. Attention to planning was limited to certain areas occupied by Europeans. The parts of Batavia where Indonesians lived were left alone. A considerable section of the population was made up of slaves divided into different ethnic groups. When environmental problems in the coastal sections of Batavia led to deadly epidemics, the colonial regime simply abandoned that quarter and moved the capital city inland to a more spacious and healthful area (Blusse 1985). The ruins of Batavia were used to build a new governmental complex. Yet the move was again marked by a piecemeal planning process that prioritised European concerns. The country villas of the Dutch enclaves were constructed with modern sanitary arrangements, but most of the population lived in poor conditions with no basic infrastructure. Urban development in Batavia was generated by a system of free enterprise; individual initiatives superseded collective will. That aggravated problems caused by the lack of land regulation and town planning. Common in reports on Indonesian towns in the colonial era were concepts such as "untidiness", "disorder" and "disintegration" (*Toelichting* 1938). There was nothing to learn from the past. There was never a comprehensive planning process to guide urbanisation.

However, the Dutch legacy of Jakarta is just one convenient nationalist story behind the dream of building from scratch a fully planned new capital city. There are other considerations or political conjunctures that might have contributed to the idea of escaping from Jakarta.

First of all, the truth about postcolonial Jakarta is that it has had no lack of government policies to regulate its land, traffic and rivers. The problem is that they have not always been implemented as planned. For instance, during Suharto's era, there was an Urban Master Plan for long-term growth, an Urban Regional Section Plan for medium-term expansion and Detailed Plans to control development at a local, block-by-block level. Permits were required for projects associated with each of those levels, but the regulations were often ignored, bargained over, or manipulated.

This gap between policy and implementation was not unintended. The loopholes in regulations and flexibility in practices were designed to allow transactions that would yield extra benefits for insiders. The gap also gave rise to a form of brokerage based on local norms and informal institutional networks that connect government officials, business groups and military personnel with local leaders, land brokers and thugs. Policy implementation is structured by these practices of informality. Over time, they became a way of working, a "tradition" that constitutes the political culture of urban development.

The association of Jakarta with weak government or lack of planning thus is inaccurate. Law enforcement may be inadequate, but this doesn't mean that the city lacks the capacity to govern. The lack of planning indeed can be understood as an art of governing, for it ensures the operation of informality. This form of statecraft enforces a regulation only when it is deemed necessary by a consensus of the informal network. By the end of Suharto's rule, that tradition of informality in urban management had been firmly established. It evolved among the government, the military, businesses and other official and unofficial local players. The fortunes of Jakarta's commoners are shaped within these multiple dimensions of agency and their gaming of gaps between planning and implementation.

This tradition has survived the Asian financial crisis [*krisis moneter*] at the end of the 20th century. The game continues to work to "harmonise" different social groups, ensuring mutual support and shared benefits without jeopardising the authority of the post-authoritarian government. And in many cases, it also helps civic organisations and commoners operate in the city. The urban poor are occasionally accommodated by the gap between policy and implementation: it allows low-income groups to develop their own capacity to build their residential areas incrementally and informally, as long as they don't undermine the interests of the ruling elites. The *kampung* dwellers are left to manage their resources and built environment with some discursive help from the government.

## New Urban Politics

The tradition of gaming the gap, power sharing and elite informality inherited from Suharto's time is so strong that it is difficult to determine whether the city government of Jakarta, despite decentralisation, has had its own formal political life.[6]

The collapse of Suharto's dictatorship in 1998 has nevertheless opened up popular politics. The experience of Lieutenant General Sutiyoso as governor of

Jakarta signalled the opening of this new chapter. When he was in office under Suharto, he saw his job as simply following the orders of the president who had appointed him. But soon after Suharto stepped down, Sutiyoso was shocked by street protests against him that erupted almost every day. He was perhaps the most embattled governor in Jakarta's history.

A regional government law enacted in 2004 has pushed popular politics further from the street to the city hall. The law provides for the direct election of the governor. Now politicians can succeed only by winning popular support. This shift from presidential appointment to direct election has made it possible for someone with no political base among the national ruling elites to become governor. Jokowi (before he became president) and his former deputy, Basuki Tjahaja Purnama (known as Ahok), are good illustrative examples. They started with no existing politics of rent-seeking. Their political style was populist, and their urban management approach was organised around issues of social tension and environmental degradation.

As discussed in Chapter 6, to win the heart of the *rakyat* (the ordinary, relatively poor people), Jokowi and Ahok promised cards that would provide access to the health and education systems. They pledged to build low-cost apartments and promoted a slum improvement programme. They criticised the gap between City Hall and the people, and they found a way to communicate with the urban poor. They showed their confidence that the government was capable of financing social welfare projects as long as there was no corruption. In the 2007 gubernatorial election, their populist approach was successful due in large measure to the contrast they made with the incumbent governor, Fauzi Bowo, who symbolised the old elite establishment.

When Ahok assumed the governorship upon Jokowi's ascent to the presidency in 2014, the two sought to bring together the city and the nation in a new way, that is to improve governmental capacity to collect tax and distribute it as public goods. By doing so they sought to undermine the entrenched legacy of the Suharto New Order. The oligarchic tradition, as discussed earlier, combined large commercial interests with state power in a system of interlocking formal and informal relations. Jokowi asserted that these arrangements had produced only a culture of "corruption, intolerance of difference, greed, selfishness, legal violations, and opportunism".[7] During his 2014 campaign, Jokowi called for a "mental revolution" against this system. He pushed for reforms to create a more accountable bureaucracy as a basis for carrying out their populist agenda. The rise of Jokowi and Ahok in Jakarta showed that the majority of voters desired radical change. They were also fed up with perennial problems such as flooding, traffic congestion and inequality. For them, such urban ills were more important than issues of ethnic and religious identity. But that soon changed.

## The Fall of Ahok

If he had not been Jokowi's deputy, it is unlikely that Ahok could have won the governorship on his own. His rise and fall illustrate the peculiar position of the ethnic Chinese minority in the history of Jakarta—and Indonesia. Indonesia's ethnic Chinese have long been considered "not national enough", due in no small measure to the legacy of colonial policies that endorsed racism and discrimination. Categories that separated ethnic Chinese (known then as "foreign orientals") from the indigenous population were institutionalised by the colonial regime and lived on under the discriminatory assimilation policy of the postcolonial state. Suharto's regime perpetuated an idea of the Chinese as the ethnic other who controlled the nation's economy, despite the fact that many are extremely poor.

Such stereotypes resulted in a long history of violence against the ethnic Chinese, starting with the 1740 Batavia massacre (Blusse 1981). This minority nevertheless played a major role in Jakarta's urban development, as developers and builders as well as commercial bourgeoise. Its members paid for the construction of Batavia's City Hall, built the city's wall, dug its first canals, and in modern-day Jakarta developed many megaprojects, often in collaboration with Indonesian political elites. Their contribution to the city was both accepted and resented. While some were economically powerful, all but the connected few were political pariahs.

As the first ethnic Chinese and Christian governor of Jakarta in decades, Ahok drew controversy. Being an outsider, he cared little for the old bureaucracy. He brought an image of clean, disciplined and efficient governance to City Hall. His record of bureaucratic reform and urban development won him support from voters. Yet by undoing the entrenched legacy of the Suharto era, he also created many enemies. Resistance from the old forces took various forms, such as rejection or slow consideration of his budget plans.

Faced with this obstruction, Ahok looked for other sources of revenue that did not require approval from the city council. He negotiated with business groups, as his predecessors had done, but he openly pressured them to provide more funds that could be used to finance infrastructure such as roads, parks and low-cost apartments. This brought him into disfavour with business leaders and those who were comfortable with the old way of operating the city.

Meanwhile, his campaign of urban transformation forced *kampung* residents to register with the government for benefits, disregarding their tradition of autonomy and anonymity. His administration carried out mass evictions in flood-prevention operations, contradicting the pro-poor populist approach that had brought Jokowi and him to power. He also undercut the influence of independent *preman* brokers by taking over their field of operation and reorganising marketplaces for street vendors. He installed parking machines, revitalised traditional markets and built more shopping malls for vendors as well as to some extent (following Jokowi's approach as Mayor of Surakarta) repairing their carts or offering them new ones. This had compromised or eliminated the role of *preman* in the city. It reduced thuggery, but it also displaced the very identity of *preman*, that is their freedom to rule the streets.

Ahok's political enemies exploited every critique directed at him. To stop him (and weaken Jokowi's presidency), his political enemies targeted his Christian Chinese background. Meanwhile the rise of China made his position more complicated as it raised the spectre of Chinese domination in Indonesia. In the lead-up to the 2017 Jakarta election, Ahok's Islamist opponents mounted a series of mass demonstrations, denouncing him as an enemy of Islam. He was charged by prosecutors with blasphemy, and ultimately convicted and sentenced to two years in prison.

The fall of Ahok marked the rise of Islamic identity politics. Suppressed under Suharto's regime, Islamic groups have now entered the mainstream politics of the city and the nation. Their opposition to Ahok led them to unite in a movement called Alumni 212, becoming a major force behind antigovernment rallies. But they lost cohesiveness after Ahok's fall; their orientations and activities remain diverse and often depend on the political parties they can latch onto in a coalition.

By then, it was clear to Jokowi that the web of power relations established under the Suharto New Order is not easy to dismantle. It implicates every level of society, and it grows by incorporating new technology and practices. With Ahok, he has tried to reform by establishing an accountable bureaucracy and formalising civic and economic relations. However, undoing the old system also entails uprooting local communities whose livelihoods have become entangled with the informal power networks.

Jokowi was reportedly rattled by the protest against Ahok whose case was seized by his political opponents to hold anti-government rallies. Confronted by this challenge, Jokowi worked to win over major Islamic leaders and their organisations. He visited many Islamic boarding schools. He ordered the Ministry of Public Works and Housing to build flats for the schools in Padang, a major Islamic regional capital of Sumatera where he didn't win in the 2004 presidential election. And finally he chose the head of the Indonesian Ulama Council, the country's largest Islamic organisation, as his running mate for the 2019 election. By abandoning Ahok and co-opting the Islamists, Jokowi managed to stay in power.

## Yearning for Utopia

It finally feels like it's come full circle. The city has gone beyond Sukarno's dream of it to become "the greatest city possible". This is more than just a gap between a dream and realities. It is a mismatch between they city and the nation. For Jokowi, Jakarta's time is up. It was the congestion. It was the flooding. It was the sinking. It was the urban politics. It was all of them. The city can fall, but not the nation. On 16 August 2019, a day before Indonesia celebrated its 74th Independence anniversary and just a few weeks before being sworn in for a second term, Jokowi made the proposal in his state of union speech at Parliament: "I thereby request your permission to move our national capital to Kalimantan... A capital city is not just a symbol of national identity, but also a representation of the progress of the nation. This is for the realisation of economic equality and justice. This is for realising *Indonesia Maju* (progress). For Indonesia to live as long as possible".[8]

This is a yearning for a new "exemplary center"—one that presumably would be defined by its contrast with Jakarta, by the memory and current reality of the "turmoil in the realm"—one that could be planned and appreciated from a safe distance. But what would happen to Jakarta without the nation-state?

Some supporters of relocating the capital are yearning for another utopia. They are confident that Jakarta would not only survive, but also prosper once relieved of the burden of being the seat of government. They promise that Jakarta will be like New York, where property values never fail to rise—that it will be in a strong position to compete with Kuala Lumpur, Bangkok and Singapore as a regional financial centre. They have faith that the invisible hand of the market will not only save Jakarta from sinking, but also fulfill its potential as a city of capital.

## Notes

[1] Ihsanuddin, "Kepala Bappenas: Presiden Setuju Ibu Kota Jokowi Putuskan Ibu Kota Negara Dipindah ke luar Jawa", *Kompas*, 30 April 2019.

[2] Septian Deny, "Wawancara Khusus Menteri Bambang: Ibu Kota Baru Jadi Identitas Bangsa", liputan6.com, 31 May 2019, at https://www.liputan6.com/bisnis/read/3980834/wawancara-khusus-menteri-bambang-ibu-kota-baru-jadi-identitas-bangsa.

[3] Desi Angriani, "Lima Tokoh Idola Jokowi: Bung Karno, Bung Karno, Bung Karno, Bung Karno, Bung Karno", medcom.id., 29 July 2014, at https://www.medcom.id/nasional/politik/eN4WJ0wK-lima-tokoh-idola-jokowi-bung-karno-bung-karno-bung-karno-bung-karno-dan-bung-karno.

[4] "SBY: Pindahkan Ibu Kota Solusi Kemacetan", *Kompas*, 3 Sept. 2010.

[5] Tim Visi Indonesia 2033, "Pemindahan Ibu Kota ke Kalimantan: Lorong Keluar dari Berbagai Paradoks Pembangunan, menuju Indonesia yang Tertata" [Moving the Capital City to Kalimantan: An Exit from Developmental Paradoxes Towards an Orderly Planned Indonesia], at

http://perpustakaan.bappenas.go.id/lontar/file?file=digital/211340-[_Konten_]-Konten%20
E3602.pdf.

[6] Okamoto indicates that unlike other Indonesian cities, which have two tiers of government (the provincial and city levels), Jakarta has the status of a province, with one elected governor to oversee the city's five territories and one district, each of which is managed by a mayor appointed by the governor. The central government's rationale for not holding direct elections for the mayors is to prevent local politics from destabilising the capital city. The implication of this arrangement is that local concerns are largely unheard or are given lower priority by the governor. Consequently, Jakarta's electoral politics is more relevant for national elites than for the inhabitants of the city. See Okamoto 2013.

[7] Fabian J. Kuwado, "Jokowi dan arti 'Revolusi Mental'", *Kompas*, 17 Oct. 2014.

[8] Chandra Gian Asmara, "Ibu Kota Pindah ke Kalimantan, Ini Pidato Lengkap Jokowi", CNBC Indonesia, 16 Aug. 2019, at https://www.cnbcindonesia.com/news/20190816114218-4-92474/ibu-kota-pindah-ke-kalimantan-ini-pidato-lengkap-jokowi.

# Chapter 9 | Jakarta: A Conversation

## Urban Politics and Governance

*Question (Q): Can you paint us a picture of how Indonesian cities are changing today? What makes them such exciting sites of research?*[1]
Abidin (A): Indonesian cities are recognisably diverse, but Jakarta (our focus here) is the capital city, the political centre of Indonesia and the site for capitalist modernisation. It is naturally a site where changes are most rapid and visible especially in the urban form, but at the same time we could say that the city seems never to have changed. Spatially, more and more spaces are being opened up by property developers to signify development, but this is accompanied by the growth of new *kampung* in unexpected places, despite the demolition and displacement of the old ones. Such production of space is highly dynamic but it defies a linear view of time and space. The old persists in all that is new—the new and old layers co-exist. A friend suggested that contemporary transformation of urban space, in the form of mixed-used superblocks, has constituted another layer of urban form on top of as well as within the existing ones. He calls this new layer a fifth layer, suggesting that previously Jakarta had four layers of space that co-existed uneasily over a long period of time (Santoso 2011). He could also add more layers as we progress, but the recent addition might find itself integrated into the existing one, raising thus a question of how we should conceptualise the idea of "change".

Perhaps it should come always with a footnote or another set of concepts such as layering, incorporation, hybridisation, co-existence or transformation, complete with notes about the inherent paradoxes in bringing these concepts to bear on a complicated subject such as Jakarta. The easy answer to such a condition is the perceived "disorder" which for some is due to the lack of planning or law enforcement. It is striking to read the report of the "Visi[-on] Indonesia 2033", launched in 2008 prepared by Adrinof Chaniago who served in the administrations of both presidents Soesilo Bambang Yudhoyono and Joko Widodo. The report basically proposed to move Indonesia's capital city from

Jakarta to Kalimantan. The title ran: "Moving the Capital City to Kalimantan: An Exit from Developmental Paradoxes Towards an Orderly Planned Indonesia" (see Chapter 8, endnote 5). It points to the absence of "order" and "planning" in Jakarta and says that the only path available is to escape from the city. Yet the lack of order constitutes a kind of rule, a form of governance, a statecraft that works in and through different actors that cut across the formal and informal institutional cultures. Perhaps it is like a hidden order that grows out of disorder—an order that expresses itself in an assemblage of power relations and different interests that are not always compatible and are often paradoxical. Yet they constitute a logic of rule that is at the same time opened for contestation.

*Q: In times of democracy, what are the external ideas or drivers having an impact on the development of Jakarta—which are today's major external forces, as you see them?*

A: If we consider democracy to be an external idea that is taking root in Jakarta, such an idea takes a local form. It is not only about political participation, but also about the "liberation" of the city from the dictates of the nation-state in making decisions about urban development. This changing relation between the city and the nation is often seen as a result of decentralisation of governance where the municipality is assuming more agency and taking more actions. This development, as we know, is also happening in other parts of the world. It is associated with the withdrawal of the state and neoliberalisation of the city. Jakarta too is undergoing such a change, although some argue that for Jakarta, decentralisation means only delegating administrative authority to the municipality while the urban developmental paradigm continues to follow the national agenda. In other words, the municipality utilises its new-found authority by mobilising what it finds useful from national policies instead of creating its own framework on behalf of its residents. The governor of Jakarta for instance could choose to please or undermine the central government through certain urban programmes for his own political career. The influence of the national government, being located in Jakarta, is considered extensive and capable of overcoming the territorial limit of a city government. We thus see Jokowi reasoned his decision to run for president (while serving as Jakarta's governor) as a means of coordinating the different surrounding regions to solve Jakarta's *banjir* [flooding] and traffic problems. As a capital city, Jakarta had to share its "autonomous" power with the central government which stands above the city. Since Jokowi became president of the country, a new trend in times of democracy has emerged: the position of Jakarta's governor is a great jumping stone to become president of the country.

*Q: So, to what extent has the city "freed" itself from the nation-state?*
A: There are local elections to choose the head of local government, including the governor of Jakarta who in turn appoints civil servants. Along with this is the emergence of a new style of local politics where politicians can gain (politico-economic) power with little support from the central government. For instance, Ahok (Basuki Tjahaja Purnama), a Christian-Chinese from outside Java, became governor of Jakarta, although he went directly from his vice-governor post to that of governor. Ahok and Jokowi [former governor before becoming President of Indonesia] are both clearly products of this policy change. And recently (2017), academician and former Minister of Culture and Education, Anies Baswedan, after being ousted by President Jokowi from his cabinet, returned as governor of Jakarta with the political support of a coalition of parties, including Islamic groups, that are critical of the President. Such a dynamic was unthinkable during the time of Suharto.

*Q: Is the city fulfilling a mission that the nation-state has failed in, such as delivering good governance? Can you talk about this in relation to Ahok?*
A: It is interesting to examine how Ahok legitimised his method of governing through use of the jargon of "good governance", which included transparency, accountability and, to a lesser extent, participation. All of these leave us with an impression of the rise of new civic and democratic values, but they are actually "popular" values, which are not always the same as "people's" values. Popular values are often translated into populist programmes—ironically hierarchical—that give free education, free health care, almost free bus rides and low apartment rental costs (to compensate for eviction), as we had seen in Ahok's administration. Decentralisation has given rise to such popular performances of the city government. The capital city has become the arena for the representation of popular values.

*Q: Populist politics, especially during electoral campaigns, generally start with complaints about social divisions and injustices, such as unequal access to collective urban resources such as land, water, and public facility or infrastructure. In what way did Ahok (or Jokowi) and even Anies follow this path as governor of Jakarta?*
A: Issues of fairness, justice and equality were indeed part of political campaigns, but populist politicians also know very well the limits to addressing such issues. They understand that people will continue to complain about public services, as they are demanding more and more services. So, over time, politicians would generally look for "popular problems" that they think cut across different groups and reach a broader audience. They would look for what they think are their main supporters and eventually their attention shifts from the urban poor to the

middle class, who are complaining not so much about poverty, social divisions and injustices but more about issues relating to the condition of urban space, the environment and sustainability: flooding, traffic jams, pollution and green space. In the end they create what they imagine to be their broad support base. Environmentally related sustainability has increasingly become the base of populist politics, displacing livelihood issues that have been the main concern of the urban poor. And so it follows that the populist politician seeking election/re-election will incorporate environmental issues into his platform. What is important for populist politicians is the *idea* of fairness, justice and equality, which could be used only for political campaigns as a counter image, for they knew perfectly well, in *practice*, fairness, justice and equality are contextual, relative, and political. Today it seems to me the era of Jokowi and Ahok is being presented by Anies Baswedan as contributing nothing other than furthering social division, inequality and injustices. But "equality" and "justice" are favorite terms for campaigns against the present incumbent, easily mobilised by populist politicians to gain support from the people, but once they hold office, they know that inequality and injustice are hard to seriously deal with.

*Q: What other new practices legitimise the rule of a populist politician, and what implications might they have for the city?*
A: With decentralisation, a city like Jakarta can behave as if it can exist on its own. So it seeks a brand which will help it emphasise its strength and distinctiveness, to look unique, dynamic and new, but mostly along the lines of the popular "global city" paradigm. This is why we see businessmen, corporate managers, celebrities and creative people running for governor or mayoral positions. We should not be surprised too, to see Ahok, for instance, using managerial language like "results", "rewards" and "performance" in his speeches on urban governance. The city leader can also be rewarded not only by re-election by the people, but also by the state, which offers national budget funds based on performance. This has given rise to a politics of time in which the governor is constantly chased by time; he must act and show quick results, as speedy completion has become the sign of success. Bringing works to completion seems to sustain popularity; the key concern is how to gain influence within a very limited period of time. The implication of such politics for the city is seen in what kinds of urban programme or project are prioritised, and who or what is left behind. For instance, the focus on mass evictions from *kampungs* on the riverside, as a quick "solution" to urban flooding, tends to ignore the more time-consuming investment in a participatory approach to reach cooperative negotiation with communities or in collaboration with authorities in the outer regions where headwaters are located. In some ways, one could

argue that Jakarta is not like Solo, or Ahok is not Jokowi. Ahok considered his method acceptable within the format of government as an institution with legitimate power to use force to secure what is considered "public interest". Unlike Governors influenced by Suharto's tradition of rule, he didn't use the middle power, i.e. the *preman* [thugs] which he sought to eliminate. Instead he mobilised the military and the police, and this in effect created a spectacle of a binary contrast of domination versus resistance on the street. On the other hand, in Jakarta, the long history of "criminalising" the *kampung* has also made it relatively easy for the authorities to evict *kampung* residents, even though the cost is high, not only materially but also socially and ultimately politically. It is nevertheless seen as strategic because it can be done speedily to show the government's performance in tackling various issues at once: flooding, land use, housing and green space all in one shot.

*Q: Why do you think Ahok had so much support even though he had failed in his re-election bid (2017)?*
A: I think the support that Ahok was gaining is not due to his eviction of *kampung*; people were actually very nervous about this even though the middle class in Jakarta largely supported the act on the grounds of river normalisation and better physical environment for *kampung* dwellers. The support was due to the reforms he had implemented in City Hall, including disciplining his own staff. He is also known for his strong anti-corruption stance which he demonstrated in front of the Jakarta City Council (DPRD-DKI) that sought to manipulate the budget plan. He knew how to save time and money to restore the power and popularity of City Hall. Indeed, when Jokowi and Ahok took over City Hall in 2012, they knew that if they wished to move fast in their programmes, seen as central to the legitimation and sustenance of the platform on which they were elected, the greatest challenge would be ensuring the capacity of the bureaucracy to implement them. Prior to Ahok taking over initially as Deputy-Governor, municipal staff were widely known as being less than energetic. They normally slowed things down. They knew that they would be in their positions longer than the governor, so why bother moving fast? In the past, there were empty desks after lunch hours, no staff in attendance. But in fact, the staff was not lazy, instead they were very active, they were doing their own business inside or outside City Hall. They were *ngobyek* (doing individual projects). I am not sure what they were up to, but for sure they were not serving the public interest.

People also believed that Ahok's leadership would make a striking shift in the operation of City Hall. He was a graduate of Prasetya Mulya, a private institution of continuing education for those aspiring to become CEOs and who sought more efficient methods to manage companies. However, I think Ahok mistakenly believed that he could run City Hall like running a company. He believed he had the authority to direct his company, but the municipality is not a company. He thought he could fire staff, but often he had only the authority to reshuffle staff positions. What he could do was recruit new staff who would outperform the old ones. This way he could set examples and rules. This method has slighted many, especially senior bureaucrats who have an expectation of respect for the years of service they have given. Unsurprisingly, they don't like Ahok. They don't like being pushed around. And of course, members of the Jakarta City Council who were accustomed to underhand financial deals also disliked him. However, the urban majority who are tired of a lax civil service and corruption see in Ahok a reformist figure, and they fear that no other leader would do what Ahok has done—shake the bureaucracy and clean up the apparatus from within. They supported Ahok I think for such reasons, but we should note that many supporters remained ambiguous and disapproved of Ahok's take on *kampung* (and would rather prefer a Jokowi-like approach) and his view that capitalism should be allowed to prosper in Jakarta as long as its profits are shared with the city (such profit-sharing however won't be enough to save the environment).

*Q: In 2017, Jakarta elected a new governor, Anies Baswedan. Could you reflect a bit on the broader political implications of how the campaign was conducted, the elements of identity politics and how this may affect how politicians in the future try to build popular support?*

A: One of the major components of populist politics is that it relies on having an enemy, imagined or real. We can see in the campaign how Anies Baswedan, in many ways self-consciously, formed himself by looking for difference. He preferred not to tackle issues in the same way (or not tackle issues at all) for fear of alienating his supporters and jeopardising his larger political ambition. First of all, he played religion and race cards to win the election. He also sought to undo the practices Ahok had set. For example, he overturned Ahok's policies concerning flood mitigation strategies and the use of public spaces for motorcycles, food hawkers and city parks. He sought to rebuild the *kampungs* that were previously depopulated by Ahok. He sought to represent Ahok's pro-poor initiatives as being backed by big moneyed developers, against his egalitarian platform which he claims to be rooted in Islamic social values. Elements of "identity politics" (this term might not be received well by Muslims) inevitably played out, especially when a Muslim challenged a non-Muslim candidate. But this is also not new, as we just have to remember how Fauzi Bowo mobilised his "Betawi" identity when he bid for his reelection as governor against another Muslim candidate. What is significant nevertheless about Ahok is that he represents something that is hard to imagine, an ethnic Chinese Christian who is so close to the President of Indonesia and who might conceivably even become Vice President himself! It is worth remembering that Ahok alone would never have become governor of Jakarta had he not served as vice-governor during Jokowi's tenure as governor. When he moved on to his own re-election bid, he was already a figure to rally against, and he became a unifying force for people ranging from the old corrupt forces of Suharto to new Islamic hardliners who were looking for a "common enemy"; he was therefore easy to be put on the spot for the opposition groups to build a shared platform against. But such a platform is temporary. Some people believe that it was assembled in and through Ahok in order to challenge, if not to unseat, Jokowi.

What is crucial is what came after the "end" of Ahok. Would the assembly remain after the "enemy" had been defeated? Is Ahok the "real enemy"? Time has indicated that without Ahok as a frame, the alliance's attempt to challenge Jokowi had become transparent. We know that since then the government has banned the hardline group led by Rizieq Shihab for disrupting peace and security. In a way, Ahok served as a "resolution" in this war between Jokowi and the alliance. What happened to members of the once "anti-Ahok" group in relation to the new governor they have supported? Unlike Ahok, who could ignore them, Anies was indebted to them for his position. As a politician, Anies keeps them on his side. Indeed, he channeled funds from City Hall to Muslim organisations that he knows will defend his position simply because he is a "Muslim governor".[2] As we now know, every year he distributed grants (*dana hibah*) to mosques located in areas where he had won electoral votes in 2017 (Hidayat 2019). Future politicians will have to build their popular support by considering if such politics could be reconciled with Islamic values and with Jakarta's pluralism and diversity of Muslims. We have learned that towards the end of his term, Anies allocated some funds to church organisations to show that he is a figure of tolerance—an image that he badly needs to gain a wider support should he be chosen to run in the 2024 presidential election.

*Q: Has the disappearance of Ahok influenced the strategy pursued by the following city administrations in any way?*
A: First, we should acknowledge vice-governor Djarot Hidayat who was in charge of the City Hall before Anies Baswedan's tenure. Within a short period of time (i.e. four months) Djarot sought to deliver Ahok's "best" programmes to strengthen their legacy while making people remember that Djarot is not Ahok. (Djarot is anyway calmer and would have approached *kampung* issues quite differently.) He held onto the image of clean, uncorrupted and effective administration to the point that the incoming governor would have no choice but to carry the burden of responsibility to keep this legacy alive. He did that by establishing local regulations

(known as Perda) for on-going programmes, which include mass rapid transit, light rail transit as well as the so called "coordinated children-friendly public space" (*Ruang Publik Terpadu Ramah Anak*).³ He also tried to do the same for the 2018 provincial budget (known as *Anggaran Pendapatan dan Belanja Daerah* [APBD 2018]) and intended to consolidate a financial system that would prevent corruption. All these contributed to a standard of governance that Anies had to deal with. It is also hard to maintain as it came out of Ahok's sustained "creative destruction" of a very old and persistent bureaucratic tradition—a shake-up of an apparatus that could be politically costly. However, one would also imagine that failure to meet Ahok's new standards would be equally costly for any new governor thanks to Ahok and Djarot's successful branding of their administration to the public.

In some crucial ways, we can say that Anies' style of governing of Jakarta was profoundly shaped by the legacy of Ahok and Djarok. His efforts to undo the examples Ahok had set reveals only further the influence of Ahok. Programmatically, as a matter of fact, many of Anies' programmes carried the appendix "plus": Smart Jakarta Card+ (KJP+); Jakarta Health Card+ (KJS+) and Jakarta Elderly Card+ (KJL+). This means that many of their programmes were developed out of those initiated by Ahok and Djarot. But Anies also knows perfectly well the socio-political cost of following Ahok's more groundbreaking legacy. Some of his elite supporters expect a different style of governing, including a return to the old way of doing things. Thus, instead of alienating dominant members of Jakarta Council with Ahok's method, he pleased them by returning to the old bureaucratic tradition; instead of improving transparency and accountability, he opened a hole for corruption; instead of dealing with the thorny issues of Jakarta flooding which would demand that he relocate some settlements from the riverside, he preferred to offer a different concept in order to do nothing about it. After all, Anies managed to keep his culture of politeness. Maybe that's what he needed to stay in power, by reidentifying with the tradition established prior to Jokowi–Ahok. It is interesting to hear that as soon as he entered City Hall he sought to reconnect with governors from the pre-Ahok and Jokowi era. The consequence for Jakarta under Anies is the return of old actors such as *preman* and an old way of doing things, such as elite informality reproducing thus an art of governing of *zaman jahiliah* (to use Djarot's term referring to the age of ignorance prior to Islam) which has displaced the "era of light (*era terang benderang*)" that Djarot had established with Ahok and Jokowi. From this perspective, Anies' heavily reliance on Islamic supporters to the point of allocating budgets for radical Muslims is a case of his failure to meet Ahok's standards. He needed supporters who believe that his failure to meet Ahok's standard is a success story.

*Q: What does the imprisonment of Ahok mean for Jakarta?*

A: And also what does it mean to the nation? Some analysts see the jailing of Ahok in terms of Muslim and non-Muslim issues, and the imprisonment of Ahok means the end of Jakarta as a multiethnic and multifaith cosmopolitan city. But this simplification is somehow problematic. For sure, what happened to Ahok worries not only Indonesia's minorities, but also the majority of moderate Muslims and should not be framed as a Muslim/non-Muslim issue. It shows the rise of a particular form of political Islam that goes beyond what we have recognised in Nahdlatul Ulama (NU) or Muhammadiyah which refused to endorse the protests against Ahok (even though their members attended the rallies). It relates to the influence of the Prosperous Justice Party (PKS) which for a long time has sought to control Jakarta, but has been able to register its presence only in the surrounding regions of the capital, such as Bekasi, Depok and the Tangerang areas. It relates to the rise of vigilante groups such as the Islamic Defenders Front (FPI), self-styled leaders and other new Islamic multitudes with no affiliations to existing organisations or political parties. This includes those who learn about Islam through the internet, books and other discursive gatherings, those who create a mission for themselves to safeguard Islam. They may have serious disagreements with each other on various issues, but they would spontaneously mobilise to join a demonstration to defend Islam. So the framing of the issue in terms of Muslim and non-Muslim ignores the new formation of Islamic groups and also the diversity of Islamic forces.

What did the jailing of Ahok mean to ethnic Chinese? For some, what happened to Ahok is just another lesson in Indonesian history, that after the onslaught of Suharto's othering, politics is just not the thing for them. Others become very proud of being Chinese, that Ahok becomes the signifier of the fearless, the principled "political Chinese", and the embodiment of "true" Indonesian nationalism. In any case, Ahok inspired a young generation who moved from being "friends of Ahok" to forming a political party called *Partai Solidaritas Indonesia*. It is also interesting to see that the rallies staged by Pro-Ahok supporters (who are mostly non-ethnic Chinese) are accompanied by a cry for "NKRI (*Negara Kesatuan Republik Indonesia*)", the "unified nation" which suggests at once that Ahok signifies NKRI and that he fights against the forces that threaten to break up the nation.

But how about Ahok's own awareness of what it meant to be in jail? I heard from a friend that Ahok knew perfectly well, sadly for him and his family for sure, that the best option was to be in jail. He knew that Jakarta would become chaos again and again should he be freed. And this would put Jokowi in a much more difficult position as opposition against him would intensify—a situation that would in the end paralyse Ahok as well. The jailing of Ahok (and presumably also the ending of his political career) has at least relieved Jakarta for the time being from becoming the site of demonstrations against the government by Islamic vigilante groups with implicit support from the opposition. The opposition suddenly lost justification to stage demonstrations. And Jokowi for the time being is freed from charges of being pro-Ahok and anti-Islam, a condition that was crucial for him to secure a position in the 2019 Presidential election. Meanwhile the blasphemy law that was used to put Ahok in jail could also be used by the government to charge radical Islamic leaders who are widely known for occasionally humiliating other religions in their public speeches.

Finally, what does it mean to Jakarta? If Ahok were a governor elsewhere he would not have found himself in today's situation. People outside Java knew perfectly well what it means to have a local government that is clean and truly serves the public. They are fed up with their corrupt leaders. Jakarta however is a different place. It is a place that displays cosmopolitanism, but it is also the place where people have become narrow-minded and focused more on gaining and strengthening power through all kinds of political alliances and deal-making. The ruling elites care very little about the importance of having a good city or local government that serves the public. Many of them see the gubernatorial election as a proxy campaign for a presidential election, not so much a path for serving the public and creating a better place for everyone to live in the city. Jakarta thus has become more the jumping stone for those who are in power to keep their power, or for those who seek power to take over power. Big and small groups meet there to find fortune while rehearsing quite freely their freedom to express radicalism, racism and corrupt behaviour, for such practices seem to be what Jakarta has come to signify.

## Marginalised Inhabitants / The Urban Poor

*Q: What are the internal drivers that are having an impact on the spatial changes in the city? As you have indicated, there is often a notably populistic rhetoric in the way the political elite relates to the growing middle class and the huge group of marginalised/vulnerable citizens in Jakarta. My take is that the elite benefits from the marginalised social groups, and so they are included in the city through the work and services they provide. But will governments also meet their needs for a liveable city in any meaningful way? Will the needs of the huge number of marginalised inhabitants be considered in the future Jakarta? If yes: In what way will the elite pay attention to their needs and include the marginalised groups in the future of Jakarta?*

A: The kind of capitalist modernisation that operates in Jakarta relies on workers from semi-formal households. This is a workforce that works not in isolation or by exclusion, but by cultivating relations with their surroundings including the formal sector as Jakarta has become part of the circuit of the international division of labour. Workers in Jakarta sustain the regime of cheap labour as one or two members of their household would be connected to the shopping malls, office buildings or factories, while others are street vendors, maids, or micro entrepreneurs in the *kampung*. In other words, this is a workforce sustained by households with multiple sources of income that cut across the formal/informal divide. It sustains a condition that favours capitalist enterprises as labour costs can be kept low. One could argue that while *kampung* folks are self-sustaining through *gotong royong* (helping one another) they are subordinating themselves to capital. But what this also crucially means is that the multitudes of *kampung* inhabitants, while marginalised or exploited, are important forces for development itself.

The state is aware of the importance of semi-formal workers in sustaining a regime of cheap labour, which has become the pillar of support for development. The state is also aware that it has no capacity to take care of all the needs of the *kampung*. It thus has to rely on the relative autonomy of *kampung* folk to manage by themselves. The state is also perfectly aware that this *kampung* folk is the *rakyat*—the embodiment of Indonesian revolution. They cannot be ignored. The state has to show that it cares. During normal times, we thus see certain *kampung* programmes, such as sewerage upgrading and alleyway repair. Today, rewards are also given to green *kampung*, "clean" *kampung* or exemplary *kampung* (*kampung teladan*), and so on. One may imagine that some of the rewards come from funds generated by corporate social responsibility. At times of crisis, such as during the late 1990s and early 2000s monetary crisis, the state (after the fall of Suharto) is on their side for fear of unrest, such as by allowing many laid-off workers to occupy government owned "unused land" (*tanah terlantar*) including areas beside rivers and railways and under toll roads. These places quickly became *kampung*. In every *kampung* in Jakarta, we thus see a complex infrastructure—from transport to utility no matter how inadequate—that is neither formal nor entirely informal. It is difficult thus to say that the political elites ignore the poor and their *kampung*. The power relation is so subtle. It involves mutual help as well as mutual ignoring of each other. This kind of relation has a rather long history, going back, as some friends in Jakarta would argue, to pre-colonial times (though this would demand a different framework of analysis). The issue is that these workers from semi-formal households and the complex links they have established with the state and capital have made it difficult for them to unite as a political force against these sites of power. I think Jakarta will continue to rely on this power arrangement. The spatial manifestation of this arrangement is the everywhere-ness of *kampung* in the city, while distance between the city and the *kampung* is kept for ensuring propinquity. So, we may have to rethink our categorical assumptions to understand how exclusion is neither outside nor marginal to the operation of power.

*Q: But there is a growing group of vulnerable families in the city and, if measures are not taken, they are likely to become increasingly exposed to environmental and social hazards. Meanwhile, there are evictions and relocations, which mean more displacement. Is it likely that we will see any game changers, such as the cessation of relocation, more public services such as water, sewerage, public transportation, clean and comfortable public spaces, parks, clean air or schools and health care?*

A: Indeed, while earlier I emphasised the power arrangement where all social actors "participate" in mutual production and exploitation as an art of governance, the poor are clearly more vulnerable to social and environmental hazards. And they are normally targeted for eviction to "improve" the environment. So there is a profound unevenness in the operation of the "power sharing" system. The game changer of our time is the increasing importance of trans-local urban activists, NGOs and community leaders who work across different places. They have been working with vulnerable communities against eviction and displacement, using various tactics from protests and demonstrations on the streets to negotiations with authorities through litigation and political contracts. They organise affected communities so the struggles for the rights to the city can be heard and can lead to improving the social and physical environment of vulnerable families. While their struggles are meaningful, the approach is often framed locally and rather narrowly so problems receive only patchy and temporary solutions, but this seems to be the framework that works at this juncture.

Unlike cities in core countries, historically Jakarta (like many postcolonial cities) has never been provided with a universal infrastructural ideal. Given the current domination of the neoliberal developmentalist idea, there is a reason to doubt that a universal infrastructural ideal could be implemented in a city that has long been built on (uneven) deal-making between capital, the state and a divided civil society. All the public service items on your list would be subjected to such negotiation that a remedy of one item could mean a harm for others on the same list. The "river normalisation" programme is believed to be the best way to mitigate flooding in the capital even though around 8,000 residents are living along the Ciliwung riverside. So, the eviction or relocation that comes with the programme is framed as both saving the riverside settlers from environmental hazards and restoring the urban ecology. Yet, even with this understanding, the government knows perfectly well that relocation or eviction is materially, socially and politically costly. It is not a sustainable course of action. Furthermore, the administration alone won't be able to financially support it. What it has been doing is to use business corporations to help finance relocation, so low-cost (rental) apartments are built by funds from corporate social responsibility and parks are built by developers. This was the arena in which Ahok found himself and which he helped create. One would have expected an invention of a different game from

Anies as he wanted to be *different* from his predecessor. But he was left with no choice other than continuing Ahok's policies and practices or do nothing at all. He seemed to prioritise the latter to buy time by initiating different conceptual thinking about the nature of water flow which, after knowing that it still demands eviction or relocation, he preferred to do nothing about.

We have a social formation that enables all the public services to be put on the table for political calculation. When public services need a political contract with politicians, this enacts patron–client relations that are hard to sustain. The players are familiar with such a game of time, of temporising. They know the problem and also the benefit of keeping the game and playing it. To outsmart it by building a universal infrastructural ideal in which public services are for everyone is not without political risks. Therefore, I doubt that universal infrastructural ideal will ever become part of the deal, not within the time frame of our generation.

## Cities (Fragmented) from Below

*Q: If cities are for a large part created "from below", then how could politicians and city planners work with this knowledge, and perhaps integrate it in their planning—or will that always be impossible?*
A: I think politicians and planners know that our cities are indeed created "from below" and I also think that they have integrated this knowledge into their "private" planning. What is more challenging is planning "from above", truly serving everyone—a public realm, from water and transport to health and schools, that serves the public. We haven't had that tradition. We are only accustomed to planning "from below" if that could include the legacy of divide and rule from colonial times. We need to first unpack the notion of "from below". If cities are created "from below", what is "below" is not in fact a singular.

Historically, a large part of Jakarta developed "from below" along different paths, different markets, different norms, different traditions, different attachments and a different sense of place, and this has given the city a "thousand dimensions" (Seno Gumira Ajidarma [2004a; 2015]). We can picture a constellation of "plural societies" in colonial times in which people lived together but apart, where they could only imagine unity in fragmentation. What can we learn from or how can we intervene in such a fragmented space "from below" and save it as an alternative source of knowledge for well-intended planners?

From this perspective, what came from below has historically been seen by well-intended politicians and planners as unsustainable, so there have been great experiments throughout Indonesian history in which "supra-local" spaces have been created. This was what President Sukarno attempted to do in Jakarta during decolonisation. His main concern was the unsustainability of fragmentation, the tyranny of diversity at the time of decolonisation. He felt a need to imagine a united nation by creating a new space "from above". Many of his messages to architects then were about how space could unify the imagination of the public that we are "one nation"—sharing the same feelings and living in equality (*sama rasa sama rata*). This can only be understood in the context of the profound segmentation of the city left behind by Dutch colonial power, which had ruled by dividing the city. But, as we also know, the modernist experiment, alas, was limited to a spectacle of an "exemplary center". It has failed to create a universal infrastructural ideal. The modernist space "from above" has only furthered spatial division and inequality in the city. Jakarta continues to be dominated by the rule of fragmentation from below in the hands of private business groups, communities and residents who secure their own spaces with little coordination from above. It is far more difficult to plan from above for the interest of the "public realm"—if this can be agreed on. So it seems more challenging to plan from above than from below. Jakarta has only a tradition of creating cities "from below", one that contributes only to serving private interests.

But it is important to keep researching attempts by politicians and planners to plan from above by way of coming to terms with conditions from below. We can take note that there were some instances of planning "from below", not so much via participatory approaches but when planners and politicians consider the *kampung* as a neighbourhood to reckon with. In the 1960s and 1970s, there were attempts to contextualise design so that the new neighbourhood would adapt to the local spatial fabric of the *kampung*. The streets then were not designed for cars to pass through. They were more like an extension of the *kampung* pathways. A few of these early productions can still be seen today, but the paradigm was soon defeated in the 1980s by the developers' version of real-estate planning, which was focused on accommodating automobiles. Since then, the city has been organised around the flow of cars. The *kampung* began to be seen as backward, and not as a space for design inspiration. It is considered at best a "space of transition" that will give way to the "modern city". The upgrading of certain *kampung* neighbourhoods, known as the "kampung improvement programme", was never an influential paradigm for planners. The programme fell apart when more *kampungs* needed upgrading.

Over time, "from below" became a term for forces of the other that are at once functional for and feared by politicians and planners in their efforts to create defensible spaces. For instance, in the aftermath of 1998, what was produced right after the push for "reformasi" was a series of spatial reforms that were quite undemocratic: the fencing of a public park, the eviction of the poor, the proliferation of gated communities and concessions to urban development that have degraded the environment. Such disjuncture—democratic reform and undemocratic space—has a lot to do with the history of ruling through the fragmentation "from below". *Reformasi* has produced more spaces from below, but it hasn't yet produced any universal infrastructural idea that would serve the public. If planning from above means the provision of a universal infrastructural ideal for everyone, I think it is not a bad idea. It would be revolutionary.

*Q: If we find that civil society actors are key players in urban planning but are also fragmented and not all steered by the same political agenda, then how can activists— be they inhabitants or external actors wanting to "do good" for the vulnerable—work with civil society in constructive ways?*

A: Conversations among activists, architects and planners have often led to the challenge of locating one's position in the fragmented whole. For such a position to be meaningful, it needs to be positioned in relation to other positions. It may be also useful to reflect further on the question of fragmentation in Indonesian civil society by positioning such fragmentation in the context of Indonesian political culture.

Indonesian historiography is generally marked by elite politics and one could also imagine that planning history, if it is not written critically, would be restricted to descriptions of planners making plans for the city, but the reality is that the city is built by many actors. Meanwhile developers have been portraying themselves as the master builders of the city and the nation. Politicians, developers and planners (to a lesser extent) are powerful actors, but they are fragmented. Like the urban majority of the lower middle class who are often (mistakenly) not considered players, even if they constitute a bloc, they are internally fragmented. So, how could activists work under such circumstances?

Historically, the postcolonial city was dominated by an authoritarian state that was formed by a coalition of political, military and economic elites that sought to control civil society. Yet the sphere of civil society is large, and it consists of multiple layers of agencies ranging from workers, middle class entrepreneurs and the urban poor operating in a relatively autonomous domain, even if they are not entirely outside the state and capital. They are connected to the elites in a division of labour that is both international and local, but they are also left alone to self-manage their own survival. Their relationship with the state, the political elites and the business group is ambiguous and complex. If members of civil society constitute a bloc of their own, they are internally divided along the lines of class, ethnic and religious identities. There are norms however that govern their relations which bring coherency and tolerance to the sphere, but they are not always fully integrated into the elites' leadership.

For the state to "control" these multitudes, it would need to sub-contract its power to a range of relatively autonomous local leaders consisting of religious leaders, *oknum* (shadowy personalities related to the state) and *preman* (thugs), among others, who often play important roles in mediating between the state and civil society. During the regime of Suharto, these "brokers" served as a conduit of patron–client relations for the state to maintain order, harmony and stability at the very local level.

Indonesian civil society, from the colonial through to the post-colonial era, has thus been formed in this context of indirect rules. It recognises the power of hierarchy—top-down leadership via local agents—but it also self-manages below the government. A shared vision can be achieved within this order by way of coercion or persuasion, through the instruction from above (*atasan*) or initiatives from below, as long as they contribute to the order and stability of the political realm. Activists, whether from inside or outside, would find themselves operating within this architecture of power relations. If they are able to find a connection with figures within the system, they may work quite well to save a *kampung* from eviction (see the case of *kampung* Kali Code in Yogyakarta or the current discourses on the political contract). This is the kind of civil society we have had (a good point of comparison would be with the "political society" of Partha Chatterjee). Any activist would have to work in and through this structure, and not so much by setting civil society against the state.

In the post-Suharto era, such a structure continues to operate. Power is still in the hands of the political elites, but they are relying more on forming alliances to maintain their position and they often operate on the basis of difference. They are competing with each other while forming alliances to overcome the uncertainty of the democratic post-authoritarian era. They harness the multitudes of civil society and they nurture certain values and interests to win support. And the result is a map of power that is less clear. The state may have less authority due to decentralisation, but it is still a major force and a throne to fight for, especially by the political elites from old and new times. Ambitious politicians are keen to use the realm of civil society for their own career development, that is to win election. They fragment further the already fragmented sphere by supporting certain groups after a political expediency. Thus, the realm of civil society is both more fragmented and more powerful. It is increasingly harder to imagine the shape of civil society in which activists work. Activists who wanted to do good work could end up supporting a regressive urban agenda which first appears as progressive. Working only "from below" I think is inadequate because the political culture of Indonesia is fluid.

*Q: What seems to have brought the past and present together is the site of struggle, the kampung which remains the site for "doing good" for the vulnerable. Can the kampung be seen as the site for building "civil society"?*

A: You are probably thinking about "civil society" as a domain of sociality where activities are aimed at preserving the common good in opposition to money and power? I was involved in a research project carried out by Tarumanagara University in Jakarta to document the changing character of different *kampung* in Jakarta in the post-Suharto era, and we have been wondering along the same lines—that is about the possibility of a civil society forming in the *kampung*. Our starting point then was the idea that what is at stake for most of the *rakyat* (the common people) is the chance to live and to prosper (*sejahtera*) in the city. And we also recognised the fact that most vulnerable groups happen to be living in a *kampung*. In other words, *kampung* is still the only settlement that is capable of accommodating the *rakyat*. We also recognised that a form of social organisation (be it top-down or bottom-up) has long evolved in the *kampung* regardless of all the changes that have taken place. As noted earlier, *kampung* folk work by pooling household incomes and community resources and in doing so they cultivate a capacity for self-management. This raises the question of whether *kampung* could be seen as a space of hope for the formation of a "civil society" that transcends individual or group interests and is concerned with the "commons" as a basis for attaining prosperity for all. Behind this identification is our critique of the visions promoted by developers through their privatised "new town" and gated neighbourhoods in the city which we consider "uncivil" if not anti-urban. One way for us to re-imagine the city then is to consider the *kampung* as a possible site for building civic society, even though such a proposition entails the risk of projecting *kampung* beyond its reality.

We have first to accept that there is a broad range of *kampung*. Geographically there are *kampungs* that are closer to the centre, to money and power, such as the CBDs. These *kampungs* survive by serving the activities in the core, to the degree of building starred hotel-like accommodation in the *kampung* to accommodate the managerial staff of office buildings. For this type, what we have gathered so far are not sequences of resistance against eviction, but "symbolic resistance" from accommodation to commodification. What we found is less a formation of class solidarity, and more a collection of individual collaborations, "self-evictions" and bourgeoisification of the *kampung*. A most profound change is the certification of *kampung* land, the process that has meant the dissolution of the informal land market that used to sustain the commonality of *kampung*. The transformation of the land status is carried out through persuasion because occupants tend to feel more secure with "*hak milik*" (ownership rights) as they can sell their titled land at the formal land market price. This is a form of displacement by possession.

This I think is a more serious form of displacement or relocation that is carried out voluntarily by the *kampung* land owners. The survival of Jakarta's *kampung* increasingly depends on the degree of its gentrification. The closer it is to CBDs, the higher its commercial value. High-end rental units are being built in different parts of *kampung* to accommodate the managerial class in the nearby CBDs. We are now seeing a new kind of *kampung* in the city that is populated not by the vulnerable. The people who live in this gentrified *kampung* represent a group of new "civil society" and they may appropriate a type of old *kampung* lifestyle.

There are also *kampung* that are most vulnerable. This is partly because they are located along the riverside and, under a regime of environmentalism supported by the middle class, they are subjected to eviction. What we have learned from the range of urban activism by well-intentioned community organisations and NGOs is that they don't want to leave an impression that confrontation or demonstration on the streets is their way of working. Instead they work to negotiate with government and politicians to secure a place for the poor *kampung* to co-exist in the city. They work through papers and laws as well as political contracts with politicians looking for voters. In some cases, this method works. This is more like a "political society" that Partha Chatterjee theorises about. In any case, Indonesian civil society is never quite a separate domain, as it has been part of the state with which it must find its position and negotiate on issues. I think it is only in and through the state or government that a *kampung* can be integrated into the urban fabric (including the infrastructure), not as the other but as a constitutive part of a whole, as it has been. Whether *kampung* can serve as the site for "civil society" is an interesting question but we would need to reckon with the diversity of *kampung*.

## Asian Urbanism

*Q: The twenty-first century has also been called the "Asian Century", in contrast to the preceding "American century", which was dominated by the global spread of the American way of life and its urban forms. The strategies for development are likely to change now with investment interests and other technical solutions emerging from an increasingly powerful Asia. The earlier modern mainstream American forms of urban development with superhighways and huge CBDs that have marked Jakarta may come to an end. Maybe this will be replaced with solutions that require less urban travel, as we are seeing the dismantling of the "car society" in some OECD countries and new forms of urban planning emerging in Europe. What is the significance of the growing importance of the Asian world region in the "Asian Century"?*
A: The "Asian Century" is also understood as the rising influence of Asia, which refers more specifically to the rise of China and the possibility of a new hegemonic power in the region. Hegemony, as we know the concept, refers to a leadership

that is influential economically, politically and culturally. A new hegemon might consist of a cluster of nation-states or a single nation-state, and its influence could be regional instead of world-wide. I am not sure if China is becoming a world hegemon when it is barely capable of dealing with its own internal challenges, from income inequalities to environmental issues. Regionally, we see an increasing Chinese investment in Indonesia, in Greater Jakarta. This is an important phenomenon to try to understand because it raises the question of whether a new development model may challenge the existing capitalist modernisation led by the US. But we often forget that the recent influx of capital from China is not unprecedented. We have already seen the investments by Japan, Singapore, Taiwan and Korea in the construction of Greater Jakarta, many of which relied on the car civilisation of the US.

It is certainly an interesting hypothesis that the rise of Asia would produce a different strategy of development, or should we say, the production of a different kind of space, or space being produced differently. The notion of "difference" has indeed occupied academics as well as policy makers in registering the rise of Asia. However, such interest in the rise of Asia does not necessarily mean the decline of the urban development paradigm. What we have seen is a version of neoliberal developmentalism where the Asian states continue to play a major role in shaping the condition of capitalist modernisation. The Chinese government, like Indonesia's for instance, is perfectly well aware of the unsustainability of continuous economic growth. The authorities are worried about the environment. Yet the idea of copying Los Angeles in order to become part of car civilisation is far more powerful than say, continuing the tradition of bicycling. Car civilisation is discredited in some OECD countries, but it is still living on in Asian cities. It is in this context too that "inter-Asian" cross-referencing is actually still mediated by the car civilisation of the US, just as certain local governments in Vietnam, acknowledging the historical tie with the Indonesian revolution, preferred the Indonesian developer to build new towns in the peri-urban areas of Hanoi. And this developer, Ciputra, is known in Indonesia as the promoter of car civilisation. What can we expect from the outcome other than the reproduction of car civilisation as it is evolving in Asia, its exceptional form, some might argue?

The question of influence raises another issue of whether a measure taken in one place works in other places where the same conditions do not exist. Could Indonesia create the conditions that have enabled OECD countries or Singapore to build differently? Would Indonesia follow the Chinese government in its response to the elite corruption or pressures from the subordinated class? A lot of regional sharing of new urban ideas is focused on a particular project with no connection to change in social formation. It assumes transferability regardless of historical conditions. According to this assumption, the urban form that Singapore has taken is seen as a "model" that can be copied and pasted onto cities in China, India or Indonesia without the historical conditions that have produced Singapore.

*Q: Are there any lessons that Jakarta or other Asian cities have learned from the new directions in planning, such as decreasing car dependency, that we are seeing in some OECD countries?*

A: Jakarta has been formed through a series of quotations and appropriations of different practices, for better or worse. So anything new in the OECD (or in cities of the Global South) would not escape potential inclusion in Indonesian globalising practices. For instance, right after the collapse of Suharto's order, Governor Sutiyoso picked up from the Brazilian city of Curitiba the idea of creating an exclusive bus route known in Jakarta as a busway.[4] He knew perfectly well that in the new era opportunities to become popular were great. By comparisons with a subway system, the busway offered a "quick fix" and it could be appropriated quite easily. In Curitiba, the busway and the BRT (bus rapid transit) system were introduced to serve populations at the periphery so that they could gain access to the city. Sutiyoso reversed this order and brought the busway right into the centre of the city to showcase his dedication to "public transport". Did he initiate a new planning culture? It is hard to tell, but environmentalism is widespread today. It became a fully-fledged slogan under Governor Fauzi Bowo. We can call it "bourgeois environmentalism" as the notion of "green" became trendy among the middle class. The city was decorated with billboards of real estate companies promoting properties with names associated with "green". The idea of "back to the city" promoted by developers in order to build a series of "superblocks", a mighty high-end commercial complex where residents could have everything they need, is just another example of environmentalism. These complexes offer "green living" to Jakartans who believe that these complexes can relieve them from the hassle of the maddening traffic. Imagine a short walk away to the all-in facilities. These are all initiatives that on the surface seem to aim at dismantling car society, but at a deeper level they are more like a "spatial fix" for continuing capitalist modernisation with an ecological face.

## Environmental Politics

*Q: Jakarta has several vulnerable features, such as growing inequality and the many environmental issues. What do you think will come out of these issues?*

A: It may be worth noting that "environmental issues" entered the consciousness of the urban middle-class population only rather recently. The majority of the upper-middle class and ruling elites, sustained by the media, became concerned only after seeing that their CBDs and housing complexes, as well as the presidential palace, could be inundated so regularly. The expansion of the geography of flooding from *kampung* to the planned areas of the city has shifted the discourse from that of modernisation to the possibility of enhancing sustainability. This is not to suggest that there was no environmental consciousness prior to 2000. We have had a "Ministry of Environment" since the Suharto regime, but only recently has the urban become the site for all agencies to think about the environment. In Jakarta today, environmental issues are being framed in the urban context, which ultimately shows how ill-equipped the city government is for dealing with such issues. The outcome of this is that tackling environmental issues often involves placing the blame on the urban poor who live along the riverside.

The "growing inequality" issues, on the other hand, have had a longer history. They gained recognition soon after Independence. Back then, Mr. Mohammad Hatta, the first vice-president, already proclaimed his intention to create universal "housing for all" to stop the growth of inequality carried over from the colonial era. However the issues of growing inequality were contained for many years under the relatively successful state ideology of "development", which preached "stages of development". In other words, inequality was seen as a tolerable stage of development. Central to this understanding is the idea of social mobility, of moving upwards, which also meant moving to the city—to Jakarta—to turn the wheel of fortune. The state tolerated or even promoted rural and urban integration. So people from the countryside would migrate to the city or peri-urban areas to serve as labourers in construction and manufacturing generated by the influx of Foreign Direct Investments. Many migrants stayed in *kampung* settlements, which were then seen less as a space of inequality and more as a "space of transition" or perhaps a "space of hope" for a better life. In this sense, *kampung* serves as a stabiliser of what is otherwise a profoundly uneven development of capitalist modernisation. It is also seen as an antidote to (not just a product of) inequality.

The emergence of the environment as a critical category has a significant impact on the way in which inequality is understood and handled. In this instance, urban poverty, a signification of inequality, is seen as an environmental issue. *Kampungs* on the riverside, for instance, are seen not only as a manifestation of inequality but as also causes of environmental degradation. "If you wish to have no *banjir* [floods], then you wouldn't want the riverside to be occupied", the governor would say. For the governor, relocating people from *kampung* to apartment buildings thus tackles issues pertaining both to the environment and to inequality. Instead of seeing *kampung* as a space to moderate the contradiction of development, the *kampung* today is seen as a place of "padkumis" (padat, kumuh dan miskin – crowded, shabby and poor) —an embodiment of inequality that threatens the well-being of the city (Musni Umar 2015). We therefore hear statements such as "People would chose eviction if they realised they would get better homes, more comfortable bedrooms as well as parks and a healthy environment".[5] So while issues of inequality are linked to those of the environment, one is used to displace the other.

*Q: Will there be more sustainability or smart city development in Jakarta despite the fact that such developments are considered both modern and attractive but also an externally imposed, top-down continuation of colonialism rather than as responses to the local values and the needs of lower-middle class kampung families?*
A: In the belief of the governor of Jakarta, sustainability and the smart city concept are what the city is aiming at. Towards the end of 2014, the governor launched the Jakarta Smart City (JSC) programme, but in fact it was first introduced during the tenure of Governor Sutiyoso. The system was operational only after Rama Raditya, the CEO of TerralogiQ (an information technology company initially working for the retail and property sectors and supported by Google) approached Ahok. The Governor was interested in the capacity of technology to collect data not only from mathematicians and researchers but also from the public through their complaints about their living conditions. The governor had sought to enhance "transparency and public participation" so that everyone in Jakarta acts as a *warga*, a citizen. Today *Pak lurah* is not used to mean the head of a district. Instead the term "manager *warga*" is used, and this is not just a regular *warga*, but a smart *warga*, who has a smart phone to help manage the city. During Ahok's tenure, a popular magazine summarised what it means to be a *warga* of a smart city:

> Jakarta residents can feel proud, for now they can participate in managing their city. All they need is only a smart phone (*ponsel pintar*) in their hand. All the problems they see in their environment (from smelly rubbish and unauthorised banners to potholes and clogged drains) can be instantly reported to receive an immediate response.[6]

The magazine also indicated that every day, the system installed in the smart city programme records between 3,000 to 5,000 reports. If we consider how the smart city programme relies on smart phones, which have become more and more affordable, we can immediately see its attraction—the programme is built on the idea of a "direct" communication between the ruled and the ruler. The extent to which the programme is central to the everyday life of *kampung* families is debatable, but it seems clear that the public is being asked to participate in e-government, which has disciplined the civil servants as well as the *warga* who are invited to take responsibility for the policies and actions of the authorities, including the violence embedded in the decisions.

*Q: How do you think the national and city governments will handle the city's Achilles' heel, namely, the impact of climate change on society and the fragile environment?*
A: The national and city governments are aware of Jakarta's vulnerability but they focus on something else that is often seen as more critical, namely development and economic growth. They accept that Jakarta is suffering from a "chronic illness", the care for which comes periodically through responses such as "river normalisation", bringing back green spaces and so on. Yet such responses are carried out in order for the economic growth to continue.

In this era of climate change, the priority is still placed on economic growth. As far as the environment is concerned, the governments want to believe in the possibility of ecological modernisation: economic growth and environmental issues could work together in mutually beneficial ways. Under this paradigm, climate change and its impact on Jakarta are considered disturbances that threaten the ongoing routine of modernisation, but such a problem could be overcome by technological advancement, so the story goes. The reason for dealing with climate change is to ensure that the present speed of development could be accelerated. Today, the keyword for the government at all levels is "acceleration" (*percepatan*) of everything from instant services to programme results. With such a temporal framework, climate change occupies a different temporality. It requires recognition of the limits of growth, but such recognition contradicts the infinity of modernisation.

The governments will handle the fragility of the city in the face of climate change by recognising "disasters" as something manageable through a coordinated technological system. We can see this in the national law that followed the tsunami. It relies on response mechanisms and disaster management, as there is a whole industry offering such services. It relies on international disaster professionals, managers and industries which use climate change scenarios to introduce ways of reducing risks, such as through "contingency planning" and updating info and data in order to measure steps to be taken for the present and the future. However, such an industry is created to sustain ecological modernisation. It is designed to not question the unmanageability of the endless accumulation of capital.

## The City of a Thousand Dimensions

*Q: Scholars working on Jakarta seem perplexed by the gap between policies and implementation in the city. There are policies and the formal structures of governance, so why is there this discrepancy? There are partial explanations, such as corruption, bureaucracy, unclear mandates and the fact that several regions "intersect" in Jakarta. In our email correspondence, you mentioned undercurrents that are difficult to assess with planning theory or conventional methods. I would like to ask about the "undercurrents" that affect urban planning in Jakarta. Could you expand on what you mean by "undercurrents" and how you would suggest that the social sciences might explore their impact?*

A: What I have attempted so far is to suggest that there is a certain order behind the apparent messiness and fragmentation of Jakarta. Despite the apparent disorder, we heard that in Jakarta/Indonesia everything can be organised or arranged— *"semuanya bisa diatur"*. This phrase was first used by Indonesian vice-president Adam Malik in the 1980s. He referred to a way of working in which problems could always be resolved consensually to avoid conflicts. The phrase soon became popular but it is now vested with a different meaning—one that is associated with irregularity or informal deal-making to get things to work beneath the appearance of following the rules; such a deal could be "accepted" consensually to avoid conflicts. The term is still used today to indicate hidden practices that work, though one should ask: for whom? Today's politicians who seek to show that they are following the rules and practising good governance refer to *"semuanya bisa diatur"* as a practice of the previous era. I use the term undercurrents to capture the sense of *semuanya bisa diatur* that flows beneath the appearances of messiness.

I was also thinking about Suharto's New *Order* which is an ideology to ensure development under a stable authoritarian structure. Beneath this order is a range of relations and deals known only through the smiling face of the general. Social scientists approach such representation of power through conceptions such as patrimonial power or patron–client relations. These are helpful concepts, but they tend to fall into a "culturalist" trap, thus undermining the politico-economic dimension of the undercurrent order. What I seek to show is that undercurrents are formed through a relation between capital, the state and society. They operate beneath or beyond the appearances of policies, and they shape implementation and outcomes. In this sense, policies are better understood as a starting point for a relation to be formed and developed. They are not meant to regulate or serve as a framework for evaluation. They work as policies only when the relations break down and conditions arise that lead to charges of *NKK* (*Nepotisme, Korupsi dan Kolusi*). The forces of *reformasi* are aimed at eliminating NKK for "good governance", but undercurrents continue to make things happen. The economic order still relies on the semi-formality of workers' households which helps externalise costs for the benefit of capital and the state; the city is still run by urban brokers known such as *oknum* and *preman;* and on the board of every major company, such as banks and property companies, there is always a *komisaris* —a retired, high-ranking government officer—who can work the undercurrents. A lot of deals are made informally, if not illegally, between the ruling elites and they shape the way policies are implemented.[7]

Indonesian writer Seno Gumira Ajidarma (2004a; 2015) called Jakarta "a city of a thousand dimensions" perhaps with *semuanya bisa diatur* in mind: the city can't be measured only by the three, or four, standard dimensions. A failure in implementation is a success when measured differently because it would open up an opportunity for another project. So there is a gap between policy and implementation because loopholes could become a space to breathe not only for the elites but also the poor to have a place or hold their place in Jakarta. There are a thousand dimensions to configure. We therefore need to understand how *semuanya bisa diatur* still operates as undercurrents that are often more effective than the order of rules.

## Notes

[1] Questions are from Andy Fuller (University of Utrecht), Jörgen Hellman (University of Gothenburg), Marie Thynell (University of Gothenburg) and Roanne van Voorst (University of Amsterdam).

[2] Siswanto, "Novel: ACTA Dukung Anies Beri Dana Ormas dari APBD", Suara.com, 19 March 2017, at https://www.suara.com/news/2017/03/19/125649/novel-acta-dukung-anies-beri-dana-ormas-dari-apbd.

[3] Djarot Saiful Hidayat, "Kita Jangan Balik ke Zaman Jahiliah", *Tempo*, 10–16 July 2017, p. 103.

[4] In Curitiba, the busway is part of a well planned and integrated transportation system.

[5] See report by Nurul F. Ramadhani, "Do You Want to be Evicted?", *Jakarta Post*, 8 Feb. 2017.

[6] Arnaldi Nasution and Ilham Pradipta, "Jakarta Smart City: Memangkas Birokrasi Lewat Aplikasi," *Initisari*, June 2016: 150.

[7] Ananya Roy calls this a practice of informality. See Roy 2005.

Chapter | **Our Streets: Reflections on a**
10 | **Pandemic City**

(with Wahyu **Astuti**, Frans **Prasetyo** and Suryono **Herlambang**)

The spaces of our city are once again subject to order and regularity, but this time in response to a COVID-19 rampage that recognises no boundaries. This essay is a reflection on the streets of Jakarta seen as an embodiment of "dreamworld and catastrophe" (Buck-Morss 1995). We tease out a relevant history of streets in the nationalist imagination, the impacts of the pandemic and what could be in the epoch to follow.

## The Road to the Hospital

I sat next to the driver in the ambulance to transport my spouse, a COVID-19 patient, from our home in the city of Tangerang [on the outskirts of Jakarta] to a hospital. The driver said to me, "This ambulance can take 40 trips a day". But how did the driver keep track of the high number of trips? "There are not many ambulances, but what really counts is the road condition". Indeed, on the way, we competed for space with other vehicles, especially trucks. Along the entire route, I saw how the roads continued to operate at full capacity. From the ambulance, I saw the usual street scenes: vendors, pedestrians, cars, carts, cats and, above all... motorbikes. The two motorbikes in front of us served as our "ambulance guards". They were volunteers. "Let us guide you!" said one of them before we started the trip. He wore a coat saying "*ambulans dan damkar* [ambulances and fire trucks]". They knew that an ambulance does not automatically get priority over other road users, even though it is equipped with a siren. All the way the "ambulance guard" maneuvered for us to pass through the traffic congestion. At some junctions, we met other volunteer guards who stopped the traffic to help us pass. These traffic volunteers are true markers of an emergency. They are "people as infrastructure" (Simone 2004). The ambulance alone would not have saved us that day.

Wahyu (Ayu) Astuti, 7 November 2020

Ayu managed to write down this experience in her notebook. Time was supposed to stand still during the lockdown, or "restriction of mobility", in Indonesia. But even under these emergency circumstances, the clock continued to tick. Time then was of the essence. Yet it couldn't be accounted for as the road conditions were unreliable. In major Indonesian cities, time is lost to space. Transportation to the hospital in an ambulance guaranteed nothing, as ambulances have no control over the roads. They are constantly caught in traffic. The loud, high siren disappears into the general soundscape of the streets. Ayu ended her entry with the realisation that "there could never be a lockdown in this city. The street is not empty. Everything goes on as usual".

## The Road to a Nationalist Utopia

The Sudirman-Thamrin Road bore a deserted look during the first few days of the restriction of mobility. Passers-by could see only some screens displaying information about COVID-19. The restrictions on the main financial streets, however, did not prevent the upper-middle classes from making attempts to ride bicycles—a newfound hobby to keep them moving during a time when they were supposed to be "working from home". The governor of Jakarta, Anies Baswedan, had managed to launch a bike revolution over the previous few years to facilitate the emergence of "sustainable" private transportation methods like cycling among Jakarta's new middle class. By the time Jakarta was hit hard by the pandemic in July 2020, a car-free day on weekends for specific areas of the main streets, pedestrian route design and permanent bike lanes on main financial streets had become symbols of a new urban utopia. This new lifestyle, sustained by high-end bicycles and special cycling gear, has not only maintained the status of the Sudirman-Thamrin Road, but also strengthened class distinctions. During the COVID-19 mobility restriction, cycling was not permitted. The only exceptions for road use were granted to drivers taking the sick to the hospital. The restriction helped prevent traffic congestion on protocol roads.

These two scenes—an ambulance racing against time on an uncontrolled and crowded street and the temporary closure of a protocol road to non-essential activities—happened during the same period of time. The Sudirman-Thamrin Road embodies authority, order and national progress. This was the venue for every spectacle of utopian urban experiment in Jakarta: the first designated busway line, the first Mass Rapid Transport (MRT) line, the first dedicated bike lane. Every governor of Jakarta since Independence has left their mark on this main road, from building another layer of the road (as in the time of Governor Ahok) to creating a bike lane during Anies Baswedan's administration. Our leaders have shared a common aim: to maintain the utopian vision of moving forward to a future without traffic congestion. They were entranced by *zaman pergerakan* (age in motion) in the early 1900s, which refers to *gerak*—moving forward—through asphalted roads.[1] By the turn of the twenty-first century, however, *macet* (heavy traffic) had jammed such roads to progress. By the time of Governor Baswedan, who took office in 2017, the image of utopian *gerak* could only be saved by the dedicated bike lane.

**Figure 10.1.** Barricades in Bandung's major Asia-Africa Street (photo by Frans Ari Prasetyo, 25 April 2020).[2]

According to Thomas More, utopia occupies an island that is as isolated as an enclave. It is a real or projected segregation within the world. But utopia could also serve as an imagined restoration of the lost self. For the Sudirman-Thamrin Road, it would be to remove the fear of congestion, of disappearing into the undifferentiated masses, of contamination, of breaking down, or of massive demonstrations that could lead to the collapse of a regime in power, which American anthropologist John Pemberton called the "political traffic accident".[3]

## *Ramai*—The Composite Road

Heavy traffic is an everyday occurrence on Jakarta streets. It has been normalised by the term *ramai* (crowded). Although it contrasts with the enclave of utopias, *ramai* can't exactly be called a dystopia, for it carries festivity and productivity. If the main road is controlled according to the logics of consumption and lifestyle, everything appears productive at every time on the *ramai* road for, here, livelihoods are at stake. Every time we pass through such streets in the afternoon, we know we must rush—otherwise, we could get stuck in the traffic. At 4 p.m., food carts are already stationed along its edges, clothes vendors are rolling out tents, and colourfully decorated horse carriages arrive, their owners intent on attracting child riders. As the sun sets, the streets are already packed with traders, street musicians, parked motorcycles and pedestrians as the streets become a *ramai*, or a lively space. The truth is that *ramai* can't be controlled, much like a traffic jam.

Street life creates multitudes—it was never intended to be a utopian enclave. As such, it is contagious. It can spread easily because it is composite, open for reconstitution, adaptation and appropriation. It inspired the establishment, which sought to plan something similar, but more controllable and fashionable. The Puri Night Market—just such a creation—is situated in the middle of Jakarta's West Central Business District, known as Puri CBD. Developed in the late 1990s as an alternative activity centre for the upper-middle class, the developer, too embarrassed to acknowledge the influence of *ramai* street life, cited New York City as the inspiration: "Infrastructure in Puri CBD is relatively better and organized, as it is designed with city block concepts so that it becomes more comfortable for drivers and residents to walk, like in New York".[4] Yet, soon the Puri Night Market had become a *ramai* walk filled with composite smells, and the uncontainable sound of things and people, all of which contradict the utopian imagining of an enclave. The Puri Night Market soon grew beyond the utopian grid of Manhattan. The authorities tolerate the excess, for it is a "silent form of collective collaboration" that seems to benefit everyone.[5] Such excess recalls the comments of a powerful governor, Ali Sadikin, who said, "I agree with the existence of street vendors, as long as we can control them. But in Jakarta, it does not look like they can be controlled because of urbanization". He continued, "I only see more diseases than none", in what he considered an excess of street vending.[6]

Since COVID-19 first subdued Jakarta, the roads have been subject to spatial and temporal control. Those who depend on street life for their livelihood have had no choice but to *turun ke jalan* (go to streets). The *ramai* space has given President Joko Widodo, also known as Jokowi, pause: "We have barricaded access to roads, but I still see day and night, still *ramai*, and I went to *kampung* (urban community neighbourhood), also *ramai banget* (very festive)".[7]

On some major streets, Starbucks, Pizza Hut and mall tenants also *turun ke jalan,* joining ambulances, vendors and street musicians.[8] The road has become *riuh* (noisy)—an intensification of *ramai*, as it is filled with asynchronous calls that are unavoidably class-based. People *turun ke jalan* to feed their families rather than working virtually from home. This tension exists across the globe, but in Jakarta, it carries us downstream to issues concerning the exemplary centre of Sudirman-Thamrin and the *ramai* roads, or what counts as utopia or dystopia. Beneath the *riuh* and the *ramai*, motorbike taxi (*ojek*) drivers keep the nation moving.

**Figure 10.2.** Mobile stall in Tangerang (photo by Wahyu Astuti, 14 August 2021). *Note:* Domino's, the international pizza chain stall open with motorcycle and standing banner on the street, side by side with a *tempe* fritters stall in a local street in Tangerang. With the restriction on shopping malls opening, tenants went to the street ("turun ke jalan") to approach buyers.

## Motorcycles and Alleyways

"*Paket!*" I rushed out to see the package I ordered yesterday. It arrived faster than I thought it would. So, I took it inside and started unpacking. Soon after I finished, I went out to dispose of the box, and the courier was still there. He was busy reorganising loads of packages on his motorcycle, tying them here and there with ropes, making sure they did not fall off his motorbike. One does not need statistics to assert that the number of motorcycle couriers has proliferated during the pandemic. The sight of motorcycle couriers carrying bulk goods—sometimes with an iron frame extension or heat insulator for food delivery at the back of their motorcycle—is the "new normal".

Wahyu (Ayu) Astuti, 25 July 2021

When almost every sector of the economy fails, logistics and courier services thrive—especially for last-mile or store-to-consumer delivery. Gojek and Tokopedia, Indonesia's unicorns in ride-hailing and e-commerce, have merged and are expected to excel in the logistics business. For couriers, the road is full of calculations and speculation: how many packages can be delivered, what is the distance to be travelled, what are the related fuel costs and how much money can the drivers save? This set of considerations, however, also means competition and precarity. With more individuals signing up as couriers and drivers due to layoffs in other sectors and the increase in online shopping during the pandemic, the number of couriers increased, but their compensation has plummeted.

**Figure 10.3.** Motorcycle courier riding through the streets in Tambora, West Jakarta (photo by Wahyu Astuti, 21 September 2021).
*Note*: Bulky goods are piled on the motorcycle.

Motorcycles are the backbone of delivery services—only motorcycles can access *jalan tikus* (rat runs) in *kampung*. It is also easier to avoid road closures if one travels through *kampung*. Upon closing the roundabout (Bundaran) Hotel Indonesia to motorcycles in 2015, for example, Governor Ahok said, "there are other routes, *jalan belakang* (back routes). There are back routes for the streets we close, and couriers can get through them" (qtd. in Kurnia Sari Aziza 2014). Although scenes of alleyways might be dystopian to modern planning, alleyways are pivotal to the idea of (im-)mobility, even during a pandemic. When Jakarta's protocol roads were closed, the drivers' knowledge of *jalan tikus* kept the economy afloat. When the roads are not familiar, the "maps platform" leads them to the address. Angi, a motorbike driver, points out, "many times, I was happy to deliver food to places that were featured on the maps platform. But because [the neighbourhood] is restricted, I had to find a way around".[9]

This capacity for free movement points to a configuration of the city and its society that cannot be planned. Jakarta is built to a plan that produced the Sudirman-Thamrin Road, but many parts of the city are the result of organic growth. Indonesian writer Seno Gumira Ajidarma (2004a, 2015) calls Jakarta a "city of a thousand dimensions" since it is difficult to measure.

The COVID-19 situation, however, made it clear that something has shifted within the hierarchical order of motor vehicles in Jakarta. With road blockages, it was no longer easy for automobiles, the most favoured type of vehicle, to move around the city. Instead, motorcycles are now the number one vehicle that will lead Jakarta and Indonesia out of the catastrophe caused by the pandemic. Ayu, in her quotation towards the beginning of this chapter, indicates how ambulances alone wouldn't have saved the life of her family member that day; the motorcycle drivers led the ambulance out of and through the traffic. During the time of "mobility restriction", they were on the move, connecting households through deliveries, serving as a bridge between barricades, enclaves and portals. They have made dystopia a liveable condition. Although their patterns of movement contradict the ordered utopian ideal, motorcycle drivers have become a constitutive part of social stability and a new normal.

Historically, motorcycles were a spectacle of dystopia. They stemmed from the dystopia of *macet* (gridlock) that cars contributed to. With few safe or reliable modes of transportation, more middle class Jakartans were attracted to cars for the status and the air conditioning. By the end of the 1900s, Jakarta was known to have some of the worst traffic in the world. The first decade of the 2000s saw the meteoric rise of motorcycles. By 2010, Jakarta had eight million registered motorcycles with 300,000 motorcyclists killed on the roads between 1992 and 2010 (Rusyanto 2010).

One scene of dystopia leads to another. There is a class dimension to the dystopic motorcycle accidents. In 2009, Fauzi Bowo, then governor of Jakarta and owner of ten Harley-Davidson motorcycles, commented that "motorcycles increase not by one or two like having children, but they grow like cats giving birth".[10] For Governor Bowo, purchases of motorcycles have grown wild, like the state of nature. For lower class people, having a motorcycle is not only natural, it is instrumental for one's livelihood and can enable one to build up status. Like a medium for class struggle, motorcycles defeat the cars of the upper class trapped in endless traffic queues. Such revenge on the streets, however, contributes nothing to solving deadly traffic congestion. Furthermore, many urban workers have gone into debt purchasing motorcycles to try to make a living. The roads of Jakarta have become more *ramai* as sites of contestation between different classes riding Harley-Davidsons, cars, motorcycles and lately, the high-end bicycles of the Anies regime. Each vehicle symbolises a class-specific utopian aspiration, but together they have contributed to a collective dystopia.

## Road to Digital Utopia

Over time, motorcycles have become an alternative "public transport", a practice that grew out of a much longer history of *ojek sepeda* (bicycle taxi). At first, the motorbike taxi was simply called *ojek*. It could hold more passengers than a car. Obviously, it was more dangerous too. But the challenge for the *ojek* driver was how to find customers, as these could look for the *ojek* only at designated make-shift stations. It didn't take long for Harvard-trained Nadiem Makarim (today's Minister of Education), who was a regular customer, to become inspired. He belongs to the generation that knows perfectly well what apps can do to revolutionise Indonesian streets. In this scenario, the dystopia of *macet* was an opportunity to build a utopian city. With the launch of a specific app in 2015, he declared that "there's no reason for cars to exist in this city at all" (qtd. in Van Mead 2016). This same declaration also killed the business of *tukang ojek* (informal motorbike taxi). Some policymakers argue that he has killed public transport. "Our customers are smartphone users", Makarim said. "They are middle class people switching from private cars. They wouldn't have traveled on buses anyway" (ibid.). Such a calculation produced the Gojek app. "We bring everything to you. If you didn't want to, you wouldn't have to leave your apartment" (ibid.). This is the suggestion to which every government now returns frequently during COVID-19 restrictions.

## Barricades

As the number of COVID-19 cases surged and the government imposed a series of mobility restrictions, the so-called Online Ojek (or online motorbike taxi known now by *Ojol*) was often caught in contradictory regulations. It was restricted but allowed to operate, or vice versa. In some areas, the decision for something to operate was in the hands of the local authorities. The latest version of "lockdown" generally allows *Ojol* to cross barricade points, provided they are delivering or taking orders.

The city itself has been divided into barricade points where one can cross. They keep changing, but as of July 2020, "in the city there are 19 points, on the toll road there are 15 points, at the city limits 10 points, in the buffer area there are 29 points, and the Sudirman-Thamrin Road section there are 27 points, so there are 100 points in total".[11] This has not included routes through the *kampung*, which have their own barricade points, called portals, each with its own rules that are often beyond the government's control. This interlocking network is hard to map since it is not sustained by government-imposed (or any other type of stable) regulation. The unpredictability that characterises the urban configuration of Jakarta seems to inform the inconsistent rules.

The government is not in favour of "lockdowns", not only because it would burden the state as the sole responsible agent of control, but also because it would not be able to stay flexible, accommodating and negotiable. As community researcher Frans Prasetyo indicates, the government has implemented various scenarios: the Large-scale Social Restriction (PSBB) (April–June 2020), then PSBB Transition (June–September 2020), PSBB Strict (September–October 2020), and PSBB Transitional #2 (October 2020–January 2021). In early 2021, we heard new terms: Community Activities Restriction (PPKM) (January–February 2021), PPKM Micro (February–June 2021), PPKM Emergency (1–20 July 2021), PPKM level 3–4 (21–25 July 2021) and PPKM Extended level 1-2-3 (various times in 2022). They offer neither a coherent system nor a linear transition. Instead, they constitute a series of incalculable turns between dream and nightmare. To pass a barricade point, to flow and to live, is to interpret and stretch what counts as "essential" or "critical". For some, the PPKM stands for *Pandai-Pandai Kalian Mencari Jalan* (be smart in finding your own road/way to pass).

## *Go to the Street*: Revolution or Counter-Revolution

Anti-lockdown protests are everywhere in the world. In Indonesia, they are called *turun ke jalan* (go to the street). But as we have indicated above, *turun ke jalan* also means going back to street life. *Turun ke jalan* in the first sense does not need a leading hand. It is recurrent in that it is at once heterogeneous and iterative—repetitive but not monotonous—which constitutes the experience of street life. There are no hidden agendas beyond the chaotic logic of survival. The authorities consider another form of *turun ke jalan* more significant because of its association with intentional rallies, marches, or protests. This *turun ke jalan* is goal-governed, and questions are often raised about the participants' motivations and characteristics: the provocateur, the *dalang* (the mastermind), or the *bandar* (funder). Both kinds of *turun ke jalan* could be subject to control or scrutiny, but they could also be tolerated under various names—for the right to livelihood or the right to make transactions on the street.

The COVID-19 situation has blurred these two meanings of *turun ke jalan*. The fights for present survival and future idealism co-exist and overlap; they are no longer mutually exclusive. This superimposition echoes Indonesians' concerns over the extension of COVID-19 restrictions, which have been understood as extensions of state power and societal control. The state also goes to the street, attempting to control or save lives.

**Figure 10.4.** Scene on the street near a Police HQ in Bandung, April 2020 (photo by Frans Ari Prasetyo, 25 April 2020).
*Note*: The signs, from the Andir Covid-19 Task Force, read: "Stay Home!" and "Let's wear masks!"[12]

Political parties also *turun ke jalan*. They advertise their parties and candidates for the next presidential election via billboards on main streets across Indonesia.[13] Nothing could be more sinister than to see such billboards compete with those bearing COVID-19 messages as the country overtook India's daily case numbers and surpassed Brazil's daily death rate. Politics and the pandemic lurk in the spectre of our future. They ride on our streets which have become the site of political accidents and deadly contestations.

## Notes

[1] According to Mrázek, "modern roads and railroads . . . were the veins and the arteries of the movement. The movement's pain and hope, as well as its gathering sense of revolution, were supposed to concentrate on the modern roads" (Mrázek 2008: 37).

[2] The restriction of mobility was carried out by spatial barriers, but such a practice was applied only to a few major streets, giving thus an impression of discipline and control. The secondary and smaller streets were left open to traffic, congestion and the condition of crowdedness (*ramai*).

[3] See Pemberton 1994: 6 for a discussion of the association of *macet* with "political traffic accident". See also Sidel 1998.

[4] "Jakbar Dikembangkan, Membatasi Laju Pertumbuhan Jakarta Selatan", *Kompas*, 24 March 2008, p. 25.

[5] Simone (2014: 10) contended that the street has become "the arena where more silent forms of collective collaboration were worked out, but always under close scrutiny".

[6] Ali Sadikin, "Gubernur: Saya Setuju Pedagang Kaki Lima, asal Terkendalikan", *Kompas*, 16 June 1976, p. 12.

[7] As cited in "Jokowi Minta Penyekatan Dievaluasi, Kini Perlu Diwaspadai Klaster Keluarga", *Detiknews*, 18 July 2021, available at https://news.detik.com/berita/d-5647537/jokowi-minta-penyekatan-dievaluasi-kini-perlu-diwaspadai-klaster-keluarga (accessed 9 Oct. 2022).

[8] As reported in "Turun ke Jalan demi Mendongkrak Penjualan", *Tempo*, 29 Sept. 2020, at https://koran.tempo.co/read/ekonomi-dan-bisnis/458332/turun-ke-jalan-demi-mendongkrak-penjualan and "Pandemi, PHK, dan Pengamen", *Tempo*, 8 Feb. 2021, at https://koran.tempo.co/read/metro/462173/pengamen-jalanan-semakin-banyak-di-masa-covid-19 (accessed 8 Dec. 2022).

[9] "Cerita Driver Ojol Bertualang Portal Gang Tiap Ada Pembatasan, Basah Kuyup karena Sering Disiram Disinfektan", Kompas.com, 6 July 2021, at https://megapolitan.kompas.com/read/2021/07/06/16122571/cerita-driver-ojol-bertualang-portal-gang-tiap-ada-pembatasan-basah-kuyup.

[10] As cited in "Karena Motor Beranak Seperti Kucing", https://www.viva.co.id/indepth/sorot/68294-karena-motor-beranak-seperti-kucing.

[11] Director of Traffic of the Polda Metro Jaya Kombes, Sambodo Purnomo Yogo, as cited in "Jakarta residents are more 'locked' in the emergency PPKM period", *VOI*, 17 July 2021, https://voi.id/en/news/67973/jakarta-residents-are-more-locked-in-the-emergency-ppkm-period.

¹² Police forces were mobilised to offer the sense that the city was under control. This shows an instance of phantasmapolis, the performance of which requires a ghostly presence of the deadly street that needs to be exorcised or cleansed through a show of containment.

¹³ Nawir A. Akbar, "Baliho Politikus Saat Pandemi Narsisme Politik", *Republika*, 3 August 2021, https://www.republika.co.id/berita/qx8m4h428/pengamat-baliho-politikus-saat-pandemi-narsisme-politik.

# Afterword:
# On "Multitude" and the Urban Question:
# A Reading in a Time of Pandemics

When I started to put together this book, little did I realise that I was thinking about the relations between the "urban question" and the "multitude" and how they might be relevant for understanding an Indonesian city. To consider these two terms however is also to acknowledge that while ideas (especially those emanating from Western metropoles) can be discussed theoretically, empirically or experientially anywhere, they can also get us easily lost in language, in translation.

In 1982, Edward W. Said wrote an important piece called "Traveling Theory" in which he indicated that all theories or ideas are developed in response to specific social and historical circumstances, and when they travel from their point of origin, the power and the meaning attached to them change as they become assimilated or localised into a new context:

> First, there is a point of origin . . . a set of initial circumstances in which the idea came to birth or entered discourse. Second, there is a distance transversed, a passage through the pressure of various contexts as the idea moves from an earlier point to another time and place where it will come into a new prominence. Third, there is a set of conditions—call them conditions of acceptance or. . . resistances—which then confronts the transplanted theory or idea, making possible its introduction or toleration, however alien it might appear to be. Fourth, the now fully (or partly) accommodated (or incorporated) idea is to some extent transformed by its new uses, its new position in a new time and place. (Said 1983: 226–7)

It would be an enormous task to travel from point one to point four, but it is a journey that we need to bear in mind if we use any "imported" concept such as the "multitude" or the "urban question" to address situations in Indonesia. Let me organise my thoughts around the following three questions:
1.    What does "multitude" mean to me, analytically and empirically?

2. How might my choice of focus—the "urban question" of Indonesia— engage with the concept of "multitude" as I understand it?

3. How might the link between the "urban question" and the "multitude" concepts become useful for considering the challenges and opportunities for the "urban majorities" (Simone 2013, 2014) of the pandemic era and its association with the "new normal"?

## What does "multitude" mean to me, analytically and empirically?

Michael Hardt and Antonio Negri popularized the term "multitude" through their books *Multitude* (2004) and *Empire* (2000). To track down a possible meaning of their use of the term, we could perhaps consider only the following two quotations:

> The concept of multitude is meant to re-propose Marx's political project of class struggle. The multitude from this perspective is based not so much on the current empirical existence of the class but rather on its condition of possibility . . . such a political project must clearly be grounded in an empirical analysis that demonstrates the common conditions of those who can become the multitude. (Hardt and Negri 2004: 105–6)

> In order to verify this concept of multitude and its political project we will have to establish that indeed the differences of kind that used to divide labor no longer apply, in other words, that the conditions exist for the various types of labor to communicate, collaborate, and become common. (Ibid. 107)

From these quotations we get a sense that when Hardt and Negri conceptualised the idea of multitude, they had in mind a formation of a new labour relation. They were trying to change the focus from labour (such as the proletariat) fully constituted within the class system to a consideration of "various types of labor" and the shared new conditions within which they might be able to "communicate, collaborate, and become common" so as to work out a "condition of possibility" for carrying out a political project.

Let me consider this conceptualisation of multitude in terms of "urban theory", such as the theory of "city in transition", which is connected to Marxist urban theory and its teleological form of developmentalism.

In classical Marxist theory, urbanisation is a precondition of capitalist development. It follows that such a process of urbanisation, which was in the interest of the exploitative capitalist class, requires a deal with the exploited labourers. The "class peace" took the form of state-mediated "collective consumption" so the work force is proletarianised, not only through wage work, but also through the provision of facilities such as schools, hospitals, transport, housing, leisure, etc.— all of which are "collective".[1] It follows that the growth of collective consumption has been due to "the growing power of [the] worker movement which extends its bargaining power to all areas of social life" (Castells 1977 [1972]: 445). For Manuel Castells, the "urban question" of capitalism (in the later Fordism of the 1960s and 1970s), therefore, is extremely important as the site of struggle and it should be grasped in terms of contradictions between "collective consumption" and private expropriation.

Yet, moving forward to the 1980s and later, state involvement in the means of "collective consumption" has been devalued, and private expropriation has become dominant in most of the core countries. The truce between capital and labour was over by the time of the "neoliberal" regimes of Margaret Thatcher (in the UK) and Ronald Reagan (in the US). Since then, labour relations have been reorganised from what was once identifiable as "mass labor" (as in Fordism) to a discursive "assemblage of labourers" which are dispensable, disposable or replaceable according to market forces.

In Fordism, labourers were strictly controlled to avoid uncertainty and their lives were accounted for through statistics in order to constitute the body of "society"; in post-Fordist conditions, however, uncertainty is accepted as a new norm, and flexibility is the underlying structure. And for Thatcher: "Who is society? There is no such thing! There are individual men and women and there are families and no government can do anything except through people and people look to themselves first [. . .]."[2] This quotation represents a new era of post-Fordist neoliberalism that emphasises the role of the individual in "society". It follows that the privatisation of public goods is considered positive and liberating for it represents the entrepreneurial spirit of the individual in generating more capital and investment. The labourer is understood as an individual who must look inwardly instead of relying on government or a union, entities which have been weakened or dismantled. The identity and identification of the post-Fordist labourers, thus, are always in flux, continuously constructed and recomposed in and through the market. In this new condition, labourers could be seen more like an assemblage which is not united under an identity or a position. Instead, they relate to each other through antagonism, competition and friction.

The state too can no longer govern in a unitary manner; instead, the notion of the "withdrawal of the state" becomes a commonplace. Meanwhile, infrastructure has become an arena for business sector investment. This shift has also made the concept of "collective consumption" obsolete as indicated in a special issue of *Sociological Review* in the 1990s that opined: "The collective consumption approach has not continued to develop in a unified way since the mid-1980s, and has shown some signs of overall loss of direction and vigor"(Dowding and Dunleavy 1996: 43).

It is this context of the hegemonic rise of neoliberal post-Fordism that Hardt and Negri were grappling with—the implications of the passage from Fordism to post-Fordism for labourers. The concept of multitude is an attempt not only to identify such a shift to a new condition shared by those who become the multitude, but also to explore its condition of possibility, which for Hardt and Negri, as the quotations above make clear, is a political project.

I am basing my line of thought on a gut feeling of what the "multitude" is about. But to move on, let's ask ourselves a question: how could/should we "localise" the concept of "multitude" to address the specificity of the condition of our own space and time, say in Indonesia? In the next section, I consider the urban condition of Indonesia, which, unlike the Western metropole, did not experience the Fordist/post-Fordist shift, but only a continuation of private expropriation from the past to the present (since colonial times!). In what way then is the concept of multitude helpful for understanding the different condition of urban Indonesia?

## The Urban Question of the Periphery

Moving to our own space, in the periphery or semi-periphery of the world's capitalist economy, the Fordist/post-Fordist shift of production has resulted in the move of manufacturing industries away from the core countries to the developing countries, in such a way that a *new* international division of labour has emerged. This spatial decentralisation affected the core and peripheral countries differently. In the core countries, there was significant deindustrialisation, unemployment (or shift of employment to precarious jobs), and the declining power of labour unions to bargain for pay and job security. In the peripheries, manufacturing production went to any country that offered a friendly climate for investment—low cost labour and weak environmental laws.

With a new concentration of industrial labourers in the Global South, we can ask: does the classic Fordist urban question (and the concomitant contradiction between "collective consumption" and private expropriation) make sense for cities in the Global South? My answer to this is *no*. Indonesian cities (unlike most Western cities), as indicated in Chapter 4, "never implemented a unitary infrastructural ideal aimed at benefitting the wider public. Instead, the city has, from the beginning, been represented by a series of fragmented, privately funded infrastructural projects, constructed to benefit only certain stakeholders" (ch. 4, p. 72, above).

The classic collective consumption issues, such as public transport, green spaces, water, electricity or gas have never been prioritised, not to mention other services such as housing and land use, which are either neglected or unregulated if not "privatised". In the absence of universal public goods to foster social equality, there is no ground to formulate the "urban question" to which "collective consumption" is central. Indonesians have been living with heterogeneous and improvised infrastructures that do not constitute a coherent universal framework for a formulation of "collective" consumption. What we have are agglomerations of unevenly constituted local or localised infrastructures.

Furthermore, industrial labourers constitute only a fraction of workers in urban Indonesia. They are not the majority, and neither are they unionised strongly enough to strike for fair pay and job security. The majority work in the informal sector. In such a context, while capitalist development is taking place in the city, it has never fully proletarianised peasants or workers; and while deruralisation is taking place, it has only incompletely urbanised the city.

So, we have here a set of disjunctures between the multitudes of the Global North and those of the Global South. There is a disjuncture on issues of labour identity and organisation; disjuncture on the urban question (since there is no "collective consumption" in the form of a universal infrastructural ideal for the state to mediate); and since the urban majority survives in the informal sector, there was never a truce between capital and labour. The condition within which the multitude of the Global South is constituted is very different from that of the North. In the South, there is no such dramatic shift from Fordist production to Post-Fordism. The South continues to experience a capitalist mode of exploitation sustained by partially constituted semi-proletarianised households. In other words, in Indonesia and unlike in the West, the multitude is formed due to incomplete urbanisation and the city's incomplete proletarianisation, not to any condition that post-Fordist labourers have encountered.

Despite the historical disjuncture, the idea of "multitude" nevertheless invites us to raise the question of how the post-Fordist informalisation of the workforce in the Global North might resonate with the long-standing history of informal workers in the Global South.[3] A consideration of multitude in the Global North might need to start with an understanding of the working of the multitude in the Global South. While the conditions of the multitudes in the North and the South could be comparatively analysed, it is important to remember that urban development in a place like Jakarta is different from what has been assumed in classical Marxism, namely that capitalist formation requires the incorporation of land assets into capitalist ventures and peasants/workers into the urban proletariat. In Indonesia, such a process is necessarily incomplete because only incomplete urbanisation and incomplete proletarianisation could support the reproduction of capitalism in the peripheral zone.

## A Different Multitude, A Different Truce: Capital, (informal) Labour and the State

A consideration of multitude in an Indonesian city would need to unpack the organisation of relations between capital, (informal) labour and the state. Following Chapter 1, let me consider once again the kind of truce between the state, capital and (informal) labour under the notion of "middling urbanism". Central to middling urbanism are the existence and production of the irregular settlement of urban *kampung*. I have argued that the relation between the state and (global) capital requires that (formal and informal) labour be located spatially in and around the city. In the absence of land use for social housing, the relatively "self-built" and "self-managed" *kampung* offers affordable housing for low-wage labourers and workers from both formal and informal sectors who are unable to survive elsewhere in the city.

*Kampung*, therefore, absorbs the costs of infrastructure and housing that the state and capital would otherwise have to cover. For both the state and capital, *kampung* is useful for it accommodates labour migrations, reduces unemployment and sustains the low-wage regime of economic growth. The *kampung* thus forms a mutually constitutive relation with the state and capital in the co-production of a distinctive urban condition that is not based on state investment in "collective consumption" (which is lacking) or "private expropriation" alone. Instead, it absorbs the contradictory relations between them.

In Hardt and Negri, the concept of multitude and the condition of its existence offer a way to explore the possibility of a political project beyond Marx's definition of class struggle. For us, since *kampung* serves to moderate conflicts between the urban and the rural, the industrial and the preindustrial, the modern and the premodern, its existence moderates conflicts instead of serving as a site for class struggle. As an intermediate space, *kampung* serves to moderate the increasingly polarised urban-rural system. One could argue, therefore, that such an arrangement prevents "class struggle" at the level of a rural/urban divide. The *kampung* is not in opposition to the city nor to the countryside. The collective aspirations for upward mobility of migrants to the city and *kampung* inhabitants are all tied to their (relatively autonomous yet dependent) relations with the state and capital.

Yet *kampung* could be understood as the milieu of the multitude as it too constitutes (in Hardt and Negri's words) "the conditions for the various types of labor to communicate, collaborate, and become common" (Hardt and Negri 2004: 107). The survival of the inhabitants of *kampung* (unlike the classical paradigm of the urban West) is based on the development of "household", of an income pooling unit (Smith and Wallerstein 1992). The household consists of a group of persons whose livelihood is sustained by way of pooling together multiple incomes from a variety of occupations such that, due to their substantial reliance on informal sectors, they are not fully wage-dependent "proletarians". In short, the work of members of a household cuts across formal and informal sectors.

Hardt and Negri's conceptualisation of the multitude is a response to the increasing informalisation of workers in the Global North, a situation that is not unfamiliar to the intersectionality of formal and informal sectors in the Global South. It remains a challenge to consider the extent to which the multitudes could constitute a united front that can serve as a basis for class struggle. In the case of urban Indonesia, for labour to "become common", members of the *kampung* multitude relate with each other, not only through communication and collaboration, but also through competition and friction. Their truce with the state and capital is formed through a beneficial if problematic politics of collaboration and co-exploitation of resources.

The conclusion that we can draw from the Indonesian multitude is that it is formed through both old (colonial) and new (postcolonial) worldwide divisions of labour, and involves urban majorities whose work cuts across formal and informal sectors. They come together not because of any shift in labour relations (such as that which constituted post-Fordism), but by the internalisation of conditions of uncertainty and improvised connectivity of the urban as a result of inadequate support from infrastructural goods.

The Indonesian urban multitudes are a large workforce. They are exploited but not overly so. They retain a certain autonomy in self-managing with few state-provided infrastructural services, but they do not organise themselves around collective consumption against private expropriation. The patchily realised infrastructural systems have generated related improvisations at a local level and suffice for only a localised collective identity formation—too weak to constitute a political block. Furthermore, what is to be defended when universal infrastructure is non-existent? As a result, there is no "class struggle" around collective consumption since the means of collective consumption (i.e. the universal infrastructure ideal) is limited or scarce and has never been fully state-controlled or manifest.

## The (Post-)Pandemic Question

The pandemic reveals contradictions in the current structure of the global division of labour. The connectivity of global cities has not been matched by the infrastructure of the built environment and of health services. Globally, the pandemic has indicated to us the failure of neoliberal policies of the privatisation of public goods and the elimination of social safety nets. It has brought to our attention both the unevenness of global development generally and the shared infrastructural poverty, especially in Indonesia. The Indonesian multitudes that have sustained such a formation are the result of the old normal (or the abnormality of the long twentieth century) and its concomitant infrastructural scarcity. They have suffered most during the pandemic, since the restrictions dismantled their connectivity to the streets and their surroundings, and changed the organisational patterns of their livelihood.

We have been accustomed to seeing the struggles of the multitudes as part of the old normal, as a tradition or a different way of doing things for urban majorities. Yet the pandemic has taught us that the previous neglect of socio-spatial infrastructure for the urban majority is a problem. We need a new approach to realise the well-being for all, and yes, that the goal shouldn't be the speed of capital accumulation and competition for economic growth. But what sort of new normal do we want, and by what means are we going to get there?

We could consider such a question by making the urban question relevant for the Global South. But then we must confront the question of infrastructure, since it is the means for constituting the common, the means for collective consumption. It seems to me there are two approaches to the question of infrastructure. The first is to consider difference as the strength of the urban majority or the urban multitudes (if these terms could be made interchangeable). We appreciate the works of urbanists whose deep knowledge of cities in the Global South has highlighted the potentiality of the self-reliance of the urban multitudes as in a term like "people as infrastructure" (Simone 2004). Such an approach cannot be easily summarised. But

> the ways in which [their] different economic practices, demeanors, behavioral tactics, forms of social organization, territory, and mobility intersect and detach, coalesce into enduring cultures of inhabitation or proliferate as momentary occupancies of short-lived situations make up a kind of algorithmic process that continuously produces new functions and new values for individual and collective capacities, backgrounds, and ways of doing things. (Simone and Rao 2021: 151)

It follows that such a set of capacities, "albeit facing new vulnerabilities and recalibration, will become increasingly important in shaping urban change in a post-pandemic era" (ibid.).

This formulation for a post-pandemic era seems reasonable considering that the communing between urban majorities has become infused into practices of everyday life, and for them embodies infrastructure and vice versa. Yet, we must acknowledge that such capacity has been developed out of the condition of state neglect and physical infrastructural scarcity. Should such a condition be accepted as the basis for thinking about urbanism in a post-pandemic era?

I would suggest rather that we seize the moment of the post-pandemic to retrieve the promise of Indonesian revolution, unfulfilled since the 1950s, which is the state's desire to provide a truly universal infrastructure aimed at "collective consumption" to achieve a holistic approach to health, social cohesion and the environment for the benefit of the whole country, including the urban. In this sense, the role and position of the state must be returned as a medium for achieving societal goals and as a guarantor of public access to Universal Basic Assets covering education, health, housing, technology and information.[4] This perspective recognises that the pandemic has taught us that fragmented efforts and improvisations are inadequate when they are not aligned to form a universal infrastructural ideal. But would such an ideal be a very good idea? Perhaps not, as it may not offer improvement and may not address one of the great political challenges of our time: private expropriation of public infrastructure. But such an aspiration is as local as it is universal. It is in the political imaginary of Indonesian revolution, striving to achieve a more egalitarian society.

In the end, I think the third "middle" way could be a wiser path to take, that is to learn from both identity and difference, to seek lessons from both the improvised local infrastructure of the urban *kampung* majorities and the universal infrastructural ideal for the construction of the "common" for people to collaborate, to seek a social and political life around it (be it in the form of the urban question or the question of collective consumption) so that multitudes of the Global South are not just subjects brought together by the deprivation of what could be a "common" infrastructural ideal.

I was wondering what Seno Gumira Ajidarma would think if we suggested to him that a version of his "city of a thousand dimensions" could offer a different way for thinking about the futurity of post-pandemic urbanism? He knew about the controversy of escape from Jakarta, and that the government has issued a generous idea and policy to build a new capital city, and to build homes and jobs for many thousands or millions of new inhabitants. Can't such a capacity be mobilised to repair the ruined Jakarta, to rebuild its civil society and to prevent further poverty and despair? If asked "what do you think of a universal infrastructural ideal for Jakarta?" I have a strong feeling that Seno would say "I think it would be a good idea", even though this could change significantly his "city of a thousand dimensions".

## Notes

[1] Manuel Castells, writing in the late 1960s and in the 1970s, used the term "collective consumption" to measure the substance of "class peace" during the Keynesian era. See Castells 1972, 1977.

² Margaret Thatcher, "Interview for *Women's Own* ('No Such Thing as Society')", 1987, from the website *Margaret Thatcher Foundation: Speeches, Interviews and Other Statements*, available at https://www.margaretthatcher.org/document/106689 (accessed 10 Oct. 2022).

³ Consider, for instance, world-systems analysis as in the essays collected in Tabak and Crichlow 2000.

⁴ "To Build the World Anew: Joint Statement of Public Intellectual Forum", unpublished paper prepared by Indonesian intellectuals during the COVID-19 situation, 2020. The joint statement is prepared by the Public Intellectual Forum, a scholars' collective across different academic fields who were engaged in an open conversation (from April to August 2020) about the COVID-19 situation, the new normal and the outcome we hope for. It encourages a move towards a *substantive* new normal:

> A substantive new normal means that the new normal should not be that of remedying a failing system. Instead, it should take us to a world that is more democratic and relatively egalitarian, a realistic aspiration that can be approached however only by moving towards decommodification of resources that should never be appropriated for private sale – from the human body and hospital to the institution of education and the environment: such as the ocean, atmosphere and forests. Our view contains proposals to experiment with a new social structure of relation that is based on an old wisdom and practices derived from the principle of a *"lumbung"* (i.e. a commons) whose objective is community survival rather than profit. It is proposed here without assuming that it is perfect or better, but merely to suggest a need for continuous discussion about alternative structures to realize a substantive new normal.

# Bibliography

Abeyasekere, Susan. 1987. *Jakarta: A History*. Singapore: Oxford University Press.

Aditjondro, George. 1995. "Bali, Jakarta's Colony: Social and Ecological Impacts of Jakarta-Based Conglomerates in Bali's Tourism Industry", Working Paper 58. Perth: Asia Research Centre on Social, Political, and Economic Change, Murdoch University.

Adkins, Brent. 2015. *Deleuze and Guattari's A Thousand Plateaus: A Critical Introduction and Guide*. Edinburgh University Press. https://doi.org/10.1515/9780748686476.

Agrawal, A. 2005. *Environmentality: Technologies of Government and the Making of Subjects*. Durham, NC: Duke University Press.

Agustina et al. 2013. "Wong Solo Di Belantara Jakarta", *Tempo*, 27 Jan.: 32.

Ajistyatama, Wendra. 2014. "Foreign Developers Eye Local Prospects", *The Jakarta Post*, 11 July.

Al Azhari, Muhamad and Eko Prasetyo. 2017. "Ahok's Defeat Signifies Tough Road Ahead for Democratic and Tolerant Future", *Jakarta Globe,* 21 April. Available at https://jakartaglobe.id/news/ahoks-defeat-signifies-tough-road-ahead-democratic-tolerant-future/ (accessed 17 Oct. 2022).

Alsadad Rudi. 2014. "Ahok: Biasanya PKL Setor ke Preman, Sekarang Kita yang jadi Godfather", *Kompas.com*, 4 July. Available at https://megapolitan.kompas.com/read/2014/07/04/12240521/Ahok.Biasanya.PKL.Setor.ke.Preman.Sekarang.Kita.yang.Jadi.Godfather (accessed 8 Dec. 2022).

AlSayyad, N. 2004. "Urban Informality as a 'New' Way of Life", in *Urban Informality: Transnational Perspectives from the Middle East, South Asia and Latin America*, ed. N. AlSayyad and A. Roy. Lanham, MD: Lexington Books, pp. 7–30.

Amin, Ash and Nigel Thrift. 2002. *Reimagining the Urban*. Cambridge, UK: Polity Press.

Anand, Nikhil. 2015. "Leaky States: Water Audits, Ignorance, and the Politics of Infrastructure", *Public Culture* 27, 2: 305–30.

Anderson, B. 2009. "Afterword", in *Populism in Asia*, ed. K. Mizuno and P. Phongpaichit. Honolulu: University of Hawaii Press, pp. 217–20.

Andriyanto, Heru and Lenny Tristia Tambun. 2019. "City Officials Struggle to Explain Rp. 82b Budget for Glue", *Jakarta Globe*, 31 Oct.

Arai Kenichiro. 2011. "From Water Buffaloes to Motorcycles: The Development of Large-scale Industrial Estates and their Socio-spatial Impact on the Surrounding Villages in Karawang Regency, West Java", *Southeast Asian Studies* 49, 2: 161–91.

_____. 2015. "Jakarta 'Since Yesterday': The Making of the Post-New Order Regime in an Indonesian Metropolis", *Southeast Asian Studies* 4, 3: 445–86.

Armas, Adnin. 2016/17. "Aksi 212 adalah Karya Bersama Segenap Umat Islam Indonesia", *Jurnal Ekonomika* 4, 1: 37–41.

Bainbridge, Amy. 2013. "Indonesia's Bikers Drive Booming Sector", ABC News, 12 April. Available at http://www.abc.net.au/news/2013-04-12/indonesian-bikers-drive-booming-sector/4626444 (accessed 12 Oct. 2022).

Barker, Joshua. 1998. "State of Fear: Controlling the Criminal Contagion in Suharto's New Order", *Indonesia* 66 (October): 7–43.

_____. 1999. "Surveillance and Territoriality in Bandung", in *Figures of Criminality in Indonesia, the Philippines and Colonial Vietnam*, ed. V. Rafael. Ithaca, NY: Cornell University Press, pp. 95–127.

Barker, Joshua and Sheri Gibbings. 2018. "Cultures and Politics of Indonesian Infrastructures", *Indonesia* 105 (April): 1–17.

Batuman, Bülent, ed. 2021. *Cities and Islamism: On the Politics and Production of the Built Environment*. New York: Routledge.

Blusse, Leonard. 1981. "Batavia, 1619–1740: The Rise and Fall of a Chinese Colonial Town", *Journal of Southeast Asian Studies* 12, 1: 159–78.

_____. 1985. "An Insane Administration and Insanitary Town: The Dutch East India Company and Batavia (1619–1799)", in *Colonial Cities: Essays on Urbanism in a Colonial Context*, ed. Robert J. Ross and Gerard J. Telkamp. Dordrecht: Nijhoff, pp. 65–85.

Boeke, Julius H. 1953 [1910]. *Economics and Economic Policy of Dual Societies*. New York: Institute of Pacific Relations.

Boomgaard, Peter. 2007. "In a State of Flux: Water as a Deadly and a Life-giving Force in Southeast Asia", in *A World of Water: Rain, Rivers, and Seas in Southeast Asian Histories*, ed. Peter Boomgaard. Leiden: KITLV Press, pp. 1–26. Doi: 10.26530/OAPEN_376971. .

Boomgaard, Peter, ed. 2007. *A World of Water: Rain, Rivers, and Seas in Southeast Asian Histories*. Leiden: KITLV Press. https://doi.org/10.1163/9789004254015.

Bowen, John. 1986. "On the Political Construction of Tradition: Gotong Royong in Indonesia", *Journal of Asian Studies* 45, 3: 545–61.

Brand, Peter. 2007."Green Subjection: The Politics of Neoliberal Urban Environmental Management", *International Journal of Urban and Regional Research* 31, 3: 16–32.

Buck-Morss, Susan. 1995. "The City as Dreamworld and Catastrophe", *October* 73 (Summer): 3–26. https://doi.org/10.2307/779006.

Bunnell, Tim et al. 2013. "Urban Development in a Decentralized Indonesia: Two Success Stories?", *Pacific Affairs* 86, 4: 857–76.

Bunnell, Tim and Michelle Ann Miller. 2011. "Jakarta in Post-Suharto Indonesia: Decentralization, Neo-Liberalism and Global City Aspiration", *Space and Polity* 15, 1: 35–48.

Burhani, Ahmad Najib. 2020. "Anies Baswedan: His Political Career, COVID-19, and the 2024 Presidential Election", *Perspective* (ISEAS) 48, 19 May.

Butler, Judith. 2018. *Notes Toward a Performative Theory of Assembly*. Cambridge, MA: Harvard University Press.

Caljouw, M. Peter, J. M. Nas and Pratiwo. 2005. "Flooding in Jakarta: Towards a Blue City with Improved Water Management", *Bijdragen tot de Taal-, Land- en Volkenkunde* 161, 4: 454–84.

Castells, Manuel. 1977 (French version, 1972). *The Urban Question: A Marxist Approach*. Cambridge, MA: MIT Press.

_____. 2010. *The Rise of The Network Society*. 2nd ed. Oxford; Malden, MA: Blackwell.

Chalana, Manish and Jeffrey Hou, eds. 2016. *Messy Urbanism: Understanding the "Other" Cities of Asia*. Hong Kong: Hong Kong University Press. https://doi.org/10.5790/hongkong/9789888208333.001.0001.

Clarke, Giles T.R. 1985. "Jakarta, Indonesia: Planning to Solve Urban Conflicts", in *Cities in Conflict: Studies in the Planning and Management of Asian Cities*, ed. John P. Lea and John M. Courtney. Washington, DC: World Bank.

Cochrane, Joe. 2016. "What's Clogging Jakarta's Waterway? You Name It", *New York Times*, 3 Oct.: A4

*Coconuts Jakarta*. 2015. "Ahok: Government is Ready to Go to War with Parking Thugs", 11 Aug. Available at https://coconuts.co/jakarta/news/ahok-government-ready-go-war-parking-thugs/ (accessed 2 Oct. 2022).

Colombijn, Freek. 2010. *Under Construction: The Politics of Urban Space and Housing during the Decolonization of Indonesia, 1930–1960*. Leiden: KITLV Press. https://doi.org/10.1163/9789004263932.

Cowherd, Robert. 2002a. "Planning or Cultural Construction? The Transformation of Jakarta in the Late Suharto Period", in *The Indonesian Town Revisited*, ed. Peter J.M. Nas. Münster: LIT Verlag and Singapore: ISEAS, pp. 17–40.

_____. 2002b. *Cultural Construction of Jakarta: Design, Planning and Development in Jabotabek, 1980–1997*. PhD dissertation, Cambridge, MA: MIT.

_____. 2005. "Does Planning Culture Matter? Dutch and American Models in Indonesian Urban Transformations", in *Comparative Planning Cultures*, ed. Bishwapriya Sanyal. New York: Routledge: 165–92.

Cowherd, Robert and Eric Heikkila. 2002. "Orange County, Java: Hybridity, Social Dualism and an Imagined West", in *Southern California and the World*, ed. Eric Heikkila and Rafael Pizarro. Westport, CT.: Greenwood Press, pp. 195–220.

Danusari, Aryo. 2013. "Performing Crowds: The Circulative Urban Forms of the Tariqa Alawiya Youth Movement in Contemporary Indonesia", in *Global Prayers: Contemporary Manifestations of the Religious in the City*, ed. Jochen Becker et al. Zurich: Lars Mueller, pp. 338–51.

Das, Ashok Kumar. 2006. "What's Real and What's Rhetorical? The Effects of Decentralization and Participation on Slum Upgrading in Surabaya", paper presented at the Annual Conference of the Association of Collegiate Schools of Planning, Chicago, 9–12 Nov. Available at: http://blog.hawaii.edu/durp/files/2014/03/Das_ACSPpaper_CKIP-06.pdf

Deleuze, Gilles and Félix Guattari. 1987. *A Thousand Plateaus: Capitalism and Schizophrenia*. Trans. Brian Massumi. Minneapolis, MN: University of Minnesota Press [originally published in French 1980].

De Soto, Hernando. 2000. *The Mystery of Capital: Why Capitalism Triumphs in the West and Fails Everywhere Else*. New York: Basic Books, 2000.

Dewi, Sita W. 2014. "Jakarta Administration Aiming to Clear All Slum Housing by 2017", *Jakarta Post*, 21 Nov.

Dick, Howard. 1981. "Urban Public Transport Part II", *Bulletin of Indonesian Economic Studies* 17, 2: 72–88.

Dick, Howard and Peter J. Rimmer. 1980. "Beyond the Formal/Informal Sector Dichotomy", *Pacific Viewpoint* 1: 26–41.

_____. 1998. "Beyond the Third World City: The New Urban Geography of Southeast Asia", *Urban Studies* 35, 12: 2303–22.

Dickson, E. et al. 2012. *Urban Risk Assessment: Jakarta*. Washington: World Bank.

Djarot Saiful Hidayat. 2017. "Kita Jangan Balik ke Zaman Jahiliah", *Tempo*, 16 July: 101–3.

Dorléans, Bernard. 2002. "Urban Land Speculation and City Planning Problems in Jakarta before the 1998 Crisis", in *The Indonesian Town Revisited*, ed. Peter J.M. Nas. Münster: LIT Verlag and Singapore: ISEAS, pp. 41–56.

Douglass, Mike. 2000. "Mega-Urban Regions and World City Formation: Globalisation, the Economic Crisis and Urban Policy Issues in Pacific Asia", *Urban Studies* 37, 12: 2315–35.

_____. 2010. "Globalization, Mega-projects, and the Environment: Urban Form and Water in Jakarta", *Environment and Urbanization* 1, 1: 45–65.

Dovey, Kim. 2014. "Incremental Urbanism: The Emergence of Informal Settlements", in *Emergent Urbanism*, ed. T. Haas and K. Olsson. London: Ashgate, pp. 45–54.

Dowding, Keith and Patrick Dunleavy. 1996. "Production, Disbursement and Consumption: The Modes and Modalities of Goods and Services", *Sociological Review* Special Issue 44, S1: 36–65.

Dreyfuss, Jeff. 1990. "Jakarta: Two Personae – 'the Big Village' and 'Rock City': A City Caught between Worlds", *Journal of South Asian Literature* 25, 1: 177–87.

Elson, Robert. E. 2009. "Another Look at the Jakarta Charter Controversy of 1945", *Indonesia* 88 (Oct.): 105–30.

Endah, A. 2012. *Jokowi: Memimpin Kota Menyentuh Jakarta* [*Jokowi: Leading the City, Touching Jakarta*]. Jakarta: Metagraf.

Evans, Peter. 2002. "Introduction: Looking for Agents for Urban Livability in a Globalized Political Economy", in *Liveable Cities? Urban Struggles for Livelihood and Sustainability*, ed. Peter Evans. Berkeley: University of California Press, pp. 1–30.

Firman, Tommy. 1989. "Mobilitas Tenaga Kerja Industri Konstruksi: Studi Kasus Interaksi Desa dan Kota di Jawa" [Mobility of the Construction Industry Labour Force: A Case Study of Rural and Urban Interaction in Java], *Prisma* 3, XVIII: 48–63.

_____. 1998. "The Restructuring of Jakarta Metropolitan Area: A Global City in Asia", *Cities* 15, 4: 229–43.

_____. 2000. "Rural to Urban Land Conversion in Indonesia during Boom and Burst Periods", *Land Use Policy* 17, 1: 13–20.

_____. 2002. "Indonesian Cities in the Early Reform Era", in *The Indonesian Town Revisited*, ed. Peter Nas. Münster: LIT Verlag and Singapore: ISEAS, pp. 101–12.

_____. 2004. "New Town Development in Jakarta Metropolitan Region: A Perspective of Spatial Segregation", *Habitat International* 28, 3: 349–68.

Firman, Tommy et al. 2010. "Potential Climate Change Related Vulnerabilities in Jakarta: Challenges and Current Status", *Habitat International* 35, 2: 372–8.

Fishman, Robert. 1987. *Bourgeois Utopias: The Rise and Fall of Suburbia*. New York: Basic Books.

Foucault, Michel. 1977 [1975]. *Discipline and Punish*. New York: Pantheon Books.

Friedmann, John. 2011. "Introduction: Becoming Urban—Periurban Dynamics in Vietnam and China", *Pacific Affairs* 84, 3: 425–34.

Friedmann, John and André Sorensen. 2019. "City Unbound: Emerging Mega-conurbations in Asia", *International Planning Studies* 24, 1: 1–12.

Fuller, Andrew. 2004. Postmodernism and How Ajidarma used it Against the New Order. MA Thesis, University of Melbourne.

Gandy, Matthew. 2006. "The Bacteriological City and Its Discontents", *Historical Geography* 34: 19–20.

Garreau, J. 1991. *Edge City: Life on the New Frontier*. New York: Doubleday.

Gilbert, Alan and Josef Gugler. 1992. *Cities, Poverty, and Development: Urbanization in the Third World*. New York: Oxford University Press.

Graham, Stephen and Simon Marvin. 2001. *Splintering Urbanism: Networked Infrastructures, Technological Mobilities and the Urban Condition.* New York: Routledge.

Guinness, Patrick. 2009. *Kampung, Islam and State in Urban Java.* Singapore: NUS Press.

Gunadi, Iwan. 2003. "Produk Ketertekanan tanpa Ideologi Bulat", *Sastra Kota: Bunga Rampai Esai Temu Sastra Jakarta.* Dewan Kesenian Jakarta and Bentang Budaya, pp. 67–91.

Gunawan Mohamad. 1979. "Jagorawi", in *Catatan Pinggir 1.* Jakarta: Gramedia.

Gunawan, Restu. 2010. *Gagalnya Sistim Kanal: Pengendalian Banjir Jakarta dari Masa ke Masa* [Failure of the Canal System: Flood Control in Jakarta from Time to Time]. Jakarta: Kompas.

Hardt, Michael and Antonio Negri. 2000. *Empire.* Cambridge, MA: Harvard University Press.

_____. 2004. *Multitude: War and Democracy in the Age of Empire.* Cambridge, MA: Harvard University Press.

Harms, Erik. 2011. *Saigon's Edge: On the Margin of Ho Chi Minh City.* Minneapolis, MN: University of Minnesota Press. https://doi.org/10.5749/minnesota/9780816656059.001.0001.

_____. 2016. "Urban Space and Exclusion in Asia", *Annual Review of Anthropology* 45, 1: 45–61.

Hart, Keith. 1973. "Informal Income Opportunities and Urban Employment in Ghana", *Journal of Modern African Studies* 11, 1: 61–89.

Harvey, David. 2005. *A Brief History of Neoliberalism.* Oxford: Oxford University Press. https://doi.org/10.1093/oso/9780199283262.001.0001.

_____. 2010. *The Enigma of Capital and the Crisis of Capitalism.* Oxford: Oxford University Press.

Hassan, Fuad. 1995. *Pentas Kota Raya.* Jakarta: Pustaka Jaya.

Hefner, Robert. 2000. *Civil Islam: Muslims and Democratization in Indonesia.* Princeton, NJ: Princeton University Press.

Hellman, Jörgen, Marie Thynell and Roanne van Voorst, eds. 2018. *Jakarta: Claiming Spaces and Rights in the City.* Abingdon and New York: Routledge.

Herlambang, Suryono, ed. 2006. *Politik Kota dan Hak Warga Kota* [Urban Politics and Urban Citizens' Rights]. Jakarta: Gramedia.

Herlambang, Suryono et al. 2018. "Jakarta's Great Land Transformation: Hybrid Neoliberalisation and Informality", *Urban Studies* 56, 4: 627–48. https://doi.org/10.1177/0042098018756556.

Hidayat, Reja. 2019. "Politik Dana Hibah Tempat Ibadah Anies Baswedan" [Anies Baswedan's Politics of Grants for Places of Worship], *tirto.id*, 10 Sept. Available at https://tirto.id/politik-dana-hibah-tempat-ibadah-anies-baswedan-ehME (accessed 6 Oct. 2022).

Hiebert, Murray. 1995. "Give and Take", *Far Eastern Economic Review*, 25 May.

Hoek-Smit, Marja C. 2002. "Implementing Indonesia's New Housing Policy: The Way Forward-- 'Findings and Recommendations of the Technical Assistance Project', Policy Development for Enabling the Housing Market to Work in Indonesia", Kimpraswil, Government of Indonesia and the World Bank. http://housingfinance.wharton.upenn.edu/Documents/Indonesia%20Housing%20Policy%20Study.pdf.

Hogan, Trevor and Christopher Houston. 2002. "Corporate Cities – Urban Gateways or Gated Communities Against the City? The Case of Lippo, Jakarta", in *Critical Reflections on Cities in Southeast Asia*, ed. Tim Bunnell, Lisa Drummond and K.C. Ho. Singapore: Brill, pp. 243–64.

Hosseini, Hamid. 2012. "Arthur Lewis' Dualism, the Literature of Development Economics, and the Less Developed Economies", *Review of European Studies* 4, 4: 132–40. https://dx.doi.org/10.5539/res.v4n4p132.

Hugo, Graeme. 1977. "Circular Migration", *Bulletin of Indonesian Economic Studies* 13, 3: 57–66.

Huyssen, Andreas. 2008. "Introduction: World Cultures, World Cities", in *Other Cities, Other Worlds: Urban Imaginaries in a Globalizing Age*, ed. Andreas Huyssen. Durham, NC: Duke University Press, pp. 1–23.

Ibrahim, Nur Amali. 2018. *Improvisational Islam: Indonesian Youth in a Time of Possibility*. Ithaca, NY: Cornell University Press. https://doi.org/10.7591/cornell/9781501727856.001.0001.

*Indonesia Property Report*. 1995. "New Towns and Satellite Cities", *Indonesia Property Report* 1, 2, 3rd Quarter.

Institute for Policy Analysis of Conflict (IPAC). 2019. "Anti-Ahok to Anti-Jokowi: Islamist Influence on Indonesia's 2019 Election Campaign", *IPAC Report*, No. 55, 15 March.

Irawaty, Dian Tri. 2018. "Jakarta's Kampung: Their History and Contested Future", MA Thesis, Geography, UCLA.

*Jakarta Post*. 1990. "Operation of Land Brokers Upsets Mayor", 14 May.

"Jakarta Smart City, Memangkas Birokrasi lewat Aplikasi" [Reducing Bureaucracy by Using Apps]. 2016. *Intisari*, 1 June. Available at https://www.myedisi.com/intisari/1326/2104/jakarta-smart-city-memangkas-birokrasi-lewat-aplikasi (accessed 7 Oct. 2022).

Jellinek, Lea. *The Wheel of Fortune: The History of a Poor Community in Jakarta*. Honolulu, HI: University of Hawaii Press, 1991.

Kamil, Ridwan. 2008. "Merebut Ruang yang Hilang" [Reclaiming Lost Space]. 27 Sept. https://ridwankamil.wordpress.com/2008/09/27/merebut-ruang-yang-hilang/

Keil, Roger. 2018. "After Suburbia: Research and Action in the Suburban Century", *Urban Geography* 41, 1: 1–12. doi 10.1080/02723638.2018.1548828.

Khusyairi, Johny. 2011. "Modernity on the Road Traffic of Surabaya in the 1920s", *Humaniora: Journal of Culture, Literature and Linguistics* 23, 3. Available at: http://jurnal.ugm.ac.id/jurnal-humaniora/article/view/1031 (accessed 19 Oct. 2022).

King, Ross and Dyah E. Idawati. 2010. "Surabaya Kampung and Distorted Communication", *Sojourn: Journal of Social Issues in Southeast Asia* 25, 2: 213–33.

Klein, Naomi. 2007. "Disaster Capitalism: The New Economy of Catastrophe", *Harper's Magazine*, Oct.

Kooy, Michelle and Karen Bakker. 2008. "Technologies of Government: Constituting Subjectivities, Spaces, and Infrastructures in Colonial and Contemporary Jakarta", *International Journal of Urban and Regional Research* 32, 2: 375–91.

Kurnia Sari Aziza. 2014. "Ahok: Motor-motor lewat Jalan Belakang Saja" [Ahok: Motorbikes Only on the Back Streets], 13 Nov. Available at https://megapolitan.kompas.com/read/2014/11/13/15133781/Ahok.Motor-motor.Lewat.Jalan.Belakang.Saja (accessed 9 Oct. 2022).

_____. 2015. "Ahok: Sekarang Zaman Mafia, Bukan Zaman Preman Lagi" [Now's the Time of the Mafia, No Longer the Time of Thugs], *Kompas.com*, 3 Nov. https://megapolitan.kompas.com/read/2015/11/03/16215091/Ahok.Sekarang.Zaman.Mafia.Bukan.Zaman.Preman.Lagi.

Kusno, Abidin. 2000. *Behind the Postcolonial: Architecture, Urban Space and Political Cultures in Indonesia*. New York: Routledge.

_____. 2010. *The Appearances of Memory: Mnemonic Practices of Architecture and Urban Form in Indonesia*. Durham, NC: Duke University Press.

_____. 2013. *After the New Order: Space, Politics, and Jakarta*. Honolulu, HI: University of Hawaii Press.

_____. 2018. "Southeast Asia: Colonial Discourses", and "Postcolonial Southeast Asia", in *Routledge Handbook of Planning History*, ed. Carola Hein. London: Routledge, Chapter 17, pp. 218–29; Chapter 18, pp. 230–43.

_____. 2019. "Foreword: Exemplary Centre and Beyond", *Asia Pacific Viewpoint* 60, 1: 3–6.

_____. 2022. "A 90th Birthday Tribute: Anthony D. King: An Appreciation", *Planning Perspectives* 37, 3: 641–54.

Kwak, Nancy. 2015. *A World of Homeowners: American Power and the Politics of Housing Aid*. Chicago, IL: Chicago University Press. https://doi.org/10.7208/chicago/9780226282497.001.0001.

Laclau, Ernesto. 2005. *On Populist Reason*. London: Verso.

LaFraniere, Sharon, John Pomfret and Lena H. Sun. 1997. "The Riadys' Persistent Pursuit of Influence", *Washington Post*, 27 May: A01.

Lang, E. 2003. *Edgeless Cities: Exploring the Elusive Metropolis*. Washington D.C.: Brookings Institution Press.

Langdon, Philip. 1995. "Asia Bound", *Progressive Architecture*, March: 45.

Larkin, Brian. 2013. "The Politics and Poetics of Infrastructure", *Annual Review of Anthropology* 42: 327–43.

Latifah, Yuni. 2019. *Lights of Life*, WWG Publisher.

Latour, Bruno. 2004. "Why has Critique Run Out of Steam? From Matters of Fact to Matters of Concern", *Critical Inquiry* 30, 2: 225–48. https://doi.org/10.1086/421123.

Leaf, Michael. 1991. *Land Regulation and Housing Development in Jakarta: From the 'Big Village' to the 'Modern City'*. PhD Dissertation: University of California Berkeley.

_____. 1993. "Land Rights for Residential Development in Jakarta, Indonesia: The Colonial Roots of Contemporary Urban Dualism", *International Journal of Urban and Regional Research* 17: 477–91.

_____. 1994a. "Legal Authority in an Extralegal Setting: The Case of Land Rights in Jakarta, Indonesia", *Journal of Planning Education and Research*, 14: 12–18.

_____. 1994b. "The Suburbanization of Jakarta: A Concurrence of Economic and Ideology", *Third World Planning Review* 16, 4: 341–56.

_____. 2011. "Periurban Asia: A Commentary on 'Becoming Urban'", *Pacific Affairs* 84, 3: 525–34.

Lee Han Shih. 2009a. "Mochtar Riady: The Banker without a Bank", *The Asia Magazine*, 17 March. http://www.theasiamag.com/people/mochtar-riady-the-banker-without-a-bank <no longer available>.

_____. 2009b. "James Riady: The Evangelical Felon", *The Asia Magazine*, 17 March. http://www.theasiamag.com/people/james-riady-the-evangelical-felon, <no longer available>.

_____. 2009c. "Exodus out of Indonesia", *The Asia Magazine*, 31: 39.

Leisch, Harald. 2002. "Gated Communities in Indonesia", *Cities* 19, 5: 341–50.

Leitner, Helga and Eric Sheppard. 2018. "From Kampungs to Condos? Contested Accumulations through Displacement in Jakarta", *Environment and Planning A: Economy and Space* 50, 2: 437–56.

Ley, Lukas. 2017. "Building on Borrowed Time: The Temporal Horizons of Infrastructural Breakdown in the Delta of Semarang" (PhD Dissertation, University of Toronto).

_____. 2018. "Discipline and Drain: River Normalization and Semarang's Fight against Tidal Flooding", *Indonesia* 105, April, pp. 53–75.

Lim, William. 2012. *Incomplete Urbanism: A Critical Urban Strategy for Emerging Economies*. Singapore: World Scientific.

Lindsey, T. 2001. "The Criminal State: Premanisme and the New Indonesia", in *Indonesia Today: Challenges of History*, ed. G. Lloyd and S. Smith. Singapore: ISEAS, pp. 283–97.

Liong Ju Tjong et al. 2020. "Space Grabs: Colonizing the Vertical City", *International Journal of Urban and Regional Research* 44, 6: 1072–82.

Lippo Homes. 2018. *Meikarta*. Available at https://www.lippohomes.com/Project/Index/1026 (accessed 30 Sept. 2022).

Mahasin, Aswab. 1992. "Two Faces of the Cities", *Prisma: The Indonesian Indicator* 51: 2–3.

Malo, Manasse and Peter J.M. Nas. 1996. "Queen City of the East and Symbol of the Nation: the Administration and Management of Jakarta", in *The Dynamics of Metropolitan Management in Southeast Asia*, ed. Jürgen Rüland. Singapore: ISEAS, pp. 99–132.

Maulia, Erwida. 2020. "Indonesia's Wealth Gap Spurs Muslims to Join 'Economic Jihad'", *Nikkei Asia Review*, 28 Jan.

Mbembe, Achille. 1992. "Provisional Notes on the Postcolony", *Africa* 62, 1: 3–37.

McFarlane, Colin. 2010. "Urban Shadows: Materiality, the 'Southern City' and Urban Theory", *Geography Compass* 2, 2: 340–58.

McGee, Terry. 1991. "The Emergence of Desakota Regions in Asia: Expanding a Hypothesis", in *The Extended Metropolis: Settlement Transition in Asia*, ed. N. Ginsburg, B. Koppel and T. McGee. Honolulu, HI: University of Hawaii Press, pp. 3–26.

_____. 2002. "Jalan, Jalan: Invading, Destroying and Reconstructing the Southeast Asian City", *Bijdragen tot de Taal-, Land- en Volkenkunde* 158, 4: 637–52.

McGee, Terry and Ira Robinson, eds. 1995. *The Mega-Urban Regions of Southeast Asia*. Vancouver: UBC Press.

Miyake, Yoshimi. 2006. "Political and Cultural Aspects of Japanese War Compensation to Indonesia" [in Japanese]. *Meiji Gakuin Daigaku Gengo Bunka Kenkyu* 23.

Mizuno, K. and P. Phongpaichit, eds. 2009. *Populism in Asia*. Honolulu: University of Hawaii Press.

Mrázek, Rudolf. 2008. *Engineers of Happy Land: Technology and Nationalism in a Colony*. Princeton, NJ: Princeton University Press.

_____. 2013. "Water and the Colonial Urban Imaginary: Rudolf Mrázek in Conversation with *Architecture + Adaptation*", in *Jakarta: Architecture + Adaptation*, ed. Etienne Turpin, Adam Bobbette and Meredith Miller. Depok: Universitas Indonesia Press.

"Murphy/Jahn: Jakarta Communications Tower". 1995. *Architectural Design AD*, 65, 7/8, July-August.

Murray, Alison. 1991. *No Money, No Honey: A Study of Street Traders and Prostitutes in Jakarta*. Oxford: Oxford University Press.

Musni Umar. 2015. "Konflik dan Kemiskinan di DKI Jakarta, Bagaimana Mengatasinya?" [Conflict and Poverty in Jakarta: How Can it be Overcome?], *Kompasiana*, 7 August.

Available at http://www.kompasiana.com/musniumar/konflik-dan-kemiskinan-di-dki-jakarta-bagaimana-mengatasinya_55c48ce42cb0bd2b102cba7c (accessed 7 Oct. 2022).

Mydan, Seth. 2007. "Flood Toll Rises and Indonesia Braces for Disease", *New York Times*, 6 Feb., p. A 11.

Nas, Peter. 1990. "The Origin and Development of the Urban Municipality in Indonesia", *Sojoum: Journal of Social Issues in Southeast Asia* 5, 1: 86–112.

Newberry, Jan. 2006. *Back Door Java: State Formation and the Domestic in Working Class Java*. Guelph, ON: Broadview Press. https://doi.org/10.3138/9781442603141.

Noor, Farish A. 2011. "The Partai Keadilan Sejahtera (PKS) in the Landscape of Indonesian Islamist Politics: Cadre-Training as Mode of Preventive Radicalisation?". Singapore: S. Rajaratnam School of International Studies (RSIS) Working Paper 231.

_____. 2012. "The Forum Betawi Rempug (FBR) of Jakarta: An Ethnic-Cultural Solidarity Movement in a Globalising Indonesia". Singapore: S. Rajaratnam School of International Studies (RSIS) Working Paper 242.

Nugroho, Johannes. 2017. "Abolition of Accountability Reports a Setback", *Jakarta Globe*, 7 Dec.

Nur Yasmin. 2019. "An Indonesian Governor Confronts His Illuminati Accusers", *Jakarta Globe*, 11 June. Available at https://jakartaglobe.id/context/an-indonesian-governor-confronts-his-illuminati-accusers/ (accessed 2 Oct. 2022).

Okamoto Masaaki. 2013. "Jakarta's Local Politics and its Institutional Lack of Democracy", Center for Southeast Asian Studies Kyoto University *CSEAS Newsletter* 67 (Spring): 11–13.

Ong, Aihwa. 2011a. "Introduction: Worlding Cities", in *Worlding Cities: Asian Experiments and the Art of Being Global*, ed. Ananya Roy and Aihwa Ong. London: Wiley-Blackwell, pp. 1–26.

_____. 2011b. "Hyperbuilding: Spectacle, Speculation, and the Hyperspace of Sovereignty", in *Worlding Cities: Asian Experiments and the Art of Being Global*, ed. Ananya Roy and Aihwa Ong. London: Wiley-Blackwell, pp. 205–26.

Onghokham. 2003. *Wahyu yang Hilang, Negeri yang Guncang* [*The Loss of Divine Power, the Shock of the Nation*]. Jakarta: Tempo and the Freedom Institute.

Paat, Yustinus. 2020. "Anies Defends Coastal Reclamation in Ancol", *Jakarta Globe*, 13 July.

Padawangi, Rita and Mike Douglass. 2015. "Water, Water Everywhere: Toward Participatory Solutions to Chronic Urban Flooding in Jakarta", *Pacific Affairs* 88, 3: 517–50.

Pannell, Sandra. 2007. "Of Gods and Monsters: Indigenous Sea Cosmologies, Promiscuous Geographies, and the Depths of Local Sovereignty", in *A World of Water: Rain,*

*Rivers, and Seas in Southeast Asian Histories*, ed. Peter Boomgaard. Leiden: KITLV Press: 71–102.

Pearson, Clifford A. 1993. "Going Global", *Architectural Record*, March: 3.

Pemberton, John. 1994. *On the Subject of Java*. Ithaca, NY: Cornell University Press. https://doi.org/10.7591/9781501729362.

Pepinsky, Tom. 2017. "Jakarta's New Governor Doubles Down on Identity", *New Mandala*, 17 Oct. Available at https://www.newmandala.org/jakartas-new-governor-doublesidentity/ (accessed 3 April 2020).

Peters, Robbie. 2013. *Surabaya, 1945–2010: Neighbourhood, State and Economy in Indonesia's City of Struggle*. Singapore: NUS Press.

Phelps, Nicholas et al. 2006. *Post-Suburban Europe: Planning and Politics at the Margins of Europe's Capital Cities*. New York: Palgrave Macmillan. https://doi.org/10.1057/9780230625389.

Pollock, Naomi R. 1993. "KPF Bank Complex Rises in Jakarta", *Architectural Record*, March: 4.

Porio, Emma. 1997. "Rethinking the Enabling Strategy in Social Housing: State–Civil Society Dynamics in Southeast Asia", in *Governance on the Ground: Innovations and Discontinuities in Cities of the Developing World*, ed. Patricia L. McCarney and Richard E. Stren. Baltimore: The Johns Hopkins University Press, pp. 171–93.

Prasetyo, Frans Ari. 2017. "Bandung Mau Berubah dengan Bersolek, Hanya Saja Terlalu Menor", *Tirto.id.*, 13 Dec. Available at https://tirto.id/bandung-mau-berubah-dengan-bersolek-hanya-saja-terlalu-menor-cBAq (accessed 16 Dec. 2022).

_____. 2019a. "From Creative City to Religious City: Mesjid, Alun-alun dan Palestina Walk di Bandung" (unpublished paper).

_____. 2019b. "Alun-alun, Palaguna dan Kuasa Lahan (Kota)", *Indonesia.id.*, 27 April. Available at https://www.indonesiana.id/read/109311/alun-alun-palaguna-dan-kuasa-lahan-kota (accessed 16 Dec. 2022).

Pugh, Cedric. 1994. "The Idea of Enablement in Housing Development: The Political Economy of Housing for Developing Countries", *Cities* 11, 6: 357–71.

Rabinow, Paul. 1989. *French Modern: Norms and Forms of the Social Environment*. Cambridge, MA: MIT Press.

Rachmadi, Benny. 2012. "Jokowi Hadapi Banjir", *Kontan*, 28 Nov. Available at http://images.kontan.co.id/main/kartun_benny/302 (accessed 3 Oct. 2022).

Rachmatunisa. 2015. "Ridwan Kamil, Anak Twitter yang Jadi Walikota" [Ridwan Kamil, a Child of Twitter who Became Mayor], *detikinet*, 16 June. Available at https://inet.detik.com/cyberlife/d-2943296/ridwan-kamil-anak-twitter-yang-jadi-walikota/2?device=desktop (accessed 3 Oct. 2022).

Rahn, John. 2008. "'Mille Plateaux', You Tarzan: A Musicology of (an Anthropology of (an Anthropology of *A Thousand Plateaus*))", *Perspectives of New Music* 46, 2 (Summer): 81–92.

Ramadhan K.H. 1992 (republished 2012). *Ali Sadikin: Membenahi Jakarta Menjadi Kota yang Manusiawi* [Ali Sadikin: Fixing Jakarta to Make it a Human City]. Jakarta: Ufuk Press.

Rao, Vyjayanthi. 2012. "Slum as Theory: Mega-cities and Urban Models", in *The SAGE Handbook of Architectural Theory*, ed. C. Greig Crysler, S. Cairns and H. Heynen. London: Sage, pp. 671–86.

Reerink, Gustav and Jean-Louis Van Gelder. 2010. "Land Titling, Perceived Tenure Security, and Housing Consolidation in the Kampongs of Bandung, Indonesia", *Habitat International* 34, 1: 78–85.

Reid, Anthony. 1998. "Political 'Tradition' in Indonesia: The One and the Many", *Asian Studies Review* 22, 1: 23–38.

Riach, James. 2014. "Zaha Hadid Defends Qatar World Cup Role Following Migrant Worker Deaths", *The Guardian*, 25 Feb. Available at https://www.theguardian.com/world/2014/feb/25/zaha-hadid-qatar-world-cup-migrant-worker-deaths (accessed 27 Sept. 2022).

Riady, Mochtar. 2016. *Mochtar Riady: My Life Story*. Hoboken, NJ.: Wiley.

————. 2018a. "The Story of Lippo Group and Modern Indonesia: Mochtar Riady's story (1)", *The Nikkei Review*, 10 Sept.

————. 2018b. "Lippo Gets its Start as an Import Agency: Mochtar Riady's Story (21)", *The Nikkei Review*, 30 Sept.

————. 2018c. "The Opportunity for Growth Finally Comes: Mochtar Riady's Story (22)", *The Nikkei Review*, 1 Oct.

————. 2018d. "Turning Wasteland into a Valuable Asset: Mochtar Riady's Story (23)", *The Nikkei Review*, 2 Oct.

————. 2018e. "A New Direction for Lippo After the Asian Financial Crisis: Mochtar Riady's Story (25)", *The Nikkei Review*, 4 Oct.

————. 2018f. "Becoming a Christian in my 60s: Mochtar Riady's Story (29)", *The Nikkei Review*, 8 Oct.

"Riady Scion Seeks to Save Lippo Empire on the Brink". 2019. *The Business Times* (Singapore), 12 Sept. Available at https://www.businesstimes.com.sg/real-estate/riady-scion-seeks-to-save-lippo-empire-on-the-brink (accessed 30 Sept. 2022).

Ridha, Muhammad. 2018. *Melawan Regim Infrastruktur: Studi Ekonomi Politik* [Opposing the Infrastructure Regime: Studies in Political Economy]. Makassar: Cara Baca.

Rieky, Ferdinandus Benny. 2014. From *Kolantas: Koplak Berlalu Lintas*, by Taupik, Wisnu, Kasmiyanto dkk. Jakarta: Visimedia Pustaka, p. 49.

Rigg, Jonathan. 1988. "Rural-Urban Interactions, Agriculture and Wealth: A Southeast Asian Perspective", *Progress in Human Geography* 22, 4: 497–522.

Rizqo Kanavino Ahmad. 2017. "Ini Pidato Lengkap Anies Usai Dilantik Jadi Gubernur DKI" [This is Anies' Full Speech on Being Sworn in as Governor of the Special Capital Region]. 16 Oct. (accessed 2 April 2020).

Robison, Richard. 1986. *Indonesia: The Rise of Capital*. Sydney: Allen & Unwin.

Robison, Richard and Vedi Hadiz. 2004. *Reorganising Power in Indonesia: The Politics of Oligarchy in an Age of Markets*. Abingdon: Routledge.

Robinson, Geoffrey. 1995. *The Dark Side of Paradise: Political Violence in Bali*. Ithaca, NY: Cornell University Press.

Roosmalen, Pauline. 2015. "Expanding Grounds: the Roots of Spatial Planning in Indonesia", in *Kota Lama Kota Baru: Sejarah Kota-kota di Indonesia Sebelum dan Setelah Kemerdekaan*, ed. Freek Colombijn et al. Yogyakarta: Ombak Press: 75–117.

_____. 2017. "Modern Indisch Town Planning", in *The Life and Work of Thomas Karsten*, ed. Joost Coté et al. Amsterdam: Architecture & Natura, pp. 265–303.

Rosser, Colin. 1983. "The Evolving Role of a National Agency for Housing and Urban Development in Indonesia", *Habitat International* 7, 5/6: 137–49.

Roy, Ananya. 2005. "Urban Informality: Toward an Epistemology of Planning", *Journal of the American Planning Association* 71, 2: 147–58.

_____. 2009. "The 21st Century Metropolis: New Geographies of Theory", *Regional Studies* 43, 6: 819–30.

_____. 2011. "Slumdog Cities: Rethinking Subaltern Urbanism", *International Journal of Urban and Regional Research* 35, 2: 223–38.

Rusyanto, Edo. 2010. *Hiruk Pikuk Bersepeda Motor*. Jakarta: Tristart Kreasi.

Ryter, L. 1998. "'Pemuda Pancasila': The Last Loyalist Freemen of Suharto's Indonesia", *Indonesia* 66: 44–73.

Said, Edward. 1983. "Traveling Theory", in *The World, the Text and the Critic*. Harvard University Press, pp. 226–47.

_____. 1989. "Representing the Colonized: Anthropology's Interlocutors", *Critical Inquiry* 15, 2: 205–25.

Santosa, Iwan. 2005. "Keliru Konsep, Jakarta Terus Macet", *Kompas*, 18 June. http://www.pda.or.id/pustaka/books-detail.php?id=20050066.

Santoso, Jo. 2011. *The Fifth Layer of Jakarta*. Jakarta: Centropolis.

Santoso, Jo and Miya Irawati, eds. 2015. *Transformasi Urban Metropolitan Jakarta: Adaptasi dan Pengembangan*. Jakarta: Pusat Studi Metropolitan, Universitas Tarumanagara.

Sausan Atika. 2020. "Three Years on, Anies Still Missing Mark: Councillors", *Jakarta Post* 26 Oct. Available at https://www.thejakartapost.com/news/2020/10/26/three-years-on-anies-still-missing-mark-councillors.html (accessed 2 Oct. 2022).

Scott, James. 1972. "Patron-Client Politics and Political Change in Southeast Asia", *American Political Science Review* 66, 1: 91–113.

————. 1998. *Seeing like a State*. New Haven, CT: Yale University Press.

Seno Gumira Ajidarma. 2004a. "Dimensi Ruang: Kisah-kisah Jakarta", in *Affair: Obralan Tentang Jakarta*. Yogyakarta: Penerbit Buku Baik Yogyakarta; rpt. 2015 in *Tiada Ojek di Paris*. Jakarta: Mizan, pp. 179–87.

————. 2004b. "Manusia Jakarta, Manusia Mobil", in *Affair: Obralan Tentang Jakarta*. Yogyakarta: Penerbit Buku Baik Yogyakarta.

————. 2008. *Kentut Kosmoplitan*. Depok: Koekoesan.

Server, O.B. 1996. "Corruption: A Major Problem of Urban Management: Some Evidence from Indonesia", *Habitat International* 20, 1: 23–41.

Shatkin, Gavin. 2017. *Cities for Profit: The Real Estate Turn in Asia's Urban Politics*. Ithaca, NY: Cornell University Press.

Shaw, Robert. 2015. "Bringing Deleuze and Guattari Down to Earth through Gregory Bateson: Plateaus, Rhizomes and Ecosophical Subjectivity", *Theory, Culture & Society* 32, 7–8: 151–71. https://doi.org/10.1177/0263276414524451.

Sheppard, Eric. 2019. "Globalizing Capitalism's Raggedly Fringes: Thinking Through Jakarta", *Area Development and Policy* 4, 1: 1–27.

Sidel, John. 1998. "Macet Total: Logics of Circulation and Accumulation in the Demise of Indonesia's New Order", *Indonesia* 66 (Oct.): 158–95.

Silas, Johan. 1984. "The Kampung Improvement Programme of Indonesia: A Comparative Case Study of Jakarta and Surabaya", in *Low Income Housing in the Developing World*, ed. G. K. Payne. New York: Wiley, pp. 69–84.

————. 1987. "Indonesia", in *Housing Policy and Practice in Asia*, ed. Seong Kyu Ha. London: Croom Helm, pp. 135–58.

Silver, Christopher. 2008. *Planning the Megacity: Jakarta in the Twentieth Century*. New York: Routledge.

————. 2018. "Waterfront Jakarta: The Battle for the Future of the Metropolis", in *Jakarta: Claiming Spaces and Rights in the City*, ed. Jörgen Hellman, Marie Thynell and Roanne van Voorst. New York: Routledge, pp. 120–37.

Simanjuntak, I. et al. 2012. "Evaluating Jakarta's Flood Defence Governance: The Impact of Political and Institutional Reforms", *Water Policy* 14: 561–80.

Simatupang, Wita, Miya Irawati and Rully Mardona. 2015. "Symbiosis of *Kampong* and Large-scale Development: The Case of Kampung Menteng Atas and Rasuna Epicentrum Development", Conference Proceedings Paper, *True Smart and Green City?* 8th Conference of the International Forum on Urbanism, Incheon. https://doi.org/10.3390/ifou-A009.

Simmel, Georg. 1971 [1903]. "The Metropolis and Mental Life", in *Georg Simmel on Individuality and Social Forms*, ed. D. Levine. Chicago: University of Chicago Press.

Simone, AbdouMaliq. 2004. "People as Infrastructure: Intersecting Fragments in Johannesburg", *Public Culture* 16, 3 (Fall): 407–29.

_____. 2010. *City Life from Jakarta to Dakar: Movements at the Crossroads*. London: Routledge.

_____. 2013. "Cities of Uncertainty: Jakarta, the Urban Majority, and Inventive Political Technologies", *Theory, Culture & Society* 30, 7–8: 243–63.

_____. 2014. *Jakarta: Drawing the City Near*. Minneapolis, MN: Minnesota University Press.

Simone, AbdouMaliq and Vyjayanthi Rao. 2021. "Counting the Uncountable: Revisiting Urban Majorities", *Public Culture* 33, 2 (94): 151–60.

Sjahrir, Kartini. 1995. *Pasar Tenaga Kerja Indonesia: Kasus Sektor Konstruksi* [The Indonesian Labour Market: the Case of the Construction Industry]. Jakarta: Grafiti Press.

Slater, Dan and Diana Kim. 2015. "Standoffish States: Non-literate Leviathans in Southeast Asia", *Trans Regional and National Studies of Southeast Asia* 3, 1: 25–44.

Smith, Joan and Immanuel Wallerstein. 1992. *Creating and Transforming Households: The Constraints of the World-Economy*. Cambridge, UK: Cambridge University Press. https://doi.org/10.1017/CBO9780511520860.

Smith, T.M. 1977. "Corruption, Tradition and Change", *Indonesia* 11: 21–40.

Soegiarto, Yanto. 2017. "Lippo Group to Develop $21B Meikarta Industrial City", *GlobeAsia*, June, pp. 77–9. Available at https://beritasatumedia.cld.bz/bWKbTTo/81/#zoom=z (accessed 30 Sept. 2022).

Soja, Edward. 2000. *Postmetropolis: Critical Studies of Cities and Regions*. Oxford: Blackwell.

Specter, Michael. 1984. "Letter from Jakarta", *Far Eastern Economic Review*, 8 March.

Sukarno. 1962a. *Amanat Presiden Sukarno, pada Peringatan Ulang Tahun ke 435 Kota Djakarta di Gedung Olah Raga Djakarta, 22 Juni 1962*. Djakarta: Departemen Penerangan, no. 218.

_____. 1962b. "Transformation of Djakarta Raya", in *Indonesia 1962*. Department of Foreign Affairs, Republic of Indonesia.

Sulistyo, Hermawan. 2006. *Benang Kusut Lalulintas*. Jakarta: Pensil 324.

Sullivan, John. 1980. *Back Alley Neighbourhood: Kampung as Urban Community in Yogyakarta*. Melbourne: Monash University Centre of Southeast Asian Studies.

Sungkar, Aulia R. 2015. "National Developers Looking to Team Up with Foreign Investors", *The Jakarta Post*, 5 Nov.

Tabak, Faruk and Michaeline Crichlow, eds. 2000. *Informalization: Process and Structure*. Baltimore, MD: Johns Hopkins University Press.

Tani, Shotaro. 2018. "How Lippo's Field of Dreams Could Become a House of Cards", *The Nikkei Asia Review*, 7 Dec.

_____. 2019. "Indonesia's Lippo Group Throws 33-year-old Heir into Deep End", *Nikkei Asia*, 22 March. Available at https://asia.nikkei.com/Business/CEO-in-the-news/Indonesia-s-Lippo-Group-throws-33-year-old-heir-into-deep-end (accessed 30 Sept. 2022).

Texier, P. 2008. "Floods in Jakarta: When the Extreme Reveals Daily Structural Constraints and Mismanagement", *Disaster Prevention and Management* 17, 3: 358–72.

Thompson, Rachel. 2018. "A Dutch Garuda to Save Jakarta? Excavating the NCICD Master Plan's Socio-environmental Conditions of Possibility", in *Jakarta: Claiming Spaces and Rights in the City*, ed. Jörgen Hellman, Marie Thynell and Roanne van Voorst. New York: Routledge: 138–56.

*Toelichting op de "Stadvormingsordonnantie Stadsgemeenten Java"*. 1938. Batavia: Landsdrukkerij.

Toer, Pramoedya Ananta. 1955. "Letter to a Friend from the Country", in *From Surabaya to Armageddon*, ed. and trans. H. Aveling. Singapore: Heinemann.

Tunas, Devisari and Andrea Peresthu. 2010. "The Self-Help Housing in Indonesia: The Only Option for the Poor?", *Habitat International* 34, 3: 315–22.

Van Breen, Herman. 1917. *Kleine Werken ter Verbetering van den Gezondheidstoestand der Hoofdplaats Batavia*. Weltevreden: Albrecht, 1917.

_____. 1919. "Kleine Werken te Verbetering van den Gezondheidstoestand ter Hoofplaats Batavia", *Indisch Bouwkundig Tijdschrift*, 15 Sept.

Van Klinken, Gerry. 2011. "Mengkolonialisasi Borneo: Pembentukan Propinsi Dayak di Kalimantan" [Colonising Borneo: the Establishment of the Dayak Province in Kalimantan], in *Pembongkaran Narasi Besar Integrasi Bangsa*, ed. Sita van Bennelen and Remco Raben. Yayasan Pustaka Obor Indonesia, pp. 161–97.

Van Mead, Nick. 2016. "The World's Worst Traffic: Can Jakarta Find an Alternative to the Car?", *The Guardian*, 23 Nov. Available at <https://www.theguardian.com/cities/2016/nov/23/world-worst-traffic-jakarta-alternative> (accessed 9 Oct. 2022).

Van Voorst, Roanne. 2016. *Natural Hazards, Risk and Vulnerability: Floods and Slum Life in Indonesia*. New York: Routledge. https://doi.org/10.4324/9781315716411.

Vltchek, Andre. 2018. "Palangkaraya: Dreaming about the Soviet Capital of Indonesia and the 1965 US Backed Killing Fields", *Countercurrents.org.*, 8 Dec. Available at https://countercurrents.org/2018/12/palangkaraya-dreaming-about-the-soviet-capital-of-indonesia-and-the-1965-us-backed-killing-fields/ (accessed 16 Dec. 2022).

Wallerstein, Immanuel. 2004. *World-Systems Analysis: An Introduction*. Durham, NC: Duke University Press.

Wertheim, W.F., ed. 1958. *The Indonesian Town: Studies in Urban Sociology*. The Hague and Bandung: W. van Hoeve.

Widyanto, Untung. 2007. "Hoki di Perut Naga", *Tempo*, 25 Feb.: 40–2.

Widyanto, Untung et al. 2013. "Bah di Perut Naga", *Tempo*, 3 Feb.: 45.

Wijanarka. 2006. *Sukarno dan Desain Rencana Ibukota RI di Palangkaraya* [Sukarno and the Design Plan of the Capital of the Republic of Indonesia in Palangkaraya]. Yogyakarta: Ombak Press.

William, Anton, J. Supriadin and M.O. Istman. 2013. "Peluit Bahaya dari Latuharhary" [Alarm Whistle from Latuharhary], *Tempo*, 3 Feb.: 50.

Wilson, Ian. 2008. "'As Long as It's Halal': Islamic Preman in Jakarta", in *Expressing Islam: Religious Life and Politics in Indonesia*, ed. Greg Fealy and Sally White. Singapore: ISEAS-Yusof Ishak Institute, pp. 192–210.

_____. 2011. "Reconfiguring Rackets: Racket Regimes, Protection and the State in Post-New Order Jakarta", in *The State and Illegality in Indonesia*, ed. E. Aspinall and G. van Klinken. Jakarta: KITLV Press, pp. 239–60.

_____. 2015. *The Politics of Protection Rackets in Post-New Order Indonesia: Coercive Capital, Authority and Street Politics*. Abingdon: Routledge, 2015.

Winarso, Haryo. 2006. "Access to Main Roads or Low Cost Land? Residential Land Developers' Behavior in Indonesia", *Bijdragen tot de Taal-, Land- en Volkenkunde* 158, 4: 653–76.

Winayanti, Lana and Heracles C. Lang. 2004. "Provision of Urban Services in an Informal Settlement: A Case Study of Kampung Penas Tanggul, Jakarta", *Habitat International* 28, 1/2: 41–65.

Wirosardjono, Soetjipto. 1991. "The Informal Sector: Victims of a Double Standard", *Prisma* 51: 61–7.

Wirth, L. 1938. "Urbanism as a Way of Life", *American Journal of Sociology* 44, 1: 1–24.

Withers, Ian. 2014. "Southeast Asian Construction Economics: Chasing Tigers", *Building. co.uk.*, 6 Nov. Available at http://www.building.co.uk/south-east-asian-construction-economies-chasing-tigers/5071810.article (accessed 20 Sept. 2022).

Yen Tzu-Chien. 2017. "Reflections on a Reunion in Jakarta", *New Mandala*, 5 Dec. Available at https://www.newmandala.org/reflections-reunion/ (accessed 19 Oct. 2022).

Zaenuddin H.M. 2013. *Banjir Jakarta: dari Zaman Jendral JP Coen (1621) sampai Gubernur Jokowi (2013)* [Jakarta Floods: from the Time of General J.P. Coen (1621) to Governor Jokowi (2013)]. Jakarta: Change Publication.

# Index

1965, bloody coup of, 52
212 Alumni, 178
212 brand, 159, 167
212 Mart, 159–60
212 Movement, 157–62, 167

Abeyasekere, Susan, 146n1
*adat istiadat* (traditional festivals), 34
agriculture, 23
Ahok, Jakarta Governor, 71, 76, 83, 87,
    95–6, 128, 138, 186, 192, 212
  administrations of, 143, 145, 183
  anti-Ahok rally, 158–9
  anti-Ahok, reunion of, 159
  anti-Ahok, sentiments, 144
  aspiration for a "Jakarta without
      slums", 143
  aspiration to modernise and formalise
      housing in Jakarta, 141
  blasphemy allegation against, 144
  desire to transform Suharto's
      traditions of urban politics, 142
  end of tenure of, 144, 177–8, 189
  forcible eviction of residents from
      riverbank neighbourhoods, 143
  friends of, 189
  imprisonment of, 189
  new urban politics, 144
  pro-poor initiatives, 186
  protest against, 178
  protest by Islamic hardliners against,
      144
  removal of patronage control over
      street vendors, 140
  urban "beautification" agenda, 143

war against the parking *preman* bosses,
    140
AlSayyad, Nezar, 131
*Alun-alun* Bandung, 154–6
American century, 198–200
anti-Chinese sentiments, 144
anti-flooding system, 82
anti-foundational work, 15
anti-government rallies, 178
anti-lockdown protests, 214
anti-mathematical axiomatics, 15
*Appearances of Memory, The* (2010), 16
Arai, Kenichiro, 120
Armas, Adnin, 159
Artaud, Antonin, 14
Asia-Africa Conference (1955).
    *See* Bandung Conference of Asian and
    African Nations (1955)
Asian Century, 198–200
Asian financial crisis (1997), 1, 6, 65, 110,
    114, 175
Asian Games (1962), 144, 171
Asian suburbanisation, 111
Asian urbanisms, 23, 198–200
assemblage, 13–16, 20, 43, 50, 90, 103,
    108, 167, 182
assemblage of labourers, 220
authoritarian, 17
"auto-constructions", 1, 8–10
Automated People Mover (APM)
    monorail, 123
automobiles
  hegemony, 58
  industries, 59–60, 69
  transport systems based on, 57, 61

promotion of, 60

automobilisation, of city and suburb, 57

avant-garde architect, 152–3

*Babad Giyanti* (eighteenth-century
    chronicle), 169

back to the city, idea of, 47n2, 60, 98, 148,
    200

Badan Nasional Penanggulangan Bencana
    (BNPB). *See* National Disaster
    Mitigation Agency

Bakhtin, Mikhail, 25

Bali, 4, 14

*bandjirkanaal* (flood canal), 105n26

Bandung, 20, 151
    *alun-alun* (the town square) of, 154–5
    *Bandung Juara* (Bandung Champion),
        154, 157
    as capital city of West Java, 153
    as creative city, 157
    as green city, 157
    Masjid Al Safar in, 152–3
    middle class of, 154
    transformation from creative city to a
        religious city, 154
    urban connectivity of, 157

Bandung Conference of Asian and
    African nations (1955), 155, 171

"Bandung Unggul dan Agamais"
    (Bandung Champion and Religious),
    155

*banjir* (flooding), 15, 71–7, 103, 182
    "agent" of, 93
    in Batavia, 88
    as *bencana* (disaster), 81–2
    as *berkah* (blessing), 89–91
    as *bocor* (leaking), 88–9
    as *budaya* (culture), 91–3
    causes of, 94
    cultural aspects of, 93
    cyclical life of, 89
    deaths due to, 88
    displacing, 93–6
    economy of cleaning up after, 89

effects of, 92
engineered flooding, 84–7
environmental degradation due to, 201
flood relief and mutual help during
    periods of, 91
*longue durée* of, 93
management of, 82–3
money extortion by opportunists for
    personal benefit, 89
opportunities for "*bocor*-ing" money, 89
repairing of potholes after, 89
socio-political dimension of, 91
Zaenuddin's book on, 92

*banjir kiriman* (flooding water from
    outside their areas), 80

*banjir mengamuk*, notion of, 76

banks
    Asian Development Bank, 55, 94
    Bank Central Asia (BCA), 112
    deregulation and privatisation of, 112

BAPPENAS, 41, 170, 173

barricades, 213–14

Baswedan, Anies, 129, 144, 146, 157–8,
    186–7, 207
    American century, 198–200
    style of governing of Jakarta, 188

Batavia, 50, 76, 83–4, 88, 90, 92
    City Hall, 177
    colonial architecture of, 6
    environmental problems, 174
    flooding in, 88
    massacre of 1740, 177
    urban development in, 174

*Bataviasche Electrische Tramweg*, 50

Bateson, Gregory, 14

*becak* (pedicab), 49, 52–4, 64–5

Bekasi Regency, 110

*bela bangsa* (defending the state), 161

*bemo*, 49, 52–3

*benang kusut* (tangled threads), 50

Benmaamar, Mustapha, 68

Benton, Gordon, 118

*bersih kampung* (cleaning the environment),
    34

"Betawi" identity, 186
bicycle taxis. *See ojek*
bike revolution, 207
binary opposition, 17, 27, 31
blasphemy law, 190
Bodjonegoro, Bambang, 170
Body without Organs, 14
Boeke, Julius Herman, 29, 31
bourgeois environmentalism, 200
*Bourgeois Utopias* (Fishman), 123
Bowo, Fauzi "Foker", 61, 81, 106n33, 176, 186, 200, 212–13
brokers
    *calo*, 2
    *perantara*, 132
BRT (bus rapid transit) system, 200
bubble economy, 5
*Building* (magazine), 1, 10
Bumi Serpong Damai, 59
bureaucratic reforms, in Jakarta, 139, 177
business as usual, tradition of, 139
busway lanes, in Jakarta, 62

capital, 4–6
    accumulation of, 33, 36
    dead capital, 12
    future of, 10–11
capitalism, 12, 18, 24, 33, 41, 45, 61, 102, 143, 166, 186, 220, 222
capitalist development, 52, 219, 222
capitalist modernisation, 18, 25, 36, 56, 103, 190, 199
    development of, 201
    plans for, 59
capitalist ventures, 222
capitalist world-economy, 138
car civilisation, of the US, 199
car-free day, on weekends, 207
carpools, 62–3
car society, 198, 200
Castells, Manuel, 123, 157, 220
    *Urban Question, The*, 21, 219, 220, 221, 222, 225, 226
catchment zone, 80

Central Jakarta, 116–17
    mayor of, 96
    Menteng area of, 80
Chaniago, Andrinof, 173, 181
Chatterjee, Partha, 196, 198
China, 6, 10
    investment in Indonesia, 199
    rise of, 198
Chinese Christians, 186–7
Cideng River, 78
Ciliwung River, 50, 84, 94–6, 105, 192
Ciputra Group, 10, 59–60, 199
"Cities without Slums" campaign, 142
City Administration Office (Dinas Tata Kota), 107n44
city in transition, theory of, 219
city of a thousand dimensions, 11–13, 203–5, 212, 226
civil society, 17, 19, 44, 45, 131, 192, 195–8
    formation of, 197
climate change, 71, 92, 103, 203
clothing (*sandang*), 42
coalition of parties, 183
coastal development plan, 100
Coen, J.P., 92
collective collaboration, 209
collective consumption, growth of, 219–22, 226
colonial economy, 29
colonial era, 17, 29, 51–2, 84, 174, 201
colonial modes of knowledge production, 15
colonialism, age of, 6
Communism, in Indonesia, 52
Communities that Care for Pluit's Environment, 78
Constitution of Indonesia, 149, 158
construction boom, in Asia, 1, 6
construction culture, in Indonesia, 4, 12
construction economies, 1, 7–8
construction industry
    in Indonesia, 2
    in Japan, 7

construction workers
 formalisation of, 4
 recruitment of, 3
 relation with *mandor*, 3
 transnational, 6–7
contingency planning, 203
core, 31. *See also* periphery
corporate social responsibility, 154, 191–2
corruption, 60, 76, 100, 110, 129–32, 135, 139, 142, 143, 146n8, 147n11, 156, 158, 176, 185, 186, 188, 204
Country Garden Holdings, 122, 124
COVID-19 pandemic, 19, 21, 206, 216, 224–6
 anti-lockdown protests, 214
 mobility restrictions due to, 213
critical infrastructure studies, 16
cultural hegemony, production of, 129
cultural ideology, 3
"culturalist" trap, 204
cultural rituals and ceremonies, 34
Curitiba, Brazilian city of, 200

*daharuning praja*, 169
*Dajjal* (one-eyed devil in Islamic mythology), 152
*dana hibah*, 187
Danusari, Aryo, 165–6
Darmadi, Jan, 4
debt payment, 125
decentralisation, 41, 44, 46, 128, 135, 175, 182–4, 196, 221
Decentralisation Act (1903), 146n1
*de facto* settlements, 23
Deleuze, Gilles, 13–14, 152–3
Delta Silicon (Silicon Valley of Indonesia), 123
 Industrial Park, 120
democracy, 17, 151, 182
democratic era, post-Suharto, 62
Department of Transport (*Dinas Perhubungan*), 61
*desakota*, 23, 29, 55–7, 111
de Soto, Hernando, 9, 12, 44

development, ideology, 12, 17, 24
development balanced, 131
Dick, H.W., 52
digital utopia, road to, 213
dike-and-dam system, 82
disaster capitalism, 102
disaster management, 93
division of labour, 19, 25, 27, 37, 39, 191, 195, 221, 224
Douglass, Mike, 97
Dreyfuss, Jeff, 27
driving on roads with heavy traffic, challenge of, 63
dual economy, theory of, 29
Dutch colonialism, 170, 174
Dutch colonial power, 14, 194
Dutch East India Company, 169
Dutch floodgate system, 83

East Jakarta, 76
ecological consequences, 1
ecological modernisation, 203
e-commerce, 124, 211
economic jihad, 160–1, 167
edge cities, 110
edgeless cities, 110
Effendy, Rustam, 61
egalitarian society, 226
Electronic Road Pricing, 62
elite informality, 110, 113, 115, 175, 188
elites, power of, 132
*Elle Décor* magazine, 152
Environmental Impact Assessment (EIA), 98, 103
environmental politics, 200–3
equality, principle of, 131
ethnic Chinese, 49, 78, 90, 112, 177, 186, 189
European representation of identity, unity of, 14
everyday life, agency of, 63–4
eviction, 17, 27, 40, 95, 96, 100, 103, 132, 141–3, 146n7, 147n14, 148n19, 148n21, 157, 164, 177, 183–5, 192–4, 196, 197, 202

eviction, self, 45, 197
eviction and relocation, of *kampung* dwellers, 27, 95
extended metropolitan regions (EMRs), 55, 111
exurbia, 110

*Far Eastern Economic Review* (FEER), 6–7
fighter for Islam, 162
financial capitalism, 61
flood-control system, 84, 87
flood culture, 93
floodgates, 82
 canal system, 98
 operators, 83, 87
flood management, 82
 colonial system of, 83
 floodgate system for, 86
flood risk, 86
floods, in Jakarta. *See also banjir* (flooding)
 *banjir* as *bencana* (disaster), 81–2
 *banjir kiriman* (flooding water from outside their areas), 80
 deaths due to, 88
 "deep tunnel" project for mitigation of, 74
 infrastructure to control, 78
 "Nyi Loro Kidul *mengamuk*" (rampage of the Sea Goddess), 76
 scope and problems of, 94
 urban system of flood management, 79
flow of water, in Jakarta, 75–7
folding architecture, concept of, 152
food (*pangan*), 42
foreign cars, dealerships of, 60
foreign direct investments, 201
foreign orientals, 177
formalised city, 24–5
formal land market, 24, 36–7, 197
Formula E electric motorsport championship, 144
Forum Betawi Rempug (FBR), Jakarta, 134

*Forum Masyarakat Peduli Lingkungan Pluit. See* Communities that Care for Pluit's Environment
fragments, 15
freeways, 59, 69
 formation of, 55
French Indochina, 6
*Front Pembela Islam* (FPI). *See* Islamic Defenders Front
Fuller, Andy, 13

Gandy, Matthew, 104n5
Garuda bird, of Hindu-Javanese mythology, 100–1
gated communities, proliferation of, 194
*gedongan*, 27
Geertz, Clifford, 151, 169–70
gentrification of *kampung*, 39, 45
Geospatial Information Agency, 80
global, art of being, 18
 local and, 18
global cities, 20
 connectivity of, 224
 paradigm of, 184
global division of labour, 191, 224
globalisation of architecture, 6
Global North, 222
 informalisation of workers in, 224
Global South, 131, 200, 222, 225
 industrial labourers in, 221
 intersectionality of formal and informal sectors in, 224
 nature of urbanisation and suburbanisation in, 24
 urban expansion in, 23
Godfather (Italian mafia), 140
Gojek, 66, 211, 213
good governance, practice of, 128, 156, 183, 204
*gotong royong* (mutual help), 9, 34, 36, 42–3, 63, 89, 191
governance, political culture of, 1, 15, 21, 24, 29, 72, 118

governing, art of, 21
governmentality, 15, 20, 40, 72, 104
government-owned "unused land" (*tanah terlantar*), 35, 36
Governor of Jakarta, 61, 71, 81, 130, 139, 141, 157, 182–3, 202, 207
  Anies' public presentation as, 145
Grand Hyatt Bali, 4
Greater Jakarta, 117, 173
  Chinese investment in, 199
  construction of, 199
Great Sea Wall, 100–3
green architecture, 121
green living, 200
green, notion of, 200
grey zone of governmentality, 40
ground rent, 41, 45
growth coalition, 57, 59
Guangzhou, 116
Guinness, Patrick, 31
Gunadi, Iwan, 62
Gunawan, Iwan, 93
Gunawan Mohamad, 57
Gunawan, Restu, 76

*habitus*, 24
*hak guna bangunan* (right to build), 44
*hak milik* (ownership rights), 44, 197
*hak pakai* (right of use), 44
*hak sewa* (tenant rights), 44
*halal* certifications, 160
hamlet chief (ketua RW), 145
*hansip* (security personnel), 173
Hardt, Michael, 21, 219, 221, 224
Hart, Keith, 31
Harvey, David, 45
Hassan, Fuad, 56
Hatta, Mohammad, 149, 201
hawkers, 32
health care and education, 140
Herlambang, Suryono, 128
Hidayat, Djarot, 187
high-rise rental apartments, 10, 141

*hijrah*, performance of, 161
Hindu-Buddhist Majapahit, 135
Hindu-Islamic Javanese style of construction, 8
Hizbut Tahrir Indonesia (HTI), 150, 157
*hoki*, 79–80
homeownership, 43
  benefits of, 44
Hong Kong, 7, 112, 115–16, 118
horse-tram lines, 50
Hotel Indonesia, 6, 88, 212
house construction, 8
household
  development of, 223
  mystery of, 32–3
  semi-proletarian, 33, 36
  Wallerstein's concept of, 33
housing
  for "lower income" population, 42
  *papan*, 42
  right to adequate, 43
  shortage of, 42
  socialist-oriented, 42
  universal, 42
  zero down-payment housing programmes, 144
housing agencies, establishment of, 42
housing industry, 43
housing properties, marketability of, 69
Hundley, Tom, 68
hybrid space, 23

identity politics, elements of, 186
Imperial Golf, 118
income pooling activities, 33, 36
income pooling unit, 33, 223
incomplete urbanism, 23
incorporation and modernisation, idea of, 52
incremental urbanism, 23
Independence Day festival (*17 Agustus-an*), 34
*Indiese Stedebouw* (Karsten), 51

indirect rule, 36, 196
Indonesia
  anti-graft agency, 124
  Chinese investment in, 199
  decentralised power developed in, 134
  economic growth of, 60
  Independence Day, 108
  as Islamic state, 150
  Japanese occupation of, 34
  "one-and-the-many" authority of, 133
  political culture of, 142
  politics and culture in, 13, 20
  post-Suharto presidents, 102
  Proclamation of Independence, 129
  rise of Islamism in, 150
  socio-political and economic systems,
    159
  under Suharto's rule, 153
  transfer of sovereignty from the Dutch
    to, 41
  unicorns in ride-hailing and
    e-commerce, 211
*Indonesia Maju*, 179
Indonesian Bank Restructuring Agency
  (IBRA), 115
Indonesian Communist Party (PKI), 171
Indonesian Corruption Eradication
  Commission, 110
Indonesian government
  first Congress on Housing, 42
  "growth coalition" with private
    developers, 59
  marketisation and private housing
    development, 41
  plan of "modernisation", 41
  post-Suharto decentralisation policy,
    41
  primary needs, 42
  role in transforming the city of Jakarta,
    41
Indonesian Islamism, 150
Indonesian municipalities, formation of,
  146n1
Indonesian Muslim Forum (FUI), 158

Indonesian nationalism, 41, 136, 189
Indonesian Red Cross, 80
Indonesian revolution, 191, 199, 226
Indonesian Ulema Council (MUI), 160
industrialisation, significance of, 23, 221
industrial labourers, 221–2
industrial park
  building of, 116
  Delta Silicon, 120
  division of, 117
inequality, growth of, 201
informal economy, 29, 31, 65
informality, practices of, 2, 12
informal sector, 1
  concept of, 29
  invulnerability of, 29–32
informal transports, displacement of, 52
informal urban political traditions, of
  Jakarta, 138–42
infrastructures, 25, 35
  communities of, 77–9
"inter-Asian" cross-referencing, 199
international division of labour, 19, 25–7,
  37, 39, 191, 221
International Labor Organization, 31
intersectional binarism, 27–9
Irawaty, Dian Tri, 43, 141
Iskan, Dahlan, 66
*Islam, aksi Bela* (act of defending Islam),
  158
Islamic art and architecture, 152
Islamic boarding schools, 178
Islamic Defenders Front, 144, 150, 157,
  160, 162, 189
Islamic identity, 151
Islamic identity politics, rise of, 178
Islamic law (*sharia*), 149
Islamic Mataram, 135
Islamic New Year of *Idul Fitri*, 34
Islamic politics and religious movements,
  149, 150
Islamic social values, 186
Islamism, rise of, 167
Islamist Caliphate, 150

Islamist movement, emergence of, 21
Islamist urbanism, 20, 150, 153
    formation of, 163
    sense of, 167
    story of, 164

*Jabotabek*, 111, 121
*Jagorawi* toll road, 56–7, 59
Jakarta, 40
    bureaucratic reforms in, 139
    as city of rivers and canals, 82
    city zoning infringements, 97
    decentralised power developed in, 134
    desire for a change, 16–17
    development of, 132
    Forum Betawi Rempug (FBR), 134
    Golden Triangle, 4
    growth rate of private vehicle
        ownership, 48
    historicity of, 41–4
    infrastructure to unify, 74–5
    Kampung Improvement Programme
        (KIP). *See* Kampung Improvement
        Programme
    migrants, 42
    mutually constitutive older and newer
        elements, 17
    negotiations between globality and
        locality, 18
    post-era demands, 17
    skyline, building of, 5–6
    smart city development in, 202–3
    urban development of, 57
    urban system of flood management, 79
    West Central Business District (Puri
        CBD), 209
    without slums, 142
    as world city, 108
    Zoning Office, 80
*Jakarta baru*, ideal of, 74, 100
Jakarta Bay, 82, 99–100, 103, 144
    reclamation of, 144
Jakarta Charter, 149
Jakarta City Council (DPRD-DKI), 185–6

Jakarta Education Cards. *See Kartu*
    *Jakarta Pintar* (KJP)
Jakarta Elderly Card+ (KJL+), 188
Jakarta Gubernatorial Election (2017),
    160
Jakarta Health Card+ (KJS+), 188
Jakarta Health Cards. *See Kartu Jakarta*
    *Sehat* (KJS)
Jakarta Housing and Administrative
    Buildings Agency, 141
Jakarta MRT, 49
Jakarta One Card, 142
*Jakarta Post*, 10, 141
Jakarta Propertindo Group, 80
Jakarta Setiabudi International (JSI), 4
Jakarta Smart City (JSC) programme, 202
*jalan belakang* (back routes), 212
Jalan Sudirman, 58, 88
Jalan Thamrin, 88, 170
*jalan tikus* (rat runs), 48–50, 64, 69, 212
Japan
    "new California city", 122
    occupation of Indonesia, 34
    war compensation funds, 5–6
Japan International Cooperation Agency
    (JICA), 55
*Jasa Marga*, 56, 59
job security, 221–2
Jokowi–Ahok administration, 142
Jokowi era (2012–14), 92, 188
Jonggol, 172
Justice and Prosperity Party, 150, 153, 157

Kajian Lingkungan Hidup Strategis
    (KLHS), 103
Kalimantan island, 171
Kamil, Ridwan, 152–3
    avant-garde impulse of, 153
    beautification of the *alun-alun*, 154–5
    popularity of, 153
*kampung*
    bourgeoisification of, 197
    commonality of, 197
    hotel-like accommodation in, 197

ideas to upgrade, 145
irregular settlements, 23
*jalan tikus* (rat runs) in, 212
Kali Code, 196
land owners, 198
lifestyle of, 198
new urban form, 96–100
residents living on riverbanks, 81
self-reliance, 25
sense of belonging, 137
tradition of, 137–8
*kampung deret* (row villages), 141
Kampung Deret Program, 141
*kampung* dwellers, 175, 185
eviction and relocation of, 95, 157
livelihood of, 35
self-displacement of, 164
Kampung Improvement Programme
(KIP), 12, 35, 42–5, 47n4, 194
*Kampungkota* city, formation of, 29
*kampungkota*, notion of, 29
*kampung* land, "dead capital" of, 44
*kampung* neighborhoods, 8, 24, 27, 60,
167, 194
security for, 135
*Kampung* Pulo, 26, 95, 96, 141
*kampung* settlements, 3, 8–10, 23, 201
analytical map of, 30
association with the informal
economy, 29
banality of, 25–7
"best practice" associated with housing
provision, 40
building construction in, 26
characteristic of, 26, 34
conceptualisation of, 25
culture and politics of, 39
culture of "helping one another"
(*gotong royong*), 34
deficiency of, 24
destruction and construction of, 25
development packages for, 35
eradication of, 33

existence as an intermediate space, 24
formation of, 83
governance of, 34–5
income-producing "pooling"
activities, 36
influence of the "middle" power in,
35–6
intersectional binarism, 27–9
*majelis kampung*, 34
"middle-class" rental spaces in, 38
neighbourhood unit of, 34
new *kampung*, 37–9
as "non-official" cultures of self-
reliance, 26
preservation of, 37
role in the functioning of the city, 24
self-management of, 40
street scene in, 26
work force in, 33
*kampung susun* (elevated villages), 141
*kampung*-upgrading initiatives, 141
Karsten, Thomas, 51
*Kartu Jakarta Pintar* (KJP), 140
*Kartu Jakarta Sehat* (KJS), 140
*kawula gusti*, 136, 140
*kekerabatan* (communal bond), 34
*kelurahan*, 34, 78
Kelurahan Pluit, 78
*kemanunggalan kawula gusti* (unification
of the ruler and the ruled), 140
Kepala Dinas Pekerjaan Umum (the head
of Public Works), 87
Kepala Seksi (section chief), 87
Kepala Suku Dinas (department head), 87
*kerja bakti* (communal work), 34
Kertajati International Airport, 123
Klein, Naomi, 102
Koalisi Selamatkan Teluk Jakarta. *See* Save
Jakarta Bay Coalition
Kohn Pedersen Fox (architects), 4
*komisaris* (retired, high-ranking
government officer), 204
*korupsi* (corruption). *See* corruption

*kota*, 27
*kota seribu dimensi. See* city of a thousand
    dimensions
Kuma, Kengo, 121
Kwak, Nancy, 43–4
*Kyai Garuda* (king's carriage), 170

labour migration, 1, 223
labour supply, 2–3
    unlimited supply in developing
        countries, 31
Laclau, Ernesto, 130
laissez-faire capitalism, 41
*lalulintas*, 50
land
    commodification of, 58
    formal land market, 36, 37
    formal tenure, 37
    informal land market, 36, 37
    semi-formal tenure, 37
    unified national land status, 42
land unused or abandoned (*tanah
    terlantar*), 35, 191
land bank, 8, 117
land certification programme, 9, 12, 37,
    44–6, 138
land complicity, 36–7
land dualism, 37
land legality, system of, 36
land market, 24
    informal, 42
    in *kampung* areas, 42
land reclamation project, 80, 102, 143, 173
land status
    standardisation of, 42
    transformation of, 197
land tenure, 137
land-use regulations, violations of,
    107n44, 110, 131, 145
land values, 26
Langdon, Philip, 6
Latour, Bruno, 16
    matters of concern, 16
    matters of fact, 16

law enforcement, 100, 102, 110, 175, 181
legal dualism
    dissolution of, 45
    of land, 42
Lewis, W. Arthur, 31
Liem Sioe Liong (Sudono Salim), 112–13,
    126n4
Li Ka-shing, 118
Lippo Bank, 113–15
    bad loans, 115
    corporate borrowers, 115–16
Lippo Cikarang Tbk, 119, 123
Lippo Group, 10, 108, 110–11, 122, 154
    American Adventure, 113–15
    California transfer, 119–20
    dedication to serve the new
        community, 118
    Eastern connection, 120–2
    idea of world-class facilities, 118
    interests in China and Hong Kong, 115
    Lippo Village project, 117, 118
    Meikarta mega-project, 111–13
    Orange County project, 117, 120
    overseas operations, 117
    scandal, 124
    Super Mall, 118
Lippo Karawaci project, 118–19
liveable city, concept of, 121
Location Permits, issuance of, 42, 59
lockdowns, 207, 214
*lokasi rawan banjir* (flood prone
    locations), 77
low-cost housing, 40

*macet* (traffic jam), 15, 62, 208, 212
Makarim, Nadiem, 213
Malik, Adam, 204
Malo, Manasse, 41, 131, 136
*mandor* (head of construction workers),
    4, 8, 11
    labour market of, 3
    recruitment of workers, 3
    relation with construction workers, 3
    role of, 2–3

Manggarai floodgate, 84, 87, 105
Manhattan transfer, 10
*manunggaling kawula gusti*, 136
*manusia Jakarta*, 48
maps platform, 212
marginalised inhabitants, 190–3
market liberalisation, 59
Marxist urban studies, 21, 33
Marxist urban theory, 219
Masjid Al Safar (a mosque for travellers),
    Bandung, 152–3
*masjid origami* (origami-style mosque), 152
Mass Rapid Transport (MRT), 207
Master Plan for the Acceleration of the
    Expansion of Indonesian Economic
    Development, 121
Mbembe, Achille, 25
McGee, Terry, 23, 55
megacity, 23, 169
mega-urban regions, 23, 111
Meikarta, 122–5
    future of, 124
    map of, 109
    "Meikarta" project, 108, 110
        issuance of property permits for,
            110
    showroom in a shopping mall, 122
Meng Ta-cheang, 120
mental revolution, idea of, 129–31, 138,
    139, 174, 176
messy urbanism, 23
Metropolitan Priority Areas, 121
micro entrepreneurs, 191
middle class, of Indonesia, 59
    real estate housing complex, 27
    rental spaces, in *kampung*, 38
middle-income earners, 60
"middle" power, in the *kampung*, 35–6
middling urbanism
    defined, 24
    phenomenon of, 24
    positioning of, 24–5
middling urbanism, concept of, 24, 33, 37,
    40, 46, 223

migrant workers, 4, 7, 24
*mikrolet* ("micro-opelet" buses), 53, 63–4
Ministry of Environment, 201
Mitsubishi Corporation, 120
Mitsubishi Jisho Sekkei Inc., 121
"modernisation" of the city, 27, 31, 36
modernisation theory, 33
monetary crisis of 1998, 60
money politics, 135
moral economy, of the state, 136
More, Thomas, 208
mosquito fleet, 51–2, 64
motorbike taxi *(ojek)* drivers, 210
motorcycles
    accidents, 68, 212
    and alleyways, 210–13
    as backbone of delivery services, 212
    Harley-Davidson, 213
    mobility restriction, 212
    *ojek. See ojek*
    popularity of, 66–9
        *versus* cars, 67
        to earn money for living, 67
        filtering through traffic
            congestion, 68
    purchases of, 213
    *tukang ojek* (informal motorbike taxi),
        213
motor vehicles in Jakarta, hierarchical
    order of, 212
Muhammadiyah, 189
Muirhead, Desmond, 118
multitude, concept of, 17, 21, 219, 221
Murray, Alison, 27
*mushollas* (prayer houses), 151, 164–5
*musyawarah* (consensus decision making),
    34
"mutual help" *(gotong royong)*, 9, 42, 63,
    89–91, 130, 191

Nahdlatul Ulama (NU), 189
Nas, Peter, 41, 131, 136, 146n1
National Capital Integrated Coastal
    Development (NCICD), 100

National Capital of Indonesia, 101
National Disaster Mitigation Agency, 94
nationalist utopia, road to, 207–8
National Land Agency, 36–7
National Monument Square (*Lapangan Monas*), 151, 158, 166
National Movement to Safeguard Ulema Fatwas (GNPF), 158
national road systems, creation of, 55
*Negara Kesatuan Republik Indonesia* (NKRI), 189
Negri, Antonio, 21, 219, 221
neighbourhood chief (ketua RT), 145
neoliberal "as exception", 1
neoliberal developmentalism, 192, 199
neoliberalism, practices associated with, 20, 41, 47n4, 151, 156, 166, 182, 220, 221, 224
neoliberal populism, 142
neoliberal urbanism, study of, 40
neoliberal work ethic, 139, 104n4
*Nepotisme, Korupsi dan Kolusi* (NKK), 204
new capital city, 15, 20
New Order (1998 to the present), 4–5, 42, 129, 161
    changes after the end of, 44–5
    coordination, 52–5
    developmentalism, 56
New Order Racket state, 133
New Pluit City project, 98–100
new towns, 59–60
    3-in-1 zones, 62
    advertisements for, 63
    construction of, 12, 63
    development of, 60
    promotion of private car ownership, 60–1
new urban politics, 144, 175–6
*nggak masuk akal*, 71
*ngobyek* (doing individual projects), 185
Nomadology, 14
normality, sense of, 91
North American architects, 5–6

North Jakarta, 78, 97, 143
Nugroho, Sutopo Purwo, 94

Oded, Muhammad, 153
OECD countries, 199
Office of Water Management (Tata Air), 87
*ojek* (freelance motorbike taxi), 49, 63, 65–6
*ojek sepeda* (bicycle taxi), 213
*Ojol*, 214
Okamoto Masaaki, 180n6
*oknum* ("shadowy" quasi state personnel), 35, 196, 204
One District One Entrepreneurship (OK OCE), 144
Online Ojek, 213
*opelet* (the post war wooden cabin automobile), 52–3
Orange County project, 117, 120–1, 123
Orientalised Other, 14
oriental mentality, notion of, 29

Padawangi, Rita, 97
Pakubuwana II (Javanese king), 169
Palangkaraya, 171
Pancasila (the philosophy of the state), 5, 52
*Pandai-Pandai Kalian Mencari Jalan* (PPKM), 214
pandemic city, 21
*Panitia Agung* (the Grand Committee), 171
Panjaitan, Luhut, 124
Pantai Indah Kapuk, 59
Pantai Mutiara residential area, 80
"para-transportation" system, in Jakarta, 19, 48, 55, 64–6
*Partai Keadilan Sejahtera* (PKS). See Justice and Prosperity Party
*Partai Solidaritas Indonesia*, 189
"patron-client" political tradition, of Southeast Asia, 133
patron-client relationship, 3, 133, 147n11, 193, 196, 204
Pembangunan Pluit Jaya Company, 80
Pemberton, John, 208

*pemborong* (a wholesale service in
    construction), 2, 4
*pembuat batako* (precast brick maker), 2
Pemuda Pancasila, 133
*Pendidikan Kesejahteraan Keluarga*
    (PKK), 34
*pengawas lapangan* (field officer), 2
*penggali tanah* (person who digs the hole),
    2
*Pergerakan* (motion, movement), 17
periphery
    notion of, 31, 32, 39, 40, 163, 200
    urban question of, 221–2
Periurban, 19, 23, 24, 39, 54, 199, 201
peri-urban Jakarta, town development of,
    56
peri-urbanisation, 102
*per-kampung-an* (settlements with a
    *kampung* environment), 140–1
Perumahan Nasional or National Housing
    (PERUMNAS), 42–3, 46
*Perusahaan Pengangkutan Djakarta*
    (PPD), 52
planning culture, 18, 200
planning regulation, 26, 57
Pluit communities, 78
Pluit Dam, 78, 80–1
plural Islamisms, 150
plural societies, 193
political Chinese, 189
political economy, of transport, 57
political society, 196, 198
political traffic accident, 208
politics of time, 129, 142–6, 184
*politik kota. See* urban politics
*Politik Kota dan Hak Warga Kota.*
    *See* Urban Politics and the Rights of
    Urban Citizens
Pollock, Naomi, 4
Pollux Mega Kuningan project, in Jakarta,
    10
Pollux Properties Indonesia, 10
pony carts (*dokar*), 51–2
populist politician, rule of, 184

populist politics, 128, 130, 136, 140,
    145–6, 183–4, 186
portals, 214
post-Fordist labourers, 220, 222
post-metropolis, 110
post-suburbia, 110
    birth of, 115–17
power relations, architecture of, 196
"power sharing" system, 192
Prasetyo, Frans, 21, 154–6, 214
*preman* (thugs), 35, 132, 139–40, 161–2,
    173, 185, 196, 204
Preparatory Committee for Independence,
    149
Presidential Decree, 102, 143
*pribumi* (natives), 144
private car ownership, promotion of, 55,
    57, 60–1, 63
private expropriation, notion of, 223
privatisation and deregulation, campaign
    for, 57
pro-*kampung* programme, 142
proletarianisation, 33
property developers, 103
property development
    in Indonesia, 110
    in Jakarta, 10
property market advertisements, 59
Prosperous Justice Party (PKS), 189
public goods, privatisation of, 220
Public Intellectual Forum, 227n4
Public Order Agency, 96
public-private partnership (PPP), 41, 121
public scrutiny, 138
public servants, disciplining of, 139
public space, 15, 35, 141, 145, 149–52,
    154, 157, 162, 165, 167, 186, 188, 192
public transport, in Jakarta, 57, 192, 200
    deterioration of, 60
    highways, 61
    political economy of, 57
Public Works Unit (Dinas Pekerjaan
    Umum), 79
*pungli* (extortion), 135

*pungutan liar* (illegal fee extortion), 135
Puri Night Market, 209
Purnama, Basuki Tjahaja. *See* Ahok,
    Governor
Purwakarta, 173

Qingjian Group Co. Ltd, 10
Qlue (a crowd sourcing smartphone app),
    140
Queen of the South Sea, 76, 103

Raditya, Rama, 202
railway, expansion of, 57
*rakyat* (the common folk), 27, 41, 54, 135,
    136–7, 140, 197
*rakyat kecil*, 66
*ramai* (crowded) road, 25, 208–10
Ramto, Bunyamin, 97
Reagan, Ronald, 220
real estate developer, 9
real estate development, 60
real estate housing, 9, 27
Real Estate Indonesia, 42–3
real estate investment trusts (REITs), 117
real-estate planning, 194
real estate turn, 1
reclamation project, 103
*Reformasi*, post, 12, 13, 17, 19, 195
regional integration, 6
religious identities, 134, 150, 176, 195
religious pluralism, 167
    of Indonesian society, 149
religious transgression, routinisation of, 154
rent
    rental buildings, 8–10
    rental prices, 39
    rooms for, 39
rent-seeking, politics of, 176
reserve wage-labourers, 33
residential housing, for living with family,
    111
restriction of mobility, 207
*revolusi*, 17
rhizome, rhizomatic, 15, 17, 19

Riady, James, 108, 117, 120, 123–4
    illegal contributions to 1996
        Democratic campaign finances,
        114
Riady, John, 124, 125
Riady, Mochtar (born Lie Mo Tie), 110–12
    American Adventure, 113–15
    banks in the US, 114
    financing of Clinton's campaign, 114
    role in improving Indonesia–US ties,
        114
    vision of a new community, 118–19
"rise of capital", 52
riverbank-dwelling poor people, 92
"river normalisation" programme, 93, 192
riverside settlements, 103
roads, in Jakarta, 50
    construction for motorised vehicles, 54
Robison, Richard, 52
"rock city" (Dreyfuss), 27
rooms for rent, 39
Roosmalen, Pauline, 51
Roy, Ananya, 131
Rukmana, Siti Hardiyanti, 56
*Rukun Tangga* (RT), 34
*Rukun Warga* (RW), 34
rural/urban divide, 201, 223

Sadikin, Ali, 52–3, 209
Said, Edward
    Traveling Theory (1982), 15, 218
Salafi-modernist network, 150, 157
Salim Group, 112
Salim Group bank, 115
Sarinah Department Store, 6
Save Jakarta Bay Coalition, 100
Scott, James, 5, 35
seasonal flooding, issues of, 91
secular liberalism, 150
secular nationalism, 150
security of the construction site, 2
self-employment, 66
self-help *kampung*, 43
semi-formal tenure, 36

*Index*

semi-formal workers, 32
semi-proletarian household, 27, 32–3,
  36–7, 39
*semuanya bisa diatur*, sense of, 204
Seno Gumira Adjidarma, 11, 48, 193, 205,
  212, 226
  depiction of Jakarta as a city of a
    thousand dimensions, 12–13
  *Kentut Metropolitan*, 13
  postmodernist style, 13
  Schizoanalysis, 15
  thousand dimensions, 14
shadowy officials (*oknum*), 132
*shalat berjamah*, 156
Shenzhen Yantian Port, 124
Shenzhen Yantian Port Group, 122
Shihab, Rizieq, 144, 160, 187
Shimizu Corporation, 4
  Jakarta Design Office, 6
  New York office, 7
sidewalk vending, legalisation of, 145
*sikap mental* (mental attitude), 130
Simmel, Georg, 138
Sinar Mas Land Group, 10
Singapore, 1, 7, 10, 22n5, 117, 179, 199,
  200
smart city development, in Jakarta, 202–3
Smart Jakarta Card+ (KJP+), 188
social housing, 40, 46
  state provision of, 40–1
socialist city, 171
social order, 20, 40, 129
social safety nets, 224
social stability, 212
social welfare projects, 176
*Sociological Review*, 220
Solo (Surakarta), 74, 130, 140, 169–70,
  178, 185
Southeast Asia, 1, 6, 7, 10, 23
Southeast Asian cities, 1
Southeast Asian Games, 7
South Jakarta, 80
South Korea, 10, 101, 117, 121
space-time coordination, 159

spatial differentiation, practice of, 84
state, 25, 32, 34–6, 149, 179, 183, 199
  moral economy of, 26, 136, 147n16
  nation, 27
  nation building, 31, 129, 167, 172
  Statecraft, xii, 15, 18, 19, 36, 39, 40,
    43, 175, 182
state power, maintenance of, 133
Stormwater Management and Road
  Tunnel (SMART) project, 74
Strategic Environmental Assessment
  (SEA), 102
street life, in Indonesia, 209
street vendors, 32, 135, 209
  removal of patronage control over, 140
  reorganising marketplaces for, 178
suburbanisation, 24
suburb, concept of, 111
suburbia, concept of, 110–11
Sudirman-Thamrin Road, 207, 214
Sueb, Benjamin, 93
Suharto, post-, 17, 197
  decentralisation policy, 41
  "*prorakyat*" programmes, 136
Suharto, President, 17, 41, 102
  bloody coup of 1965, 52
  collapse of dictatorship, 175
  "*dwi tunggal*" ("two and yet one"), 136
  fall of, 60, 128
  New Order regime, 129
  path of "development", 42
  Presidential Decree (1995), 143
  rise of, 52
Suharto, regime, 12, 17, 57, 201
  collapse of, 60
Sukabumi, 173
Sukarno, President, 5, 12, 149
  dream, 171–2
  as first president of postcolonial
    Indonesia, 51
  nation-building project, 172
  "Old Order" regime of, 52
  *Panitia Agung* (the Grand
    Committee), 171

*penyambung lidah rakyat* (the tongue of people), 136
prestige projects of, 6
reconstruction of Jakarta, 172
removal of trams from Jakarta's streets, 51
superblocks, 10, 28, 60, 97, 98, 173, 181, 200
"supra-local" spaces, 193–4
Surabaya, 2, 4, 7, 43, 55, 100
   Kampung Improvement Programme (KIP), 47n4
Surakarta (Solo), 74, 130, 140, 169–70, 178, 185
Sutiyoso, Governor, 74, 81, 175–6, 200, 202
Swissasia Global, 115
Syarifuddin, Ari, 89

*taman* (garden), 118, 156
Tambunan, Rio, 107n44
Tanjung, Charirul, 101
Tariqa Alawiya Youth Movement, 166
Tarumanagara kingdom (358–669 CE), 92
Tarumanagara University, Jakarta, 197
taxes, collection of, 133
taxi services, door-to-door, 51
technoburbs, 110
technopoles, 123
tenure security, 43, 47n3
terminological innovations, 111
Thatcher, Margaret, 220
third world cities, development of, 52
"third world" countries, 31
Third World liberation, 172
thousand dimensions, 11–16, 13–16
*Thousand Plateaus, A* (Deleuze and Guattari), 13–16
three dimensional buildings, 5, 12, 15
thugs (*preman*). *See preman*
time, politics of, 142–6
Tjhi, Khiong Fat, 78–81
Tokopedia, 211
toll roads, automobiles and the business of, 57–9

Toto, Bartholomeus, 121, 122, 124
Town Management Division, 118
*tradisi*, 129–30
traffic accidents, 51
traffic congestion, in Jakarta, 48, 61–2, 208, 213
   *macet* (traffic congestion), 62
traffic jams, 59–60
transitional policies, 32
transit-oriented development (TOD), 121
trans-local urban activists, 192
transportation and road system, in Jakarta, 48–50. *See also* urban transport systems
   capital-intensive technologies of, 52
   during Dutch colonial times, 50–1
*tukang ojek* (informal motorbike taxi), 213
*turun ke jalan* (go to streets), 209–10, 214–16
Twitter, 156–7

UN Habitat "Cities without Slums" campaign, 142
United Overseas Bank Plaza, 88
universal housing, 42
unused land (*tanah terlantar*), 35, 191
urban and rural complementarities, 23
urban anthropology and sociology, 32
urban, becoming, 17
urban circularity, 165
urban citizenship (*warga kota*), 137
urban construction, Japanese–Indonesian relations in, 5–6
urban development, 41, 121, 194–5
   in Batavia, 174
   in Jakarta, 23, 155
urban economy, integration of rural households into, 3
urban form, 23, 24
urban governance, 60
urbanisation, 24, 33, 39
urbanites, 24
urban *kampung*, settlement of, 223
urban middle-class population, consciousness of, 200

urban planning, 128
  at block-by-block level, 175
  Detailed Plans, 174–5
  Urban Master Plan, 174
  Urban Regional Section Plan, 174
urban politics, 15, 20
  of Anies Baswedan, 129
  and cultures, 17
  economy and, 16
  formation and contestation of, 149
  and governance, 181–90
  and Mental Revolution, 129–31
  *versus* national politics, 128
  traditions of
    bureaucratic, 135–6
    *kampung*, 137–8
    oligarchic, 131–2
    pre-Jokowi-Ahok, 146
    *rakyat*, 136–7
    subcontracted, 132–5
  in Western societies, 128
Urban Politics and the Rights of Urban
  Citizens, 128
urban poor, 36
Urban Poor Consortium, 97
urban-rural system, 223
urban-rural transactions, 111
urban society
  external dynamics of, 31
  internal dynamics of, 31
urban spaces
  of the city, 12
  disorderliness (*rommeligheid*) of, 51
  of Jakarta, 29
urban sprawl, 23
urban theories, 25
urban transformation, political economies
  of, 164
urban transition, 23
urban transport systems, 52, 63
  electric tram, 50
  *mikrolet* ("micro-opelet" buses), 53
  minibus fleet, 53
  modernisation and incorporation of, 53

  motorisation of, 54
  PPD bus system, 53
  in the Suharto era, 54
urban "turf war", 135
U.S. Agency for International
  Development (USAID) programme,
  53, 55
*Ustad* (Islamic preacher), 152

Van Breen, Herman, 83–5, 88, 98, 102
van Haegen, Melanie Schultz, 100
vendors' carts, reparation of, 140
Vereenigde Oostindische Compagnie
  (VOC). *See* Dutch East India
  Company

wage-dependent "proletarians", 224
wage-labourers, from semi-proletarian
  households, 32
Wahdah Islamiyah, 158
Wahid, Abdurrachman, 161
Wallerstein, Immanuel, 32
  concept of household, 33
*waqf* (charitable endowment), 164
*warung* (food stall), 11
*Washington Post*, 68
wastelands, 116
water infrastructure, moderniation of,
  104n5
waterways, 15, 19
  engineering of, 82–4
"water world" park, 120
Western metropole, 221
West Flood Canal, 80–1, 84
West Java, 152
  Bogor Regency in, 172
  political organisation of space, 153
  rise of Islamists in, 153
Widodo, Joko (Jokowi), 124, 128, 138,
  140, 158, 181, 209
  administrations of, 143, 145
  aspiration to modernise and formalise
    housing in Jakarta, 141
  mental revolution, 131

plan to move Indonesia's capital city away from Jakarta, 169, 173
presidential campaign, 130
second term as President of Indonesia, 169
tenure as governor, 187
war against the legacy of Suharto, 131
Wijaya, Endang, 97
Winarso, Haryo, 59
Wirosardjono, Soetjipto, 31
Wirth, Louis, 138
Wisma Nusantara (office building in Indonesia), 6
withdrawal of the state, notion of, 220
*wong cilik* (common people with little connection to wealth or power), 136
work forces, proletarianisation of, 33
working from home, 207
World Bank, 42, 44, 54, 59, 75, 93

Structural Adjustment Programme, 52
world-capitalist system, dynamics of, 32
worlding cities, 18
Worthen Bank, 114

YouTube, 139
Yudhoyono, Bambang Soesilo (SBY), 61, 87, 101, 121, 173, 181

Zaenuddin's *Banjir Jakarta*, 92
*zakat*, 156
*zaman edan* (a time of madness), 137
*zaman jahiliah*, 188
*zaman pergerakan* (age in motion), 208
zero down-payment housing programmes, 144
zone of urbanisation, 23
zoning in planning, 26